The
Canadian
FOOD
ENCYCLOPEDIA

A. H. Jackson & James Darcy

The Canadian Food Encyclopedia

First Printing 2013

Library and Archives Canada Cataloguing in Publication
Jackson, A. H., 1944-, author
The Canadian food encyclopedia / A.H. Jackson, James Darcy.
Includes bibliographical references and index.
ISBN 978-1-927126-54-7 (bound)
1. Food--Miscellanea. 2. Cooking--Canada. 3. Cooking, Canadian.
I. Darcy, James, author II. Title.
TX360.C3J335 2013   641.300971   C2013-902810-2

Published by
Company's Coming Publishing Limited

Corporate Head Office:
Suite 5, 2910 Commercial Drive
Vancouver, British Columbia, Canada V5N 4C9
Tel: 604-687-5555 Fax: 604-687-5575
www.companyscoming.com

Distribution Office:
BookLogic
2311 - 96 Street
Edmonton, Alberta, Canada T6N 1G3
Tel: 780-450-6223 Fax: 780-450-1857

Director of Editorial and Production: Matt Bromley
Project Editors: Sheila Quinlan, Jordan Allan
Book Design and Layout: Volker Bodegom
Cover Design: Gerry Dotto
Cover image: red leather texture - © Photos.com; white leather texture - © Kittiyut Phornphibul/Photos.com; apple - © anjoirina/Shutterstock.

Company's Coming is a registered trademark owned by Company's Coming Publishing Limited.

We acknowledge the financial support of the Government of Canada through the Canada Book Fund for our publishing activities.

Printed in China

PC: 21

CONTENTS

INTRODUCTION

This book is for Canadians made uncomfortable by the ubiquitous end-game offerings on all Chinese restaurant menus—the "Canadian" food section: cheeseburgers, fries and fried chicken. There is more—you know there *has* to be—but somehow you cannot put a finger on what else defines Canadian cuisine other than poutine, butter tarts and maple-flavoured doughnuts. You are not alone; almost every Canadian is afflicted with a kind of nationalistic dementia generated by successive tidal waves of 20th-century convenience foods. A cuisine of centuries has been suborned by frozen entrées and branded quickie foods to a point that dinner tables have become redundant in most Canadian households.

Unlike the vast majority of American settlers, most Canadian pioneers, who arrived in ethnic waves at varying intervals, came with a plan and were prepared for hardships, thanks to informative pamphlets compiled by the French and British governments, and later, the writings of amateur botanist and pioneer advocate Catharine Parr Traill. Her two best-selling books—*The Backwoods of Canada*, published in London, England, in 1836, and *The Canadian Settler's Guide*, also titled *The Female Emigrant's Guide, and Hints on Canadian Housekeeping*, published in 1854—provided Canadian settlers with insight and knowledge from Traill's personal pioneer experiences in the Canadian wilderness along with information gleaned from the experiences of earlier settlers. Her first book, a compilation of letters written to her mother, addressed the problems encountered by pioneer settlers with financial means, whereas her later books concentrated on informing those less fortunate.

In an 1833 letter home, a year after immigrating to Canada, Traill inventoried the skills required of pioneer women: they must know how to tap maple trees to make sugar; they must know how to make vinegar, candles and soap; they must learn to produce hop-rising dough and bake bread, to salt meat and fish, to spin, dye and knit yarn; they must make clothes, manage chickens, rear and keep cattle and be expert at milking cows and churning butter. Among her many helpful tips to prospective settlers, one in particular became a supreme benefit to both pioneer families and the whole of Canada: bring seeds. Early French settlers brought along the seeds of apples, peas and onions; Scotsmen brought oats and turnips; the English brought pears, peaches, cherries and rhubarb; and the Irish brought their potatoes.

Thanks to Traill's books, immigrant settlers from Britain headed for bush farms in Canada during the mid-19th century, especially the women, knew what challenges awaited and came prepared. Before embarking on the great adventure, they took crash courses in sewing, clothes-making, soap production, first aid, gardening, hearth building and cookery. They brought along cooking pots, eating utensils, spices, small grinders and seeds for planting; however, nothing could have prepared them for the never-ending forest with trees so tall and wide that it took a man most of the day to cut down only one.

With any luck, settlers had neighbours to help in felling trees and raising a cabin and barn, or they had the means to pay for workers. Felled trees were dragged into heaps, topped with shattered limestone

and set afire. The baked limestone, when mixed with water, was used as caulking for the cabin and barn. Helpful neighbours or hired hands needed feeding, but how was a woman to feed all the hungry men with only an open fire? More importantly, what would she feed them? Well, thanks to Traill's books, the settler wife had already purchased an iron hearth rotisserie in Québec City, along with barrels of lyed corn and a barrel each of beans, salt, apples, molasses, salt pork and, if she was lucky, a barrel of white flour.

Canada's newcomers had studied maps and read books. They knew their destination, the climate and what difficulties lay in store. Although the U.S. invited the poor and downtrodden, Britain insisted land grant immigrants to Canada be skilled and financially secure. Tradesmen went to the towns and villages, skilled farmers to the immediate countryside and Highland Scots and Irish to the hinterlands. Britain recruited millers to operate "crown mills," assisted settlers in procuring livestock and supplied law and order. The colonization of Canada progressed westward in an orderly fashion, unlike in the U.S., where expansion always outran the law, creating wild frontiers. In Canada, the settlers went straight to work; men cleared land, built cabins and planted crops, while the women supplied brainpower and direction: what to plant first, where to plant it, how to use and sell the surplus and what to eat in the meantime.

One can almost visualize the pioneer wife, one arm akimbo, the other outstretched and shaking a finger at her husband. "Samuel," she says, "you make that fireplace hearth much larger. I will not be on hands and knees whilst I cook thy dinner." She would get her larger hearth because in the New World women ruled. Women decided where to build, what to build and how big. They laid out and planted vegetable gardens, had charge of finances, clothed and fed their family and got them all to church on time. If there were no churches, they arranged a community raising and got them built. Women were the nucleus, the driving force that populated this great nation, and when things got tough, they were always there to point out that better days were just ahead.

For early settlers who depended on fresh produce, the months of April and May were the hardest because root cellars were exhausted and cows were off their milking, and foraging in the wild took on new meaning: survival. Forests were a boon to early Canadian immigrants, who also enjoyed another benefit not as widely available to pioneers in the U.S.: a watery lifeline, the St. Lawrence River and the Great Lakes. Early settlements were never far from this river and lake system that allowed settlers access to the sea and the far-off market of Great Britain. Canada had vast quantities of fish and timber for sale or trade, and the ships that arrived to buy and transport those commodities to France, Britain and her colonies never arrived empty. They carried livestock from France, molasses, citrus, dried fruits and salt from the Caribbean and spices, tobacco, tea and coffee from the east, via Britain. General stores at the very fringes

of civilization rarely stocked refined sugar or flour, but molasses, lemons, apples, oranges, tea, spices and coconut might be there by the barrelful. The availability of food items rare in the U.S. helped to shape Canadian cuisine, but similarities existed in the use of wild game and natural forest products, and, of course, there were ties that bound them to the home country.

Canada belonged to Britain until Confederation in 1867, and although settlement in the U.S. was helter-skelter, Canada enjoyed a government-supervised colonization. Settlers had to prove their worth before receiving property deeds, British law was always close at hand, and relations with First Nations seldom derailed as they did south of the border. Friendly relations meant closer contact with native peoples, and from them, early settlers received much-needed wisdom on living in the wilds. The cuisine of First Nations saw a welcome adoption by our early settlers, and both their recipes and preparation techniques feature predominantly in the evolution of the great Canadian food experience. Helping thy neighbour was an important part of pioneer life, both north and south of the border; however, farms in Canada tended to be smaller and closer together than in the U.S., which allowed for a greater degree of neighbourly assistance when needed.

Canadian pioneers often brought belongings from the home country, whereas in the U.S. they generally arrived penniless, with only the clothes on their backs. To have books, lamps to read by, seeds to plant, pots, pans, a fireplace crane and spices to cook with helped to assure Canadian pioneer families that better days were truly just around the corner. Acquiring a cow, pigs and chickens marked the first of those better days as procuring farm animals changed lives. Milk, butter, pork, chicken and fresh eggs were the nightly dreams of every new settler until the big day arrived. Imagine the excitement about the first pail of milk, or the delight over that first egg. Pioneering in Canada had its moments, and one of the biggest, especially for the pioneer wife, had to be the fully finished kitchen, with a window from which she could watch her future unfold and keep an eye on her garden and cooling pies.

Early settlers ate a lot of pie: wild game pies, wild berry pies, chicken pies, pork pies, beef pies, turnip and potato pies, squash pies, fruit pies and custard pies. A cow for milk and butter, a field of wheat and a barrel of salt meant shortcrust pie pastry and a way to transform fruit, berries and meats into portable culinary delights that could be kept in cool root cellars for weeks. Along with stewed beans, onions and hardtack, the humble pie had come along on the first sea voyages to Canada. Called "sea pies" and usually filled with a variety of well-cooked meats and covered with a hard dough called a "coffin crust," they remained edible for weeks and served as extra rations for a ship's crew and passengers. Adopted by settlers in New Brunswick and Nova Scotia, the sea pie moved west into Québec with settlers to become

cipaille, a covered pie filled with alternating layers of pastry, meat, fowl, potatoes and onions.

Pies also featured prominently in Acadian fare, with fruit pies, such as apple and wild grape, becoming popular. Lobster was so plentiful and cheap in the Maritimes that lobster pie was the subject of much complaining from men forced to eat it for breakfast, lunch and dinner. As the pie moved west, the complaining ceased when pigeon, duck, eel, pheasant or sturgeon replaced the hated lobster. Pie is good eats, and a pioneer cook with an imagination could produce a cornucopia of pastry-covered delights with a variety dependent only on the availability of fish and game and what fruits and berries were in season. Originally made with flour, water, salt and a dash of vinegar, the almost-inedible coffin crusts began a transformation with the addition of butter and lard, with not a few cooks becoming famous for their flaky shortcrust pies. The pie, with or without crusts, remains a bulwark of modern-day Canadian cuisine: one-pot meals, casseroles, braised meats and even microwave convenience foods evolved from the pie—a culinary masterpiece with a long history.

Curiosity not only killed cats, but it also killed the plentiful deer and wild turkeys that came to investigate the chopping noises made by woodcutters. Roast venison and turkey turned on a spit is good, but when basted with molasses and crushed forest berries, it becomes downright yummy, especially when coupled with baked Indian meal cakes laced with the same forest berries. Depending on the cook's ingenuity, any number of flavour combinations was possible by the inclusion of berries with the staples of venison, wild fowl and Indian meal.

Indian meal was simple cornmeal, or lyed corn, a First Nations staple produced by boiling corn in water laced with lye derived from wood ash. The lye removed the indigestible hulls from the corn, making its nutrients available to the human body. Indian meal was a useful food that could be prepared dozens of ways: as a bread substitute, a breakfast cereal, a soup and stew thickener or a dessert when mixed with molasses. Native tribes, especially the Iroquois, were so adept at producing Indian meal that it was an intertribal trade commodity long before the arrival of settlers and was easily obtainable. Indian meal sustained the settlers while they cleared land for spring planting and prepared for winter.

A large family was key to survival in the wilds of Canada. Children were more mouths to feed, but they compensated by gathering what the forest provided in abundance. Nut trees were everywhere in Canadian forests: walnut, beech, hazel, chestnut, shagbark hickory and butternut, and all of them were infinitely useful during the arduous winter. Walnut and chestnut meats were ground into flour in a hollowed-out stump and were used as an extender for scarce wheat flour or to add some character to Indian meal cakes and gruel, whereas the more oily nut meats, especially butternut, could be pressed to supply oil for lamps and cooking.

The first Canadian winters were difficult for early settlers accustomed to the mild winters of coastal and southern Europe. Forced to endure months of snowbound isolation, they also had to fend off packs

of wolves intent on devouring their livestock. Among these animals there would be at least an ox or horse, purchased in Québec City to pull their wagon, and perhaps a cow. Come spring, settlers took to the forest to tap the sugar maple for sap that could be made into syrup to refill empty molasses barrels, as well as solid blocks of maple sugar for sweetening Indian meal breakfast gruel.

Spring planting was anxiously anticipated during the long winter. The husband had two or three acres of cleared, stumpy ground, whereas his wife had the cabin's sunny periphery and perhaps a small meadow for a garden. He planted a sustenance crop of potatoes, wheat, oats, corn and turnips, and she planted items designed to put the smiles back onto her family's faces: sage, mint, basil, rhubarb, beans, carrots, onions, cabbage and beets, along with a few well-placed red currant bushes and as many fruit trees as she had space to plant.

A first spring in the wilds of Canada was a flip of the coin for bush settler families: if all went as planned, they harvested enough to see them through the next winter; if not, they had to pack up and either return to England or take menial jobs in the nearest village or town. If the weather held and the crops grew, by the next spring five more acres could be cleared and planted and the small cabin replaced by a more commodious structure. By the next spring, with more acres cleared, chickens would be scratching about and laying eggs, pigs would be eating any kitchen scraps and another cow purchased from a not-so-fortunate

settler family would be supplying more fresh milk and butter, requiring the building of an icehouse.

Foods that had been staples in the home country were now "luxury" ingredients that ingenious pioneer cooks combined with foraged berries and nuts to produce the culinary magic that is the true heart of a Canadian cuisine that began with roasts, soups and pies. The undesirable parts and bones of a felled deer were hearth-roasted and popped into a soup pot for weekday dinners. What remained of a pioneer family's Sunday dinner of roasted venison flavoured with wild ginger and basted with raspberry sauce was carefully set into pans with onions and carrots, topped with pastry and placed into the dying embers of the hearth to bake alongside rhubarb, wild grape and blueberry pies sweetened with molasses or maple sugar.

History has moulded our national character and provided Canadians with decent values. We cherish law and order, we respect our neighbours and we tolerate different political and religious beliefs. We are nice people of many origins united in one goal: to make Canada the best it can be in everything. We are doing a good job, because Canada ranks among the prime living spaces on the planet and has become one of the world's great food producers. We feed so many, yet so few of us know anything about our great Canadian food experience or how it evolved from backwoods survival to become the national cuisine. For your erudition, allow me to present our national cuisine timeline. ❖

CANADIAN CUISINE MILESTONES

1497

Giovanni Caboto, *aka* John Cabot, sails off from Bristol, England, to find a short trade route to the Orient. Three months later, he returns to report finding a whole New World of tall trees and waters so thick with fish they could be hauled aboard in buckets. In 15th-century England, fish was a magic word, and Cabot's stories earned him a second five-ship voyage in 1497. It was a fateful one because he failed to survive, but several of his ships returned to corroborate his fishy tales, and not long after, whole fleets from France, Spain and England were braving the western sea to search out the fish that could be caught in buckets…namely, cod.

and cakes, all washed down with spruce beer. Cartier repays that hospitality by kidnapping two of the chief's sons and taking them back to France as souvenirs. They're smart kids, because on the way they hatch a plan that guarantees their return; they simply play on the Frenchmen's greed and tell them about all the gold in a place called "the Kingdom of the Saguenay."

1534

Jacques Cartier encounters the Mi'kmaq and some trade ensues, an occasion that will eventually set off a mad rush for furs. He also sails into the Gulf of St. Lawrence to Chaleur Bay, where he encounters a group of Iroquois hunting seals. While only the encounter is noted in Cartier's log, he and his crew must have been treated to a dinner: seal, cod and sturgeon, maple sugar–glazed moose loin, corn soup

1535

Cartier is back with the kids looking for riches, and while he finds none, his discovery of another gold, the Iroquois cornfields, will eventually reap far more benefit to Europe than the real thing. This time, Cartier kidnaps the Iroquois headman, Chief Donnacona, who succeeds in making his kids' fabricated story of Saguenay gold even more convincing.

1541

Cartier returns to New France but without Chief Donnacona, who died in France. This news puts off the Iroquois, who quickly lay siege to Cartier's settlement.

Cartier is chased off, but he doesn't care because he finds what he thinks is gold and diamonds. He returns to France triumphant, but is forced into retirement when his riches turn out to be worthless quartz and iron pyrite: fool's gold. The end of Cartier's explorations marked the beginning of Europe's run for the fish.

1580

Over 10,000 Europeans are now making the annual journey across the pond to fish for cod. The New World has become a beehive of exploitation, and new foods are discovered almost monthly: corn, potatoes, peanuts, chocolate, avocados, tomatoes, chili peppers, pineapples—the list goes on and on.

1606

Cartographer and explorer Samuel de Champlain, having barely survived a disastrous first winter on an island in the St. Lawrence, establishes a new settlement on the mainland, calling it Port Royal. Applying lessons learned during the previous hard winter, he institutes an eating club called *L'Ordre de Bon Temps*, the Order of Good Cheer, and orders that 15 of the most prominent members of his all-male settlement take turns hosting special meals. It is a good idea because it causes a culinary competition within the whole group, resulting in joyous camaraderie, better nutrition and an easier wait for spring. Disbanded in the spring of 1607, the Order of Good Cheer has become legend in

THE FIRST WAVE (1663–1745)

The age of plenty in an empty land

Thanks to the high-handed tactics of Jacques Cartier, France's colonial government in Canada inherited a continuous problem with the war-like Iroquois that was addressed by colonization in a manner that mimicked the ancient European feudal system. Huge tracts of land along both banks of the St. Lawrence River (*seigneuries*) were granted to the Catholic Church, noble families and wealthy military officers, who then subdivided their tracts into leased farms for settlers. The settlers (*habitants*) were required to pay a portion of their crops as rent, support the church through crop tithes, enlist themselves in a militia for common defence and provide the landlords (*seigneurs*) with a few days labour each month. The wealthy seigneurs constructed manor houses, mills and churches and employed both habitants and slaves to clear land and fence in gardens and orchards. They brought olive oil, wine, brandy, gardeners, domestic servants, livestock, millers and trained chefs from the old country, along

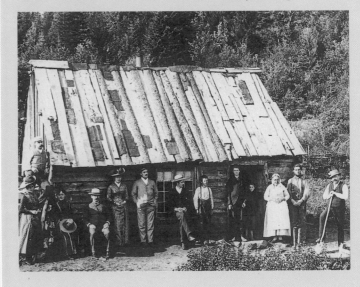

Québec, where the feasts of *Bon Temps* are recreated every winter.

1670

England's King Charles II grants the lands of the Hudson Bay watershed to "the Governor and Company of Adventurers Trading into Hudson's Bay," and the great rush to riches is off and running. Calling itself the Hudson's Bay Company (HBC), the group sends out capable managers they call "factors" to establish

with a few soldiers to train servants in the use of firearms. Pioneering a new land involved only short durations of sacrifice and deprivation for both seigneurs and habitants, and after a few years most were enjoying a quality of life that far exceeded what they had abandoned in France.

Originally, seigneurial tracts for habitants were long, narrow sections fronting the St. Lawrence River, allowing the habitants access to the bounties of both river and forest. From the river came eel, trout, salmon and sturgeon, whereas the forest supplied deer, bear, hare, birds, mushrooms, wild garlic, mustard, berries, maple syrup and the occasional caribou or moose. From the seigneury, the habitants purchased milled flour and copious quantities of hard apple cider and brandy, through either trade or credit. To drink water in France was to invite disease, and old drinking habits were hard to break, a situation that suited the seigneurs just fine because it bound the habitants to the land, especially when they bought on credit.

continued next page

fur trading posts called "factories" and to keep them well supplied with trade goods and food. To keep the factors happy and to reward the voyageurs who ferry furs to Montréal and return with supplies, the HBC makes sure every factory is well stocked with butter, tea, biscuits, coffee, cane sugar, salt beef and other goodies from home, a nice tradition that in later years provides pioneer families with a bit of the home country when HBC begins stocking imported goods.

1673

Réne-Robert Cavelier de La Salle constucts a stone fort at the mouth of the Cataraqui River—the present-day location of Kingston, Ontario—and begins to actively explore the Great Lakes and the Mississippi Valley, claiming the whole area for France.

On their land, the habitants planted wheat, oats, beans, turnips, cabbage, carrots, onions and peas. They also raised hogs and chickens and constructed beehive ovens for baking bread and pies and simmering great pots of pea soup. Although the original settlers to Québec usually hailed from the Brittany region of France, the seigneurs generally recruited their habitant families from the agricultural area of Normandy, a land with a rich culinary history of peas, beans and apples, which, along with squash and corn, make up Canada's iconic historical foods. Today, Canada is the world's largest producer and exporter of green and yellow peas, lentils, navy beans, sugarless apple pies and giant Atlantic pumpkin seeds.

Québec's seigneurs were unlike France's landed gentry in that they usually enjoyed a good rapport with their tenant farmers and often pitched in when labour was required for community building projects, such as fencing apple orchards to keep out deer or the collection of maple sap. The seigneurs attended the same church as the habitants, as well as habitant festivities, baptismals and weddings, and they often hosted their own soirées. Habitant families were often invited for Sunday dinner with the seigneur and his family, for which the habitant was honour-bound to reciprocate. It was a real backwoods camaraderie, and it provided the habitant with worldy news, the seigneur with trusted tenants and their wives with new kitchen fare through recipe exchange. The habitant's wife might learn the secrets of puff pastry while the seigneur's wife learned what forest mushrooms were safe to eat and how best to prepare them.

New France (Canada) provided a good life for both seigneurs and habitants, except that the latter would never see clear title to their lands that, unlike with the British system of primogeniture, were divided equally among survivors upon the death of the original seigneur or habitant. A shrinking tenancy to farm forced many habitant sons to become *coureurs-de-bois* or to move to Île Royale (Cape Breton Island) or other parts of Acadia (which encompassed the present-day provinces of Nova Scotia and New Brunswick and the U.S. state of Maine). As a result of this migration and the 1755 expulsion of habitant migrant settlers from Acadia, the Québec food experience—the original Canadian cuisine—spread far and wide, enriching the culinary vocabulary of a multitude of settler families. ✍

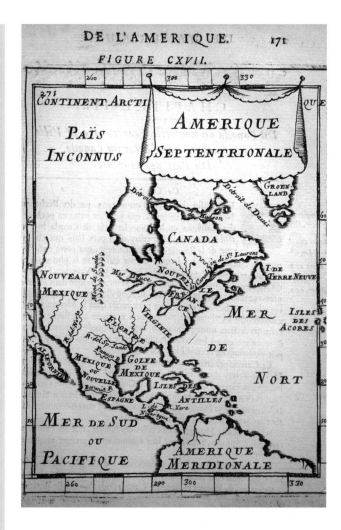

1710

The European War of Spanish Succession (1701–1714) spreads to North America, where it is known as Queen Anne's War. The English colonies of New England fight against a combined French and First Nations army based in Acadia and Canada, with the main conflict ending with the taking of Port Royal by English forces in October 1710. After their victory, the English rename Port Royal "Annapolis Royal" in honour of the Queen.

1713

As the War of Spanish Succession draws to a close, the signing of the Treaty of Utrecht awards England

total possession of Hudson Bay, Newfoundland and Acadia, although ambiguous wording concerning the boundaries of the Acadian cession sets the stage for future conflicts. The French retain control of Île-Saint-Jean (Prince Edward Island) and Île Royale (Cape Breton).

1755

The deportation of French-speaking Acadians from Nova Scotia, New Brunswick and New England begins. Many are transported to France, but most are dispersed to southern areas of North America, with thousands finding their way to Louisiana, where they become known as Cajuns. Years later, almost half the Acadians return to Canada, bringing not only their old Acadian cuisine but also their new Cajun style of cooking.

THE SECOND WAVE (1745–1755)

The age of oats and pie

The breakup of the Scottish clan system and the expulsion of small tenant farmers in the Scottish Highlands by the English caused an exodus to Canada, especially to the area they called New Scotland, or Nova Scotia. The exodus uprooted whole Scottish towns and villages, providing Canada with a fortuitous supply of millers, blacksmiths, wheelwrights, merchants, carpenters, brewers, bakers, weavers and shepherds. English Canada's economy, based solely on salt fish exports, began a change toward one that included agriculture and forestry.

Halifax, the centre of all things British in Nova Scotia, fared badly regarding fresh produce because the surrounding landscape was unfit for farming. Although farmers settled there initially, they eventually moved away to more agriculturally viable locations. Between 1750 and 1753, hundreds of German farmers were enticed to Canada by the promise of free land near Halifax, but after a few years, they all moved to the more fertile Lunenburg area of Nova Scotia, leaving the British in Halifax with their meals of oatmeal porridge, Scotch pie, German sausage, a breakfast cake called bannock and not much else.

The British, being mostly military men and merchants, wanted meat and fresh produce on their dinner tables, not salt fish and beans. Farmers in fertile areas south of Halifax, known as Acadians and being mostly French, despised the British and sent their produce and livestock anywhere but Halifax. By 1755, the British had had enough of salt fish, beans and Indian meal gruel and moved to expel every citizen of Acadia who refused an oath

of allegience to the Crown, awarding new immigrants the departing Acadians' homes and farms. The expulsion targeted both Acadian people and elements of Acadian society that the British government considered anti-monarchistic.

The 1660 restoration of the British monarchy and the mass execution of those responsible for the beheading of Charles I had caused a mass migration of Cromwellians, Puritans, Scottish Presbyterians and expelled clergymen from the Church of England to Canada and New England. These were dour-natured, rabble-rousing people who considered acceptable cuisine to be limited to meat, potatoes and plain cheese, with all other foods being either Catholic, Royalist or devil inspired. These people and their offspring fanned out into the mainstream and affected the political and social mores of English Canada until the Acadian expulsion of 1755. War with France seemed imminent, and since the Acadians were mostly French and likely to cause trouble for the British, ethnic cleansing was deemed necessary. That it also cleared out all remaining anti-Royalist and Puritan elements and put fresh produce and meat on the dinner tables of the British in Halifax was either coincidental or the main objective, depending on whose history you read. ✍

1759

The washerwomen of Québec City's Lower Town inadvertently supply British troops a way to surprise and defeat the French garrison at Québec City. Having observed the women washing clothes in the river, the British simply wait for nightfall and proceed single file up the path the women used to descend and ascend the cliff with their washing. With the British in complete control of Canada, the French/Indian threat to the 13 southern colonies disappears, enabling those colonies to concentrate on freeing themselves from British control. Immigration to Canada from the Thirteen Colonies and Britain increases; ships loaded with settlers arrive almost daily, and the evolving Canadian food experience switches from a pork, fish, wine and sauce-based cuisine to one built upon mutton, beef, peas and beer. English-style taverns become popular, the beer flows and roast beef with mushy peas almost destroys the Canadian food experience.

1769

The Experienced English Housekeeper, written by Elizabeth Raffald, is published in London, England, and becomes essential reading for the wives of settlers and military personal headed for Canada.

1774

The British pass the Québec Act, which guarantees the rights of French Canadians and awards them control of the Ohio River Valley south of the Great Lakes, an action that placates the French but adds fuel to the U.S. revolutionary movement.

1775

The American Revolution begins, and the action creates a political and military front, or border, with Canada where none had previously existed. Political and military posturing uproots families on both sides, while both overseas and St. Lawrence shipping slows to a trickle. Staples such as salt, molasses, spices, citrus, tea and coffee become unavailable. The few general stores serving pioneer settlements close up, and families must rely on foraged foods and ingenuity to survive.

1776

Starting November 1775, two U.S. armies under generals Richard Montgomery and Benedict Arnold attack Montréal and Québec City. While they are successful at Montréal, they are defeated at Québec City and forced to withdraw back to the United States. Montgomery dies in battle, and Arnold is severely wounded.

THE THIRD WAVE (1756–1780)

The age of beer, beef and spuds

As a result of losing the Seven Years' War, France ceded Canada to Britain and precipitated a mass migration, especially from Ireland and northern Scotland, with Britain offering emigrants free passage along with some assistance—such as tools, salt, food rations, guns, gunpowder and a vast military presence for protection—to bush settlers. British garrisons, whose soldiers received a daily beef and six-pint beer ration, became the nucleus for towns and villages because millers, brewers and farmers were required to keep soldiers supplied with beef, beer and spuds.

Sounds yummy, but in reality it was less so because of the British utilitarian attitudes of the time: to kill a domestic animal for consumption while the beast was still useful was considered almost sinful. Milk cows and oxen became roast beef only when they were crippled or old, pork products came from the most mature hogs, mutton came from ancient sheep, and horses were butchered for the stewpot just before taking their last step. Big meat ruled, and it was all tough as nails—luckily, the English had learned the trick of tenderizing meat from the Romans,

and after a few weeks of hanging and a bit of mould scraping, there was your Sunday dinner. It was a bit ripe, but a good long roasting fixed that, and from this habit of culinary utilitarianism came the British reputation for overcooking food.

Potatoes had become so popular in Britian that they arrived in Canada early and became as ubiquitous as corn and apples. Potatoes were an ideal crop for the Maritimes because the soil was particularly suited to growing the tubers, and just like grain and apples, surpluses could be easily distilled into alcohol. Distilleries were everywhere in Canada: in grain mills, general stores, taverns and inns and behind farmers' barns. Waste-not, want-not booze, along with cheap Caribbean rum, kept half of Canada in a state of constant inebriation for most of its formative years. Work, eat, drink and sleep, with a day off for Christmas and public hangings, was the yearly grind for most Canadians, and they pursued those activities with gusto, especially the consumption of roasted meat and potatoes. ✍

1783

United Empire Loyalists fleeing the American Revolution arrive in all parts of Upper Canada and the Maritimes. They bring both their cuisine and their slaves, with each having an impact on the evolution of Canadian cuisine—roast duck laced with cayenne pepper is a culinary revelation for Canadian settlers.

1786

John Molson buys a small brewery in Montréal and begins creating a financial, nation-expanding empire that will include banks, lumber, steamships, a railway and larger breweries. Called the nation's greatest entrepreneur, John Molson and his business endeavours create a demand for timber and grains, while his banks bring needed capital to small towns and villages.

1789

Peasant revolts in France, probably inspired by the consumption of ergot-infected grain, cause an emigration of nobility to New France, where they establish new seigneurials and business endeavours, such as lumbering and the breeding of livestock.

1790

A salt boiling operation is established at Twelve Mile Creek (now St. Catharines, Ontario) by William Merritt, an immigrant from Liverpool, England, a city with a long history of salt production. The British government in Upper Canada discontinues the practice of supplying each settler family with a barrel of imported salt.

1793

Slavery is abolished in what is now Ontario; wealthy landowners depending on enslaved workers and kitchen help either downsize, leave the province for the U.S. or go to Québec, where the practice of slavery continues until 1833. Down but not out, slavery is simply renamed "indentured servitude" and exists nationwide until well into the 20th century.

THE FOURTH WAVE (1780–1843)

The age of culinary change

The American Revolutionary War (1775–1783) caused a massive migration north by United Empire Loyalists and returning Acadians, with as many as 50,000 settling inland from the Maritimes to the newly created province of Upper Canada. Wealthy loyalists brought their slaves, livestock, domestics and cooks, and they parlayed small farm allotments into plantations and large orchards. The plantations ultimately failed for various reasons—including unfavourable weather and a 1793 ban on the purchase of slaves—but they did create larger, more productive farms from the government land grant system, and these farms attracted mills, workers and roads for the benefit of travellers.

Centres that grew into villages saw the opening of inns and taverns whose kitchens offered employment to displaced plantation cooks, escaped U.S. slaves and returning Acadians, with not a few becoming famous for their "groaning board" dinners. These dinners often included Southern-inspired dishes like slow-baked Virginia-style ham and biscuits, crayfish pie, fried fish, frog legs, cornbread, yams, tomato salad, corn on the cob and syrupy dessert pies, along with traditional roasts of beef, mutton and wild game. A treat for well-heeled travellers, Southern-style foods found acceptance in home kitchens, a fact that soon led to the design of Canadian cooking stoves with tops that facilitated iron frypans and boiling pans.

At the dawn of the 19th century, relations with the U.S. had deteriorated to a point that war seemed inevitable, requiring Britain to send troops to fortify what had previously been an open border. Trade with the U.S. ceased, the St. Lawrence River was all but closed to traffic, and Canadian settlers again looked to the forest for sustenance, only this time with some help from native peoples. Food writers are prone to include First Nations cuisine as part and parcel of the Canadian food experience, but until they were bound by having to battle a common enemy, contact between settlers and indigenious peoples was at best a cordial isolation.

After the War of 1812, however, mutual suspicion waned along with the threat of further invasion from the U.S. Although the borders remained closed for years afterward, First Nations hunters and fishermen stepped up their activities and instituted a brisk trade in forest fare with Canadian towns and villages. The natives also made sure that their customers knew how to properly prepare what settlers considered exotic foods, such as porcupine, raccoon, squirrel, beaver tail, muskrat, bear, sturgeon roe, turtle and wild rice.

When immigrant settlers attempted to move west onto the prairie lands in 1811, they found that cordial isolation was replaced by outright hostility from the Cree, Blackfoot, Sioux and the Hudson's Bay Company's rival, the North West Company. This hostility was not resolved until 1882, when market hunters had almost completely removed the reason for the presence of the Plains tribes—the bison. Market hunters took only hides, tongues and the tender humps, leaving the remainder of the animal to rot. ✍

1812

The U.S. declares war on Britain, and conflict breaks out along the Canada–U.S. border. Shipping on the St. Lawrence slows to a trickle, and men leave their farms and families to fight. U.S. forces burn York (Toronto) and capture the British fleet on Lake Erie. Canadian militia, British regulars and First Nations warriors capture Detroit and burn the American cities of Washington and Buffalo. General stores in Upper Canada close for lack of merchandise, and pioneer families again look to the forests for survival.

1816

The infamous "year without summer" caused by an 1815 volcanic eruption in Sumatra forces many settlers to abandon farms in eastern Canada and move westward into the central regions.

1817

The side-wheel steamship *Frontenac*, built in Bath, near Kingston, begins plying the waters of Lake Ontario. She ferries in supplies to settlers and takes out potash, furs and timber.

1818

Canada's first sugar refinery opens in Halifax but is of little benefit to settlers down the line. They make

do with homemade maple sugar—an arduous, time-consuming endeavour—or they purchase barrels of molasses or expensive, poor-quality muscovado, sometimes called Barbados sugar, from suppliers in Montréal. *Muscovado* means "unrefined" in Spanish, and it arrives at the port of Montréal in molasses-dripping kegs with their dirty brown contents half fermented.

1821

The Hudson's Bay Company and its archrival the North West Company merge, giving HBC a continent-wide reach.

1825

John Molson builds the British American Hotel in downtown Montréal. Modelled after the Palais Royal in Paris and managed by an Italian hotelier, Molson's hotel and dining room, the finest in North America, becomes a benchmark for future great Canadian hotels. Unescorted ladies are allowed access to Molson's new hotel, something unheard of in Europe and a custom continued in all newly built Canadian hotels.

1828

The Welland Canal opens, connecting Lake Ontario and Lake Erie, but with a depth of only four feet, it proves unsatisfactory; reconstruction begins immediately.

1832

The opening of the Rideau Canal in Ottawa—connecting the Ottawa River and Lake Ontario—enables shipping from Halifax to Welland and beyond via the Welland Canal.

1833

The Welland Canal reopens with a depth of eight feet. It is now able to handle vessels coming all the way from Halifax via the Rideau Canal. For residents of Canada West, life improves considerably; more general stores open, and goods become more varied and

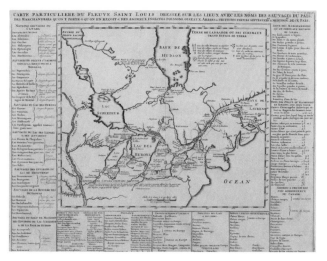

less expensive. Millers get larger grinding stones and equipment to harness waterpower, Great Lakes fishermen receive cheaper salt and lumbermen have a way to ship their products to the east coast and beyond.

1835

Justus von Liebig—a German chemist and inventor of chloroform, nitrogen fertilizer and the meat extract OXO—experiments with various combinations of powdered acids and sodium bicarbonate (baking soda) and invents what every housewife has been waiting for: baking powder. Milk no longer needs clabbering (souring, acidification) to provide a rising for baked goods and breads, and cakes and cookies no longer taste like ammonia through the use of ammonium bicarbonate, the precursor to baking powder. However, Canadian housewives continued to wait, clabbering away.

1837

Armed insurrection in both Upper and Lower Canada (the Rebellion) is crushed, with most of the instigators, including leaders William Lyon Mackenzie and Louis-Joseph Papineau, escaping to the United States. Armed incursions by American irregular forces keep tensions high along the border and hamper ship traffic on the St. Lawrence, forcing settlers to rely on the forests for survival—again.

1841

An Englishman named Orlando Jones gets the idea to grind hominy (the endosperm of corn) into starch in an alkaline bath. Jones manages to secure both British and American patents on his brainwave, but Canadian mills pay them no heed and quickly install corn boilers and alkaline baths and reset their grinding stones to very fine. In no time at all, cheap cornstarch had replaced expensive arrowroot and tapioca starch in every Canadian kitchen. More pies and puddings put smiles on the faces of overworked farmers and settlers, prompting the government to ignore Orlando Jones' demands for patent protection.

1843

English chemist Alfred Bird produces a workable baking powder by combining sodium bicarbonate (baking soda) with cream of tartar and cornstarch. That was fine and dandy for European bakers, but housewives in North America were still clabbering dough and waiting.

1846

Waves of Irish immigrants arrive in Canada to escape the potato famine. They bring with them cholera and typhus, which spreads to both urban and rural areas of Canada and kills almost 20 percent of the population. Canadians stick to their farms and homes, and kitchens take on a new importance.

1847

A stamping machine to mass produce tin cans is patented by American inventor Henry Evens, and tin cans slowly become available countrywide. Canning bees are popular, with area families sharing in the cost of a canning machine. Local women spend days preparing food and filling, boiling and cranking the machine, while their men haul cans and install shelves in root cellars. A taste of summer enjoyed in the dead of winter considerably improves the lives of settlers, prompting the creation of new and distinctly Canadian recipes.

1850

Specifically designed cooking stoves begin to appear, completely changing the culinary practices of Canadian cooks. Up to this date, wood- or coal-fired stoves were designed solely for heating, with housewives still labouring in the kitchen hearth over one-pot or roasted meals. In 1854, Toronto resident Ruth Adams receives the first patent granted by the British government to a Canadian woman for what she calls the reverse cooking stove. More efficient than a regular stove, it can heat, bake, boil and fry, but her design never saw

THE FIFTH WAVE (1844–1871)

The age of cholera, cooking stoves and isolation

In 1844, the potato blight struck Ireland and Scotland, causing famine and pushing a massive migration to Canada as far west as Manitoba. Immigrants brought along cholera and typhus, and fear of those diseases prompted Canadians to stay close to their new-fangled iron cooking stoves and peruse newly published Canadian cookbooks, such as *The Cook Not Mad* (published in 1831), *The Frugal Housewife's Manual* (1840) and Catharine Parr Traill's *The Female Emigrant's Guide* (1854).

During the mid-1800s, Red Fife wheat caused a home-baking craze, especially after 1855, when U.S.-manufactured calcium phosphate baking powder and dry yeasts became available in Canada, along with sugar from John Redpath's newly constructed Montréal refinery. Good cheap sugar, flour and quick-rising yeast were a revelation to Canadian housewives and created a huge demand for cooking stoves. No more red faces from hearth cooking, no playing with coals—you just had to feed in a few pieces of wood and out came such a cornucopia of baked goods that the demand for fine-milled wheat flour skyrocketed, causing shortages. Housewives nagged husbands, who in turn nagged the politicians into promoting settlement of the western prairie lands to meet this insatiable demand for wheat flour. ✍

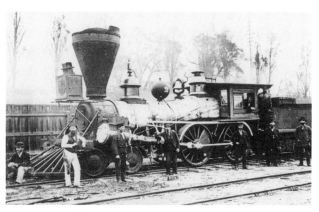

manufacturing, probably because of the cost of production. The average Canadian family has little money to spend, and while the kitchen stove quickly gains acceptance, most are procured from local iron foundries and are cheap iron boxes with doors. But even so crude a device would cause users to think they had died and gone to heaven; no more red faces from cooking in an open hearth, no more pie and bread with soggy centres, no more hauling tons of wood, no more chimney fires, and the stoves had room for multiple cooking pots. However, it would be another 20 years before factory-manufactured cooking stoves became widely available. Probably the best was the Findlay Stove, made at the Findlay Foundry, Carlton Place. This Canadian success story continues to this day—Findlay Stove is still in the business of manufacturing wood-burning ovens and stoves, along with many modern appliances.

1853

The Grand Trunk Railway is created through the amalgamation of six railways, completing a line from the east coast to Toronto. That same year, the Great Western Railway completes a track from Niagara Falls to Windsor, with a spur to Toronto.

It is now possible to travel and ship goods from Halifax to Windsor. It is a huge break for settlers in Canada West (Ontario), who now have access to food items as diverse as fresh oysters, lobsters, salt, sugar, woollen goods and heavy machinery.

1854

John Redpath, a construction contractor for the Rideau Canal, opens a sugar refinery in Montréal, and life is suddenly a whole lot sweeter for Canada's settlers.

REFINING THE SUGAR.

How Sugar, when refined, is cool'd
In moulds of the familiar shape,
    Is known to most. So having pass'd
    Through many a peril, pinch, and scrape,
    We find it now exposed for sale
    By Grocers, wholesale and retail.

1855

Eben Norton Horsford of Providence, Rhode Island, discovers that calcium acid phosphate and baking soda work to raise bread and begins to market Rumford Baking Powder in bulk. Also, canned meats, soups and pork and beans become available in urban food and rural general stores.

1859

The government of the Province of Canada creates Thanksgiving Day, a Canadian original; the United States does not institute the holiday until the end of the Civil War in 1865.

1860

Glass canning jars become available to settlers in eastern Canada. Called Mason jars after their inventor John L. Mason, the screw-top containers revolutionize home canning and turn root cellars into glittering depositories of summer delights. Not until

the completion of the railway in 1885 do the canning jars become widely available in western Canada.

1861

William Davies opens a meat-packing plant in Toronto, an operation that will eventually become the mighty Canada Packers Limited.

1864

French aristocrat Justin de Courtenay cultivates European grapes on the western shore of Lake Ontario and forms a company called Vine Growers Association. At the 1867 Paris Exposition, his Gamay grape wine wins a prize, a feat not repeated by a Canadian winery for another century.

1866

Samuel Platt discovers salt while drilling for oil in Goderich, Ontario. Platt starts a company to process brine from his drill site, and according to judges at the 1867 Paris Exposition, produces the world's finest salt. Salt is no longer an expensive import for settlers and becomes widely available. Cheaper salt prompts the formation of Great Lakes fisheries, along with many meat and fowl preserving companies, which is a boon to pioneer families headed west. Also in 1866, two brothers, Joseph and Cornelius Hoagland, along with a young marketing genius named William Ziegler, give both American and Canadian housewives a convenient, branded product they call Royal Baking Powder.

1867

The Dominion of Canada is created by uniting New Brunswick, Nova Scotia and the Province of Canada, which is then divided into the two provinces of Ontario and Québec. Two New Englanders, John Dwight and James Church, launch their Cow Brand, a baking powder that becomes immensely popular in Canada.

1869

The Hudson's Bay Company signs a "deed of surrender" with the Canadian government, giving up all claims of ownership to that vast area of North America called Rupert's Land. The company's focus changes from furs to goods, with trading posts (called factories) stocking more varied merchandise.

1870

The first salmon cannery is established at Annieville, British Columbia. Cans containing one pound of fish are hand-packed and soldered, with its first year's production being around 300 cases. Ten years later,

three canneries are shipping cases across the country and to Europe, and production climbs to 100,000 cases. By the year 1900, over 90 canneries are in operation, shipping out over two million cases of a product that changes the eating habits of Canadians. Cheap and readily available, the one-pound tins of BC salmon inspire many enduring recipes.

1874

Toronto medical student Henry Woodward invents the electric light bulb and illuminates his mother's kitchen. The next year, he sells his patent to American inventor Thomas Edison and buys his mother a Findlay stove for her brand-new kitchen.

1880

Red Fife wheat seed, an accidental discovery by Ontario farmer David Fife, is made available to all prairie farmers. Grain storage elevators holding around 35,000 bushels are constructed every 15 kilometres along rail lines, causing towns and villages to spring up almost overnight.

1881

La Compagnie de Sucre de Betterave de Québec begins refining sugar from beets in Farnam, Québec.

Two decades later, Ontario has four large sugar beet refineries, and within a short time, both Manitoba and what is now Alberta have refineries. Today, only Québec, Manitoba and Alberta have factories processing sugar beets, a shrinking industry because of competition from American high-fructose corn-syrup producers.

1882

Ottawa engineer and businessman Thomas Ahearn invents the electric cooking range for the kitchen of

THE SIXTH WAVE (1872–1914)

The age of westward expansion and culinary diversity

Railways, steamships and the 1867 acquisition of Rupert's Land, along with the displacement of native Plains tribes, meant easier transportation west for settlers. A concerted effort was made by the Canadian government, the Hudson's Bay Company and the Canadian Pacific Railway (CPR) to attract large numbers of immigrants from both the U.S. and Eastern Europe to the prairies. Canada grew a variety of wheat called Red Fife that the entire world craved, and the completion of the CPR in 1885 provided farmers a way to get it to the world.

As CPR-constructed grain silos became the nucleus for prairie towns, a diversity of food preparation spread through rural populations by way of barn raisings, neighbourly visits, church socials, restaurants and the new catalogue issued by the Toronto-based T. Eaton Company. The catalogue enabled settler wives to order stoves, cooking implements, cookbooks, spices, canned goods

and supplies for home canning. The most popular items were John Landis Mason's patented glass canning jars, which spawned the famous prairie canning bees and church socials wherein all manner of recipes bridging all ethnic barriers became "Canadianized" by adding locally available ingredients that were often superior to those of the old country.

Initially, the prairies were a fertile grassland, a sea of vegetation as far as the eye could see. Ranchers raised beef cows, farmers grew wheat, wives looked after gardens, milked cows and tended kitchens, and children fished local streams and lakes for trout and pickerel. Immigrants with special trades voluntarily chose to settle areas that needed their talents, whereas many areas of eastern Canada had historically recruited skilled tradesmen by offering incentives, such as free transportation and land.

CPR and the Hudson's Bay Company were the big players in the West, and between them they had millions of acres of land to toss around, but they wisely reserved the best for those immigrants with skills. Experienced farmers got prime land for growing wheat, along with free specially hybridized seed. German millers and brewers received free building lots and subsidized lumber. Dutch dairy farmers got land with water and grass. Icelandic fishermen received free land among Manitoba's 100,000 lakes. French orchardists got all the protected valleys to grow their fruits. For this carefully laid foundation, skilled tradesmen arriving at later times knew exactly where their talents were needed, especially after World War I, when Canada's western provinces garnered immense benefit from a mass migration of European skilled workers.

Ottawa's Windsor Hotel. That same year, he invents and patents an electric heater, water heater and flat iron. Six years later, Ahearn's Ottawa Electric Company illuminates the entire city, and two years after that, he has electric streetcars running the length of the city. However, many years would pass before the average Canadian housewife would benefit from his electric range or other inventions, as generating electricity and stringing power lines became a slow process. Natural gas is cheap, easier to produce and pipe, and it beats electricity into Canadian kitchens by decades.

1883

Successive crop failures put the future of prairie farming in doubt. Just in time, old bones emerge from the parched landscape to save farmers from rack and ruin. By 1890, bison bones become the Prairies' largest export. Shipped by rail car to eastern cities, the bones are converted to phosphate fertilizer and the carbon is used to refine sugar. During the decade from 1883 to 1893, the gathered-up bones of over one million bison are loaded onto rail cars and shipped east for processing. The greatest crime perpetrated on wildlife was the indiscriminate slaughter of millions of plains buffalo, but the bones saved an agricultural endeavour slated to become one of the world's great breadbaskets.

1884

The T. Eaton Company begins filling mail orders for goods and provisions with shipping by rail to the nearest depot. Canadian Pacific Railway tracks had reached Calgary, and Eaton's establishes a special department to handle orders and shipments to western settlers. Eaton's issues a catalogue of goods available and gives western farmers a taste of the good life. Orders pour into Eaton's for all manner of dry and canned goods. The lives of western farm wives improves considerably when Eaton's begins to ship cooking stoves.

1885

Our transcontinental railway is complete and the future of Canada's grain industry assured. Prairie housewives now have access to necessities that make their lives endurable. New settlers arrive accompanied by their worldly possessions, while at the same time, cook stove, piano and cream separator salesmen fan out across the Prairies. Elsewhere, a German pharmacist, Dr. Oetker, discovers that aluminum sulphate causes baked goods to rise in a hot oven.

1888

Baking powder salesman William Monroe Wright (a cousin of Wilbur and Orville Wright) has an idea

to combine sodium aluminum phosphate and cream of tartar. This double-action baking powder raises baked goods before and during the baking process. His company, the Calumet Baking Powder Company, becomes the world's largest manufacturer of baking powder. Double action is a good idea, and the year before Wright's Calumet brand hits the market, the E.W. Gillette Company of Chicago launches its Magic brand, another double-action baking powder, beating Calumet to the Canadian market. Both Cow Brand and Magic baking powders rule ovens from Ontario to the eastern seaboard, while the Royal brand holds sway in western Canada, with all brands manufactured in Canada after the turn of the century.

1890

Emile Paturel opens a lobster-canning factory at Shediac, New Brunswick, and although he goes broke three times, he eventually manages to turn the bottom-crawling crustacean into a culinary treat he ships around the globe.

1902

Charlie Woodward, *aka* Chunky, opens a department store in Vancouver, BC, and in 1926, he opens another Woodward's in Edmonton, Alberta. Woodward emulates the Eaton's stores and establishes a mail order business and is soon opening more stores. In 1993, suffering the effects of the 1980s economic recession,

Woodward declares bankruptcy, with the name and some assets acquired by the Hudson's Bay Company. Defunct for many years, there are now plans in the works to revive the company that so many remember with affection: Chunky Woodward's wonderful department stores.

1907

The Meat and Canned Food Act becomes law, enabling federal inspection of meat-packing plants, and Canadians stop dying from bacteria-infected meats and botulism.

1909

George Saunders, a federal government cerealist, hybridizes cold-tolerant, disease-resistant wheat called Marquis that sees distribution to all prairie farmers. In a decade, Saunders' discovery accounts for 90 percent of Canada's wheat crop.

1910

Arthur Ganong, a St. Stephen, New Brunswick, chocolate maker, has the idea that fishermen might like a convenient form of his product and invents the chocolate bar. The company, Ganong Bros. Limited,

has somehow avoided conglomerate takeover and is still producing candy in St. Stephen to this day, remaining an all-Canadian family business.

1914

World War I begins, and Canadians learn the meaning of food rationing. Kids collect metal, grandmothers knit army socks, domestic servants disappear into munitions factories, and moms across the country plant victory gardens, create new ration-extending recipes and learn to bake barley bread.

1916

An American immigrant to Labrador named Clarence Birdseye notices that fish caught and quickly frozen in barrels of seawater by local Innu people retain their freshness and flavour. He hatches a plan to commercialize the process and begins designing a plate-and-belt freezing system. In 1918, Birdseye returns to the U.S. to help in the war effort but continues thinking about new ideas for his freezing system.

1918

The first rock salt mine in the British Commonwealth opens at Malagash, Nova Scotia. Already-cheap salt cod becomes even cheaper, dozens of new processing plants open and the die is cast for the eventual demise of the fishery.

1919

Theodore Pringle Loblaw opens Canada's first self-serve groceteria in Toronto, and within a decade he has 80 stores in Ontario and the American states of New York and Pennsylvania.

1920

James Lewis Kraft, born in Stevensville, Ontario, adds a Montréal cheese factory to his burgeoning U.S. food-processing empire and gives his homeland a taste of his patented invention—processed cheese.

1924

Clarence Birdseye founds the General Seafood Company and perfects his freezing technique through a device he calls the Quick Freeze Machine.

THE SEVENTH WAVE (1915–1959)

The age of Spam and national belt-tightening

The Great War (1914–1918) turned Canada into an industrial power through the production of war materials. With few men at home to run the factories, women took off their aprons and stepped into the workplace. They worked swing shifts, ate cafeteria food, endured food rationing and embraced dinner from a can.

Post-war industry focused on consumer goods such as electric and gas ovens, and Canadians once again gathered around tables for the family dinner. Then along came the Great Depression (1929–1939) and World War II (1939–1945). For most early 20th-century Canadians, the 1930s were the worst of times—money was so tight that housewives resorted to inventiveness to put meals on the dinner table. The big food companies understood their pain and helped with the inventiveness by developing tight-money recipes. Canadians were back to eating dinner from a can: pork and beans, beef stew, salmon, sardines, corned beef and, beginning in 1937 and developed by the U.S. meat-packer Hormel Foods, a canned chopped pork-shoulder-and-ham combination called Spam. Corned with salt and sodium nitrate like canned corned beef, Spam possessed a much superior taste and looked almost like ham. Spam is still considered such good eats that the Hormel Food Company recently shipped out its seven-billionth can. ✄

In Canada, around 53 herbaceous plants are considered food crops (a mushroom and 52 seed plants). The problem is that they all ripen during the warmer months. Clarence Birdseye's Labrador idea enables access to almost-fresh veggies all winter long and provides a larger market for growers. However, at the time, there is no way for storekeepers to stock frozen products, so Birdseye gets to work and invents a freezer that will suit both the public and storekeepers. He even designs an electric light assembly to illuminate the front windows of stores that sell his frozen foods. In 1929, Clarence Birdseye, called the Father of Frozen Foods, sells his patents to the Postum Company that will eventually become General Foods. When asked about his invention, Birdseye always credited the Innu people of Labrador for supplying the idea that changed cooking and eating habits around the world.

1929

The Great Depression is not a market crash in Canada; economic collapse has been creeping up for a decade. In the West, successive years of severe drought and low grain prices have slowly leached the economic lifeblood from every prairie province, forcing 66 percent of the rural population onto relief. In British Columbia, the government has simply overspent the province into bankruptcy. In the Maritimes, the provinces have been broke since before 1929, when the downward spiral of the American stock market signalled the beginning of

three extremely hard years. One-third of Canada's labour force is unemployed for those years, and one in five citizens depends on government relief for survival. Hard times have a profound effect on the nation's eating habits, and Sunday dinners spiral down from roast beef, to casserole, to creamed salmon on toast, to liver loaf with ketchup.

1930

Wonder Bread, the first sliced and packaged bread, finds its way onto grocery store shelves. It was a 1921 innovation of the Taggert Baking Company of Indianapolis, Indiana, and named by that company's vice-president, Elmer Cline, who, after attending a hot air balloon race, said he had gazed in amazement at those balloons and the word "wonder" simply jumped from his yeast-soaked mind. Bought by Continental Bakeries in 1925, the Wonder brand was licenced to George Weston's Canada Bread in 1929 and to this day remains one of largest-selling breads in Canada.

1935

The Domestic Wine and Byproducts Company in British Columbia's Okanagan Valley changes

its name to Calona Wines and switches production from apple to grape wines.

1937

Kraft Dinner appears on grocery store shelves.

1939

Canada is once again at war; men sign up to fight, and women leave their kitchens to join the armed services or work in factories. Manufactured foods that can be speedily prepared become an intrinsic part of wartime family meals. Canadian cuisine goes into overdrive and new recipes speed up the delivery of meals from oven to table.

1940

Fred Moffat, an electrical researcher employed by Canadian General Electric, invents the electric kettle, and breakfasts become even speedier.

1942

Food rationing becomes law, and Canadian families tighten their belts. Here is a brief summary about rationing, by Mary F. Williamson, extracted from letters written to her mother during World War II:

Another big problem, as far as imported foods were concerned, such as vegetables, oranges and other fresh fruits, was that access to U.S. currency was severely restricted. Canned foods became very scarce as much of what was available was being sent to the troops. Sugar rationing—the first food to be rationed—began on January 26, 1942, with ¾ lb. per week per person. The amount was reduced in April to ½ lb., and at the same time tea and coffee rationing began. It was still "voluntary rationing"; the books of ration stamps were introduced in June of 1942. But already meat was hard to find. A 20 percent tax was levied on sweets and voluntary rationing was extended to bacon, pork and cheese. By August, tea and coffee were on the formal ration list: a mere 1 oz. per week per person! Butter rationing began in late December, with an allowance of ½ lb. per week per person. Meat was put on the ration list in May of 1943 at 2 lb. per week per person. Consumers were complaining that little could be found in the shops; most pork was being sent overseas. During summer 1943, the prices of local fruits rocketed, but more sugar was permitted to households for preserving and bottling. In September, store-bought jams and jellies were rationed. Food shortages of all kinds persisted through 1943. It was certainly difficult to plan a traditional Christmas dinner. Unless you were prepared to canvas every store in your wider neighbourhood, many of the basics were unobtainable.

1944

American ex-serviceman William L. Maxson invents three-part frozen dinners for the U.S. military and calls them Strato-Plates. In a little more than a decade, television and Maxson's invention revolutionized the family dinner in Canada.

1945

Canadian servicemen and women involved in the Italian campaigns return from the war with a taste for an Italian food specialty called pizza.

1946

American scientist Percy Spencer accidentally discovers that microwaves cook food when a radio transmitter he is perfecting melts a candy bar on his worktable. His messy "eureka" moment has far-reaching effects on the Canadian food experience.

1947

Kraft Foods tests the effectiveness of television advertising by reintroducing a defunct cheese brand called MacLaren's Imperial. Packed into a red cardboard container, the cheese is a huge success and marks the beginning of nationwide media campaigns by food processors to convince the public that industry-produced food is the modern, safer way to get dinner on the table.

1948

The Liberal government under Louis St. Laurent removes all barriers to U.S. investment and unofficially recognizes U.S. financial sovereignty.

1952

Our first television station, the Canadian Broadcasting Corporation (CBC), begins broadcasting in Toronto and Montréal, and one of the first commercial advertisers is the Campbell Soup Company with their famous Campbell Kids cartoon characters.

1954

The Saputo family, recently immigrated to Montréal from Italy, turns to making cheeses for the Italian community. In 1957, capitalizing on the rising popularity of pizza, they establish a factory to meet the demands of Québec pizzerias. During the 1970s, Saputo expands production to meet the demands of pizzerias across the nation and enters the retail market. During the 1980s, Saputo expands into whey processing and the production of more varieties of cheese. In the 1990s, Saputo grows ever larger, acquires more companies, goes public and enters the new millennium as a home-grown food conglomerate of massive proportions.

1956

Loblaw Groceterias begin selling "TV Dinner Brand Frozen Dinner," a C.A. Swanson product that revolutionizes the family dinner for many Canadians. Heat them, peel off the foil and dig in while watching TV becomes a national phenomena. In 1962, the Swanson Company removes the "TV Dinner" brand from all their packaging and uses just the Swanson name. However, the TV Dinner name remains synonymous with frozen dinners.

1957

McCain Foods Limited opens a plant in Florenceville, New Brunswick, to process potatoes into frozen French fries. By the start of the new millennium, McCain is a global processor of potatoes with 30 factories located around the world.

THE EIGHTH WAVE (1960–present)

The age of newer and faster foods

Asians and Middle Easterners arrived into Canada in such ever-increasing numbers that they added an entirely new dimension to Canadian cuisine, or what I like to call the "yin and yang effect." The yin is when new immigrants adjust their homestyle recipes with easier-to-obtain and fresher local ingredients, and over time their home country favourites slowly spread into the Canadian mainstream. Condiments such as soy, tamari, hoisin, harissa and wasabi that were almost unheard of a few decades ago have become as ubiquitous as ketchup in Canadian kitchens. Meanwhile, back in the old country, the yang takes effect when family and friends are treated to the old "you gotta try this" in emails, and visits abroad create whole new markets for Canadian food exports. It's yin and yang, and we all benefit.

In 1965, the U.S.-based Raytheon Corporation bought the Amana Refrigeration Company, and by 1967, they were marketing what its inventor, Dr. Percy Spencer, called the "speedee weenie"—the microwave oven. That appliance was the proverbial last straw for the great Canadian food experience; it completely disappeared in a blizzard of plastic packaged instant foods, with kitchens relegated to the keeping of plates, utensils and the freezer storage of ever-faster foods. ✍

1959

The St. Lawrence Seaway opens, enabling direct-to-the-world wheat shipping from the Lakehead, reaching as far inland as the western end of Lake Superior. The seaway also allows in the lamprey eel and hastens the demise of the Great Lakes fisheries.

1962

Edward Asselbergs, a research scientist at the Canadian Department of Agriculture in Ottawa, invents instant mashed potato flakes.

1964

Hockey great Tim Horton opens a doughnut shop in Hamilton, Ontario, and the national dementia of the great Canadian food experience accelerates—fried flour breakfasts, fried flour and processed meat lunches and dinners served on aluminum trays while watching television.

1967

American fast-food impresario Ray Kroc takes his rapidly expanding McDonald's hamburger franchise international when he opens a restaurant in Richmond, BC.

1976

Dr. Helmut Becker of Germany's famed Geisenheim Wine Institute supplies BC's Okanagan wine growers with 27 varieties of grape vines for trials that will establish the base varietals for the fast-maturing Okanagan wine industry.

1980

M&M Meat Shops open a store in Kitchener, Ontario, to sell boxed frozen meats to consumers wary of conglomerate meat packers. Today, M&M has almost 500 stores across the nation, with their boxed meat products offering consumers a way to mentally distance themselves from the abattoir.

1987

Canada and the U.S. sign a free-trade agreement that unhinges all manner of Canadian food conspiracies and increases our dependence on the U.S. in both exports and imports. Faced with competition from the U.S., Canadian meat-packing plants merge and farmers are forced into growing quality rather than weight. Canadian consumers benefit, but the control of food production slips away as more processing and raw material companies are bought out by U.S. conglomerates.

1989

An Italian, Carlo Petrini, founds the Slow Food Movement, an international non-profit organization bent on counteracting fast-food conglomerates by revitalizing local food traditions. By 2011, the organization has around 100,000 members in 130 countries, with about 6000 in Canada. Slow Food websites in Canada put consumers in touch with local producers of artisinal and organic foods and events that promote traditional Canadian foods.

1990

British-controlled Canada Packers and Maple Leaf Mills merge to become mega-conglomerate Maple Leaf Foods.

1994

A tomato called Flavr Savr, the first commercially available genetically modified (GMO) food, appears in supermarkets, quickly followed by GMO corn, strawberries and potatoes. By the end of the century, almost 70 percent of our agricultural output is genetically altered, and food allergies are on the rise.

1995

Ex-CEO of McCain Foods, Wallace McCain, and the Ontario Teachers' Pension Plan buy Maple Leaf Foods from the British and create Canada's very own mega food conglomerate—bleat, bawl, oink, freeze or fry, the McCain boys have it covered.

1996

The Food Network, a start-up culinary TV channel, becomes popular in the U.S. and enters Canada as an imported cable channel. In 2000, Alliance Atlantis Corporation launches Food Network Canada, and, while some programming focuses on Canadian

cuisine, the majority is concerned with what's for dinner in other places.

2001

The Italian mega food conglomerate Parmalat—owner of the Beatrice, Sargento, Lactancia, Balderson, Black Diamond and Astro brands—withdraws from membership in the National Dairy Council of Canada. This action effectively destroys the agency that put the Canadian dairy industry on the map and leaves smaller dairy processors without government representation. Parmalat, Saputo and Agropur process 80 percent of Canada's milk and have almost complete control of the industry, a situation that prompts many Canadians living close to the U.S. border to cross over and purchase less-expensive milk and dairy products.

2008

Maple Leaf Foods meat products are found contaminated by the listeria bacteria and are subject to a massive recall. Listeria contamination found in other food-processing plants across the nation

2011

On March 11, Japan's tsunami-crippled Fukushima nuclear power plant explodes, spewing radiation over a wide area. Food imports from Japan are stopped, but traces of radiation show up in BC rainwater and seaweed. The Canadian government begins to closely monitor food crops for radiation while citizens have second thoughts about supporting nuclear power plants.

2013

In mid-April, a Canadian taxpayer-funded food truck begins a three-week pilot project parked in Mexico City. The goal is to promote the "Canada" brand and feature Canadian products. The menu includes a variation of poutine using Mexican cheese instead of curds, albacore tuna glazed with maple, tourtière made with Alberta beef, and McCain French fries. This Agriculture Canada initiative sets us back $50,000. In May, the Québec government announces a policy of "food sovereignty," aimed at achieving an increase in the amount of locally produced food Québecers eat. Intending to impose rules and quotas, the PQ government may soon force public institutions to "buy local," even in areas of the province that would otherwise get closer-grown produce from Ontario or New Brunswick. Food as an essential part of the Québec identity is just the latest in the push to protect and promote Québécois culture and sovereignty—occasionally at the cost of common sense. ❖

causes consumers to lose confidence in conglomerate-produced foods. Sales of organic foods skyrocket, home gardens proliferate and stores are hard-pressed to keep up with demand for Mason jars.

2009

Wal-Mart stores across Canada begin stocking organic foods, and the word "locavore"—meaning someone who consumes only locally grown food—enters our vocabulary.

2010

An oilrig off the coast of Louisiana explodes on April 20, killing 11 people and causing a massive oil leak in the Gulf of Mexico. The oil spill will negatively impact the environment for years to come, including placing a strain on fish and shellfish populations. Officials with the Canadian government assure citizens that strict Canadian safety rules will prevent such a disaster from ever happening in our waters… we can only hope they're right.

There you have it, the history of Canadian cuisine in a nutshell, or how Canadians have progressed from hard-working hearths to rarely used stainless steel appliances. Most food is imported, treasured family recipes have been replaced by the internet, and restaurants are pressed into providing the nutritional content of menu items for people too stressed or busy to cook. However, there is a light at the end of the tunnel: Canadians have rediscovered vegetable gardening, a healthy source of ingredients for traditional Canadian cuisine. ❖

THE CANADIAN FOOD ENCYCLOPEDIA

Many tried and true, along with plenty that are fresh and new.

A

ABALONE—once common off the BC coast, the most prevalent species is the pinto or northern abalone (*Haliotis kamtschatkana*). From the 1950s until fishing for the species was prohibited in 1990, the sea bottom off the coast of BC was crowded with divers prying the molluscs off the rocks. Prohibition may have stopped the crowds, but not the prying; fishermen turned to boot-legging in a big way. When the authorities do catch abalone rustlers, it is with thousands of molluscs mostly headed for China. The entire BC coast remains closed to abalone harvesting because of overfishing and sea otter predation. Red abalone or frozen fillets of green lip abalone from New Zealand can still be purchased, but both are inferior to the delectable pinto species.

ACE BAKERY—in 1993, Caledon, Ontario, resident Martin Connell and his wife Linda Haynes launched a research project into French bread–baking and opened the Ace Bakery in Toronto, making the world a happier place.

Then in 2010, the mighty Weston Empire bought Ace Bakery and all of its wonderful bread products became half-baked and the world was not as happy a place.

ACORN COFFEE—brewed by the truly desperate from roasted and ground seeds or nuts of various oak trees native to Canada, the most common being the bur oak (*Quercus macrocarpa*).

AFFINAGE—a French word meaning the art of curing cheeses, with the person doing the curing called an *affineur*, an important personage in the crafting of exceptional cheeses. As Afrim Pristine of Toronto's Cheese Boutique says, "I can't buy a ten-year-old cheddar—I have to age it myself." Long established in Europe and the province of Québec, affinage is in its infancy in the rest of Canada but is slowly gaining ground.

RECIPE

Alberta Beef Ribs

Brown beef ribs on all sides in a Dutch oven. Pour on a seasoned stew of chopped onions, carrots, celery, canned tomatoes, wild or Dijon mustard, honey and garlic, and hot sauce if you like it; cook for 3–4 hours. To turn tasty into scrumptious, remove ribs after 3 hours, brush with honey and wild mustard and finish on the barbecue.

AFTERNOON TEA—historically called "low tea" because it was served on a low table, afternoon tea is an English custom established in the 18th century by Anna, Duchess of Bedford, who defied the tradition of "dinner at eight" by having tea, cakes and sandwiches served at five o'clock. If a more substantial snack was called for, such as tea and a meat pie, the affair was called "high tea" and served on a regular or high table. During the 19th century, there emerged a variation of afternoon tea called "cream tea" where the fare was, and still is, clotted cream, berries and scones. Afternoon tea would eventually become dinner-time in Canada and almost everywhere else.

ALBACORE TUNA. *See* tuna.

ALBERTA BEEF RIBS—a delicious culinary conjuration of old-time Alberta chuckwagon cooks that in modern times has become a staple offering of dude ranches, upscale western steakhouses and your kitchen, once you try the following recipe.

Alberta Beef

- Almost 6 million head of cattle graze Alberta's foothills, and no better place exists to make them happy. Alberta beef cattle eat the finest grass, drink the purest water and, when the time comes for a little marbling, get to munch the world's best grain. To paraphrase Food TV's Alton Brown, "Happy cows make…Good Eats."

- Alberta's 36,000 beef producers export over $1 billion worth of good eats around the globe.

A

B C D E F G H I J K L M N O P Q R S T U V W X Y Z

ALEWIFE FISHERY

As an indicator of the size and importance of the mid-1800s alewife fishery, records from this period show over 35,000 barrels of salt-pickled alewives shipped from Nova Scotia and New Brunswick annually. Nowadays, alewives are still pickled, but a pail has replaced the barrel, and shipping is to the Middle East and the Caribbean. Thin and bony, so not as prized as regular herring, the fish made up for those shortcomings by ease of procurement and sheer numbers. Alewives breed and spawn in fresh water, making their appearance in major river systems around the beginning of May. In earlier times, alewives would move into the rivers in such numbers that simple seine nets laid across constrictions enabled a thriving commercial trade. While a commercial fishery still exists today, primarily from rivers feeding the southern Gulf of St. Lawrence and Bay of Fundy, it is not thriving because of overfishing and degradation of breeding habitats. Alewives readily adapt to fresh-water living and can be landlocked in lakes, especially those comprising the Great Lakes system. Overfishing and lamprey predation of native fish stocks during the 1950s led to a dramatic rise in Great Lakes alewife populations until the introduction of predator salmon species and aggressive culling of invasive lamprey eels brought their numbers back under control.

Alewife

• Today, adult alewives are the preferred bait for lobster fishermen, and a small industry has sprung up canning alewife eggs, or roe. The remainder of the catch is smoked, pickled, used in pet food or made into fishmeal.

• Alewives introduced into Pacific rivers now range from California to Alaska and have become a vital food resource for depleted salmon stocks.

• The alewife earned its name from having a pronounced belly reminiscent of those found on overindulgent wives of tavern owners.

ALEWIFE (*Alosa pseudoharengus*; also called gaspereau, kiak, spring herring)—a member of the Herring family, this small (10–30 cm long), rough-scaled fish takes to curing by salt readily, and during the 1800s, millions of the little fish were salt-pickled into barrels and shipped abroad, while millions more saw use as fish bait or fertilizer. Cheap and always plentiful, the alewife became the main ingredient of hundreds of different recipes.

ALGINATES—a broad term used to describe the gums extracted from various seaweeds in the category of brown algae, such as California kelp and various seaweeds growing on Britain's

coastal areas, those countries being the major producers. Alginates are widely used in the processed food industry to emulsify and stabilize foods, especially dairy products.

ALPINE STRAWBERRY (*Fragaria vesca*; also called *fraise des bois*)—strawberries are indigenous to North America, but the most delicious one is a European import that escaped to the wilds only to be recaptured again and offered at farmers' markets: the diminutive alpine strawberry. It is a tiny berry with huge flavour, and once tried it will impart a lasting lesson, the true taste of strawberry. These berries can be any colour—red, white, even yellow—but they all have one thing in common: fantastic taste. *See also* strawberry.

> ### RECIPE
>
> ### *Alpine Strawberry Parfait*
>
> *Whisk together until smooth: ½ cup heavy cream, 2 cups ricotta cheese, ¼ cup icing sugar and 1 tsp vanilla. Layer 1½ cups alpine strawberries into 4 wine glasses, cover with the ricotta cheese mixture and top with another layer of berries and more ricotta. Sprinkle with toasted almonds and serve well chilled.*

AMBROSIA SALAD—a 1950s and '60s salad phenomenon rooted to the traditional fruit salad but with additions that included pineapple, maraschino cherries, coconut, whipped cream, strawberries, bananas, mini marshmallows and even horseradish. Today, ambrosia salad is still on the menu of a few dining establishments that time has forgotten, including everyone's favourite, the Erie Beach Hotel in Port Dover, Ontario.

AMERICAN CHEESE. *See* processed cheese.

AMERICAN CHESTNUT. *See* chestnut.

AMERICAN MUSTARD (also called ballpark mustard)—this mild mustard is made from white mustard seeds flavoured with turmeric. Strangely enough, the largest selling American mustard is called French's and is made mostly from Canadian mustard seeds. *See also* mustard.

A

AMERICAN SHAD. *See* shad.

AN EXCELLENT CAKE—recipe #146 in *The Cook Not Mad*. This very rich cake is from those good ol' days when waistline was hardly a word.

RECIPE

An Excellent Cake

Mix 2 lbs flour, 1 lb butter, 1 teacup of yeast with warm milk and set it to rise. Add 2 lbs currants, 1 lb sugar, ¼ lb almonds, ½ lb raisins chopped fine, 1 tsp each of nutmeg, cinnamon and cloves, a peel of lemon chopped fine, a glass each of wine and brandy, 12 eggs (yolks and whites beaten separately and thoroughly) and the juice of 1 orange and 1 lemon, and pop into a 375°F oven until a pick comes out clean, 30–40 minutes. Whew! Reads like an American extravaganza.

ANADAMA BREAD—iconic east coast cornmeal yeast bread sweetened with molasses. A favourite of fishermen, this richly flavoured bread is also made with whole-wheat flour. *See also* bread.

ANDOUILLE SAUSAGE—originally a sausage specialty of French Normandy, it was brought to Canada by Acadian settlers, who then brought it to Louisiana and back again as returning deportees. Although more famous in Louisiana than in Canada, this spicy beef and pork sausage has so many fans in the

Anadama Bread

- It's a strange name for bread, and how it came to be is but a legend. Tired of his wife Anna's hard bread, a fisherman yelled to his mate, "Anna be damma, we get our own meal and molasses and cook on the boat's stove top."

- Towns all along the eastern seaboard claim the invention of anadama bread, and while the original source has faded into history, the bread is certainly a fisherman's creation and most probably Canadian because our maritime fishery is historically more extensive.

Cookbooks

- *The Cook Not Mad* (1831) was Canada's first cookbook. It became a bestseller and mainstay kitchen guidebook for Canadian housewives. Only later was it discovered that the publisher, James Macfarlane of Kingston, had plagiarized almost the entire book, including the title, from the American publisher Knowlton and Rice of Watertown, New York, 60 kilometres from Kingston.

Was it outright theft or a hoax? Or had Macfarlane merely demonstrated how Canadians could be easily fooled by those words "Made in Canada"? Nobody knows, but since he owned the Kingston newspaper and never advertised the cookbook, one must surmise a warning—Canada should stand apart from the U.S. and promote its own heritage.

Maritime provinces that Loblaw's President's Choice products sold nationwide regularly feature the sausage.

ANITA'S TOP 10 CANADIAN FARMERS' MARKETS—as selected by cookbook author, culinary activist and foodie extraordinaire Anita Stewart and listed west to east:

- Pier Street Market, Campbell River, BC
- Trout Lake Market, Vancouver, BC
- City Market Downtown, Edmonton, AB
- Saskatoon Farmers' Market, Saskatoon, SK
- Le Marche St. Norbert, Winnipeg, MB
- Guelph Farmers' Market, Guelph, ON
- Marche de Vieux-Port de Québec, Québec City, QC
- W.W. Boyce Farmers' Market, Fredericton, NB
- Halifax Farmers' Market, Halifax, NS
- Charlottetown Farmers' Market, Charlottetown, PEI

ANNATTO—an orange dye extracted from pulp around the seeds of the tropical achiote tree and used by dairies to colour butter and cheese.

ANTHOCYANIN—a plant chemical found in red, blue and purple fruits, such as blueberries, cherries and grapes, that is credited with preventing and arresting any number of diseases including cancer, heart disease and various infections.

A

ANTIOXIDANT—a molecule found in some food plants that may be protective against certain diseases including cancer. Antioxidant molecules inhibit the oxidation of other molecules and can prevent damage or death to human cells. Berries, broccoli, garlic and tomatoes are all rich in antioxidants.

APPLE (*Malus domestica*)—Baldwin, Canada-red, Canada Reinette, Cortland, Cox, Fameuse (snow apple), Gravenstein, Knobbed Russet, Jonathan, McIntosh, Northern Spy, Pomme-gris, Rubinette, St. Lawrence, Winesap…there are over 6000 apple varieties. Apple trees are good at remembering friends and relatives, and planting a seed of one variety may produce a tree of a completely different variety. Apple trees are agreeable to propagation via wind, honeybees and other insects, from any convenient apple-related tree. Planting an orchard with apple seeds is always a gamble; the mature trees may bear dissimilar fruit with undesirable characteristics (perhaps even crabapples), or they may be stunted and barren because they do not like the soil or weather. To avoid this biological idiosyncrasy, orchard-grown apple trees are always from grafted stock: the wood of a desired tree is surgically attached to the roots of trees well suited to the area's growing conditions. The McIntosh apples you purchase from a supermarket all come from grafts of the original tree discovered by John McIntosh in 1811, near Peterborough, Ontario. Searching farmers' markets for those varieties that most snap the taste buds is like a treasure hunt. (Tip: When selecting apples for snacking, go for the smallest as they will contain more sugar than large apples.)

CANADA'S FAVOURITE APPLE VARIETIES

- Gravenstein—came along with the settlers and was Canada's favourite until sidelined by conglomerate packers more interested in keeping qualities than taste. Grown nationwide, it is the one to look for at farmers' markets when thoughts of pie become all consuming.

- McIntosh—look for the first generation unperfected apple.

- Northern Spy—Ontario's favourite pie apple.

- Pippins (Cox's Orange, Newtown or Albemaria)—the great apple benchmarks.

- Rubinette—difficult to grow and commercially unpopular, it is the one to look for at farmers' markets because it is one of the best snacking apples.

- Russets—dull skins, but so sweet and crisp.

- Snow (Fameuse)—the finest "fresh picked" snacking apple on the planet.

- Winesap—one of the best storage apples and great for juicing.

Apples

- Apple trees are not native to Canada, and while we did have two native crabapples that were much used by First Nations, these trees provided only famine food to settlers as they waited for seeds they brought from home to mature. First Nations tribes jumped at the chance to acquire European apple varieties, and settlers were often surprised to find their apple trees had preceded them to new areas.

- The apple tree's unruliness prompted the ancient Mesopotamians to invent the art of tree grafting: the insertion of a bud, or scion, from a desired variety into the woody trunk of an apple tree with known but undesired characteristics, with the host tree acting as the rootstock for the desired variety. In other words, the Mesopotamians invented cloning, because every graft will produce a fruiting tree identical to the graft donor.

- Every decade or so, a new apple variety makes an appearance at local farmers' markets. New apples are a big hit in their area, but seldom, if ever, make the jump to national availability, as doing so would disturb the status quo of tree-to-market distribution. However, there are occasional exceptions, and a BC-grown apple called Ambrosia is currently wending its way into the national food experience. Keep your eyes peeled, and if you spot this beauty anywhere, grab a few and prepare for a taste sensation.

- Once a major player in the international apple market, Canada's world market share has shrunk considerably, and we are now only the 16th largest apple-producing country—but just wait until the world tastes the Ambrosia apple.

A

B
C
D
E
F
G
H
I
J
K
L
M
N
O
P
Q
R
S
T
U
V
W
X
Y
Z

RECIPE

Barn Raiser Apple Pie

Peel, core and slice 11 lbs apples, one apple at a time, placing slices into solution of 4 cups water and ¼ cup lemon juice to prevent browning. When finished, drain apples and add 1½ cups sugar, 1¼ cups flour, 2 tsp cinnamon, 1 tsp ginger, ½ tsp nutmeg and ½ tsp allspice. Mix well and pour into the bottom crust in a large pie plate or ceramic casserole. Cover with top crust. Slit crust, paint with egg wash and dust with fine sugar. Bake on bottom oven shelf at 375°F until filling is bubbling and crust is golden brown, about 2–2½ hours, but check regularly after 1 hour.

RECIPE

Apple Tart with Custard
(Tarte de Pommes à la Normande)

Into a prebaked short crust, lay thinly sliced tart apples (such as Granny Smith) and sprinkle over ⅓ cup sugar, ½ tsp cinnamon and bake until apples begin to colour. In a separate bowl, beat 1 egg with ⅓ cup sugar until pale yellow; slowly add ¼ cup flour and beat until smooth. Add ¾ cup heavy cream and ¼ cup Calvados (French apple brandy) and beat until smooth. Pour custard over cooled tart and return to oven until custard is set and top is brown. Serve warm with a dollop of whipped cream.

APPLE AND WILD RICE—a First Nations favourite of crabapples and wild rice, quickly adapted by pioneer families with access to hybrid, European-style apples. Still popular today, the tasty combination makes a wonderful salad or stuffing for wild or domestic fowl.

APPLE BUTTER—a hard, cooked-until-thick spiced applesauce condiment popular from the very earliest times and made wherever apples grew. While not originally Canadian as the recipe was brought by either English or German settlers, apple butter has been naturalized over many generations by the use of Canadian apples.

APPLE CIDER—an easy-to-make alcoholic beverage produced by fermenting apple juice in a closed

container equipped with a one-way valve. No sugar or yeasts are needed, and after a few weeks of fermentation, the party can begin. Apple cider has been a Canadian treat since the 16th century and is traditionally pressed from windfall apples (ripe apples picked from the ground after storms). Artisanal cider presses are located in most Canadian provinces; the largest, Growers Cider Company in Victoria, BC, markets ciders across the country.

APPLE CIDER BRANDY—a high-proof distillation of apple cider, and a backyard specialty of many apple growers from pioneer days to the present. In BC and Québec, several artisanal distilleries are engaged in the legal production of cider brandy.

APPLE CIDER PIE—this was a favourite pie of the early Québec habitant who was as likely to have a slice for breakfast as he was for dinner.

RECIPE

Apple Cider Pie

Peel, core and slice 6 medium tart apples, such as Braeburn, Mac or Gala, into eighths; then place in a pot, cover with apple cider and cook over medium heat until soft, about 30 minutes. Remove from heat and thicken sauce with a little flour. Add ½ cup sugar and ¼ tsp each of ground cinnamon, nutmeg and cloves. Pour mixture into prebaked pie shell, lattice top with pastry and bake at 450°F for 8 minutes, reduce heat to 350°F and bake another 25 minutes.

APPLE CIDER VINEGAR—a specialty of apple-growing areas that is taking on the panache of fine wines, with a pronounced taste of the specific apples used in the vinegaring process and a marketing emphasis on the healthy aspects of ingesting vinegar. Look for cider vinegars at local farmers' markets, and do not be afraid to sample the wares on the spot.

APPLE ICE WINE. *See* ice cider.

APPLE MOLASSES (also called apple syrup)—a staple sweetener of pioneer settlers and still popular with today's discerning chefs. Apple molasses or syrup is used to sweeten cereal, to drizzle over pancakes and in any recipe calling for molasses. Made from fresh cider boiled to syrup, apple molasses—usually labelled as apple syrup—is available in some supermarkets and fine food stores.

APPLE SCHNAPPS—an eau-de-vie once produced by many backyard distillers, today the best legal production in Canada comes from the stills of Winegarden Estates in Baie-Verte, New Brunswick, and the Rodrigues Winery in Markland, Newfoundland. Both firms turn apples into liquor so crisp and clean it will leave you breathless and wondering why you can only buy it in those provinces.

A
B
C
D
E
F
G
H
I
J
K
L
M
N
O
P
Q
R
S
T
U
V
W
X
Y
Z

A
B
C
D
E
F
G
H
I
J
K
L
M
N
O
P
Q
R
S
T
U
V
W
X
Y
Z

APPLE SNOW PUDDING—an unpeeled apple-sauce dessert made by beating rosy-coloured applesauce into whipped egg whites while adding sugar and powdered ginger root. This classic east coast favourite has become a darling of chefs and is widely used to finish classic Canadian meals.

APPLE SOUP—popular then and now, apples work wonderfully in combination with various vegetables such as turnips, potatoes and squash.

APPLE SYRUP. *See* apple molasses.

APPLE TAPIOCA—an abundance of apples prompted early settlers to use them in inventive ways, especially in sweet desserts.

RECIPE

Apple Tapioca

Mix ½ cup softened tapioca with 6 peeled, cored and sliced cooking apples in a baking dish. Bake for 30 minutes at 375°F. Add a pinch of salt, ¾ cup sugar, 2 tsp lemon juice and a shot of cinnamon. Stir and then bake for another 20 minutes. Cool and serve with thick or whipped cream.

APPLEJACK—an easy-to-make but crude pioneer whisky made only in the winter months. To make, simply fill an outside barrel with hard cider and remove the ice as it freezes. The alcohol will not freeze; it will separate from the water and puddle in the centre. When the parting of the ways is complete, the party can begin.

APPLESAUCE—a purée made from cooked apples and a favourite condiment and dessert of both pioneer and modern families. Sweet or unsweet-ened applesauce made from fresh-picked apples is a culinary delight best consumed immediately—a few days in the fridge will have it tasting like the ubiquitous canned version.

APPLESAUCE CAKE—a favourite of early settlers and still going strong, this delicious cake uses no eggs and relies on applesauce for its light, moist texture.

APRICOT (*Prunus armeniaca*)—grown in BC's Okanagan and Similkameen valleys and to a lesser extent in southern Ontario, this fresh fruit is sometimes readily available at markets and some-times not at all, depending on early frosts.

AQUACULTURE—the cultivation of fish, shellfish or aquatic plants in enclosed areas such as net pens, ponds and tanks for human consumption. Much practised in Europe where scarcity drove necessity, aquaculture has become a 21st-century phenomenon in North America as a result of fish stock depletions by greedy for-profit con-glomerates. In Canada, mainly salmon is raised.

THE DANGERS OF AQUACULTURE

Raising fish in pens or cages seems like a good idea to politicians: it keeps the market supplied, provides jobs and enables fishermen to keep operating to supply food for what over time has became millions of captive fish. This is too many fish to feed from wild sources, but luckily corn gluten is widely available and will supply captive fish with one-third of the protein needed for growth as long as arginine and lysine, both essential amino acids for vertebrates, are added to their meal pellets. In Canada, arginine, a growth hormone releaser, is a banned food supplement because it causes problems for people with heart conditions. But how the trace amounts of arginine found in the flesh of farmed fish fed with corn gluten is affecting national health is a question waiting for an answer. Other nasty chemicals show up in the analysis of farmed fish: PCBs, antibiotics, the fire-retardant chemical Mirex, dioxins and pesticides. Fish imported from Asian countries may contain all of those chemicals, plus high levels of heavy metals and bacterial pathogens. Have you noticed a funny taste in frozen shrimp? That is sodium bisulfate, a chemical preservative sprayed onto shrimp before freezing to prevent discoloration. Nasty, but it can be worse—some foreign fisheries have taken to using formaldehyde, saltpeter, benzoate, sorbate, a dip in antibiotics and even irradiation to preserve the freshness of fish and shrimp.

Pesticides and antibiotics should be a concern to consumers because farmed fish receive both in massive amounts: the pesticide emamectin benzoate is used to counter sea lice, while antibiotics are administered on a prophylactic basis to fight infections. Confined fish are under constant stress and open to all manner of infections, both viral and bacterial, and for protection are made to swim in a virtual soup of antibiotics, some of which are passed onto both human consumers and the environment. The feedlot system of salmon aquaculture, wherein juvenile fish are transferred from inland raising tanks to offshore compounds, is notorious for infectious fish diseases that are counteracted by the use of massive amounts of antibiotics. The danger is not only that residual antibiotics will show up in retailed fish, but also that the antibiotics are slowly creating resistant marine bacteria capable of passing resistance to other bacteria, including those that are human pathogens.

Dangers aside, Canada remains a land of countless lakes and rivers surrounded by a quarter-million kilometres of coastline wherein is still found some of the safest, best tasting seafood on the planet. We simply have to circumvent the conglomerate supply chains and rely on our own devices to get safe, yummy seafood from those waters onto our tables. That can mean buying seafood from a reputable and trusted source, a local fishmonger, or establishing your own supply chain by either angling your own or cultivating friends and relatives who catch a surplus of fish.

A
B
C
D
E
F
G
H
I
J
K
L
M
N
O
P
Q
R
S
T
U
V
W
X
Y
Z

ARCTIC CHAR (*Salvelinus alpinus*)—a member of the Salmon family, but with a milder taste and tiny scales. Native to arctic and subarctic streams and lakes, char has a most agreeable flavour and may be prepared in dozens of ways.

ARCTIC GRAYLING (*Thymallus arcticus*)—related to trout and whitefish, grayling are native to rivers and lakes of northern BC, Northwest Territories and Alberta. A popular game fish, the flesh is white, flaky and bland.

ARCTIC RASPBERRY. *See* nagoonberry.

ARROWROOT COOKIES—a mother's favourite snack for toddlers since 1906. You bake good cookies, Mr. Christie, despite being just a small cog in the big wheel of mega food conglomerate Kraft Foods.

ARTISANAL—the word used to describe food and beverages made by hand using traditional techniques and only fresh, natural ingredients.

ARUGULA (*Eruca sativa*)—called "rocket" in Britain, which is an anglicized version of the French word

roquette, a word invention used to describe the Italian leafy salad vegetable *rucola*. Arugula is especially popular in North America as a peppery salad green.

ASH WATER—wars and hard times occasionally caused certain food items to become scarce, forcing Canadians to improvise. When supplies of chemically manufactured baking powder dried up, cooks made a substitute product with wood ash from the fireplace and a few gallons of water. They simply boiled the water and ash mixture for 10 minutes, let it sit all night and then ran it through some cheesecloth in the morning.

ASPARAGUS (*Asparagus officinalis*)—well known to early Greek and Roman cooks, this nearly leafless member of the Lily family is available

today as either white or green spears, with the former produced by mounding up soil to prevent sunlight from reaching the spears. Europeans prefer white asparagus, while North Americans like the normal green asparagus shoots. Growing asparagus is an expensive undertaking for farmers, which is reflected in market prices. A new crop requires two to three growing seasons to reach marketable size and after a few years begins to decline, so at any given time half of a farmer's fields are unproductive. Asparagus can be boiled or broiled, but many chefs consider grilling to be the best preparation technique because a slight charring will caramelize its natural sugars, enhancing flavour. Simply clean and snap off tough ends, brush spears with olive oil, sprinkle with sea salt and grill until fork tender.

Asparagus

- According to trials conducted in England, a Canadian asparagus variety developed at the University of Guelph and called Guelph Millennium is the world's best-growing and finest-tasting asparagus.

- Asparagus has the highest concentration of the antioxidant rutin of any vegetable, a chemical compound with life-extending attributes.

ASPARAGUS CASSEROLE—a springtime favourite of Canada West settlers, this Cheddar cheese and fresh asparagus delight is still popular. Asparagus casserole is a scrumptious side dish for baked ham.

RECIPE

Asparagus Casserole

Cover 2–3 lbs fresh asparagus spears with Cheddar cheese sauce (first a roux, then add milk, then grated cheese), top with a mixture of breadcrumbs and butter, and bake for 20–25 minutes at 350°F.

ASPIC—originally the name of the clear jelly derived from the knuckle of a calf's foot, aspic was used to hold together cold meats or fish. In modern times, the word has come to mean the dish itself and can be used to make up various dishes, especially salads.

ASSOCIATION DE L'AGROTOURISME ET DU TOURISME GOURMAND—formerly called Fédération des Agricotours de Québec, this is a provincial agency that handles all manner of agritourism, including the publishing of a guidebook that lists bed and breakfasts, country inns and farm excursions. See also *tables champêtres et relais du terroir.*

ATHOL BROSE—a Scottish alcoholic drink made by mixing oatmeal brose, honey, whisky and cream and given a Canadian twist when immigrant Scots substituted maple syrup for honey. Athol brose is the precursor drink to Ireland's famous Bailey's Irish Cream.

ATLANTIC COD (*Gadus morhua*)—the road to riches in Canada was paved with the split and salted bodies of countless codfish and the supply seemed endless, but in 1992 the fishery died, an entire species killed off by greed and mismanagement. *See also* codfish moratorium.

ATLANTIC HERRING (*Clupea harengus*; also called brisling, pilchard, sardine, sprat)—a small Atlantic schooling fish consumed by almost every predator on the planet. Herring are the dominant fish species in our east coast waters and are available fresh, frozen, smoked or canned.

RECIPE

Sardine Pie

Fry 1 diced potato until soft, then add 1 large diced onion, 1 can sardines, 3 Tbsp curry powder and salt and pepper to taste. Thicken with a little cornstarch and water and cook until almost dry. Turn into a prebaked pie shell, cover with a slitted pastry and bake at 350°F for 20 minutes, or until top is golden brown.

ATLANTIC MACKEREL. *See* mackerel.

ATLANTIC POLLOCK (*Pollachius pollachius*)—traditionally fished to supply the cat food industry, this white-fleshed but strongly flavoured fish is showing up more frequently as frozen and fresh fillets in fish markets. The artificial crab used to make sushi is actually dyed Atlantic pollock.

ATLANTIC SALMON (*Salmo salar*)—the lone salmon found in Atlantic waters, this is our preferred species for the table and for east coast fish smokers, but alas, we have wasted wild stocks to the point where most Atlantic salmon reaching markets are either farmed or imported. Sports fishermen may still catch Atlantic salmon from rivers (such as the Miramichi) and land-locked Atlantic salmon from certain lakes. In 2010, Greenpeace added Atlantic salmon to its red list after discovering that some wild-caught Atlantic salmon from unsustainable populations were showing up in supermarket coolers labelled as "farmed." Unlike the Pacific salmons, Atlantic salmon does not die after spawning and may live up to 20 years. *See also* salmon.

ATLANTIC WOLFFISH (*Anarhichas lupus*)—it's not the cutest fish in the deep Atlantic, but it's one of the tastiest. It has been trawled to the danger point, prompting the Québec government to invest some money in growing the species in tanks—something the Norwegians have been doing for 10 years.

AU PIED DE COCHON—chef Martin Picard (Food TV's "Wild Chef") is known for his gastronomic extravaganza of things many people never cook, especially duck. If heading to Montréal, make reservations at his restaurant Au Pied de Cochon and make sure to try Martin's foie gras poutine—and yes, both the fries and gravy are ducky. Martin also hosts a sugar bush extravaganza every fall to celebrate all things pork and maple, and a try at reservations during that time is equally worthwhile.

AUBERGINE. *See* eggplant.

AVONLEA CHEDDAR CHEESE—artisanal PEI cow's milk Cheddar wrapped in cloth to preserve moisture during the aging process…and it tastes sensational.

AYLMER CANNED TOMATOES—a favourite of Canadians since Aylmer, Ontario, residents David Marshall and Thomas Nairn established the company in 1881. Southwestern Ontario is one of the world's great tomato-growing areas, and despite being owned by the U.S. investment company Sun Capital Partners, Aylmer still manages to get the best of our crops into cans.

B

BABY CARROTS—baby carrots could simply be any variety of carrot picked before maturity, though the baby carrots sold in supermarkets are either manufactured from field rejects or from giant carrots grown specifically for turning into baby carrots. History credits California carrot farmer Mike Yurosek with the idea of transforming big carrots into babies during the late 1980s. However, Toronto's Royal York Hotel featured baby carrots on its menus beginning in the early 1970s, and they came out of a huge wooden Dunderbeck-type machine run by a guy from Clarkson, Ontario. Carrots the size of small children were chopped up and thrown in and, as if by magic, out came the babies.

RECIPE

Braised Baby Carrots

Place 1 cup water or chicken broth, 1 Tbsp butter, 2 tsp sugar and ½ tsp salt into a cast iron skillet and bring to a boil. Add 1 lb baby carrots in a single layer, cover skillet and reduce heat to a simmer. Cook until carrots are soft, about 5–6 minutes, and remove with a slotted spoon. Turn up the heat and reduce skillet liquid until slightly thick, then return the carrots for reheating and glazing.

BACALAO—a Newfoundland and Portuguese culinary marvel made from dried salt cod, for which there are at least 100 recipes. *Bacalao* is the Portuguese word for salt cod and quite possibly their 16th-century name for where the dish originated: Newfoundland. *See also* Basque influence.

RECIPE

Tomato Sauce Bacalao

Fry 2 lbs desalted and floured cod on both sides in ¼ cup olive oil and set aside. Add ½ cup olive oil to pan along with 1 chopped onion and 3 cloves chopped garlic; cook until translucent. Add a 28 oz tin of crushed tomatoes and 1 bay leaf; simmer 10 minutes. Add fish along with a 12 oz jar of roasted red peppers; cover and simmer for 5 minutes.

A
B
C
D
E
F
G
H
I
J
K
L
M
N
O
P
Q
R
S
T
U
V
W
X
Y
Z

BACALAO

Jenaro Pildain, owner and chef of Gurai, a famous bacalao restaurant in Bilboa, Spain, recommends soaking salt cod for 36 hours with four water changes and a final soak in mineral water to remove any chlorine taste from the tap water. Other great bacalao chefs recommend a longer soak, up to 48 hours, but somewhere in between should suffice to desalt and plump the fish for your bacalao.

BACHELOR BUTTON COOKIES—a buttery favourite of pioneer bakers because the recipe called for no soda. Bachelor buttons were a special favourite on the Prairies and were always included in the overseas Christmas packages sent to Canadian forces fighting on the battlefields of World War I.

BACK BACON—Canadian-style bacon, cured and smoked bacon cut from pork loin. Roasted back bacon was a favourite meal of settlers in early fall when hogs were butchered. Nowadays, it is mostly served as a breakfast side or paired with poached eggs and Hollandaise sauce on English muffins in a dish called Eggs Benedict.

BACON AND APPLE TOAST—apples stewed with butter and sugar and piled onto thick slices of bread fried in butter and layered with bacon.

BAGEL AND NOVA LOX—a Montréal-style sliced bagel slathered with cream cheese and topped with slices of cold or hot smoked Nova Scotia salmon.

BAKEAPPLE (*Rubus chamaemorus*; also called cloudberry)—a raspberry-like drupe that grows in places other berries refuse to grow and pickers fear to tread. The soft, juicy berries are golden yellow to pink in colour and vary in taste from tart to sweet. They are used for all manner of food products from jams and jellies to pies to liquor, with demand far exceeding supply. The jam is a favourite on the east coast, especially in Newfoundland.

BAKED BEANS—a dried pea or navy bean casserole; one of the iconic foods of Canadian cuisine.

Baked Beans

- Jacques Cartier traded with the Mi'kmaq on his first voyage to the New World in 1534, according to a note in his ship's log. Although no record exists as to what goods changed hands, food must have been tantamount, and that meant the bean pot. Pork and beans with onions and sweetener in 1534—almost a century before any Puritan set foot in a place called Boston, and two centuries before anyone thought of adding tomato sauce.

RECIPE

Classic Canadian Baked Beans

Cover 2 cups navy beans with water and bring to a boil for 2 minutes, then set aside to soak overnight. Drain liquid and replace with 5 cups hot water. Add 2 tsp each of dry mustard and salt, and ¼ tsp pepper. Simmer for 1 hour on stovetop. Transfer beans and liquid to a cast iron pot. Add ¼ lb salt pork, 1 sliced onion, ¼ cup maple sugar, 3 Tbsp maple syrup and 2 Tbsp molasses. Cover and bake at 300°F for 5 hours, adding water if beans become dry.

BAKED BEANS

Hundreds of recipe variations exist for baked beans—sweet, slightly sweet, unsweetened, spicy, plain, with or without salt pork, beef, venison—but all are rooted in the original one pot, the extremely boring ship's kettle of beans. In the 16th century, fishing fleets headed for the New World were provisioned by sensible, unimaginative men who gave the sailors dried peas, beans, salt pork, hardtack and salt, all in barrels, along with a large iron kettle to cook the salt pork and beans. However, those 16th-century sailors were an imaginative lot, and they seized upon any opportunity to elevate the palatability of their beans. Their first contact with the Mi'kmaq provided sailors with maple syrup, wild garlic and a haunch or two of venison. All went into the ship's bean pot, and life suddenly got a whole lot better for those homesick sailors.

BAKED CUSTARD—a silky smooth, baked egg and milk pudding happily consumed by generations of Canadian children and made even better with a dollop of whipped cream and a few scrapes of nutmeg.

A
B
C
D
E
F
G
H
I
J
K
L
M
N
O
P
Q
R
S
T
U
V
W
X
Y
Z

A
B
C
D
E
F
G
H
I
J
K
L
M
N
O
P
Q
R
S
T
U
V
W
X
Y
Z

RECIPE

Baked Custard

Scald 2 cups milk. Beat together 3 eggs, ¼ cup sugar and ¼ tsp salt and add slowly to milk. Add 1 tsp vanilla. Pour into ramekins or a larger dish and bake in a bain marie *(water bath) at 350°F for 1 hour, or until a knife comes out clean.*

BAKED KETTLE BREAD—bread baked in a cast iron Dutch oven (the baking kettle), which was either hung from a hearth crane or set in hot coals with more coals piled onto the lid. *See also* bread.

BAKED TURR—the turr is a sea bird; its true name is murre (*Uria aalge*), but it is called a turr in Newfoundland. The birds are skinned and baked like small chickens, and they are very popular—today, around 15,000 hunters are licenced to hunt the birds.

BAKER'S CHEESE. *See* hoop cheese.

BAKER'S FOG—before the advent of 20th-century food conglomerates, a slice of hearty home-baked

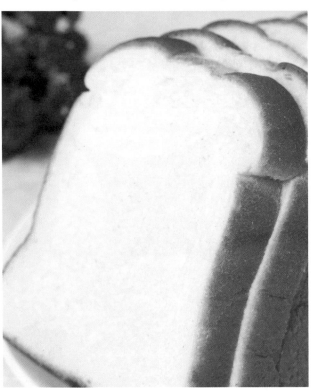

bread required a very long chew indeed unless accompanied by a soup or stew for sopping up. Sopping up cheated the human digestive process, with the roughly milled bread flour causing flatulence and digestive problems. Sifting out the bran and wheat germ not only solved those problems but also added shelf life to flour because it no longer turned rancid. Then along came a milling process that removed all but the starchy endosperm from wheat grains, producing the ubiquitous pre-chewed white flour that doubled as paper paste for bookbinders and school children. Then dry yeast arrived on the scene, enabling the rise of baking conglomerates, and Canadians began their almost century-long addiction to "baker's fog," that ubiquitous loaf of squishy, paper-paste bread that comes

Whole Wheat?

• In Canada, flour millers may lawfully remove up to 70 percent of wheat germ to improve shelf life and still label their product "whole wheat." Commercial bakeries using this wheat germ–deprived flour may in turn label their products "whole wheat" even though they lack the healthy qualities of whole grain.

• Consumers wanting the real McCoy are advised to look for labels that state the product is either whole grain, whole grain whole wheat or 100 percent whole grain.

pre-sliced, requires no chewing and is perfect for making sandwiches of processed meat derived from cattle forced to consume an overabundance of seed grains. *See also* bread, gluten allergy.

BAKER'S YEAST—yeast is a tiny organism that turns sugar or starches into alcohol and carbon dioxide. Baker's yeast is either inactive owing to a lack of moisture—an innovation of Fleischmann's Yeast during World War II and strangely called active dry yeast—or it is fresh compressed yeast that needs refrigeration.

BALDERSON VILLAGE CHEESE—established in 1881 at Balderson's Corners, Ontario, this company still produces prize-winning aged Cheddars despite being owned by the mighty Italian-based food conglomerate Parmalat.

BALLPARK MUSTARD. *See* American mustard.

BALSAMIC VINEGAR—a few Canadian wineries make balsamic vinegar from grapes specially grown for that purpose. The vinegar is not made from wine; it is just clarified juice that is reduced on low heat to about one-third of the volume and then put away in barrels for a year's fermentation, after which it is siphoned off into other barrels of decreasing size made of various woods, such as oak or cherry, where it picks up flavour and aromas. Balsamic vinegar is sensational on all manner of foods from leafy green salads to ice cream—it is even good when drunk as is from a snifter, or with a fine brandy. Try the Aceto Balsamico from BC's Venturi-Schulze Vineyards.

BALSAMROOT BREAD—a west coast specialty bread enjoyed by coastal First Nations and newly arrived settlers and made from a flour of pounded balsamroot (*Balsamorhiza sagittata*), a flowering perennial native to BC. *See also* bread.

A
B
C
D
E
F
G
H
I
J
K
L
M
N
O
P
Q
R
S
T
U
V
W
X
Y
Z

BANANA (*Musa* spp.)—Canadians love bananas, and though not homegrown produce, they have featured prominently in the Canadian food experience for almost two centuries thanks to a constant stream of ships arriving from the Caribbean. Banana pies and puddings were national favourites, and if mom was pressed for time, she simply sliced them into a bowl and poured on the cream.

Baked Bananas
(from the Ladies Home Journal, *1885)*
Peel bananas and dip into well-beaten egg whites. Roll dipped bananas in powdered sugar, making sure to coat them thoroughly. Deposit coated bananas onto a cookie sheet and bake in a hot oven for 5 minutes. Delicious, and they make a fine centrepiece for an afternoon tea.

BANGBELLY—a Newfoundland fried pancake made from flour, water, baking soda, molasses, a pinch of salt and pork fat.

BIG MIKE BANANAS

In 1922, songwriters Frank Silver and Irving Cohn penned the Broadway play *Make It Snappy*, which featured a song with the line "Yes! We have no bananas! We have no bananas today," a phrase coined by New York greengrocer Jimmy Costa. The banana song was a 1920s lament to the growing scarcity of our favourite fruit, the *Gros Michel* or Big Mike banana. Big Mike bananas yellowed naturally, resisted bruising and thrilled Canadians' taste buds with an intense banana flavour. That banana was the economic backbone of many Caribbean and Central American nations until slowly extirpated by a soil fungus dubbed the Panama disease. Those readers alive during the 1950s and early 1960s will have consumed the last harvests of Big Mike bananas and may remember the taste being far superior to those available nowadays. Younger consumers must make do with a substitute called Cavendish, a less tasty variety resistant to the insidious fungus. However, feasting for decades on the Big Mike and suddenly finding a bare cupboard, the Panama fungus simply mutated and turned to infecting Cavendish banana plantations. Banana lovers are advised to eat heartily of the Cavendish and remember the flavour, because what's coming down the pipe is a new fungus-resistant cultivar called Goldfinger, and though very sweet, it only hints at the flavour of the gone-but-not-forgotten Big Mike.

BANNOCK—originally a simple oat bread of Scottish origin, bannock was adapted by Canadian voyageurs, *coureurs de bois* (fur traders) and First Nations as an unleavened hearth cake made from a rudimentary dough of Indian meal, water, pork fat and a pinch of salt. Divided into cakes and cooked for a few minutes on a hot rock, they had something reminiscent of bread for dipping into a steaming cup of bean or pea soup. Much improved with the advent of baking soda, bannock has become the iconic bread of the Canadian North.

RECIPE

Bannock Corncakes

Mix 6 cups corn flour, 1 cup suet, 1 Tbsp salt and 3½ cups water into a dough. Knead for a bit, flatten into cakes and bake on a hot rock or in the oven until brown. Adding 3 Tbsp baking powder and handful of raisins will considerably improve the bread.

BAP—the traditional flour-dusted breakfast roll of Scotland that would over time push out sliced bread to become the bun in a hamburger.

BARBERRY JELLY—made from the bright red berries of the barberry bush (*Berberis*), this jelly was a favourite condiment of early settlers and is now a favourite of wild food foragers.

BARDING. *See* larding.

BARLEY (*Hordeum vulgare*)—an excellent source of soluble fibre for lowering cholesterol. Whole grain or hulled barley is best, but many chefs find that type of barley to be chewy and prefer pearl barley, which is grains with husk removed, or pot barley, where the miller removes only part of the hull. There is also barley flour, hominy, precooked quick barley, and even barley flakes for the breakfast table.

Barley

- Canada is second only to Russia in barley production, with most going to feed cattle and supply the brewing and distilling industries.

- Barley is more nutritious than wheat but contains a starch that is incompatible with wheat in the milling process; however, a Canadian hybridized barley called Millhouse will soon allow millers to mix the two, producing a healthier, ready-mixed flour for bread making.

BARLEY BREAD—although called barley bread, the dough is actually a mixture of wheat and barley flours. Inclusion of the latter is meant to cheapen the cost of the bread. *See also* bread.

BARLEY SUGAR—made by boiling barley water with cream of tartar and refined sugar.

BARLEY TOY CANDY—a clear, barley sugar candy moulded into dozens of different candy toys by Robertson's Candy Inc. of Truro, Nova Scotia, since 1928. Originally made as Christmas tree decorations, the candy toys in hundreds of different shapes have become a festive favourite of Maritimers. Robertson's Candy also makes many other chocolate and sugar creations including another East Coast holiday favourite, the Satin Mix ribbon candy.

BARLEY WATER—a nutritious decoction, or soup, of pearl barley. Barley water mixed with fruit juice is a popular English beverage and an ingredient in the manufacture of hard candies.

BARLEY WINE—a top fermented beer (ale) with alcohol content similar to wine. Brewed by early settlers, the beer is still produced by some artisanal breweries across Canada, including Phillips Brewing Company in Victoria, BC, Central City Brewery in Surrey, BC, Mill St. Brewery in Toronto, Amsterdam Brewing in Ottawa and Les Trois Mousquetaires in Brossard, Québec.

BARM—yeast formed on malt liquors during the brewing or distilling process, the froth; the source of a rudimentary yeast once used for bread rising.

BARMY BREAD—any bread using barm for rising; a word used to describe already risen bread.

BARON—a cut of beef consisting of two loins that have not been split apart from the backbone and is usually spit roasted. It may also describe a cut of lamb consisting of both legs and fillets.

BASKET COCKLE (*Clinocardium nuttallii*)—a mollusc similar to the littleneck clam that is found along the BC coast and is much in demand by upscale chefs. It is not commercially harvested because it is not found in abundance, but there is much

interest in the basket cockle as a candidate for aquaculture because of its rapid growth. *See also* aquaculture.

BASQUE INFLUENCE—the Basque region of Spain, the northeastern corner where the Bay of Biscay laps against the Pyrenees Mountains, spawned a civilization devoted to both the land and the sea. Basque men were extraordinary seamen and boat builders, and when it came to fishing they had no qualms about crossing the Atlantic Ocean in search of prime waters to set their nets for a fish that would become iconic to their cuisine: the Atlantic cod. When the French arrived in the New World, they found the place already cluttered with Basque ships and felt the influence of Basque cuisine on the fledgling Canadian food experience, especially their methods of preparing salt cod. Basque cooking fraternities called *txokos* gave rise to new recipes and ideas such as foie gras, smoked duck breasts and the famous bacalao, the salt cod hallmark of Basque and Portuguese cuisine known to all Maritime cooks. *See also* bacalao.

BASSWOOD (*Tilia americana*; also called lime tree, linden)—the flowers of basswood have a distinct lime flavour that earned the tree its alternate name. The tree's flowers are picked, dried and used to make a refreshing tea and also to flavour creamy desserts. Basswood flower honey is occasionally available at farmers' markets, and when discovered should be snapped up.

BASSWOOD TEA. *See* linden tea.

BATTERCAKE. *See* corn oyster.

BAY SALMON—an Atlantic salmon variety sourced from the Bay of Fundy. *See also* Atlantic salmon, salmon.

BEAKED HAZELNUT. *See* hazelnut.

BEAN PORRIDGE—originally a Scottish breakfast food made with split green peas, various diced vegetables, salt pork and bacon—known as "pease porridge"—the dish became Canadian when early settlers substituted beans for peas.

BEANS (pole, *Phaseolus vulgaris*; runner, *P. coccineus*; broad, *Vicia faba*)—fresh beans are either pod or shell type, the former consumed whole, the latter removed from their pods. Green, string and long beans are the immature pods of runner, bush or pole bean plants. Snap beans are hybridized string beans sans string; wax beans are yellow green beans; limas can be butter beans; favas and romanos are broad beans, called horse beans in early times; and the dried white, red, black, etc. are called field beans.

A
B
C
D
E
F
G
H
I
J
K
L
M
N
O
P
Q
R
S
T
U
V
W
X
Y
Z

CANADA'S FAVOURITE BEAN VARIETIES

- Aquadulce—a broad bean that is both tasty and easy to grow.

- Blue Lake—a bush-type snap bean, stringless and very flavourful.

- Broad Windsor—the tastiest broad bean.

- Fortex Filet—a long, stringless French green bean.

- Garden of Eden—the best-tasting green pole bean.

- Great Northern White—the best dried white for baked beans.

- Kentucky Wonder—a bush-type snap bean with excellent flavour.

- Lazy Wife—a bush-type snap bean with big flavour that is excellent for soups.

- Marvel of Venice—a yellow bean.

- Painted Lady—a runner bean with big taste.

- Scarlet Runner Bean—the best dried on the vine and used in soups and stews.

RECIPE

Roasted Green Beans

Roasting caramelizes the natural sugars in green beans, providing them with an irresistible crunch and sweetness. Arrange 1 lb fresh green beans, washed and with ends trimmed, in a single layer on an oiled baking sheet and drizzle with 1½ Tbsp extra-virgin olive oil. Roll beans to make sure each is coated and roast in a preheated 500°F oven for 15–20 minutes, shaking baking sheet now and then to allow even cooking. Sprinkle beans with sea salt and serve immediately.

Bears

- In Canada, sportsmen and First Nations hunters harvest around 20,000 bears annually, with an equal number hunted illegally for their gall bladders and paws. In pioneer days, young bears were hunted for both meat and fat, the latter rendered down to make lard for pastries.

BEAR STEW—a one-pot favourite of First Nations, early Canadian settlers and modern hunters. Aside from marinating cubed bear meat for 24 hours, the stew is prepared according to a regular recipe.

BEARBERRY. *See* buffaloberry.

BEAVER (*Castor canadensis*)—when the first Europeans stepped ashore to claim Canada for France, the beaver population is estimated to have been around 90 million. Being both good to eat and having a desirable pelt was just bad luck for the beaver, and it was soon trapped almost to extinction. Beavers store fat in their tail, and while First Nations would consume body meat, European trappers found the body to be too gamey and concentrated instead on beaver tails for dinner.

BEAVER TAILS (also called elephant ears, *queues de castor*)—once a baked, waste-not, want-not delicacy enjoyed by First Nations and fur trappers, the words have evolved to mean a fried slab of risen dough dusted with cinnamon and sugar or any number of toppings. Trademarked by Pam and Grant Hooker and first served at Ottawa's ByWard Market, the tails have become uniquely Canadian and a real treat for small fry. *See also* ByWard Public Market, dough gods.

BEECHNUT—American beech trees (*Fagus grandifolia*) were plentiful in pioneer days, and the nuts were easily harvested because they fall from the tree when ripe. Today, foragers still gather beechnuts, but owing to the trees' extreme suitability as firewood, the number of trees has diminished considerably.

BEECHNUT COFFEE—roasted and ground beechnuts served as a passable coffee imitation for desperate-for-a-fix pioneers, but beechnuts were more often gathered and pressed for oil or roasted as a snack food.

BEECHNUT COOKIES—iconic Canadian pioneer cookie baked every fall when beechnut trees became heavily loaded with the prickly nut husks.

RECIPE

Beechnut Cookies

Remove enough nuts from their husks to fill a 4 cup container and toast in frypan or oven. Cream 1 cup sugar with ½ cup shortening; add 4 egg yolks and the juice from ½ lemon. Sift 2 cups flour with 3 tsp baking powder and 1 tsp salt and mix with ½ cup milk. Add toasted nuts, spoon onto greased cookie sheet and bake at 350°F for 10 minutes or until golden.

A
B
C
D
E
F
G
H
I
J
K
L
M
N
O
P
Q
R
S
T
U
V
W
X
Y
Z

BEECHNUT OIL—for many pioneer families, the nuts of beechnut trees found in the forests of eastern and central Canada were a principal source of cooking and lamp oil. Once common to the Canadian food experience, this delightful mild-flavoured nut oil has all but disappeared along with the trees that produce the nuts. However, at odd times it can make an appearance at farmers' markets for the lucky shopper who happens by.

BEEF BACON—not altogether new as some halal butchers have been offering the product for years, beef bacon doesn't really taste much like real bacon. However, after much research and testing, an Alberta company called the Canadian Beef Bacon Corporation (www.beefbacon.net) is packaging up a tasty much-leaner-than-bacon from brined beef.

BEEF CONNECTIONS.CA—a Guelph, Ontario, company that connects Toronto-area consumers with selected area livestock and poultry farmers through online ordering and bimonthly delivery. This good initiative is catching on in other cities.

BEER—almost every pioneer farmer grew barley and made cottage-style or home brew, but it was the British army's six-pint ration to soldiers that caused commercial breweries to spring up in

almost every town and village. To supply the sudsy elixir, the British army imported brewmasters and set up breweries. The ensuing party saw lots of beer drunk by lots of rough men who only cared what it did and not how it tasted.

Beer

- In 1818, a London, Ontario (then Canada West), farmer named John Carling began pushing beer out his back door and down the streets in a wheelbarrow. By 1840, he had established a brewery in that city and was topping up beer mugs from muddy York to Windsor.

comes around; as the 21st century progresses, small breweries called "microbreweries" are on the rise and producing all kinds of interesting brews for thirsty Canadians, who consume $4 billion worth of suds annually.

- In 1862, Eugene O'Keefe bought a brewery in York (now Toronto) and began making Canada's first lager beer.

- In 1867, Susanna Oland began brewing beer in the backyard of her home in Dartmouth, Nova Scotia, and within a few years was brewing quality beer for the eastern part of the country.

- On the Prairies and west to the coast, many breweries started up around 1883, but in the formative years of the 20th century, an American named Fritz Sick controlled most of them. By 1930, Fritz and his son were making Pilsner beer and knocking heads with Molson, O'Keefe and Carling for market share. Big beer started buying out the little breweries across Canada, and by the century's end, big business ruled the market until it was eaten up by foreign-owned conglomerates. But what goes around

A
B
C
D
E
F
G
H
I
J
K
L
M
N
O
P
Q
R
S
T
U
V
W
X
Y
Z

BEER VS. CHOLERA

Cholera is a fearsome pathogen, with humans its only host and water and food its method of transmission—facts not known in early times but suspected. Military garrisons rarely suffered the disease because soldiers drank beer instead of water, a successful prophylactic custom adopted by the far-flung British army to prevent disease transmission. Canada, a nation populated by immigrants, suffered cholera like nowhere else on the planet: it struck the towns and the cities, and it caused almost everyone to emulate the British soldiers and abandon water for beer.

To brew beer you need grain, and the best was barley, a crop brought to Canada from Europe in the early 18th century as a bread-and-fodder grain and to make beer for the soldiers' daily ration. But when cholera arrived, barley became every farmer's dream crop; the breweries bought all that farmers could grow, and if the barley was not good enough to sell, farmers could use it to fatten beef cattle. Beef, beer and whatever came from backyard gardens was breakfast, lunch and dinner for most Canadians until the latter part of the 19th century, when cholera was finally stopped by the installation of sewage pipes.

However, as time went on, people who did care about taste arrived in Canada, prompting people like Canada's greatest entrepreneur, John Molson, to produce quality as well as quantity. Molson started up his brewery in 1786 and never looked back. By the time he passed away in 1836, he was making ale and running banks for all of Lower Canada. Ale is the tradition on the East Coast; Belgium-style beers lead the parade in Québec; lagers win in Ontario; and pilsners are the preferred quaff of Westerners.

BEESTINGS—the common name for the colostrum, the milk given by dairy cows immediately after birthing calves that contains more protein than normal milk. Beestings is thicker and sets to custard when heated, and it is of particular interest to upscale chefs.

BEET (*Beta vulgaris*)—beetroot is one of the four useful varieties of the plant *B. vulgaris*, the others being chard, fodder beets (mangelwurzel) and sugar beets. Canadian farmers grow about 1.5 million tonnes of sugar beets that are then sent south to be processed in Michigan by the grower co-op Michigan Sugar Company. In Canada, beetroots are more normally simply called beets because, unlike in the U.S. and Europe, the greens are seldom consumed.

CANADA'S FAVOURITE BEET VARIETIES

• Detroit Dark Red—the favourite of the 20th century and still popular today.

• Early Wonder—a 19th-century icon still going strong.

RECIPE

Pickled Beets

Wash 2 lbs small beets and trim tops, leaving 1 inch of stem. Boil the beets until tender, slip off skins with fingertips and place beets into jars. Bring pickling solution of 3 cups water, 8 cups vinegar, 6 cups brown sugar and 2 Tbsp salt to the boiling point (do not boil) and pour into jars. Seal with lids and let stand for several weeks before serving.

BEET MOLASSES—starting around the middle of the 19th century, pressed sugar beet juice was cooked down by Québec settlers and farmers into molasses in a process similar to maple syrup production. Extensive planting of sugar beets in that province prompted the building of a beet refinery in 1881 to produce regular sugar, and by 1902, four refineries were processing Ontario beets, with several more opening in the Prairie provinces.

BEETROOT WINE—an easily made alcoholic beverage of fermented sugar beets. It was a one-time favourite of habitant farmers and home brewers.

BEIGNET—a puffy, deep-fried pastry of French origin naturalized by the addition of maple sugar, creating the delectable maple beignet. This cousin of the doughnut is particular to France, Québec and the U.S. state of Louisiana.

BELGIAN ENDIVE. *See* chicory.

BELL PEPPERS. *See* peppers.

BELLY BUSTERS—Alberta chuckwagon camp biscuits usually served with baked beans.

BENOÎT, JEHANE (1904–1987)—born Jehane Patenaude in Montréal. After taking a degree at the Sorbonne in Paris, she returned to Montréal and opened a cooking school, then a restaurant, then began doing cooking gigs on television. Cookbooks came next, and she wrote 30 of them in French and English with her masterpiece being the *Encyclopedia of Canadian Cooking*, published in 1963.

BERKSHIRE PORK—an English heritage breed of pig adopted by niche market Canadian pork producers, who raise them by old-fashioned, ethical methods to produce the finest hams. There are more Berkshires in Canada than anywhere else, and that makes them one of our national pigs.

BERRY CAKE—an early pioneer emulation of a First Nations method of storing dried berries that, in later years, evolved into a cake topped with a fresh berry sauce.

BERRY FOOL—a dessert made with fresh berries folded into sweetened whipped cream. *See also* fool.

BERRY WINE—any fermented alcoholic beverage made with wild or cultivated berries, such as elderberry, raspberry, blueberry, etc.

BICK'S PICKLES—a national favourite since 1944, the year Jeanny and Walter Bick of Scarborough, Ontario, responded to the collapse of the cucumber market by turning tonnes of their field cucumbers into pickles. These good pickles caught the public's attention and launched the couple into the pickle business. The business prospered, and in 1966, the couple sold the business to Robin Hood Foods, now a part of the U.S. food conglomerate Smucker's.

BIG FOOD—according to analysts at the Swiss Federal Institute of Technology, almost all of the 44,000 transnational companies around the globe are controlled by 147 companies, many of which are owners of almost all the branded food products in Canada and the U.S.

MAJOR BIG FOOD CONGLOMERATES

- Agropur Co-op—an association of 3350 Québec dairy farmers with almost 8000 employees in 27 plants across North America and annual sales of almost $5 billion.

- Archer Daniels Midland (ADM) Company—grain millers, cocoa grinders and food ingredients supplier to food manufacturers and processors around the world, with over 30,000 employees and annual sales of around $80 billion.

- The Coca-Cola Company—a U.S. multinational and the world's second largest food company, with over 500 mostly beverage product brands and global sales of around $48 billion annually.

- General Mills—sells its products in over 100 countries with annual sales of over $17 billion.

- Grupo Bimbo—a Mexican multinational and the world's largest bread bakery organization with almost 130,000 employees and annual sales of $11 billion; in 2008, Grupo Bimbo bought Canada's multinational bakery conglomerate, Weston Foods.

- Ingredion—the new name for U.S.-owned Casco (Canada Starch & Best Foods) and processors of all of Canada's corn.

- Kraft General Foods—annual sales around $19 billion and 25,000 employees.

A
B
C
D
E
F
G
H
I
J
K
L
M
N
O
P
Q
R
S
T
U
V
W
X
Y
Z

- Maple Leaf Foods—meats, ready meals and bakery goods with annual sales of $5 billion and around 19,000 employees.

- McCain Foods—annual sales of $6 billion and 19,000 employees in 50 plants around the globe.

- Mondelez International—a Kraft spinoff and now a separate company selling mostly snack foods with annual sales of $36 billion and 100,000 employees in 170 countries.

- Nestlé S.A.—a Swiss multinational and the world's largest food company in terms of revenue, with around 450 factories in some 87 countries employing almost 350,000 people. Nestlé produces mostly high-profit food items, such as snack foods, chocolate, ice cream, bottled water, pet foods and instant coffee, with several of their brands having sales of over $1 billion annually.

- PepsiCo—the world's third largest food company based on revenue of around $44 billion annually, the company distributes in over 200 countries and has over 20 billion-dollar brands.

- Saputo—annual sales of $6 billion and 9000 employees, which is not bad for a company that started selling pizza cheese during the 1950s.

- Smucker's—a U.S.-based multinational food company with 5000 employees and an annual net profit of over $130 million that it uses to acquire more and more companies; this conglomerate produces food products from GMO fruits and grains and is managed by people far removed from the farm.

- Unilever—an Anglo-Dutch multinational company and the world's fourth largest in terms of revenue, with factories all over the world and almost 400 major food brands, 12 of which have annual sales of over $1 billion.

A
B
C
D
E
F
G
H
I
J
K
L
M
N
O
P
Q
R
S
T
U
V
W
X
Y
Z

BIG PANCAKE—a traditional Easter breakfast dish favoured by the people of the Charlevoix area of Québec. It is an oversized egg, flour and baking soda pancake that is oven baked, drenched in maple syrup and accompanied by crisp salt pork or ham slices.

BIOFUEL—volatile, flammable hydrocarbons derived from plants or animal wastes and used for fuel. In its quest for fuel self-sufficiency, the U.S. has turned its Midwest states into a humungous nitrogen-gulping cornfield that is continuously raising the bar on fertilizer prices. High fertilizer prices skew Canadian farm production in favour of crops that use less fertilizer, requiring taxpayers to subsidize ethanol plants into paying higher prices for grain. High-cost fertilizer affects all Canadian farmers, but the large grain farmers on the Prairies will eventually see higher grain prices owing to demand from subsidized ethanol plants. Good for them, bad for consumers, as high prices will affect grocery bills across the nation. Higher wheat prices and the disbanding of the grain commission have translated into higher land prices attracting overseas investors, especially the Chinese.

BIRCH SUGAR—a sugar obtained by boiling down the sap of various birch species that, though not as productive as sugar maples, produce a sugar and syrup that have a unique taste that is once again in demand from consumers. Look for birch sugar at more northerly farmers' markets.

BIRCH SYRUP—the sweet boiled-down sap of almost any birch tree, but white birch (*Betula papyrifera*) is preferred. It tastes nothing like maple syrup, and although common in earlier times, birch syrup became a forgotten enterprise because of the low sugar content in the sap. Whereas 1 L of maple syrup requires 40 L of sap, 1 L of birch syrup may require 100–150 L of sap. Sap is tapped from trees before buds set, or the syrup takes on a bitter taste. It also must be evaporated within 24 hours because the sap ferments quickly. Birch syrup is sometimes available at farmers' markets, and some commercial production occurs in Québec.

RECIPE

Birch Syrup Pie

Put ½ cup birch syrup in a pot with 1½ cups brown sugar and 1 cup heavy cream. Bring to a boil and simmer 10 minutes while stirring to keep it from scorching. Pour mixture into a bowl and, when cooled, whisk in 2 beaten eggs, 1 tsp lemon juice and a pinch of salt. Pour into a prebaked piecrust and bake at 375°F until filling is bubbly, about 30 minutes. Cool and serve with vanilla ice cream.

BIRCH WINE—an alcoholic beverage made from the quickly fermenting sap of birch trees. A common beverage during earlier times, it is now mostly a home-brewed oddity.

BIRD CHERRY. *See* pin cherry.

BIRD'S CUSTARD POWDER—invented in England by Alfred Bird in 1837 because his wife was allergic to eggs. The cornstarch-based pudding mix became popular around the world and especially in Canada where, after 1843, Alfred Bird sent shiploads along with his newly invented baking powder. Around 1920, the company was purchased by Kraft Foods, and in 2004, Kraft sold it to Premier Foods, the owner of the Cadbury and Oxo brands. Available at supermarkets nationwide, Bird's Custard Powder is to many Canadians a necessary ingredient for making Nanaimo bars, while others prefer Horne's Custard Powder. *See also* Horne's Custard Powder.

BISHOP'S PUDDING—a date and walnut cake with sauce from the Pointe-Claire area of Québec.

BISON (*Bison* spp.; also called buffalo)—these hefty animals roamed the Canadian prairies until the latter part of the 19th century, when market hunting almost obliterated them. Today, thanks to ranchers setting aside sections of range land for bison grazing, bison numbers have risen to around a half-million, and the animals are a valuable, sustainable source of revenue for ranchers.

Bison

- To 17th-century French explorers, the shaggy beasts they encountered west of the Mississippi River and Great Lakes were just another form of cow they called *les boeuf*. To the English speakers who came later, *les boeuf* became "la buff," and gradually over the years became the misnamed buffalo.

- Two problems hampered westward expansion of the U.S. and Canada during the early part of the 19th century: bison and native tribes such as the Cree and Blackfoot. Fifty million bison made settlement impossible, and First Nations were (obviously) resisting appropriation of their lands, so both the U.S. and Canadian governments launched efforts to reduce both populations. Plains tribes depended on bison for sustenance, so a policy of "slaughter every animal and both problems would disappear" was carried out with vigour.

A
B
C
D
E
F
G
H
I
J
K
L
M
N
O
P
Q
R
S
T
U
V
W
X
Y
Z

RECIPE

Roast Bison Tenderloin

Square up a 2 lb bison tenderloin by removing the tapered end section (it can be cooked later, either whole or sliced) and tie the roast with string to prevent separation of the chain muscle while cooking. Allow the roast to get to room temperature and then pan sear in butter over moderately high heat. Season the roast with salt and pepper and transfer into a 225°F oven, not forgetting to place a drip tray under the rack. Roast until meat thermometer registers 115°F and then turn off the heat, leaving the oven door closed. Remove roast when thermometer registers 125°F for a rare cooked roast; for medium-rare, turn off oven heat at 125°F and remove at 135°F. Cover roast with foil and allow it to rest for 20 minutes before slicing.

RECIPE

Bison Burgers

In a heavy skillet over medium heat, cook ¼ cup chopped onions until soft and remove from heat. In a bowl, combine 1 lb minced bison meat, 1 beaten egg, 1 minced garlic clove, 2 Tbsp balsamic vinegar, 1 tsp Dijon mustard, salt, pepper and the onions; mix well. Shape mixture into 4 patties and barbecue or oven broil for about 5 minutes per side. If cheese is added, use the real McCoy as anything else is an insult to a founding pillar of the great Canadian food experience. Bison meat is very lean and cooks quickly, so take care not to overcook.

BISON CHUCKWAGON STEW—a one-pot bison meat and vegetable stew favoured by 19th-century Alberta cowboys.

BISTORT (*Bistorta vivipara*)—a much-foraged perennial that grows at higher altitudes and belongs to the Buckwheat family. It was very familiar to Canada's early settlers because a similar variety grew in the home country. Peeled, the rhizomes may be eaten boiled or

fresh and taste like almonds, while the leaves make a delicious salad green. Bistort seeds may be gathered and ground into flour, while the plant's tiny bulblets make a tasty snack.

BLACK CHERRY (*Prunus serotina*)—a deciduous native cherry inhabiting forests and hedgerows from the Maritimes to southern Ontario. It is much sought after for both timber and fruit, which, although too sour for eating fresh, does make wonderful jam, jelly and pie.

BLACK COD. *See* sablefish.

BLACK CURRANT JAM—the absolute favourite jam of both early pioneers and modern foragers. The ripe berries are packed with so much pectin that any 10-year-old kid can make a batch of these preserves. *See also* currant.

RECIPE

Black Currant Jam

Mix 2 cups ripe black currants with 1 cup each of granulated sugar and water. Cook uncovered until berries are soft. Pour into sterilized jars, seal and keep in a cool place.

BLACK TRUFFLE CHEDDAR—an outstanding cow's milk Cheddar crafted by Bothwell Cheese Inc. in New Bothwell, Manitoba, since 1936. This taste sensation, along with Bothwell's other fine cheeses, is available nationwide and online.

BLACK WALNUT (*Juglans nigra*)—a native nut tree producing extremely hard-shelled nuts that are difficult to crack without damaging the nutmeats. It is the strongest flavoured walnut species and excellent for culinary purposes. Walnut trees love Ontario, especially the hard-shelled black walnut; unfortunately it has suffered the fate of so many other natural treasures and is well on its way to provincial extirpation owing to its timber going to supply a few centuries of furniture manufacturing. Unlike a few areas in the U.S. that value their trees for nuts and have established renewable plantations, Ontario's black walnut supply now depends on wild foragers and must be looked for at farmers' markets in fall. If you're thinking of planting a black walnut tree for the enjoyment of future generations, consider new hybrids that provide nuts with the same great taste, but in a shell that does not require a sledgehammer to crack.

BLACK CURRANT SCHNAPPS—an old-time favourite of backyard distillers who used black currant syrup to dampen the flames of homemade hooch. *See also* currant.

BLACK PLUM. *See* Canada plum.

BLACK PUDDING. *See* boudin.

BLACK RIVER CHEESE—located in Milford, Ontario, Black River has been creating superlative cheeses since 1901 and is a consistent prize-winner at both the British Empire Cheese Competition and the Royal Agricultural Winter Fair. Black River's emphasis is on aged Cheddar up to six years old, but they also produce fine mozzarella and goat's milk cheeses, including a fantastic sheep and cow's milk Cheddar—a shared effort with Fifth Town Artisan Cheese Company. Black River cheeses are widely available in Ontario, some national outlets and online.

BLACK WALNUT AND MAPLE COOKIES— a kitchen marvel that provided a culinary diversion to pioneer families trapped inside by winter's fury. Walnuts, flour, eggs, maple syrup, butter and a touch of salt worked magic in those log cabins, and with the addition of vanilla, you'll think you're getting a taste of heaven.

BLACK WALNUT AND PUMPKIN SOUP— a favourite soup of First Nations and quickly adopted by early settlers.

RECIPE

Black Walnut and Pumpkin Soup

Bake a clean pumpkin until the flesh is soft, then scrape it off the rind and mash it in a saucepan with maple syrup, black walnuts and a pinch of salt. Add water to liquefy, simmer for 5 minutes and serve with a garnish of chopped walnuts.

BLACK WALNUT SYRUP—Canada's First Nations tapped many species of hardwood trees for sap to make sugar and syrup, with one of the finest and best-tasting being the black walnut. Never a commercial product owing to low sugar content of the sap, walnut syrup is a spotty farm-gate product and, though very rare, it is sometimes found at farmers' markets.

BLACKBERRY (*Rubus fruticosus*)—a relative of the common raspberry and member of the Rose family. Blackberries, like raspberries, are not

single fruits, but many drupelets gathered in clusters. When picked, blackberries come off whole, while raspberries leave their core and are hollow. Although native to northern North America, blackberries are also widely cultivated in Mexico and are an important export crop. Blackberries are an excellent source of the antioxidants known to combat the effects of old age and are becoming an increasingly important crop in BC—the berry canes grow best in a temperate climate.

Blackberries

- In those growing areas of Mexico that lack a winter chill to set buds, the berry canes are chemically defoliated and forced into bloom by application of chemical growth regulators. What's in your breakfast bowl?

- Although the roots of both blackberry and raspberry plants (*Rubus* spp.) are perennial, the canes are biennial, meaning they only survive for two years: the first for growing, and the second for setting fruit.

- Blackberry is the common name for a family of bush berries that also includes dewberry, boysenberry and loganberry.

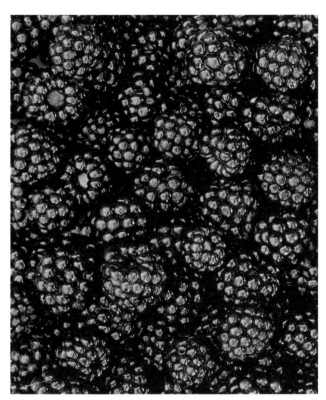

BLACKBERRY TEA—a hot water infusion of dried leaves and/or berries of the blackberry plant.

BLACKBERRY VINEGAR—an early settlers' method of preserving a bounteous crop of blackberries that has lasted the centuries to become a wintertime treat for salad lovers.

RECIPE

Blackberry Vinegar

In a large bowl, combine 2 cups each of fresh black-berries, white vinegar and water and mash up. Cover bowl and let mixture sit overnight. In the morning, run blackberry mixture through a sieve or jelly bag into a pot, add 4 cups fine sugar and boil for 10 minutes. Pour into sterilized jars and store in a cool, dry spot.

BLACKBERRY WINE—an alcoholic beverage made from fermented blackberries, and a favourite of both early pioneers and modern-day imbibers.

BLAZE'S BEANS—BC packed, pickled green beans that are hot, spicy and perfect for stirring Bloody Caesars.

BLETTING—a ripening process required of some fruits before they can be consumed, such as medlars, quince and rowanberries. Fruits can be bletted by leaving them on the tree until after a frost, or they can be picked and laid into sawdust or straw or simply stuck into a paper bag with a banana. Bletting fruit is a slow rot that increases sugar content and decreases acids and tannins, making for custard-like centres that may be spooned out and consumed.

BLEU DE LA MOUTONNIÈRE—a must-try, award-winning product of the Fromagerie la Moutonnière in Sainte-Hélène-de-Chester, Québec. Crafted from unprocessed sheep's milk and aged for three months in an underground cave, this cheese caresses the palate with complex flavours that earned it a first place at the 2010 American Cheese Society competition and second place at the 2012 competition.

BLEU ERMITE CHEESE—a blue cheese from the Fromagerie de L'Abbaye Saint-Benoît in St-Benoît-du-Lac, Québec, a dairy owned and operated by Benedictine monks. Created in 1943 and exclusive to the brothers' fromagerie, this cheese is available only in specialty cheese shops. The brothers also produce an aged version of Bleu Ermite called Bleu Bénédictin, as well as various other styles of cheese.

BLOOD PUDDING. *See* boudin.

BLOODY CAESAR—a popular clam and tomato juice–based cocktail invented in 1969 by bartender Walter Chell at the Calgary Inn (today the Westin Hotel). The drink he called a "Bloody Caesar" caught the attention of both the imbibing public and American apple juice company Duffy-Mott. With Chell's help, Mott's concocted a tomato and clam juice ready-mix for the Bloody Caesar and called it Clamato juice. It's an all-Canadian cocktail, and we quaff over 300 million of the tasty beverages every year. *See also* Clamato juice.

BLUE CAMAS (*Camassia quamash*)—a perennial member of the Lily family and an important food source for west coast First Nations, who cultivated the plant for its sweet, potato-like root. Camas roots contain significant amounts of the complex sugar inulin, which, when heated slowly in steam pits, converts to almost half the root's weight in fructose sugar. Although a good source of sweetener, blue camas never saw adoption by Europeans because it closely resembles an extremely poisonous plant species called death camas. Even First Nations harvesters always waited for the blue camas to flower before digging up the bulbs.

BLUE COD. *See* lingcod.

BLUE MONDAY CAKE. *See* wacky cake.

BLUE MUSSEL. *See* mussels.

BLUEBERRY (*Vaccinium* spp.)—in 1996, blueberries supplanted apples as the number one fruit crop in Canada in terms of area. Total production surpasses 70,000 tonnes, with most of that quantity destined for export. Of that amount about half is wild, or lowbush (*V. angustifolium*) blueberry grown in the Maritimes, and the rest is the highbush (*V. corymbosum*) variety grown in BC. Lowbush berries are the smaller variety, while highbush berries are larger and less tasty but easier to raise and harvest and are therefore more common for commercial growers. Canada accounts for about half of the world production of wild blueberries.

Blueberries

- Blueberries contain significant amounts of anthocyanins, antioxidants and photo-chemicals that offer protection from cancer and various diseases of old age. A swig of blueberry juice every day will keep the doctor away.

BLUEBERRY BUCKLE—a blueberry pudding or fruitcake favoured by pioneer families at berry-gathering time. Made more popular with the advent of baking soda, the lighter version of blueberry buckle is still enjoyed by Canadians from coast to coast.

BLUEBERRY CHUTNEY—chutney is a condiment that originated in British-ruled India but was Canadianized by substituting fresh blueberries for the typical mangos.

BLUEBERRY GRUNT—a potpie, or cobbler, made by filling a large iron pot with berries, with or without sugar, topping it with biscuit dough and cooking it over a fire. The name comes from the sound steam makes when escaping the pot. *See also* fungy.

BLUEBERRY PIE—dessert pie filled with blueberries iconic to Canadian culinary history. First Nations munched the berries, the Vikings fermented them, the French made sauce and the English made cobbler, but it was the Acadians who put the berries into a pastry crust and gave us blueberry pie.

BLUEBERRY SAUCE—First Nations were spooning a version of blueberry sauce onto roast game long before settlers arrived in Canada. Every season they harvested huge quantities of the delectable berries, dried them in the sunshine and ground them to a powder for preservation. When settlers did arrive, the sauce was immediately adopted and improved upon by mixing whole berries with molasses, adding a piece of preserved lemon peel and boiling the mixture. Nowadays, blueberry fanciers can make an excellent sauce with any number of variations for any number of applications.

RECIPE

Blueberry Zinger Pancake Sauce

Bring 2 cups blueberries, ½ cup orange juice and 2 Tbsp lemon juice to a boil over medium heat. Stir in 1 tsp lemon zest and ¼ tsp cinnamon and turn heat to low. Combine ¼ cup water and 4 tsp cornstarch and stir into mixture until thickened. Remove from heat and allow to cool before serving.

BLUEBERRY VINEGAR—a delicious vinegar made either with pure blueberry juice or by soaking the berries in cider vinegar, this latter method being the way most commercial blueberry vinegars are manufactured.

BLUEFIN TUNA—going, going and almost gone, the mighty Atlantic bluefin (*Thunnus thynnus*) has seen its numbers decline by 70 percent since the 1970s, but our Maritime fishermen are still pulling in 500 tonnes annually and wanting more. Licenced bluefin fishermen are allowed only one fish per annum, and that's a good thing, but a bad thing is allowing long-line hooking of swordfish, where a large portion of the by-catch are bluefins. *See also* tuna.

BOB'S RED MILL NATURAL FOODS—not a Canadian company, but not many of them are anymore, and how could we not like a product

called Bob's, especially when his products are so healthy and good tasting? Bob's was started by Bob Moore, a former Milwaukie, Oregon, auto service worker who had an idea that people might buy stone-ground, organically grown grains and pulses and various mixes to bake their own organic delights. Bob was right, and his Red Mill stone-ground grains and mixes are available across both the U.S. and Canada.

BOBWHITE QUAIL (*Colinus virginianus*)—the most commonly hunted quail species in North America and once plentiful in a few Canadian provinces, especially Ontario, but now on the endangered list because of habitat destruction.

BOG MYRTLE (*Myrica gale*)—found in peat bogs from Ontario to the Maritimes, the leaves were a popular medicine as well as an insect repellent. For culinary purposes, the leaves were used in place of bay leaves for stews and soups and to replace hops in beer making. Today, Beau's All Natural Brewing Company, an Ontario microbrewery, crafts Bog Beer, a brew that uses bog myrtle in place of hops.

BOGBERRY. *See* cranberry.

BOGOO—a dried and smoked meat preparation (usually caribou) of the northern Dene people.

BOILED DINNER—in the beginning, there was the fireplace hearth and a pot to cook in, and with that there were the famous boiled dinners.

Although some U.S. culinary historians like to claim the dinners as being of New England origin and consisting of corned beef, it was simply dinner of any meat, fish or fowl cooked in a hearth pot by any pioneer family with a chimney.

BOILED DRESSING—an iconic Nova Scotia salad dressing used instead of butter or mayonnaise.

RECIPE

Boiled Dressing

Beat 4 eggs in double boiler while slowly adding 6 Tbsp flour and 2 cups hot water. Beat in 1 cup cider vinegar, 6 Tbsp sugar, ¼ cup butter, 4 tsp dry mustard and 2 tsp salt and continue beating until creamy. Kept in the refrigerator, this tasty dressing will stay fresh for weeks.

BOILED RAISIN CAKE—a Newfoundland dessert cake that is easy to make and delicious. It smells divine while baking and is always half eaten before dinner time.

RECIPE

Boiled Raisin Cake

Add ½ lb butter, 1 cup sugar, ½ cup molasses, 2 cups raisins and 1 tsp each of cinnamon and cloves to 3 cups water. Boil for 15 minutes. Let mixture cool and add 1 beaten egg, 3 cups flour and 2 tsp baking soda; mix well. Pour into greased tube pan and bake at 350°F for 1 hour.

BOOT HEELS. *See* fat Archies.

BORAGE (*Borago officinalis*; also called bugloss, starflower)—a non-native plant brought along and planted by early French settlers for use as a salad green. It tastes like cucumber and makes a good flavouring for wine and cider. Now a commercial crop in the Prairie provinces, seeds from this flowering plant have both medicinal and culinary properties. High in omega-6 fatty acids, oil pressed from seeds goes to supply the health-food trade, while a small percentage of seed is used for culinary purposes and is especially good toasted. Borage flowers are used by upscale chefs to decorate salads and fish dishes, while bees produce a marvellous honey from the nectar.

BOSS RIBS—slang for roast buffalo hump, the most tender meat of the plains bison. In the early years of the 19th century, European hunters killed bison for the boss rib and left the carcass to rot. *See also* bison.

BOTTLED MOOSE—canned moose meat, a Newfoundland favourite.

BOTULISIM—an extremely dangerous form of food poisoning caused by a toxin produced by the bacterium *Clostridium botulinum*. Although a rarity today, the most common incidence of this type of posioning occurred from consuming improperly canned foods.

A
B
C
D
E
F
G
H
I
J
K
L
M
N
O
P
Q
R
S
T
U
V
W
X
Y
Z

BOUDIN (also called black pudding, blood pudding)—originally a French blood sausage called *boudin noir*, but nowadays it can be many varieties of sausage from many national cuisines. Called blood or black pudding in Britain, it is often sold by those names in English Canada.

BOUILLABAISSE GASPÉ—a stew with cod and other fish introduced to the Gaspé area of Québec by French fishermen and naturalized by the use of local fish.

BOUILLI—a traditional Acadian/Cajun ham and vegetable harvest meal widely adopted by Québec habitants and modern-day New Orleans restaurants.

BOUILLI CANADIEN. See jiggs dinner.

BOUILLOTTE DE LIÈVRE (also called rabbit stew)—an iconic 18th-century habitant dish that mixed rabbit or hare with other game meats, salt pork, onions and flour to thicken. Going west, pioneer settlers had to travel through Québec, and the habitant rabbit stew recipe went along for the ride; it was a good thing too, because many settlers found rabbit on the menu nearly every night for years.

RECIPE

Rabbit Stew

In a large soup pot, bring 1 cut-up young rabbit, 2 stalks diced celery, 1 diced onion, 2 bay leaves, ¼ tsp dried thyme and 1 tsp each of salt and pepper to a boil. Reduce heat and simmer uncovered for 2 hours. Add 3 diced carrots and 2 diced potatoes and simmer until tender, 20–25 minutes. Whisk 2 Tbsp flour into ¾ cup cold water and stir into stew until thickened.

BOUNCEBERRY—another name for the cranberry after the way it bounces when ripe. Modern processing machines use this quirk to sort unripe and ripe cranberries. *See also* cranberry.

BOVINE GROWTH HORMONE—a synthetic hormone developed by Monsanto that increases milk production in dairy cows by as much as 25 percent. Approved in the U.S., the hormone called Posilac is banned in Canada and Europe because it causes lameness and mastitis in cows and has unknown effects on consumers.

BOVRIL—a liquid beef extract invented by a Scotsman, John Lawson Johnston, in 1870 and manufactured in England for the British

Bovril

- The name Bovril is a Johnston-inspired contraction of *bos*, the Latin word for ox, and *vril*, a fictional electric fluid from English author Lord Bulwer-Lytton's then-popular novel, *The Coming Race*.

- John Lawson Johnston passed away at the turn of 20th century, but he did himself proud as his Bovril Company owned cattle ranches in Argentina and controlled the raising and slaughter of almost two million beef cows. However, in 1902, along came a company with an almost identical tasting but much cheaper product called Marmite. By 1920, Marmite sales had eclipsed Bovril, and the Bovril Company responded in proper British fashion by buying the Marmite Company. In 1990, the Bovril Company was bought by Best Foods, and in 2000, Best Foods was purchased by the mighty Unilever conglomerate.

- Sometime before the dawn of the 20th century, Bovril switched from a stubby glass bottle to an earthenware crock with a paper label, and in 1924, the company switched to the chubby brown glass bottle now recognized around the world.

and French armies. Called Johnston's Liquid Beef, the extract was a great success, but in 1879, Johnston's factory burned to the ground. To be nearer to a plentiful beef supply, he rebuilt the factory in Montréal. During the winters from 1881 to 1884, Johnston dispensed his hot beef extract drink from the ice palaces constructed at the Montréal Winter Carnival, where it became iconic to the festivities. In 1884, Johnston returned to London and began producing liquid beef for the public; capitalizing on his success in Canada, he attended expositions and fairs and dispensed his hot beverage from miniature ice palaces constructed of glass. At the South Kensington Exposition of 1887, the words "Bovril Brand" first appeared on the chubby glass retail bottles under the embossed "Johnston's Liquid Beef."

BOXBERRY. *See* wintergreen.

BOXTY—during the mid-19th century, Irish farming families abandoned their blighted fields and fled to Canada, bringing along their hopes, traditions and those recipes that had served them well in the old country. Featuring prominently was a potato pancake called boxty: mashed potatoes with an equal amount of peeled and sliced raw potatoes that have been wrung dry in a dishrag and mixed with green onions, flour, baking powder, salt and a bit of buttermilk to form a stiff batter. They were then fried in hot butter or oil.

BOYSENBERRY—a cross of blackberry (*Rubus fruticosus*) and loganberry (*R. loganobaccus*) that is usually dark in colour, softer than a raspberry, and has a unique tangy flavour that Walter Knott, a California farmer, turned into a jam and jelly success story called Knott's Berry Farm. Look for them at farmers' markets in more southern areas of Canada.

BRAISED EEL—skinned eel browned in a pan with butter, capers and parsley and then covered and simmered in white wine for 20 to 30 minutes. Eels were an important food item for early settlers. Along with sturgeon, they were fished

from the St. Lawrence River near Québec City, salted and used year-round.

BREAD—the staff of life, made from milled kernels of wheat, corn, rye, barley, oats or almost anything that can be dried and ground to flour. Flour, water, soda or yeast, a spoonful of sugar, a pinch of salt—and voilà, bread dough. A 10-minute knead, some time to rise and into the oven it goes to work its olfactory magic.

THE MILLING PROCESS

Newly arrived pioneer cooks made bread from whatever flour they brought along, usually lyed cornmeal. Wheat seed went into the ground after corn and potatoes, followed by barley, peas and oats—all crops that, after milling into flour, could make bread. Milling would have been a problem for the earliest settlers, who had to rely on a flail and blanket method to thresh grain. Beaten off the stalks, the grain was tossed up and down on a blanket by two people, with one guiding threshed grain onto the floor. To turn threshed grain into flour, settlers used a burned-out tree stump with a milling stone set into the middle. Grain was placed onto the stone, and another stone with a handle was set on top. Crank, crank, take off the stone, brush off a little flour and wipe the brow. It was hard work, usually done by women as they stared out into the forest. They would have noticed that nut trees were everywhere—beechnuts, chestnuts, walnuts, hickory—and in no time at all those women had gathered up the nuts, dried and shelled them, and into the grinder they went. Milled nutmeats were used to bulk up expensive wheat flour, produced tasty breads and made a welcome addition to the Canadian food experience.

BREAD PUDDING—sliced bread soaked in egg custard and baked until the little buttered ends get all crispy brown. It's lovely stuff and very English, but in the early days, maple sugar put a "made in Canada" stamp on our pudding.

BREAD-AND-BUTTER PICKLES—almost every Canadian over the age of 50 can remember having to slice the cukes for these pickles and hear mom's nagging to "slice 'em thinner."

RECIPE

Bread-and-Butter Pickles

Thinly slice 3 quarts washed, unskinned cucmbers into a large bowl and toss with 3 cups pearl onions and some finely chopped green and red pepper (optional but good). Pour over a mixture of 8 cups hot water and 1 cup pickling salt. Let stand 3–4 hours. In a large saucepan combine 6 cups white vinegar, 3 cups sugar, 1½ tsp turmeric, 1 tsp mustard seeds and 1 tsp celery seeds, and bring to a boil over medium heat. Add cukes, return to a boil and remove from heat. Ladle into 2-cup Mason jars and boil sealed jars in a water bath for 10 minutes. Will keep in a cool place for up to 1 year.

BREADROOT. See *pomme de prairie.*

BRETON CRACKERS—Canada's favourite since 1983, a good-for-you snack made with 12 grains and no artificial ingredients. Baked by Dare Foods,

a Kitchener, Ontario, company with more than a century-long history, the crackers are available in supermarkets nationwide.

BREWIS—usually pronounced "broos," a Newfoundland word for the breaking up or "bruising" of hardtack, a ship's biscuit baked by provisioners for long sea voyages. Impervious to water and insects, the rock-hard biscuits required softening before eating. Historically they were set upon the overturned convex lid of a Dutch oven along with a ladle or two of the pot's contents, usually a salt fish stew, from which comes the famous fish 'n' brewis dish. In the past, brewis also meant a dish of softened broken-up biscuits mixed with flaked cod and drizzled with pork fat—yummy. Brewis biscuits are baked by the Purity Company in Newfoundland and sold in the U.S. under the Pilot brand.

BRISLING. *See* Atlantic herring.

BRITCHINS—fried egg sacks, the roe, of codfish; usually fried in cubed salt pork called scrunchions.

BROADLEAF ARROWHEAD. *See* wapato.

CANADA'S FAVOURITE BROCCOLI VARIETIES

- Di Cicco—has emerald green florets and was the most popular until modern hybrids came along.

- Green Sprouting Calabrese—the best-tasting heirloom and a market mainstay.

- Purple Peacock—a modern cross of broccoli and kale that will change haters into lovers.

- Purple Sprouting Calabrese—a purple-floret variation.

RECIPE

Roasted Broccoli

The trick here, as with all roasting vegetables, is to dry thoroughly after washing. Toss 2 lbs broccoli florets in 2 Tbsp olive oil, season with salt and pepper and lay onto a cookie sheet. Roast in a 425°F oven until tender and tips are beginning to brown, about 25 minutes. Remove from oven and zest with lemon and drizzle with lemon juice and another 2 Tbsp olive oil. Sprinkle with Parmesan cheese and serve immediately.

BROCCOLI (*Brassica oleracea* var. *botrytis*)—a member of the Cabbage family developed in the Mediterranean area and brought to Canada by immigrants during the early 20th century. Broccoli and Calabrese broccoli are different, in that broccoli is an overwintered crop harvested from early winter to late spring, while Calabrese is planted in spring and harvested from mid-summer to late fall. They possess similar but distinct flavours.

BROME LAKE DUCK—a Canadian gastronomic delight since 1912, when Brome Lake Ducks Limited set up shop on the shore of the Eastern Township's Lac Brome. Their goal, to breed the meatiest and finest-tasting duck in the entire world, caught the public's attention, and today the company ships out more than two million dressed birds annually. Quack, quack and pass the dewberry sauce. *See also* dewberries and duck.

BROWN BREAD—Canadian term for whole-wheat bread, a nationalized form of the popular pre-Confederation Boston brown bread. *See also* bread.

BROWN SUGAR PIE—of Acadian origin and a precursor to the famed butter tart, this sweet, easy-to-make dessert pie has evolved from

a molasses and milk pie to brown sugar and condensed milk and is much better for the transition.

RECIPE

Brown Sugar Pie

In a bowl, mix together 1 cup brown sugar, 3 Tbsp flour and ¼ tsp salt, and spread evenly into an unbaked pie shell. Carefully pour over the contents of a 12 oz can of condensed milk, dot with 3 tsp butter and sprinkle on cinnamon. Bake at 350°F for 50–60 minutes or until a knife comes out clean. Let cool, then refrigerate before serving.

BRUSSELS SPROUTS (*Brassica oleracea* var. *gemmifera*)—a relative of wild cabbage, but only the small leafy sprouts that emerge from a tall stalk have any resemblance to cabbage. The origin of this vegetable is a mystery, but one has to surmise it is probably from somewhere near Brussels, Belgium.

A
B
C
D
E
F
G
H
I
J
K
L
M
N
O
P
Q
R
S
T
U
V
W
X
Y
Z

BUARTNUT—a disease-resistant hybrid cross between the heartnut and butternut and a very tasty and easily shelled nut, so keep your eyes peeled for it at local farmers' markets. *See also* butternut, heartnut.

BUBBLY BAKE—a favourite Maritime seafood casserole made with fresh scallops, butter, cream, mushrooms, green onions, white wine and a bread crumb topping.

BUCKSHOTS—a new snack food made from dehulled and toasted buckwheat seeds. Created at Manitoba's Food Development Centre and judged one of the top 12 best new foods at the 2012 Winter Fancy Food Show in San Francisco, the tasty, gluten-free snack food is being manufactured and distributed by Stone Milled Specialty Grains of Oak Bluff, Manitoba.

BUCKWHEAT (*Fagopyrum esculentum*)—not wheat, not even a cereal, it is the fruit or nut of a broad-leafed plant. Grown in England to feed hogs and fowl and brought to Canada by the earliest settlers for that purpose, milled buckwheat saw other uses: as a wheat flour extender, stew thickener and, of course, to make pancakes. Buckwheat grows easily in Canada, and small fields of the crop were common to almost every farm. Today buckwheat is either milled into

a flour or processed into groats or grits for use as a meat extender and an ingredient in breakfast cereals, soups and gluten-free processed foods.

BUCKWHEAT PANCAKES—pioneer breakfast cakes made from a batter of buckwheat flour, water, yeast and a pinch of salt. The batter is set aside to rise for a few hours then is puddled into a pan and fried in lard. Buckwheat pancakes were a breakfast staple. A big stack topped with butter and drizzled with maple syrup put smiles on the faces of pioneer farmers and will do the same for you.

RECIPE

Buckwheat Pancakes

Beat about 3 pints sifted buckwheat flour, 1 tsp salt and ½ cup good barm (yeast) with enough fresh, warm milk to make a batter. Cover and set aside for the night in a warm place. In the morning, grease up a hot griddle and spoon on batter in puddles until the pan is full, but do not allow the pancakes to touch each other. If your lard or butter is hot enough, the cakes will set as you spoon them on and will cook up as light as feathers. Serve hot with butter and top with maple syrup, apple syrup, molasses or treacle.

BUFFALO. *See* bison.

BUFFALO COD. *See* lingcod.

like popcorn. The popped kernels are pink and need a lot of butter and salt because they have little taste.

BUGLOSS. *See* borage.

BULL TROUT. *See* Dolly Varden trout.

BULLY BEEF—an English term for canned corned beef, but also used extensively in Canada after World War I. *See also* corned beef, iron rations, Spork.

BUMBLEBERRY PIE—a double-crust pastry pie with a varied berry filling that most often consists of a mixture of raspberries, blueberries, saskatoons and quartered strawberries. It was a Prairie favourite included in the recipe journals of most Canadian cooks.

BUFFALOBERRY (*Shepherdia canadensis*; also called bearberry, soapberry, soopolallie)—buffaloberry shrubs have spiny tips and may grow to three metres tall, making harvesting a sometimes-painful experience. Foragers will usually wait for the berries to over-ripen, then shake the berries off the shrub onto catch cloths. West coast First Nations called the berries *soopolallies* and, by mixing them with sweet berries and beating them frothy, could make a sweet dessert reminiscent of ice cream. Pioneers sometimes brewed the berries into a quick wine or beer, as it will completely ferment in 24 hours.

BUFFALOBERRY JAM—a favourite of pioneer prairie farmers, made from berries of the buffaloberry shrub. The tart, red and yellow berries are high in pectin and are easily turned into delicious jams and jellies.

BUFFALOBERRY POPCORN—fried in oil, berries of the common buffaloberry will pop

BURBOT (*Lota lota*)—a close relative of cod with little commercial value other than as dog and cat food. Fished for its liver oil during the mid-20th century, the fish slipped back into obscurity during the 1950s. Sometimes called eelpout because its long body and fins remind fishermen of a lamprey or eel, the meat reportedly has a taste similar to lobster.

BURDOCK ROOT (*Arctium lappa*)—when dried, the roots of this commercially foraged plant taste like hazelnuts or almonds and are used by some chefs and bakers to produce nutty delights without the nuts.

BURGER CAKES—a meal extender dish popular during the Depression era and made by mixing ½ lb ground beef with chopped onions, ¼ tsp each of baking powder and salt, and 3 egg yolks. Beat the 3 egg whites stiff and fold into mixture. Spoon onto hot griddle and turn once when golden.

BURNS CHUCKWAGON DINNER—a canned beef stew so popular in the late 1940s and early 1950s that it sponsored a television show, *Burns Chuckwagon from the Stampede Corral*. Manufactured by Burns Foods, the West's largest beef packer (now controlled by Maple Leaf Foods), the yummy stew in the big can fed countless lumber and mine workers along with legions of summer camp kids and cottagers. Gone but not forgotten, the stew is memorialized on the menus of many western restaurants as the "chuckwagon dinner."

BUTTER—Canadians travelling to Europe for the first time are always amazed by the wide selection of butters available to consumers: unprocessed milk butters, single herd butters, regional butters, seasonal, cultured and exotic butters, such as goat, sheep, buffalo and even yak butter. Canadian butter is but a commodity produced by profit-driven dairy conglomerates for consumers

weaned on high-salt, low-fat butter not suitable for crafting a proper croissant. Travellers who taste real butter in Europe return home with a longing for the better stuff, but are out of luck unless willing to accept an import that has been frozen, packed into a shipping container with cheeses and costs around $35/lb, a price that reflects the impossibly high customs duty designed to protect what the world laughingly calls Canadian-style butter.

BUTTER BRICKLE ICE CREAM—an ice cream flavour with bits of toffee popular in the U.S. beginning in the 1930s. The ice cream became a naturalized, original Canadian flavour in the 1950s when J.B. Jackson Limited—a Simcoe, Ontario, novelty ice cream manufacturer—began using crushed Heath candy bars in their formulation.

BUTTER CAKE (also called cupcakes, Cumberland cake, queen cake)—a U.S. culinary invention using baking powder that became naturalized depending on what berries or fruits were added

to the batter before baking, with almost every Canadian cookbook laying claim to a variation.

BUTTER DROP CAKES—recipe #179 from *The Cook Not Mad* (1831) combines 4 eggs, 1 lb each of flour and sugar, ¼ lb butter, a touch of mace and 2 Tbsp rose water; bake in tin pans.

BUTTER ICING—the icing that covered, and still does, dozens of Canadian variations of butter cakes. It's just butter and icing sugar, but it is amenable to all kinds of flavouring such as vanilla and cocoa and is especially wonderful with lemon.

BUTTER TART—a pioneer dessert tart made with easily obtainable ingredients: eggs, butter, corn syrup, brown sugar or molasses, salt and dried currants or raisins. Butter tart popularity has withstood the test of time to become iconic to the Canadian food experience.

BUTTERFISH. *See* sablefish.

BUTTERMILK—the slightly sour milk left over after butter is made, but modern dairy methods usually entail treating pasteurized skim milk with a culture for thickening and taste.

BUTTERMILK PIE—an Acadian bottom-crust dessert pie with a custard filling of boiled buttermilk, eggs, lemon, sugar, a pinch of salt and cornstarch. The recipe originally used whey left over from butter making; this delicious pie is still a huge favourite with Maritimers.

BUTTERNUT (*Juglans cinerea*; also called oilnut, white walnut)—butternuts were a boon to pioneers settling in the St. Lawrence and Great Lakes areas. Most forests contained large numbers of butternut trees, which produce a nut that yields almost 60 percent of its weight in oil. Easily gathered from the ground and in such numbers that squirrels got sick of eating them, the nuts were either dried or macerated in a stone-grain mill and pressed for cooking oil. Unfortunately for the tree and nut lovers, the wood became prized by furniture makers, and later the trees fell victim to an invasive canker disease. A few survive, but not enough to make squirrels sick of eating the nuts, and finding them on the ground these days is nearly impossible.

BUTTERNUT SOUP—a delicious soup made by pioneers from nuts of the native butternut tree, a member of the Walnut family.

> ### RECIPE
>
> #### Butternut Soup
>
> *Add 1 cup crushed butternuts to 2 cups chicken stock, 1 diced onion, 1 chopped celery stalk, 1½ cups milk, 1 tsp salt, 3 Tbsp butter and ¼ tsp black pepper. Cook 10 minutes, then put the mixture through a sieve or give it a few spins in a food processor, and serve piping hot with a dab of butter.*

BUTTERNUT SQUASH (*Cucurbita moschata*)— a most vexing winter squash for Canadians because it is one of our favourites but is hard to grow in our climate. Although it won't grow for factory farmers, it will for smaller farmers and gardeners in southerly areas, so watch for the squash at farmers' markets. *See also* squash.

BUTTERSCOTCH—the pioneer's chocolate, and a confection that has endured the centuries. To make, heat 1 lb brown sugar until melted, then add 4 oz creamed butter and stir until it reaches hard-ball consistency. Pour onto a greased cookie sheet and score into squares. When cool, break into squares and enjoy.

BUTTERSCOTCH PIE—a scrumptious dessert pie made with our pioneer settlers' favourite flavouring.

> ### RECIPE
>
> #### Butterscotch Pie
>
> *Melt 2 Tbsp butter in a saucepan. Stir in ¾ cup brown sugar and continue stirring until thick. In a bowl, combine 2 cups milk, ¼ cup cornstarch and a pinch of salt, and stir. Gradually whisk bowl contents into saucepan and cook for 2–3 minutes until thick. In a small bowl, beat 2 eggs lightly, stir in a little of the hot mixture, add to saucepan and cook while whisking for 2–3 minutes until thick. Remove from heat, stir in 1 tsp vanilla and pour into a prebaked, 9-inch pie shell. Bake with or without meringue topping for 13–15 minutes at 350°F.*

BY-CATCH FISH—large, unmarketable fish caught accidentally by trawlers harvesting trash fish for the aquaculture trade. Factory trawlers processing on board routinely pull up nets half-filled with unwanted by-catch, which they discard. Non-factory trawlers will often unload more by-catch than catch, and this practice is perfectly legal. Long-line fishermen catch all manner of fish and mammals on their hooks: turtles, dolphins, birds and sharks by the thousands, with even the odd whale suffocating on those hooks. However, for those fishermen, it's waste not, want not; the by-catch will become bait for the countless hooks of many long lines.

Renamed Fish

- By-catch species, real monsters from the deep, are often renamed and commonly show up on menus with names like Chilean sea bass, which is actually the Patagonian toothfish, or the infamous Hawaiian butterfish, which is actually escolar, a deep-water snake mackerel with flesh that contains significant amounts of a wax ester that provides diners with an urgent need to visit the washroom.

BYWARD PUBLIC MARKET—Ottawa's original farmers' market, established in 1826 and one of the nation's oldest. In a city long polarized by racial, political and economic strife, the market was both a centre of commerce and an occasional battlefield for the terminally disgruntled. Open all hours, the market is today a major tourist draw and a continuing Mecca for the terminally disgruntled and other anti-social elements of society. Knowledgeable locals seeking fresh produce gravitate to smaller seasonal farmers' markets such as Parkdale Farmers' Market, the Carp, Lansdown and Ottawa Organic Farmers' Market. *See also* market squares.

C

CABANE À SUCRE—starting in the 18th century, sugaring became a winter business for habitants all over Québec. The habitant would stake out an area of forest rife with sugar maples, then he would build a cabin to protect himself and his sugaring pots, pans and pails from the elements. Maple sugar is what he produced in the bush: large, heavy blocks of sugar to be hauled out and gathered up by wholesalers. Not until the latter part of the 19th century, when glass containers became available, did the bush shacks begin producing quantities of syrup. Farmers would retire to the sugar shack each spring, usually with their eldest sons, and stay until the sap stopped running. Occasionally, a man's family would journey into the forest to join him, and these visits were cause for celebration and feasting

CABANE À SUCRE MENU

Visitors to a Québec sugar shack will typically find these items on the *festin*, or menu: pea soup, maple-cured country ham, tourtière, *ragout de boulettes* (meatball stew), country sausage, *oreilles de crises* (fried pork rinds), *fèves au lard* (baked beans), old-style mashed potatoes, pancakes, sugar pie, lots of home-made pickles and condiments and perhaps some spruce beer.

that over the years developed into a fun cuisine of everything maple. Nowadays, even though syrup production is mechanized and most sugar shacks have rotted into history, old habits of

family and hospitality die hard and these joyful events continue to this day, having become something of a springtime tourist attraction in Québec. Around Easter, urbanites and tourists flock to surviving sugar shacks for a recreational cookout of all things maple, especially ham. The annual sugar shack fest is so much fun that the festival has spread to the Maritimes and Ontario. People no longer have to make the arduous journey to the sugaring cabins on foot; they can drive to the *cabane à sucre*, observe the sap gathering and the sugaring, and then partake of a feast of pea soup, maple-laced ham, tourtière and maple taffy.

CABBAGE (*Brassica oleracea* var. *capitata*)—the old man of the cultivated *Brassica* species and the ancestor of broccoli, Brussels sprouts and cauliflower; its own ancestor is a wild field cabbage called colewort, a headless, spindly plant reminiscent of kale but with a slight cabbage flavour and from which members of the Brassica family come by the name "cole crops." During the first century BCE, a farmer in Northern Europe found a colewort with a large terminal bud and saved the seeds for planting. He then started

CANADA'S FAVOURITE CABBAGE VARIETIES

- Chieftain Savoy—the best of the wrinkly leaved savoy varieties.

- Copenhagen—round solid heads, sweet and good for coleslaw and sauerkraut.

- Early Jersey Wakefield—sweet and equally good for coleslaw and sauerkraut.

- January King—a sweet semi-savoy type that is great for roasting.

- Mammoth Red Rock—a red cabbage with superior flavour.

- Winningstadt—solid pointed heads that keep well and are great for stuffed cabbage.

A
B
C
D
E
F
G
H
I
J
K
L
M
N
O
P
Q
R
S
T
U
V
W
X
Y
Z

RECIPE

Roasted Cabbage

Cut 1 Chieftain Savoy or January King cabbage head into 8 wedges; place into a plastic bag with 2 Tbsp oil and 1 tsp salt and shake gently. Place wedges on a baking sheet and roast in a 375°F oven for about 45 minutes, keeping a sharp eye on them toward the end. Before serving, remove the centre core from each wedge.

saving the seeds from those coleworts with even larger heads, and by the time the seeds reached Holland, they were well on their way to being the hard white Dutch, or drumhead, cabbage. Along with the European transformation of colewort into cabbage went the age-old method of pickling colewort and producing a fermented product called sauerkraut, which happens to be rich in vitamin C and the ticket needed to defeat the nemesis of all those who went to sea: scurvy. Jacques Cartier and his men were cured of scurvy with Iroquois spruce beer during his second voyage to Canada, but Cartier made sure to bring along cabbages on his third voyage in 1541–1542. So it was that every cabbage-loving immigrant group arriving in Canada found their favourite vegetable already well established across the entire country.

CAESAR. *See* Bloody Caesar.

CAJUN CUISINE—a style of cooking iconic to the U.S. state of Louisiana developed by

Cajun

• Many French Canadians expelled by the British from Acadia (Nova Scotia and New Brunswick) resettled in the southern U.S. state of Louisiana. Over time, the word "Acadian" became shortened to "Cadien" with a French twang, then to "Cajun" by locals who were unable to handle the twang.

Acadians—or Cajuns—driven from Canada's Maritime provinces in the Great Expulsion of 1754–1763. This cuisine, not to be confused with Creole cuisine, is important to the Canadian food experience because many Cajuns returned to the Maritimes in later years and brought along their hot sauce, cayenne pepper, rice dishes and *boudin* (sausages).

CALAMARI. *See* squid.

CALF'S HEAD SOUP—there is only room for one bull on a farm, and "waste not, want not" was the golden rule. The head of an unwanted bull calf was popped into a large pot and boiled all day. Then it was dumped into a colander, picked for meat and cooked again with vegetables. Today, while the odd head still gets turned into soup on the farm, most get rendered into pellets to supply the aquaculture industry.

CALGARY REDEYE—a mixture of beer and Clamato juice; it's a purely western thing.

CALGARY STAMPEDE—the world's biggest rodeo and every Canadian's chance to be a cowboy for 10 days in July. Visitors, and there are over a million each year, don white cowboy hats, drink whisky and chow down on cowboy food. Pancake breakfasts are mandatory, as are stews and barbecue for dinner, with the fabled prairie oysters being an elective.

CALGARY STAMPEDE PANCAKES. *See* chuckwagon breakfast.

CALIFORNIA ROLL—in spite of the name, this inside-out sushi is our very own, having been invented in the 1970s by Japanese Canadian chef Hidekazu Tojo, who is also credited with inventing the smoked salmon BC roll.

CALLIBOGUS—spruce beer with rum and molasses added to it. It was an early Newfoundland alcoholic libation from whence sprang the slang word "bogus," meaning counterfeit.

CAMBRIDGE FARMERS' MARKET—established in Cambridge, Ontario, during the 1830s, it is one of Canada's oldest markets and is still clinging to its farm market mandate—all of its vendors are from within a 100-km radius of the market. It is open Saturdays all year long and Wednesdays during summer. *See also* market squares.

CANADA DRY GINGER ALE—the "champagne of ginger ales" was the brainchild of Toronto chemist John J. McLaughlin, one of Canadian automobile mogul Robert Samuel McLaughlin's three sons. In 1890, John McLaughlin opened a seltzer plant in Toronto, and ginger beer seemed a natural progression. But everyone made ginger beer, so he took another path and invented a crisper-tasting product. The brand got a big boost during Prohibition days because it masked the off-flavour of bathtub gin.

CANADA GOOSE (*Branta canadensis*)—so numerous now, but at the beginning of the 20th century, it had almost joined the passenger pigeon on the list of extinct species. While market hunters caused the extinction of the passenger pigeon, it was recreational hunters who threatened the Canada goose; in fact, during the 1930s,

A
B
C
D
E
F
G
H
I
J
K
L
M
N
O
P
Q
R
S
T
U
V
W
X
Y
Z

conservationists thought the goose was beyond rescuing. It was only saved when the outlawing of live decoy geese provided an accidental breeding stock. Nowadays, the bird is considered more pest than dinner.

CANADA GOOSE CASSEROLE—a favourite of early settlers during spring and fall migrations of the geese.

CANADA GROUSE. *See* grouse.

CANADA LETTUCE (*Lactuca canadensis*)—related to the common garden lettuce and used by First Nations and early settlers as a medicinal analgesic and salad green.

CANADA ONION (*Allium canadense*; also called wild garlic)—this spindly plant with a pink or white flower can be found in meadows from coast to coast. Although it was once popular with settlers and First Nations, it can cause gastrointestinal problems for foragers and has dropped off the national menu.

CANADA PLUM (*Prunus nigra*; also called black plum)—our native plum, it makes a wonderful glaze for all meats. Early settlers found this decorative fruit tree growing everywhere, and when forests were cleared for pasture, the trees became part of the natural fencing—the hedgerow—and is where many of southeastern Canada's native plums are still found today. The fruit is not especially good fresh off the tree because it tends to be on the sour side, but it does have wonderful flavour and is great for canning.

CANADA PLUM COMPOTE—compote is a dessert made with boiled fruit in sugar water, and Canada plum compote was a fall favourite of pioneer families lucky enough to have settled near wild plum trees.

CANADA RICE. *See* wild rice.

CANADA SNAKEROOT. *See* wild ginger.

CANADIAN BACON—it's not a term used in Canada, but in Britain it means bacon from

Canada, and to Americans it is a cut of pork loin, or back bacon. *See also* back bacon, peameal bacon.

CANADIAN CANNERS—from 1914 to 1918, Canada dispatched 700,000 men and women to World War I, an astounding number from a total population of only 7.5 million. To keep the soldiers in rations, the government turned to canned food manufacturers—such as Canadian Canners, a 1903 amalgamation of canning companies and the A.R. Whittall Can Company of Montréal—and those manufacturers began turning out huge numbers of canned goods on the very day war was declared. The first train-loads of cans went to the nation's meat packers to be filled with corned beef and ham, but within months new private and government canning factories were in operation to pack beans, vegetables and various fruits. To keep the canning factories running at full production, the government contracted area farmers for specific crops and livestock and ordered fish canners on both

Label Art

- Many of Canada's greatest artists, including the members of the famous Group of Seven, got their starts designing lithographed labels for tin cans. J.E.H. MacDonald designed all manner of can labels, A.Y. Jackson did beans and tomato cans and Tom Thomson specialized in spectacular lettering for can labels. They and the other Group of Seven members all worked at one time or another for the Grip Company, a Toronto design firm that, among other things, produced some fabulous can and cigar box labels that today are highly valued collectibles.

coasts to increase production of canned salmon and mackerel. It was a time of great sacrifice; meat, sugar and gasoline were strictly rationed, and Canadian housewives learned to cook from cans as farmers had little left over to offer Saturday food shoppers. World War I transformed Canada from a nation of farmers into an industrial powerhouse, with its workers dependent on factory cafeterias and small corner stores stocking mostly canned goods for sustenance. Almost every agricultural product imaginable was stuck into a can, and to attract consumers, the canning companies relied on lithographed labels that turned corner stores into veritable art galleries. *See also* home freezers, market squares, supermarkets.

CANADIAN FONDA. *See* fonda.

CANADIAN FOOD INSPECTION AGENCY (CFIA)—Canada is awash in laws and agencies to protect food consumers from dirty tricks, negligent processing or dangerous ingredients, and most municipalities and all provinces and territories have laws and enforcement inspectors. On the federal level, there is the Canadian Food Inspection Agency, charged with setting food safety, quality and grading standards for food products meant for interprovincial distribution or export and for preventing the production and sale of dangerous, adulterated or misbranded foods. With innumerable laws and thousands of inspectors, Canadian consumers should be confident that any food product sold in Canada is healthy and safe. However, incidents such as the soybean debacle (*see* vegetable oil) are cause for concern, especially when compounded by the 1985 federal boondoggle dubbed "Tunagate" when John Fraser, the Minister of Fisheries and Oceans in Brian Mulroney's government, overrode a decision by government inspectors to impound tainted tuna packed by StarKist in New Brunswick and allowed the cans onto store shelves in order to save the jobs of cannery workers. The CFIA claims to have more than 3000 inspectors at work, but according to the inspectors' union there are fewer than 2000—certainly not enough

to protect consumers from pathogens such as listeria and salmonella, which seem to contaminate our food supplies on a regular basis. To cut government costs, many food conglomerates, including most meat packers, are self-regulated, with inspectors visiting perhaps once a week for an hour or so. In 2008, that attitude led to a listeria outbreak at Maple Leaf Foods that killed 12 people and sickened hundreds, a disaster compounded by the CFIA's inexplicable delay in notifying the public of the contamination. *See also* food safety.

CANADIAN NATIONAL RAILWAY—shortly after World War I, the Canadian government took over the bankrupt Canadian Northern and Grand Trunk railways and formed Canadian National (CN) Railway, and wisely followed Canadian Pacific's lead by introducing travellers to the great Canadian food experience on wheels. People still pine for the CN dining car's signature dishes: cream of chicken Yvette soup, sizzling lamb chops, baked lake trout and their famous Christmas pudding, an annual wintertime culinary tradition that required no less

Peddlers Peddling

• Before the railway enabled mail-order deliveries, settlers in remote areas of Canada depended on itinerant peddlers for such necessities and luxuries as pots, pans, rakes, hoes, nails, cloth, sewing needles, books, fruit trees, seeds, spices and vanilla.

than 25 tonnes of pudding to meet demand. CN Christmas pudding lovers can stop pining; the tradition has been reborn on the government-operated VIA Rail dining car service. VIA Rail took over CP and CN passenger service in 1977, and it has done a commendable job of maintaining the magic on both of their famous long-haul trains: the Canadian, which travels from Toronto to Vancouver; and the Ocean, going from Toronto to Halifax.

CANADIAN ORGANIC GROWERS (COG)— a national charitable organization that has been promoting organic agriculture in Canada for over 30 years. COG is connected nationally through eleven regional chapters, four affiliate organizations and internationally through the International Federation of Organic Agriculture Movements (IFOAM). COG's mission is "to lead local and national communities towards sustainable organic stewardship of land, food and fibre while respecting nature, upholding social justice and protecting natural resources."

CANADIAN PACIFIC RAILWAY—Canadian Pacific (CP) was a transcontinental railway that was much favoured by Brits headed for Hong Kong and Asia. Brits arrived at Halifax aboard a CP liner, boarded a CP train to Vancouver and, once there, were transferred to another CP liner headed across the Pacific Ocean—and they were offered first-class treatment all the way. Unlike most other railways, CP considered kitchens and dining rooms too important to outsource, and they maintained control over every aspect of their food from procurement to presentation. CP station agents purchased food from local suppliers as well as commercial hunters and fishermen and insisted that only the finest meats, poultry, fish, game, produce, cheese and baked goods be delivered, an insistence backed

up by the frequent visits of railway inspectors. Many people chose to travel on CP Rail just for the dining experience, and they were never

VAN HORNE'S GREAT IDEA

In one fateful letter to William Cornelius Van Horne, president of the Canadian Pacific Railway, Albert Ballin, managing director of the German-owned Hamburg America Line, raved about his stay at London's new and

ultra-fashionable Carlton Hotel, which opened in 1899. Not only had the hotel's ambience astounded him, but its French restaurant, the Ritz-Carlton Grill, had turned him absolutely giddy. So giddy, in fact, that he immediately contracted the hotel's architect, Charles Mewes, and the restaurant's overseer, César Ritz, to duplicate their work on his company's new ship, the SS *Amerika*. Haute cuisine did not go nautical until 1905, but that did not stop Van Horne from using Ballin's good idea for CP's new hotels and steamships. Like Ballin, Van Horne needed a hook to attract travellers, and combining plush ambience with haute cuisine was just the thing. Pullman dining cars had already made his small, rudimentary stop 'n' rest hotels redundant, so in 1886, Van Horne ordered CP's hotel division to concentrate on destination hotels. "Build 'em big, boys. In places where there's lots to do and see. And feed 'em like their mothers never did." It was syncronicity, and it would later see both Ballin and Van Horne vying for French chefs to operate their respective ever-expanding empires.

CP Rail

- Ballin's Hamburg America owned *Hansa*, a steamship company that specialized in Europe-to-Canada crossings with onward connections via an arrangement with Van Horne's CP Rail.

- Steam locomotives required many stops for coal and water and to clean the firebox, and while readers nowadays may think that would have been an irritation, it was actually a welcome pause as it afforded the passengers a chance to stretch their legs. It also afforded dining car chefs an opportunity to restock their pantries as CP station agents had locally purchased provisions waiting on station platforms to supplement the lobsters, oysters, whole Gaspé salmons and blueberry pies that had been loaded in Halifax.

- CP dining car fame attracted not only fish connoisseurs, but also those seeking to land a few beauties for themselves. Fishing became a big tourist draw for CP, and to keep their hotels filled with anglers while at the same time making sure their own requirements were met, they saw to the stocking of nearby streams and rivers with salmon or trout. Oddly enough, most streams and rivers in the Canadian Rockies owe their resident trout populations to CP's stocking program because glacial scouring from various ice ages had left them completely devoid of fish.

- CP's masterpiece destination hotel, the Banff Springs, constructed in 1888, was not open during winter until after 1968, when it was renovated for year-round operation.

- A rose is a rose is a rose even in the hotel business, as a name change from Canadian Pacific Hotels and Resorts to Fairmont Hotels and Resorts in 1999 changed nothing except the hotel conglomerate's international reach. The Canadian Pacific Railway built our grand hotels and now operates around the world in a manner that does us proud.

A
B
C
D
E
F
G
H
I
J
K
L
M
N
O
P
Q
R
S
T
U
V
W
X
Y
Z

CP RAIL'S MENU CHOICES

CP's transcontinental rail passengers were treated to a culinary cross-section of Canadian foods prepared by onboard chefs specially trained to operate on a whistle-stop culinary supply schedule. Getting to the dining car was a claustrophobic adventure of bumps and smells, but when the door got muscled open, it was like stepping into Oz. Breakfast menus were extensive and featured all the standard items and a host of exotics, such as lobster with shirred eggs, wildberry pancakes with mounds of smoky Berkshire bacon, venison sausage or chops, cod cheeks and eggs, finnan haddie, baked trout, oatmeal porridge with local berries and waffles topped with the same berries or maple syrup. The menu selection for lunch and dinner was even more extensive, and selection was an integral part of the dining car experience. That all meals, including breakfast, were served on real china plates placed onto starched white tablecloths by uniformed waiters who knew the ropes only added to the fun.

Wild game, maple-cured ham, roast wild duck, baked sturgeon or lake trout and fine cheeses were featured menu items through Québec.

Whitefish, fried yellow perch or pickerel, roast lamb, wild duck and peach or apple pie was presented through Ontario. The journey through the Prairies saw passengers treated to buffalo ribeye, roasted game birds, succulent CP "Red Brand" Alberta beef tenderloin and Saskatoon berry pie. Climbing through the Rocky Mountain passes required fuelling stops for trains travelling both east and west, allowing dining car supplies to be dropped off at stations so that westbound passengers could be treated to a west coast–preview dinner of crab-stuffed Pacific salmon, while eastbounders got lobster three ways, shucked oysters and slow-poached Atlantic salmon.

disappointed. CP raised their own beef, chickens and turkeys, employed market hunters to supply wild game and birds and had contracts with fishermen all along the route to supply finny fare for CP's legendary fish dishes.

CANADIENNE DAIRY COW—the first breed of milk cow imported into Canada. They were brought from Normandy, France, by Jacques Cartier in 1541 on his third and last voyage to Acadia before being ousted by the British. Apparently that herd fell victim to a British yearning for roast beef, but others soon followed, and between the years 1608 and 1670, several hundred animals were grazing in Canadian fields. The Canadienne cows were supplanted

in the 19th century by the more productive Holstein breed, but thankfully, a few of their numbers wound up in Québec, where the attributes of the Canadienne breed were properly utilized: the cow withstood harsh winters, adapted to undeveloped pasture and produced a creamy, rich milk perfect for cheese making. Today, only around 200 head of our national cow remain, having been saved from extinction by people who care.

CANDLEFISH. *See* eulachon.

CANOLA OIL—a Canadian original, pressed from seeds of a genetically engineered variety of rape plant (*Brassica napus*) and considered to be the healthiest cooking oil because it is the lowest

CANADIENNE CHEESES

Canadienne cattle were a point of promotion for Île d'Orléans–resident Anne Aubin around 1635 when she began selling cheese that she and other island farmers had produced at the Québec City farmers' market. Her washed-rind cheese, the first cheese produced in North America, became a sensation that continued for generations until government pasteurization laws implemented during the 1970s put an end to what many Québec City residents considered the best cheese in Canada.

Then along came master cheese maker Jocelyn Labbé in 1997, and Les Fromages de l'Île d'Orléans was back in business, making cheese according to a recipe supplied by Gérard Aubin, the great-great grandson of Anne Aubin, Canada's original cheese maker. Sadly, the Canadienne, our national cow, is gone from Île d'Orléans and was actually thought extirpated until a search uncovered a few small herds totalling fewer than 200 animals on the Îles-de-la-Madeleine in the Gulf of St. Lawrence.

Not unlike the great Canadian food experience, our national breed, the Canadienne, almost disappeared, only to return and be invigorated by artisanal producers, such as Îles-de-la-Madeleine's Fromagerie du Pied-de-Vent, crafters of an amazing washed-rind cheese. Or people like Dominique and Jean Labbé, operators of the Laiterie Charlevoix, a fromagerie in Baie-St-Paul, Québec, that has embraced artisanal cheese production using the finest ingredients available and that includes among its products a special washed-rind cheese made from the milk of two local herds of Canadienne cows. The cheese is called 1608, after the date the breed got its first real start in Canada, and although I have yet to sample the cheese, rumours abound as to its greatness. Dominique and Jean, along with other members of the Association for the Development of the Canadiennne Cattle Breed

in Charlevoix, are helping return our national cow from the brink, and for that we are grateful. We are also thankful for Dominique and Jean's raw-milk Cheddar.

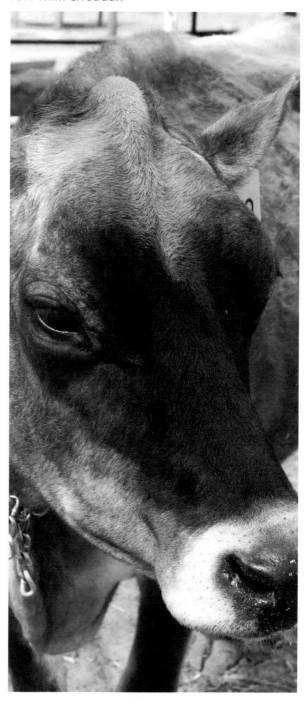

in saturated fat, highest in monounsaturated fat and a good source of omega-3 fatty acids. During the 18th and 19th centuries, seed oil from the rape plant, a close relative of mustard, was used to lubricate steam engines. That oil was inedible because it is almost 50 percent erucic acid, a bitter component found to be damaging to the human heart. But like its cousin the mustard plant, rape grew well on Canadian prairie land, and the prodigious oil content of its seeds caused Manitoba crop scientists to begin a breeding program aimed at removing the dangerous and bitter erucic acid from the rape plant, with subject plants labelled Can-O-LA, short for Canadian Oilseed Low Acid, now a trademarked name that has become generic. *See also* vegetable oil.

CAPE BRETON PORK PIE—not a shred of pork goes into this classic Cape Breton chopped date and molasses dessert tart, but at its inception in the 18th century, it may have included pork fat in the pastry.

CAPE GOOSEBERRY. *See* ground cherry.

CAPELIN (*Mallotus villosus*; also called caplin, salted caplin, *shishamo*)—a close relative of freshwater smelt, this small, silvery fish schools in the arctic and subarctic areas of both the Pacific and Atlantic oceans and comes ashore to spawn every spring. In Newfoundland, the spawn—called a "capelin scull"—is a major springtime event, with waves of the little fish rolling onto beaches while residents scoop them up in dip nets or buckets. Salt-dried capelin is used as snack food, and the fish are also canned, frozen and shipped to Japan with roe intact for a smoked finger food called *shishamo*.

CAPILLAIRE (*Chiogenus hispidata*; also called snowberry)—a round, white berry with an acidic but pleasant taste. Widely foraged by Maritimers to make jelly, capillaire were much loved by early trappers because the berries ripen late and hang onto the branches well into winter.

CAPLIN. *See* capelin.

CAPON—a young rooster that has been castrated so it becomes plumper and tastier for table use. Banned in Britain, the process is still much used in Canada to raise large birds, especially for restaurants.

CARAMILK BAR—an iconic Canadian chocolate bar introduced in the 1960s by William Nielson Ltd. and now manufactured by Cadbury Adams, a Kraft Foods company. Incidentally, the secret to how they get the creamy filling into the bar is an enzyme called invertase, the same enzyme used by honeybees to convert flower nectar into liquid honey. Now you know!

CARÊME, ANTONIN (1783–1833)—a famous 19th-century chef and the man most responsible for the involuntary shortness of breath (from overwhelming deliciousness) experienced by first-time tasters of French *patisseries*.

Caribou Herds

- Caribou are plentiful in the Northwest Territories and range over a million square kilometres in herds that may number in the hundreds of thousands.

- The largest herd—the Bathurst herd—roams between Yellowknife and the Arctic and has at times exceeded a half-million

animals, but those numbers have diminished over the last decade because of forest fires that have disrupted migration and breeding cycles.

- Other large herds roaming the north country include the Beverly, Qamanirjuaq and Ahiak herds, from which around 20,000 animals are harvested annually.

CARIBOU (*Rangifer tarandus*; also called reindeer)—Canada's most northern communities use this animal to supply the rest of us with sustainable wild game meat products. For Canadians not living in the upper reaches of the country, there is always the specialty butcher. Market caribou come from sustainable herds and are a needed source of revenue for northern peoples.

RECIPE

Caribou Burgers

Mix 1 lb ground caribou (or venison) with 1 beaten egg, 2 Tbsp olive oil, 1 clove chopped garlic and 1 Tbsp dried rosemary. Form into patties and grill.

CARIBOU (the drink)—a potent, head-spinning drink made by combining white grain alcohol with red wine; popular in the Yukon.

CARIBOU PRIME RIB ROAST—a long-time favourite Sunday dinner roast for northern

diners, now enjoyed in other areas of Canada thanks to government initiatives to establish commercial packing facilities in regions of the Far North. Lard the roast, cook for 20 minutes at 450°F, then reduce the temperature to 350°F and cook for 2 hours or until tender.

CARNATION EVAPORATED MILK—in 1884, John Meyenberg, a Swiss immigrant to the U.S., took the sugar out of Gail Borden's Eagle Brand sweetened condensed milk and began canning evaporated milk in the small town of Highland, Illinois. That effort failed to fly owing to faulty handmade cans, and Meyenberg bailed out of what would eventually become the Pet Milk Company and headed west, where he hooked up with Elbridge Stuart's Pacific Coast Condensed Milk Company to produce evaporated milk with machine-made cans. In 1907, with his company doing well, Stuart was thinking it was time to brand his product; he picked Carnation, a name prompted by a sign in a shop

RECIPE

Carnation Snow Ice Cream

A favourite Depression-days dessert made by mixing 2 beaten eggs, 6 Tbsp sugar, 1½ cups Carnation evaporated milk and 1½ tsp vanilla and cooking over medium heat until thick. Place saucepan outside until well chilled, then fill pan with clean snow and mix well. Spoon into chilled serving bowls and eat quickly before it melts.

window advertising Carnation cigars. In 1916, Stuart bought the Aylmer Condensed Milk Company in Aylmer, Ontario, just a few miles from the Borden's milk condensing plant at Ingersoll, Ontario, with both plants eventually falling victim to public company mismanagement. *See also* Eagle Brand sweetened condensed milk.

CARRAGEENAN—a common food additive that is used as a thickener and emulsifier in many processed foods, especially dairy products, in spite of evidence that it causes inflammation in humans that can lead to heart disease and cancer. It is extracted from a species of red seaweed called carrageen moss, or Irish moss (*Chondrus crispus*),

which is harvested from Atlantic coastal areas. Carageenan is deemed an organic product and is a vegan alternative to gelatin.

CARROT (*Daucus carota*)—until World War II, carrots were tough and mostly ignored as a vegetable. British hybridizing experiments increased the beta-carotene in carrots for better night vision for fighter pilots, and also produced more tender, sweeter carrots. Then the French took a hand and hybridized modern sweeter and more tender varieties, and today there are hundreds of varieties to choose from, in all colours and sizes.

CANADA'S FAVOURITE CARROT VARIETIES

- Early Scarlet Horn—has been around since the 16th century, and for tasty reasons.

- Long Orange—the progenitor of orange carrots.

- Long Orange Improved—a longer, but equally good-tasting carrot.

- Paris Market—stubby, early to market and very tasty.

- Red Core Chantenay—long, tapering, and probably the best-tasting carrot on the planet.

- Scarlet Nantes—nearly coreless and best for snacking or julienned for salads.

CARROTS AND CHRISTMAS DINNER

To early settlers with British roots, a Christmas dinner in Canada was a connection to home. Plans were made all year to make it special. A goose or turkey could be managed, either domestic or wild, while the potatoes would be stacked in the root cellar alongside the onions and the wonderful carrots that, though tough as nails, grew faster, larger and sweeter than any remembered from home. Cranberries for the sauce had been gathered, dried and stored in the cupboard to await preparation, and though the sweetener might be molasses, nobody was going to complain. The bread for stuffing, baked a few days before, would be waiting—cornbread again, but who cared. The anticipation was almost too much, especially when the children knew their mother had somehow made Christmas pudding. Pioneer life turned most wives into culinary inventors: a few candied berries, two or three mashed potatoes, a pint of molasses, a few cups of Indian meal and a pile of grated sweet carrots could be turned into a dessert masterpiece. After dinner, Dad would pour on a bit of brandy and, as Mother turned down the lantern, a lit match would turn her marvellous Christmas creation into a wispy blue volcano, eliciting squeals of delight from every child.

CARROT JAM—a favourite condiment of early settlers. It is easy to make and especially good with game meats.

RECIPE

Carrot Jam

Combine 4 cups finely chopped fresh carrots with 3 cups sugar, the juice and zest of 2 lemons and ¼ tsp each of cloves, allspice and cinnamon. Cook over low heat while stirring often until mixture is as thick as jam, about 40 minutes.

CARROT PUDDING—an early Canadian variation on the very English Christmas plum pudding, using grated carrots as a bolster for scarce ingredients.

CASKS—during Canada's formative years, all commercially produced ale and beer as well as most food products were shipped in wooden casks of various standard sizes: firkin (37 L), kilderkin (74 L), barrel (148 L) and hogshead (222 L). Butter was commonly packed and shipped in a firkin, a wooden pail with a handle and lid, while cured meats and fish, dried beans, peas, flour and cornmeal went into barrels.

A B C D E F G H I J K L M N O P Q R S T U V W X Y Z

A
B
C
D
E
F
G
H
I
J
K
L
M
N
O
P
Q
R
S
T
U
V
W
X
Y
Z

COOPERING

Barrel-making, or coopering, was essential to almost all Canadian commercial enterprises, with cooperage being part and parcel of these enterprises. If it needed shipping, it went in a barrel, and like no other product, barrels defined and affected every aspect of agriculture and industrial growth in Canada. To accommodate hundreds of barrels, shipping docks were the size of football fields. Muscle-bound workers loaded and unloaded them, specially constructed wagons transported them, big-breed horses pulled them and expert teamsters drove them. Barrels needed storage, repair, wooden-stave sourcing, blacksmithed metal hoops, etc., and for almost 300 years, those endeavours employed around 10 percent of Canadian workers. Then along came the railway, and barrels were quickly deemed round pegs in square holes, as wooden crates were a better fit for the rectangular freight cars.

It was the end of an era. Then in 1996, two Vancouverites named Trish and Cal Craik decided to leave the city rat race, move to the BC's Okanagan Valley and cooper barrels for the wine industry. An iconic occupation was reborn, and their company, the Okanagan Barrel Works in Oliver, BC, is now producing fine oak barrels for artisanal wineries and food companies that value traditional quality over quantity. That a few of these traditionalists are foreign wineries is a bit worrying, as they acknowledge that our slow-growing oak trees provide the perfect wood for ageing fine wines, and that probably has them thinking acquisition to get more of our oak trees.

CASSIA (*Cinnamomum cassia*; also called Chinese cinnamon)—a spice related to cinnamon (*C. verum*) with a similar but inferior flavour. It is often ground and passed off as cinnamon.

CATCH LIMITS—in BC, the daily possession limit of salmon of any species is eight, plus three halibut, six lingcod and 16 flounder. Not often do anglers catch their limit, but even a few salmon or halibut can be a huge catch. The Prairie provinces have some size restrictions and possession limits, but they are generous enough that proficient anglers have no problem filling a freezer. Ontario is a bit skimpy on daily limits for most species and heavy on paperwork, but that province was greed central for centuries and can hardly be blamed for wishing to rebuild over-fished stocks. Québec, on the other hand, is most generous with catch limits, and anglers from that province always have full freezers. The Atlantic provinces have very stingy catch limits, but again, you cannot blame them for wanting their fish back.

Watery Riches

- Canada's freshwater lakes, rivers and streams are home to 228 species of fish, and the marine count is around 990 species. An embarrassment of riches, yet the majority of Canadians consume only a few of our many species: salmon, trout and whitefish, along with cod, halibut, haddock and occasionally walleye.

CATSUP, CATCHUP. *See* ketchup.

CATTAIL-ON-THE-COB—boiled flowerheads of the common cattail plant (*Typha latifolia*) or the less-common thin cattail (*T. angustifolia*). Boil for 10 minutes, slather in garlic butter and eat like miniature corncobs. Delicious, nutritious and free for the taking almost everywhere in Canada.

CATTAILS AND WILD RICE SOUP—a favourite First Nations soup adopted by pioneer settlers and made with the tender shoots of the cattail plant. Easy to harvest, simply look for large shoots that haven't yet begun to flower. Peel the outer leaves from the core, from the top down, until the soft centre is reached, and cut that free with a pocket knife.

RECIPE

Cattails and Wild Rice Soup

In a heavy pan, sauté ½ cup green onions in butter until translucent, then add 1½ cups cooked wild rice, 2 tsp salt, 4 cups chicken broth and a handful of cattail shoots, and simmer for 20 minutes.

CAULIFLOWER (*Brassica oleracea* var. *botrytis*)— it was probably an ancient Cypriot farmer who first noticed a freak in his field of wild cabbage, a flower growth that had stopped at the bud stage

CANADA'S FAVOURITE CAULIFLOWER VARIETIES

- Early Snowball—a 19th-century self-blanching wonder that is still unsurpassed.

- Purple of Sicily—grows purple, cooks to bright green and is for kids who do not like cauliflower.

and produced a tender little head of confused, undifferentiated cells similar to the stem cells found in animals. A few centuries of selective breeding saw the head of the wild cabbage increase in size and make its way to Italy, where it picked up the name "cauli-fiori," and then to France, where it was called Cyprus cabbage, but cauliflower never made the culinary hit parade until it began to be served with cheese sauce in the late 18th century. Today there are hundreds of commercial varieties in many colours divided into four groups: Italian, European biennial, European annual and Asian.

RECIPE

Cauliflower Soup

Cook 1 small head of chopped cauliflower with 1 diced potato until soft. In a small saucepan melt 3 Tbsp butter and cook 1 chopped onion. Add ½ tsp thyme, and make a roux with 3 Tbsp flour. Whisk in 3 cups milk, then add 1¼ cups chicken stock. Remove from heat and stir in 2½ cups shredded Cheddar cheese.

CAVIAR—processed eggs, or roe, of various fish (sturgeon, salmon or whitefish, with sturgeon eggs being the most prized). Canadian caviar harvested from salmon, whitefish, trout, capelin and farm-raised sturgeon has become an important export product thanks to an almost worldwide embargo of the good stuff from the grossly mismanaged Caspian Sea fisheries. *See also* roe.

STURGEON ROE

Once common in Canadian rivers and lakes, sturgeon populations have been decimated as a result overfishing, habitat loss and poor management. More government intervention is needed to prevent the netting of wild sturgeon for the sole purpose of harvesting caviar, which is a most odious practice.

CELERIAC (*Apium graveolens* var. *rapaceum*; also called celery root, knob celery)—a variety of celery cultivated for its edible root.

RECIPE

Celery Root Purée

Chop 1 large celery root into 1-inch pieces and boil in salted water until tender, about 25 minutes. Drain and reserve 1 cup of the boiling liquid. In a pot over medium heat, warm ½ cup heavy cream and 2 Tbsp butter and, using a potato ricer, press out the celery root into the cream mixture and mix with a fork until creamy smooth. Thin if necessary with the reserved liquid. Season with salt and pepper, or instead of pepper a few drops of hot sauce, then cover and let it rest a few minutes before serving.

CELERY (*Apium graveolens* var. *dulce*)—modern celery differs little from its wild progenitor except for having longer and thicker leaf stems, the stems having become more valued over time than the leaves. Developed in Europe from wild celery, this vegetable was originally used as medicine, then later only its leaves were used as a soup flavouring, and in modern times the entire plant is eaten. Creating taste and value in stalks was

A
B
C
D
E
F
G
H
I
J
K
L
M
N
O
P
Q
R
S
T
U
V
W
X
Y
Z

accomplished by the French, who used the same growing technique they used for asparagus—the blanching of stalks by mounding up soil. Blanching created a tender, white stalk, but it was still short and stringy, shortcomings fixed in the late 18th century when English plant breeders produced a cultivar of tall, light green stalks they called Pascal, a cultivar that still dominates the North American celery market. Inroads have been made by the self-blanching, yellowish cultivars preferred by Europeans, with one of the best of those being the Golden Self-Blanching, which is compact, stringless and the best all-around celery, bar none.

RECIPE

Celery Soup

Cut 1 lb celery with leaves into 1-inch pieces. Peel 1 large potato and cut into the same size pieces. Fry 8 strips of bacon until crisp and set aside. Drain all bacon fat but 2 Tbsp, add celery and 1 each chopped onion and garlic clove and cook until onions are translucent, about 3 minutes. Add ½ cup white wine, season with salt and pepper and simmer until wine has reduced by half. Add 4 cups chicken stock and potato and bring to a boil. Reduce heat and simmer until potato is cooked firm but not mushy. Remove pot from heat and purée contents with a hand blender. Return to heat and simmer a few minutes while adjusting thickness with stock. Ladle into serving bowls and top with a pat of butter and crushed bacon bits.

CELERY ROOT. *See* celeriac.

CELERY VINEGAR—a long-forgotten favourite flavouring for soups and stews that is enjoying a resurrection for what it does to a Bloody Mary or Caesar. Simply soak celery seeds in white vinegar for 24 hours, then bottle and use.

CELIAC DISEASE. *See* gluten allergy.

CFIA. *See* Canadian Food Inspection Agency.

CHANTILLY—the French word for whipped cream made in the customary Canadian fashion, wherein heavy cream is whipped, sweetened with sugar and flavoured with vanilla.

CHARCUTERIE—a French culinary art born during the 15th century that encompasses the brining, smoking, salting and cooking of meats for both preservation and taste. Modern charcuterie is the artisanal processing of bacon, ham, etc., and is done mostly for taste and not by many butchers, as the industry has become top heavy with regulations to protect consumers that actually benefit conglomerate meat packers.

CHARLEVOIX LAMB—a succulent lamb produced in the Charlevoix area of Québec and designated under the province's region of origin law. Flocks are limited to 500 sheep per farmer and are fed a diet of oats and barley to supplement their grass forage.

CHARLOCK (*Brassica kaber*; also called wild mustard)—an unfortunate, bring-along seed of early pioneers that escaped into the wild to become a modern-day superweed subject to constant efforts at eradication by farmers. However, before it turned outlaw, it provided early settlers a respite from bland foods and earned a spot in the Canadian food experience. *See also* mustard.

CHEAP CAKE—a simple pioneer cake originally made with a soda rising and whatever of the following ingredients were on hand: eggs, butter, flour, milk and a pinch of salt.

CHECKERBERRY. *See* wintergreen.

CHEDDAR CHEESE—a hard cow's milk cheese first made in the town of Cheddar, England, but nationalized by Canadian cheese-making techniques, climate, grass and fodder. The once-famous quality of modern-day Ontario Cheddar has been slowly compromised by federal government supply management milk quotas, multinational dairy conglomerate cartels and ambivalent consumers. However, a few cheese makers in Ontario and in almost every

province still manage—in spite of the government's "sour milk rationing system" and the manufacturing cartels—to produce extraordinarily fine Cheddars. Most notable are the Québec fromageries, where big business and government still rule the industry but have somehow spared a few fromageries the humiliation of a cooperative milk supply.

Cheddar Cheese

- Canada has around 200 cheese makers producing approximately 135 million kilograms of cheese annually, with over a third of that production being Cheddar cheese.

- Cheddar cheese takes to freezing well. But, oddly, it works better if frozen in blocks of about 2 kilograms or more. Freezing lesser amounts results in crumbly cheese. Wrap cheese well to prevent dehydration and freezer burn.

A
B
C
D
E
F
G
H
I
J
K
L
M
N
O
P
Q
R
S
T
U
V
W
X
Y
Z

CHEEMO PEROGIES—a potato-filled dumpling popular across the country, but especially in the Prairie provinces. Out on the flatlands, if the perogies are not homemade they are Cheemos, made by Heritage Frozen Foods in Edmonton, Alberta, and available nationwide. Heritage Frozen Foods is the world's largest producer of perogies. *See also* perogies.

CHEESE CURDS—the twisty solid bits recovered from milk coagulated by rennet and drained of whey. Pressed into a mould and aged, cheese curds become Cheddar cheese and may be coloured or left naturally white. The rubbery curds are also sold as a snack food, or they are sent to restaurants for making poutine. *See also* poutine.

Cheese

• Ontario's 8500 dairy farmers produce 1.5 billion litres of milk annually, and in Québec, 10,000 farmers produce over 2 billion litres of milk. That amounts to around 55 percent of Canadian milk production, with much of it used to make cheese. Québec is Canada's "big cheese" and is doing the country proud by winning awards around the world.

• Cheese is the only segment of Canada's dairy industry that has seen a rise in consumption; other segments—milk, butter and ice cream—have taken heavy hits because of home market protectionist policies that enable foreign conglomerate dairy owners to charge high prices while preventing smaller processors from selling their products internationally.

• Failure to sample cheeses produced from the milk of bovine breeds better suited to cheese making than the Holstein breed—or from other animal species, such as goat, sheep and water buffalo—is self-inflicted oblivion to a whole world of tastes.

CHEESE

Early settlers to Canada received their land by various means, including drawing lots, outright grants or squatters' petitions. In those formative years, incentives were needed to attract settlers, one of them being a milk cow to be shared by two settlers. While this gratuity was not offered for long, it did serve to begin a trade in milk cows. By the middle of the 18th century, almost every farm enjoyed a daily supply of fresh milk and butter. By the time the 19th century rolled around, the cows had multiplied and a few farmers had became dairymen, supplying local villages with milk, cream, butter and farmer's cheese.

Around 1830, Hiram Ranney, an American dairyman from Vermont, moved to Oxford County, Ontario, with five cows. Some 20 years later, he was milking over 100 cows and decided to produce a cheese to promote his business. Ranney got to work and created "The Big Cheese," a 545-kilogram monster cheese wheel sent to the London Exhibition in London, England. That event excited both the public and dairymen, and soon Canada had hundreds of cheese factories, with many situated in Oxford County. In 1893, cheese makers from around

Perth, Ontario, pooled their resources to create another promotional cheese, the "Canadian Mite," a 1000-kilogram mammoth Cheddar destined for display at the World Columbian Exposition in Chicago. Loaded onto a railcar, the behemoth cheese wheel—1.8 metres tall and 8.5 metres in circumference—had people lining the tracks for a peek at it. While on display in Chicago, it garnered massive crowds and much publicity after it crashed through the floor of the exhibition hall. Back onto a railcar, the huge Cheddar was paraded through towns and villages all the way to Halifax, where, after much ceremony, it was loaded onto a ship for a tour of Britain. Finally, it was cut up and sold.

Then in 1995, the Loblaw supermarket chain decided to outdo all previous records and commissioned the giant Québec dairy cooperative Agropur to turn 266,000 litres of milk into a 28.5-tonne gargantuan cheese, enough to keep 2500 Canadians in Cheddar for an entire year. However, because it was a giant block and not a traditional wheel, it did not qualify for the record and became instead an icon of processed "comes square and wrapped in plastic" perversity.

CHEESE DREAM—the popular 1940s name for a baked processed cheese sandwich that was eventually called toasted cheese until it migrated to a griddle or fry pan and was redubbed the grilled cheese sandwich.

CHEESE PUFFETS—a kind of easy-to-make popover popular with Ontario settlers.

RECIPE

Cheese Puffets

Take 3 oz grated Cheddar cheese and mix with 1 egg, ½ cup milk, 1 Tbsp flour and a pinch of salt. Pour into buttered ramekins or muffin tins and bake at 400°F for 8–10 minutes.

CHERRY—not native to Canada, sweet cherries (*Prunus avium*) arrived with the earliest settlers but failed as a commercial crop because of the

RECIPE

Cherry Clafoutis

Butter a ceramic or glass baking dish and arrange 1 lb sweet cherries on the bottom. In a saucepan, heat 1 cup whole milk and ¼ cup heavy cream over medium-low heat until the edges bubble. Remove from heat and whisk in ½ cup cake flour a little at a time until smooth. In a bowl, whisk together 4 large eggs, ½ cup sugar and ⅛ tsp salt until creamy; add in milk mixture and ¼ tsp almond extract. Pour mixture over cherries and bake on the top rack of a 350°F oven until browned, about 1 hour. Dust with icing sugar and serve with a little heavy cream, or not.

large tree size and high harvesting costs. The hybridizing of small and dwarf cherry varieties has reinvigorated the growing of cherries, and today about 85 percent of domestic production is of the sour Montmorency pie cherry (*P. cerasus*). Most sweet cherries sold at produce and fruit markets are cultivars developed in BC—the Van, Stella and Skeena varieties—and all are excellent.

CANADA'S FAVOURITE CHERRY VARIETIES

- Bing—big, sweet and iconic since 1870.
- Black Tartarian—probably the best tasting, but trees grow too large for commercial use.
- Morello—the quintessential pie cherry.
- Montmorency—best sour pie cherry ever.
- Napoleon—yellow with a red flush and very sweet.
- Stella—the first self-fertile sweet cherry to be developed.

CHERRY BRANDY PIE—the dessert pioneer wives made while their husbands were busy turning their cherry crop into backyard *eau de vie*.

CHERRY COBBLER—a favourite dessert of settlers in the area around the Great Lakes. These settlers brought with them pits of both

sweet and sour cherries, but mostly they brought the sours, or Montmorency variety, which are quick growers and not as lofty as the sweet cherry. Faster growing and easier picking meant more pies and cobblers for the family. Nowadays, a new strain of slightly sweeter, dwarf Montmorency is replacing the old, and vast orchards are being established in the Prairie provinces. Look for the cherries at farmers' markets in the very near future—they will make indescribably delicious cobblers. *See also* cobbler.

RECIPE

Cherry Cobbler

Combine 3 cups pitted sour cherries with ¼ cup sugar and the juice of 1 lemon. Set aside. In a bowl mix 1 cup flour, 1 Tbsp each of sugar and baking powder, ¼ tsp nutmeg and a pinch of salt. Cut in ¼ cup cold, cubed butter, pour in ½ cup buttermilk and stir into a moist, sticky dough. Place cherries in an 8-inch square dish and spoon dough over. Bake at 375°F for 30–35 minutes or until the top is brown and bubbly. Serve hot with whipped or ice cream.

CHERRY WHISKY—a delicious alcoholic libation of early Ontario settlers from around the Great Lakes area, it is a decoction of sour cherries and backyard whisky sweetened with sugar. In other areas of Canada, different fruits were used to soothe the flames of backyard whisky.

WHISKY

Many new Canadians brought along seeds for planting, but only a few Scots and Irishmen possessed the necessary skills to ferment mash and distill a decent-tasting whisky to supply general stores. Settlers with little or no skill made backyard whisky that needed fruit and sweetening to make it drinkable. Fruit-flavoured whiskies still maintain a modicum of popularity with Canadians, as almost every distiller markets the product in some form: apricot brandy, peach delight and, of course, our long-time favourite: cherry whisky.

A
B
C
D
E
F
G
H
I
J
K
L
M
N
O
P
Q
R
S
T
U
V
W
X
Y
Z

CHESTNUT (*Castanea dentata*; also called American chestnut)—a once-prominent, edible nut–producing tree of the Carolinian belt of southern Ontario. The nuts, a mainstay food crop for both First Nations and settlers, were sweet and nutritious, and because the trees flowered in early summer and never suffered frost damage, the harvest was reliable. Mature chestnut trees could produce up to 6000 nuts and became a lumberman's delight, as the wood was easily worked and long-lasting. Both nuts and lumber from hundreds of thousands of trees were exported for over a century, but then the chestnut blight arrived, and by 1945, the trees were but a memory. However, a few proved blight resistant, and today those trees are being propagated for the benefit of future generations.

Chestnut Blight

• The blight that caused the quick demise of millions of North America's sweet chestnut trees arrived in 1904 at New York's Bronx Zoo in a shipment of Asian chestnut trees.

CHESTNUT MEAL—roasted or dried sweet chestnuts ground into flour and used as wheat flour extender and stew thickener or as a main ingredient in cakes, puddings and pie pastries.

CHÈVRE. *See* goat cheese.

CHÈVRE NOIR CHEESE—hard goat's milk Cheddar cheese made in Chesterfield, Québec, by Fromagerie Tournevent.

CHICKEN—conglomerate egg and chicken producers in Canada are in business to make money and depend on maximum output for minimum input, a business model that provides consumers a plentiful supply of meat and eggs of marginal quality. Canadians wanting the true tastes of chicken and eggs are advised to patronize poultry farmers who allow their chickens a free range and gather eggs from nesting birds. **Note:** the care and diet of chickens is more important than breed when it comes to meat and eggs, with free-range pasture producing the tastiest of both.

Chickens

- Canada's over 1000 egg farmers produce around 8 billion eggs annually. Ontario contributes about half that amount to the market, with most being products of the battery cage system, wherein laying hens are confined in stacks of small wire cages.

- A good example of how diet can affect the flavour of chicken can be found in France, where a few French farmers have created a niche business by adding fruit such as blueberries and raspberries to the diet of chickens, a practice that produces meat with a hint of fruit flavour. I have sampled it and can attest to its tastiness.

CANADA'S FAVOURITE CHICKEN BREEDS

- Chantecler—a Canadian heritage dual-purpose breed that is making a comeback.

- Dorking—one of the oldest and tastiest meat breeds on the planet.

- Non-Industrial Leghorn—an excellent layer of white eggs and progenitor of the modern battery cage industrial egg layer.

- Rhode Island Red—a laying dynamo of brown eggs.

CHICKEN BONE CANDY—a pink, cinnamon and chocolate, chicken bone–shaped candy made by New Brunswick's Ganong Bros. factory since 1885. *See also* Ganong Bros.

CHICKEN CHOW MEIN—a Canadian Chinese dish different from Americanized versions in that it is usually served on a bed of crispy fried golden noodles.

CHICKEN LOBSTER—a term for a small lobster. The smallest live-caught lobster permitted for sale in Canada is 500 g (1 lb).

CHICKEN POT PIE—before the national dementia over cuisine set in, the chicken pot pie was every cook's best friend. For readers wishing to relive the joy of a perfect pie, here's a famous one courtesy of the Fairmont Empress Hotel in Victoria, BC.

A
B
C
D
E
F
G
H
I
J
K
L
M
N
O
P
Q
R
S
T
U
V
W
X
Y
Z

> ### RECIPE
>
> *Chicken Pot Pie*
>
> *In a saucepan bring to a boil 2 cups chicken stock, 1 cup dry white wine, 2 cups sliced carrots, 2 stalks chopped celery, 1 bay leaf and a pinch each of salt and pepper. Reduce heat, cover pot and simmer 10 minutes. Add 1 lb cubed chicken and simmer uncovered until no longer pink inside. Strain pot, saving 2½ cups stock, adding chicken stock if necessary; remove bay leaf and set strained mixture aside. In a saucepan melt ⅔ cup butter and whisk in ⅔ cup flour. Now whisk in reserved stock until smooth and bring to a boil while stirring constantly until thick, about 5 minutes. Stir in ⅓ cup heavy cream and cook 2 minutes. Add chicken mixture and stir gently; add 1 cup frozen peas and spoon into small baking tins pasted with puff pastry. Top with puff pastry, seal edges well, brush with egg wash, cut slits for steam and bake in 400°F oven until golden and bubbly, about 30 minutes.*

CHICORY (*Cichorium intybus*; also called Belgian endive, curly endive, radicchio)—native to Europe, this vegetable has long been naturalized and is grown fresh for use as a salad green and for its roots. A member of the Sunflower family, chicory was a much-foraged flavouring for soups and stews, while the dried and roasted roots make an almost-acceptable substitute for coffee. Camp Coffee, a brand of chicory/coffee extract manufactured in Scotland since 1876, is still popular in Canada and in the southern U.S., where chicory has a long history as a coffee substitute. Much used by early settlers, the herb is still popular, widely foraged and available at farmers' markets. Belgian endive is more a technique of growing chicory than a different variety and is accomplished by simply cutting back the chicory in fall and allowing it to regrow in banked-up soil in a process similar to cultivating white asparagus. Traditional Belgian endive cultivation is carried on in Québec and Ontario and is fast becoming popular.

CHICKPEAS (*Cicer arietinum*)—Canada is a major player in global legume production, and chickpeas are an important export commodity, especially for Saskatchewan. A foundation food in Indian cuisine, the chickpeas are split to make dhal and ground to make gram flour for all kinds of culinary applications. Chickpeas also feature prominently in Middle Eastern cuisine, where the cooked and mashed beans become hummus and falafel. Besides growing and exporting chickpeas, Canada is now engaged in the milling of chickpeas for the production of gram flour for both domestic use and export.

> **RECIPE**
>
> ### Belgian Endive and Blue Cheese Dip
>
> *Combine 1 cup sour cream, ¼ cup whole milk, 2 Tbsp finely chopped red onion, ⅓ cup crumbled blue cheese and refrigerate for 2 hours. Separate leaves of Belgian endive and dip into sauce.*

CHICOUTAI—a cloudberry liqueur from the Côte-Nord area of Québec.

CHINESE BROCCOLI. *See* Chinese kale.

CHINESE BUFFET—originated in Vancouver around 1870, when Swedish mill workers convinced Chinese cooks to let them load their plates from a steam table to allow more room on the tables for whisky bottles and glasses.

CHINESE CINNAMON. *See* cassia.

CHINESE KALE (*Brassica oleracea* var. *alboglabra*; also called Chinese broccoli, gai lan)—this variety of kale is completely distinct from western kale and is distinguished from other Brassicas by its white flowers. The leaves have a strong cabbage flavour, but the peeled stalks have a flavour more like western kale.

CHINESE PIE. See *pâté chinois*.

CHINESE SPINACH (*Amaranthus dubius*)—any of several leafy vegetables belonging to the Amaranth family with no botanical relationship

to spinach proper. The vegetable is usually cut into short lengths and stir-fried, leaves and all.

CHINOOK SALMON (*Oncorhynchus tshawytscha*; also called king, spring or Tyee salmon)—the largest and arguably the best tasting of the Pacific salmons, Chinooks range along the entire west coast. They can attain a weight of 50–55 kg, live for about seven years and are available fresh from May to the end of July. Prized by both sport and commercial fishermen, their populations have shrunk in some areas, and the species is becoming difficult to obtain. Introduced to the Great Lakes to control alewife populations, the Chinook has done nicely and provided for an extensive sport fishery there. Chinook salmon fillets come in various shades from red to white: fish caught in deep water tend to be reddish, whereas those netted or line-caught in rivers will be pink to almost white if the spawning

rivers are long. Chinooks are carnivores and do not take to farming easily, so any found at fish markets will likely be wild-caught. If not more than a few days out of water they are delicious, especially when barbecued on a cedar or oak plank. *See also* Pacific salmon, salmon.

CHIPS 'N' GRAVY—a 1950s and '60s restaurant phenomenon that went well with Coca Cola and the rock 'n' roll blasting from jukeboxes.

CHITLIN AND PEA—fried male and female codfish reproductive organs, a Newfoundland specialty.

CHOCOLATE ROOT. *See* Indian chocolate.

CHOKECHERRY (*Prunus virginiana*)—a member of the Rose family and a close relative of the domestic plum, cherry and apricot. The small, sour cherries (called "choke" for a reason) were a welcome addition to the diets of early Canadian settlers and while not eaten off the bush, they do make wonderful jelly and syrup. Modern-day commercial fruit processors have become interested to the point that some production is being undertaken, with those in the know saying chokecherries have as great a future as the saskatoon berry.

CHOKECHERRY JELLY—a favourite with Prairie pioneers, but the jelly required long boiling to set up. It's much easier to make today, with liquid pectin.

RECIPE

Chokecherry Jelly

Boil chokecherries until the skins pop; strain through a jelly bag, squeezing the bag for every last drop of juice. For every 1 cup juice, add 2 cups sugar. Boil 5 minutes, then remove from heat. Add liquid pectin, skim and pour into sterilized bottles.

CHOKECHERRY WINE—an alcoholic, crock-fermented beverage popular with pioneer men and made from abundant, almost inedible chokecherries. To make it, you mash the berries, pour them into a crock, add sugar, water, a few cloves and a shake of cinnamon and let it sit in the sunshine for a few days.

CHOP SUEY—Canadianized Chinese "hash" of stir-fried meat, poultry or fish cooked with bean sprouts and assorted vegetables. Thought to be invented in either San Francisco or Vancouver, chop suey is actually a culinary variation of *shap sui*, a Chinese stir-fry of offal and mixed vegetables.

CHOW CHOW. *See* green tomato chow chow.

CHOWDER. *See* clam chowder.

CHUCK—the word used by cowboys and modern-day wannabes to describe the fare served on cattle drives and prepared in a horse-drawn mobile kitchen called the chuckwagon.

CHUCKWAGON BREAKFAST—flapjacks and syrup with bacon and coffee, this culinary symbol of western hospitality originated at the 1923 Calgary Stampede and is now customary at all rodeos, race events and fairs.

A
B
C
D
E
F
G
H
I
J
K
L
M
N
O
P
Q
R
S
T
U
V
W
X
Y
Z

RECIPE

Calgary Stampede Buttermilk Pancakes

In a very large bowl, whisk together 1½ cups flour, 3 Tbsp sugar, 1 tsp baking soda, 1 tsp baking powder and ¼ tsp salt. In another bowl, whisk together 1¾ cups buttermilk, 1 large egg, 2 Tbsp melted butter and 2 tsp vanilla. Pour wet ingredients into dry and whisk until only slightly lumpy. Skillet cook over medium heat.

CHUM SALMON (*Oncorhynchus keta*; also called dog salmon)—the third largest of the Pacific salmons after the Chinook and sockeye, this fish was historically the food of choice for the dogs of west coast First Nations, hence its nickname. Chum salmon weigh in at 6–7 kg, have white to pale pink flesh, live for about five years and put up a stellar fight when line-caught by sports fishermen. Low in fat and lacking taste, the chum salmon is not especially favoured by commercial fisheries or consumers, except in Japan, where it serves as an important food staple. Leaner meat makes the chum a good candidate for cold smoking, which is how a good percentage of the catch is marketed. True to this fish's nickname, much of the remainder goes to make pet food, but it is also sold as frozen barbecue tidbits. *See also* Pacific salmon, salmon.

CIDER. *See* apple cider.

CIPAILLE (also called sea pie)—an iconic French Canadian layered pie made with all turkey, duck, chicken, pigeon or partridge, or a combination in separate layers. Historically peculiar to English ships, "sea pies" baked in large cauldrons were easy to transport and their protective crust maintained freshness for weeks. *Cipaille* is still a Québec favourite and is usually made with chicken. *See also* coffin pastry.

Cipaille

- Considered the forerunner of tourtière, the English sea pie entered Canadian cuisine through a phonetic mix-up at the Gaspé Peninsula; sea pie became *la six pâtés*, or "the six layers" of the original Canadian tourtière.

- Fresh and salted passenger pigeons were plentiful, cheap and a prominent ingredient for the entire evolution from sea pie to tourtière. The word *tourte* is French for both pigeon and the crockery vessel once used to bake both pies.

CISCO (*Coregonus artedii;* also called lake herring)—a member of the Whitefish family once commercially fished from all the Great Lakes when it was called the chub fishery, a misnomer since it had nothing to do with the fish species called chub, but owing to over-fishing, the cisco fishery is now confined to Lake Superior. Ciscos are normally smoked and have a taste and texture similar to ocean herring.

CISELETTE—an Acadian sweet and savoury dessert sauce made by frying chopped salt pork until crispy, adding molasses and cooking down to a thick sauce. Still popular in parts of Québec and the Maritimes, ciselette is usually offered on crêpes, toast or fresh-baked bread.

CITY CULINARY TOURS—these are available in all major Canadian cities and feature walking tours of that city's foodie hotspots. To find a tour, simply go online.

CITY HAM—a ham that has been soaked or injected with pickling brine rather than rubbed with a dry salt mixture the way a so-called country ham is produced. *See also* country ham.

CLAM—Canadians not living near the coast are usually strangers to the culinary delight produced by ubiquitous clam shacks. Fried clams, either battered or breaded, are an essential seasonal delight on either coast. There are over 2000 varieties of clams, but only two groups: the hard-shell (*Mercenaria mercenaria*) and the soft-shell (*Mya arenaria*), also called a steamer clam.

TIPS ON BUYING AND CLEANING CLAMS

- Purchase only clams that are tightly shut or respond to a tap on the shell. If purchasing clams on ice, keep in mind that their survival time out of water is around one week. Freshly gathered clams may be stored in a refrigerator for that long, but remember to crack the container top to allow for fresh air.

- Place clams in a large bowl of water into which 3 Tbsp of cornmeal have been stirred and let it stand for a few hours. The clams will ingest the gritty cornmeal and spit it out along with any bits of wayward sand.

- Clams are much easier to shuck than oysters. Simply insert a thin knife blade (not too pointy, to avoid piercing the meat) into the slightly flared side and pry it open, taking care not to spill the liquor. Once open, run the knife under and around to free the meat from the shell and move on to the next one.

A
B
C
D
E
F
G
H
I
J
K
L
M
N
O
P
Q
R
S
T
U
V
W
X
Y
Z

Hard-shell clams bear different names according to their size, which are, from smallest to largest: countnecks (or buttons), littlenecks, topnecks, cherrystones and quahogs (or chowder clams). Soft-shell clams are usually harvested in one size and are best served steamed, fried, in chowder or on the halfshell.

RECIPE

Batter-fried Clams

In a large bowl, mix ½ cup whole milk, 1 egg yolk, 1 tsp melted butter and ¼ tsp salt, and sift in ½ cup flour. In a small chilled bowl, beat the egg white into soft peaks and fold into milk mixture. Using a two-prong fork, spear each clam, dip into batter and place in frypan. Fry several at a time in canola oil heated to 375°F until golden, about 1½–2 minutes. Drain on paper towel, season and keep warm in 300°F oven until all are fried.

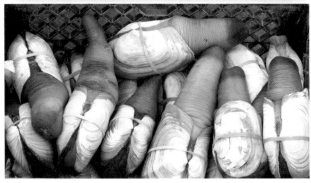

RECIPE

Breaded Clams

In a shallow bowl, mix 2 cups flour and 1 tsp each of salt and pepper. Make the egg dip by whisking 3 eggs and 1 cup milk in a small bowl. Roll each clam in flour, dip into egg, toss in breadcrumbs and set aside. Fry clams in small batches in canola oil heated to 375°F until golden, about 1½ minutes, and drain on paper towel. Serve with lemon and a side of mayonnaise, seafood sauce or ketchup.

CLAM CHOWDER—an east coast favourite, chowder is a thick, creamy soup or stew frequently but not always made with seafood, and includes diced potatoes and onions in a cream base flavoured with celery salt. While the Americans like to think of chowders as being their own, the word "chowder" is derived from the French *chaudière*, meaning "one pot," and is surely of French Canadian and Maritime origin. In the fishing villages of 16th-century Brittany, fishermen would contribute part of their day's catch to a community stock pot, a system called *faire la chaudière*, meaning "feeding the stockpot." Villagers added vegetables from their gardens, hard-baked biscuits from their ovens and whatever else was handy, such as butter or cream, with everyone getting a share of the

chaudière. The practice came to Newfoundland with Breton cod fishermen, and from there it spread to English Canada and the Thirteen Colonies, undergoing a gradual name change from *chaudière* to chowder and with potatoes replacing hard-baked biscuits or hardtack as thickener. The recipe moved south after the Acadian expulsion from the Maritimes.

RECIPE

Nova Scotia Seafood Chowder

In a saucepan, cook ½ cup diced onions in ¼ cup butter until soft. Add 4 cups diced potatoes and water to cover, and cook until potatoes are tender. Add 1 lb cubed fish fillets and 1 lb scallops and simmer 5 minutes, stirring occasionally. Add 3 cups whole milk, 4 cups cream, 2 cups lobster meat, 1 lb shucked and steamed clams and salt and pepper to taste, and cook on low heat just until hot. Whisk in 2 Tbsp flour to thicken. Serve piping hot with a pat of butter.

CLAM PIE (also called *pâté aux bucardes*)—an Acadian top-crust casserole that is still a favourite with Maritimers, who sometimes add lobster meat during the preparation. In the Maritimes, clam pie suppers are popular with tourists, and those pies come in all manner of variations. Most include onions, some have potatoes, top crusts and biscuit tops, but all are delicious.

CLAMATO JUICE—a spiced and seasoned mixture of tomato and clam juice perfected by the American apple juice conglomerate Duffy-Mott, with help from the Calgary inventor of the Bloody Caesar cocktail, Walter Chell. *See also* Bloody Caesar.

CLAPSHOT—the official name for "tatties and neeps," an old Scottish favourite that served Canadian families well during difficult times. Mash together equal amounts of potatoes and turnips, season well and throw in some chopped chives and a blob of butter.

CLENNEDAK—a children's mispronunciation of the brand name Klondike that became the nickname for a popular wax paper–wrapped molasses candy once sold in Québec.

A
B

C

D
E
F
G
H
I
J
K
L
M
N
O
P
Q
R
S
T
U
V
W
X
Y
Z

CLODHOPPERS—chocolate-covered fudge and graham cracker clusters introduced in 1996 by the Krave Candy Company in Winnipeg and available everywhere.

CLOOTIE DUMPLING—a sweet oatmeal pudding of Scottish origin served as a token haggis on Robbie Burns Day and boiled in a cloth (the clootie) rather than a sheep's stomach.

CLOTTED CREAM—made by every pioneer with a cow, and though not an original participant in the Canadian food experience, every cook should know how to make such a scrumptious dollop.

RECIPE

Clotted Cream

Pour 4 cups unpasteurized cream into a heavy saucepan and place onto a rack in a roasting pan, adding water up to a level with the cream. Simmer 4 hours and, after cooling, carefully lift the coagulated cream off the whey. Chill clotted cream and serve with almost any dessert.

CLOUDBERRY. *See* bakeapple.

CLOVER LEAF SEAFOOD COMPANY—the brand is first introduced in 1889 on cans of mackerel produced by the Anglo-American Packing Company, a conglomerate of British-financed fish canning factories on BC's Fraser River. In 1908, a larger conglomerate called British Columbia Packers is formed and begins

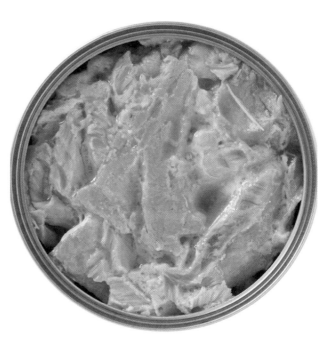

marketing canned salmon under the Clover Leaf brand. In 1946, BC Packers opens one of the world's largest fish-packing plants in Steveston, BC. In 1962, BC Packers and the Clover Leaf brand are acquired by George Weston Limited, an extremely large conglomerate, with the Clover Leaf brand now used on cans of skipjack and albacore tuna packed offshore. In 1997, George Weston Limited closes down the Steveston packing plant, putting hundreds of employees out of work, and two years later sells the fish-packing business and the Clover Leaf name to International Home Foods. Three years later, International Home Foods sells out to ConAgra, one of America's largest packaged food distributors, with the Clover Leaf brand being bounced around and gathering money until in 2010, when the fishing business and Clover Leaf brand go full circle back to British ownership in the form of Lion Capital LLP.

CN RAIL. *See* Canadian National Railway.

COADY SAUCE (also called molasses coady)—a 16th-century sweet drizzle sauce for figgy duff, a boiled raisin and breadcrumb pudding popular in Newfoundland. *See also* figgy duff.

RECIPE

Coady Sauce

Combine 1 cup molasses with ¼ cup each of water and butter, and 1 tsp vinegar. Boil and simmer for 10 minutes while stirring.

COBBLER—originally a deep-dish pie of cooked fruit completely enclosed in a coffin pastry and called crow's nest pudding. In America, the piecrust became lighter and buttery and the top crust was replaced with pudding or crumble, but in Canada, cobbler topping tended to be sweetened dumpling dough, most often just spooned on top before baking.

COCONUT SANDWICH CAKE—whole coconuts were a common offering in early general stores because of their keeping qualities and the constant stream of trading vessels from British-controlled Caribbean islands. Birthdays were a good reason to bake this cake.

RECIPE

Coconut Sandwich Cake

Mix 1 cup butter, 1 cup milk, 3 cups sugar, 4 cups flour, 2 tsp cream of tartar, 1 tsp baking soda and 5 eggs. Spread batter on a baking sheet and bake in a 350°F oven until centre springs back from a touch, about 8–10 minutes. To make the coconut icing, add 1 cup sugar to the whites of 3 eggs and whip while gradually adding the grated meat of 1 coconut. Spread icing on one half of the cake, place the other half on top and ice all over.

COD. *See* Atlantic cod.

CODEX ALIMENTARIUS COMMISSION (CAC)—an international organization often called simply Codex that was established in 1963 to implement the standard-setting component of the UN's World Health Organization (WHO) and Food and Agriculture Organization (FAO). The primary mandate of the Codex is to develop internationally recognized food standards for the protection of the health of consumers and to ensure fair practices in food trade.

CODFISH À LA MONTRÉAL—butter-basted codfish baked with peeled potatoes and served with a sprinkling of parsley.

CODFISH BALLS—an iconic east coast specialty made by combining cooked and minced codfish with mashed potatoes, beaten eggs and butter. Formed into balls and deep fried like doughnuts, they will have you reaching for more.

CODFISH HASH—like pea soup, this hash was sometimes called a devil's holiday dish as it was a ubiquitous dinner item for east coast families. It is still a suppertime favourite.

RECIPE

Codfish Hash

Mix picked codfish with mashed potatoes and cut-up pieces of fried salt pork. Add milk and stir, sprinkle some crispy salt pork on top and perhaps a few dabs of butter, and bake until crispy. Turn onto platter and serve.

CODFISH MORATORIUM—in the New World, cod seemed to be an unlimited resource, but to process this cornucopia of plenty required two items in very short supply: ships and salt, and both were historically mitigating influences in Maritime fisheries. "If it cannot be processed, do not catch it" was the byword until 1918,

when a Malagash, Nova Scotia, farmer sunk a well, discovered rock salt and made that commodity a cheap local resource. Now the only thing missing from complete unfettered harvesting of cod were the ships, and in 1950, someone got the bright idea to change back to shipboard processing. The year 1951 saw the launching of the first super-trawler designed to catch, process and freeze fish onboard, a factory ship that was so efficient it spawned even larger

UNSUSTAINABLE FISHING

The codfish fiasco may be of little or passing interest to readers as Canadians are not huge fans of fresh, frozen or salt cod, but those same circumstances that contributed to the demise of that fishery trickled down to other fish species both here and abroad. In 1804, the world's population topped one billion souls and around 50,000 fishing vessels hauled up approximately one million tonnes of fish. Two centuries later, with the world's population topping six billion, 3.5 million fishing vessels ply the world's oceans and lakes and haul in around 120 million tonnes of fish annually, with probably half again that

amount harvested illegally, an amount that is grossly unsustainable.

But then the gross unsustainability of fishing is so steeped in history that it is somehow perceived as being correct by Canadian politicians—more is good, and much more is even better. In 1871, 250,000 barrels of mackerel were shipped from Nova Scotia, but a decade later, in 1881, that figure had shrunk to 47,000 barrels. When one species dwindled, politicians simply provided financial incentives for fishermen to go after another species, and when those stocks were depleted, they provided money for aquaculture and fish farming.

vessels. From 1951 to the mid-1990s, greed and mismanagement depleted Maritime cod stocks to the point of no return. In 2003, the entire cod fishery collapsed and a 10-year moratorium on cod fishing was put into effect. Over a decade later, our Atlantic cod stocks remain depleted, and the fish has become a bottom feeder and by-catch of the driftnet and long-line fisheries.

CODFISH TONGUES AND CHEEKS—a true east coast favourite, the fishy face parts were traditionally fried in pork fat and served topped with scrunchions (pork rinds), but nowadays they are usually rolled in cornmeal and sautéed in butter.

COFFEE CRISP BAR—a better jolt than chicory, the bar that makes a nice light snack was originated by the Rowntree Company and quickly became a Canadian icon, but it lost status when Rowntree was absorbed by the mega-conglomerate Nestlé. For reasons unknown, Nestlé changed the bar's package, made it thinner and fiddled with the formula until Coffee Crisp became just another mass-produced candy bar.

COFFEE SUBSTITUTES—early pioneers had many choices for a substitute java fix: roasted wheat, barley, dandelion roots, chicory roots, various nuts, etc. In the late 19th and early 20th centuries, roasted and ground soybeans—long used in Europe as a cheap coffee substitute—became popular in Canada, especially during the periods of wartime rationing. *See also* chicory, dandelion coffee.

COFFIN PASTRY—an early-days word for the thick crust pie that was the precursor to the can: thick crusts were hard baked, filled with meat and gravy and covered with a thick pastry holed in the centre. Prior to the second baking, cooks blew into the hole and inflated the top crust, allowing for a space between contents and top crust. After baking, cooks stuck a funnel into the hole of the cooled pie and poured in hot fat that, when cooled, served to protect the pie from spoilage—the basic principle of canning. Private rations of naval officers were usually in the form of a coffin or sea pie. See also *cipaille*.

COHO SALMON (*Oncorhynchus kisutch*; also called silver salmon)—this carnivore is difficult to farm, so any Coho found in markets will likely be wild-caught. Coho may reach a weight of 15 kg, are mostly harvested in the 4–5 kg range, live for about five years and are available fresh from July to the end of September. Coho are not long-reach spawners and travel up rivers only short distances, so they need less fat reserves than either the Chinook or sockeye but are still tasty fare and much sought after by commercial fisheries and consumers. Coho get along nicely in fresh water and successful populations have been established in the Great Lakes system, providing for an enthusiastic sport fishery. Coho have firm, red to pink flesh similar to sockeye and are best served cut into steaks and poached. *See also* Pacific salmon, salmon.

COLCANNON—mashed potatoes made with lots of butter, kale and cabbage. A traditional Irish dish served at Halloween festivities with hidden coins and small gifts, it was adopted by Newfoundlanders as anytime fare but without the coins and small gifts.

A
B
C
D
E
F
G
H
I
J
K
L
M
N
O
P
Q
R
S
T
U
V
W
X
Y
Z

COLD-PRESSED CANOLA OIL (low erucic acid rapeseed oil)—an edible vegetable oil extracted from the tiny seeds of hybridized rape plants (*Brassica napus*) by gentle pressing rather than the normal chemical solvent method. Light golden in colour with a fresh nutty flavour, cold-pressed canola oil is subject to rapid oxidation by air and light and is best purchased organically grown and refrigerated, from a reliable shop. Treat yourself to a national treasure. *See also* canola oil.

COLD-PRESSED FLAX OIL—gently pressed oil from the cracked and flaked seeds of the flax plant (*Linum usitatissimum*), it is your basic linseed oil but nutritionally one of the best

sources of omega-3 fatty acids. Buy it fresh, refrigerated and in dark glass bottles because the oil is prone to oxidation. Use it in smoothies, vinaigrettes and dips, but not for frying.

COLEWORT. *See* cabbage.

COLMAN'S MUSTARD—iconic worldwide, but especially loved by Canadians ever since its creation by Jeremiah Colman of Norwich, England, in 1814. In 1825, Colman's opened a factory in Toronto to supply the whole of North America. It did well, and in 1903, Colman's bought out another Canadian favourite, Keen's dry mustard.. *See also* mustard, mustard powder.

COLOSTRUM. *See* beestings.

CONCORD GRAPES—riverbank or fox grapes (*Vitis labrusca*) have been used for pies, jams, jellies and wines since 1534, when French explorer Jacques Cartier stepped ashore in the Gaspé and found forests netted with wild vines festooned with the tiny, luscious grapes. These wild vines were quickly crossed with European cultivars to produce a cold-hardy, disease-resistant vine with larger fruit called the Concord grape. The Concord is still the most widely grown grape in the Americas.

CONEY, CONNIE. *See* inconnu.

CORAL AND TOMALLEY BUTTER—the coral is the black roe or eggs carried by female lobsters that will turn a bright red colour during cooking, while tomalley is the green substance located in the body of the lobster and functions as the living lobster's liver. Make and serve this savoury butter with lobster. *See also* lobster, lobster butter.

RECIPE

Coral and Tomalley Butter

Combine ½ cup softened butter, the coral and tomalley from 2–3 cooked lobsters, 1 Tbsp brandy or cognac, 1 tsp minced parsley, ½ tsp dry tarragon, ¼ tsp salt and a few turns of the pepper grinder.

CORN (*Zea mays*)—a huge crop in Canada, especially in Ontario and Québec, where about 3.2 million acres are devoted to the golden cobs. It is mostly grain corn to feed livestock and supply ethanol plants, with sweet corn being a small percentage of total acreage. Sweet corn is your basic dent variety (field corn) with a recessive mutation in the gene that converts sugar to starch, an idiosyncrasy first noticed by First Nations cultivators who isolated the stalks, thus effectively creating the first hybridized sweet corn. Sweet corn is Canada's largest vegetable crop, with over 50,000 acres under cultivation, and while most is canned or frozen, some fresh corn is always available for summer feasting. There are three types of sweet corn: normal sugary (*su*) comprises most heritage or heirloom varieties, with kernels that quickly lose sweetness after picking; sugar enhanced (*se*) are varieties with more sugar, and although the sweetness lasts longer, they are still at their best when consumed a few days after picking; and supersweet (*sh2*), a shrunken gene type, are genetically modified, supersweet varieties with an installed gene to prevent the conversion of sugar to starch. There is not much taste and the kernels look shrunken, but ears of *sh2* have the long shelf life demanded by supermarkets. For a treat,

if you can find them, try old-style varieties such as Seneca Chief and Golden Bantam. Cook them as soon as you can before the sugars begin turning to starch. The new, sugar-enhanced hybrids need not be cooked immediately because their sugar content is almost double that of the old varieties—sweeter, but not as tasty. Heirloom corn varieties have superior taste and texture. People wishing to know the real taste of summer are advised to search long and hard for the almost forgotten great ones, our wonderful heritage sweet corn.

CANADA'S FAVOURITE CORN VARIETIES

- Country Gentleman—small ears with eight irregular rows of kernels, but very pronounced corn taste.

- Golden Bantam—introduced by Burpee Seeds in 1902 as an early maturing yellow sweet corn with eight rows of kernels and a 15 cm cob.

- Golden Cross Bantam—Golden Bantam bred for larger cobs and a more standard 14 rows of kernels.

- Golden Queen—another Burpee introduction bred for earlier harvest than Bantam corn.

- Orchard Baby—small ears, but kernels so sweet and tender they can be eaten raw.

- Peaches and Cream—a non-GMO super-sweet variety with lots of sugar, uniform colour and rows, but not a whole lot of corn flavour.

- Seneca Chief—one of the great heirlooms with 20 cm ears, 12 rows of kernels and superb taste.

- Silver Queen—a high sugar content, non-hybrid white corn with large cobs that was later hybridized for even larger cobs and 14 to 16 rows of kernels.

Corn

- Explorers returning to France took along corn seed, but it never amounted to much until the English got hold of it. In no time at all, the "Indian corn" (at the time the English called all grains "corn") became so important a crop that it assumed sole ownership of the corn moniker.

- When French explorer Samuel de Champlain arrived in Canada in the early 17th century, he found vast plantations of hybridized sweet corn under cultivation by bands of the Iroquois nation. Subsequent explorations by Europeans found even larger sweet corn plantations south of Lake Ontario and along the Mississippi River, with some containing different varieties and colours of corn, including popcorn.

CORN CAKE—the food that sustained an empire. Every settler knew this easy recipe: to 2 cups cooled down cornmeal mush, add 1 Tbsp melted butter, 1 tsp salt, 3 beaten eggs and stir until thick. Scoop batter into well-greased bread pan and bake at 325°F for 1 hour.

CORN CHOWDER—your basic Iroquois corn soup with a few added ingredients to suit European pioneer tastes—namely butter, flour, milk, cream and diced potatoes. *See also* corn soup.

AN OMNIVORE'S DILEMMA

Canadian consumers are pretty much on their own when it comes to healthy foods and are suffering the consequences of what author Michael Pollen calls the "Omnivore's Dilemma," that of being not a selective consumer but a sausage casing for food conglomerates to fill with chemical-laced foods, along with cereals and bird seed. Corn is by far the worst because it is in almost everything on the supermarket shelf: it sweetens, it extends, it cheapens and it makes Canadians fat. Obesity is rampant in Canada—one in four Canadians is clinically obese—type-2 diabetes is almost epidemic and heart disease is a plague. Canada was originally a place where early settlers enjoyed a healthy diet of game, fish, seasonal fruits and the many varieties of mushrooms, berries and other foods the forests provided. They developed an amazing cuisine that was both sustainable and healthy, but their culinary accomplishments have faded into history because of war rationing, financial depression and opportunistic big business and its lust for profits no matter the consequences to consumers.

Food conglomerates control the distribution and processing of foods according to what generates the most profit, and if that means a limited, unhealthy choice for consumers, so be it. Today, consumers are dictated to by corporate accountants and treated like flocks of sheep—"Canadians will eat what we give them or we will sell it to some other country" is their attitude, and why not, since many of Canada's food conglomerates are controlled by foreign investors. Today, cereal and pulse crops are being genetically altered and treated with a pharmacopeia of chemicals to produce a surplus that overflows into the livestock industry, recently extended to include farmed salmon. Corn-fed salmon is an abomination and a heads-up for Canadians to throw off the yoke of conglomerate consumerism and begin to seriously consider if "what's for dinner" is not compromising their health for the financial benefit of big business.

CORN FLOUR—the British name for cornstarch and a sometimes source of confusion when consulting old cookbooks.

CORN-FRIED CHICKEN—a prairie menu fixture in the days when cornmeal was a cook's best friend. It has survived the years to become a favourite.

RECIPE

Corn-fried Chicken

Into 1 cup whole milk, stir ½ tsp salt and ¼ tsp each of sage, turmeric and pepper. Dip chicken pieces in mixture and then roll in cornmeal before frying in bacon fat or butter.

CORN HUSK COOKING—the French call it *en papillote*, meaning cooking "in paper," but Canadians call it corn husk cooking. It works for all kinds of fish but is especially good with salmon. When husking corn cobs, cut the flexible inner husks into strips for tying bundles and use the outer husks for bundling fish. Lay a fish fillet onto a strip of corn husk, dot with herb butter and lay another strip of husk on top. After tucking in the edges all around, tie up the bundle. Place bundles on the barbecue grill away from the flames, close the lid and roast for 15–20 minutes, turning once after 10 minutes. Check for doneness by opening a bundle.

CORN ON THE COB—refers to white, or sweet, corn picked immature before all the sugar in

RECIPE

Corn on the Cob

Bring a large pot of water to a rolling boil, throw in 1 Tbsp sugar and boil stripped ears for 5 minutes. Turn off heat and let ears simmer for another 5 minutes. Remove from water, slather with butter, sprinkle on salt and pepper and enjoy. Keep in mind that corn fresh from the field is always best and will need less cooking time.

the kernels is converted to starch; fresh cobs are then boiled, steamed, roasted or barbecued with or without the husk.

CORN OYSTER (also called battercake, mock oyster)—an easy-to-make, east coast, fried corn fritter usually served as a fish garnish.

RECIPE

Corn Oysters

Take 4 cups canned or fresh corn and add 3 eggs and 4 crushed crackers. Beat well, season and fry in hot oil.

CORN PIE—a pioneer version of shepherd's pie. Chopped venison or ground beef is browned in oil, placed into a casserole dish and topped with a layer of sweet corn. Top it all off with mashed potatoes and bake.

CORN SALAD. *See* lamb's lettuce.

CORN SOUP—iconic pioneer sweet corn soup borrowed from the Iroquois, who used flint corn, yellow corn, white sweet corn or dried corn boiled with venison. Europeans added white onion, flour, butter and salt pork. In modern times, corn soup has become the darling of upscale, imaginative restaurant chefs, and the soup now arrives at tables in dozens of variations.

RECIPE

The Best Ever Corn Soup

Cut the kernels off 4 ears of sweet corn into a bowl and use a spoon to scrape bits and juice from the cobs. In a pot, cook 1 diced white onion until translucent, then add 1 tsp chopped thyme and the corn. Cook for 2 minutes, then add ¼ cup flour and stir into a roux. Incorporate ¼ cup dry white wine and slowly add 3 cups chicken stock, ¾ cup each of heavy cream and cooked wild rice, and 1 cup cooked and diced pork shoulder. Bring to a simmer and serve.

CORN STICKS—a snack food that arrived in Canada with the Empire Loyalists that in modern times makes a tasty alternative to the obligatory sandwiches that accompany lunchtime soups.

RECIPE

Corn Sticks

In a bowl, sift together 2¼ cups flour, 4 tsp baking powder, 2 Tbsp sugar and 1 tsp salt. Add ¼ cup whole milk and 1 can cream-style corn. Mix well and turn onto a floured surface. Knead for 2–3 minutes and roll out to ½ inch thick and cut into 1-inch strips. Melt ⅓ cup butter in a baking pan and lay in the strips, turning to coat with butter. Bake in 450°F oven until golden brown, about 13 minutes, and serve immediately.

CORN SYRUP—BeeHive, Crown Brand Golden and Lily White brands were the ubiquitous corn syrups of late 19th- and early 20th-century Canada. Crown was the brand of choice in Québec, on the east coast and in BC, while consumers in the other provinces preferred BeeHive. Corn syrup mania occurred in the 1950s when the major brands associated themselves through advertising with the Dionne quintuplets, and tonnes of syrup went into baby formulations.

CORNBREAD—an unleavened cornmeal, or Indian meal, staple of First Nations, adapted to European tastes by the addition of eggs, sweetener, sour milk and baking soda. In pioneer days, cornbread would have been prepared and baked almost daily, and in later years, it garnered even more appeal with the addition of baking powder. *See also* bread.

RECIPE

Cornbread

Scald 1½ cups whole milk and pour into a mixing bowl. Add ¼ cup sugar, 1 Tbsp salt, ¼ cup shortening, ¾ cup water and 1 cup cornmeal, and stir. Prepare yeast (1 envelope). Stir with a fork and let it stand for 10 minutes. Pour into mix and stir. Beat in 6 cups flour, working in the last of it by hand. Turn out dough and knead for 10 minutes. Cover and let rise until doubled in volume. Punch down, cut, shape into loaves and place in greased baking tins sprinkled with cornmeal. Butter tops and let rise until double in volume. Bake in preheated 425°F oven for about 30 minutes. Enjoy.

A B C D E F G H I J K L M N O P Q R S T U V W X Y Z

A B **C** D E F G H I J K L M N O P Q R S T U V W X Y Z

CORNED BEEF—the word "corn" is Old English for any hard particle or grain, and sea salt used to preserve beef was the former. Beginning in the 17th century, beef was initially salt cured or "corned" to supply Britian's army and navy, with corned beef consumption slowly spreading to all parts of the Commonwealth. Canned minced corned beef called "bully beef" was the major field ration for British and Commonwealth troops over three wars. While canned bully beef remains a popular sandwich and mealtime ingredient in Maritime Canada, the rest of the country prefers a brined meat product sold by the slice at supermarkets or Jewish delicatessens—the exceptions being corned beef pie and hash, popular nationwide.

RECIPE

Corned Beef Pie

Mix 1 tin corned beef, mashed, 1 diced medium onion, 2 sliced medium potatoes, a dash of Worcestershire sauce or ketchup, and salt and pepper to taste in a bowl and turn into a crusted pie plate. Cover with pastry, slit the crust and bake at 350°F for 30 minutes, or until the crust is golden brown.

CORNED BEEF HASH—so ubiquitous it was nearly considered a staple food back in the day, it is once again attracting culinary attention thanks to TV chefs. It is easy to make, and once tried it becomes a breakfast favourite.

RECIPE

Corned Beef Hash

Chop a can of corned beef into 5 or 6 chopped and boiled potatoes. Add 1 chopped onion, ¼ tsp pepper, 2 Tbsp butter and ¼ cup light cream and mix well. Melt a few spoons of butter in a heavy skillet and lay in the hash. Dot the top with plenty of butter and lay on thin ring slices from 2 onions. Cover skillet and cook over low heat for 40 minutes. Before serving, sprinkle 1 tsp sugar over onion topping and place skillet under broiler for caramelizing.

CORNMEAL. *See* Indian meal.

CORNMEAL MOLASSES BREAD—a Nova Scotia specialty that travelled west with every pioneer settler who tasted a slice.

RECIPE

Cornmeal Molasses Bread

In a large bowl, mix 1 cup each of hot milk, boiling water and yellow cornmeal with 3 Tbsp butter, ½ cup fancy molasses and 2 tsp salt. In a smaller bowl, combine 2 Tbsp dry active yeast, 1 tsp sugar and ½ cup warm water, and let stand 15 minutes until frothy. Add yeast mixture to cornmeal mixture, and slowly beat in 5–6 cups flour until thick. Turn onto floured surface and knead in remaining flour until dough is smooth and elastic. Place dough into a buttered bowl and let rise in place for 2 hours. Punch dough, place into 2 or 3 loaf tins, let rise until doubled in size, and bake at 350°F for 1½–2 hours.

COSY EGGS (also called whore's eggs)—what Newfoundlanders call the green sea urchins that are cut open and the roe consumed with a spoon, like a boiled egg. *See also* sea urchin roe.

COTTAGE BEER—our earliest settlers made homebrew using the Indian meal casks muscled from Québec City to their new homestead. First, they had to boil a mixture of water, wheat bran and a handful of hops until the hops sank to the bottom. Then the hot mix was filtered into a cooling tub and, when lukewarm, a few quarts of molasses were added. Once that dissolved, the mix was poured into the casks along with a few spoonfuls of brewer's yeast. With the barrel bunged and working, the thirsty pioneer brewer had only to wait four or five days to slake his incredible thirst.

COTTAGE PIE—the original name for the minced beef and potato icon of British pub fare known as shepherd's pie. Named after the cottage housing occupied by people of reduced means who embraced any culinary creation that included inexpensive minced beef and potatoes, the original cottage pie featured both a bottom and top of mashed potatoes with a minced beef middle. The shepherd's version was a lamb stew with a topping of mashed potatoes, but over time the pubs dumped the lamb stew and went back to cheap minced beef, keeping only the pricey name. Nowadays, both upscale chefs and home cooks are more inclined to return the dish to its original preparation and name, because what does a shepherd have to do with minced beef? See also *pâté chinois*.

COTTAGE ROLL—the top end of the pork shoulder, sometimes called the shoulder butt, or sweet pickled cottage roll when pickled in brine.

COUNTERFEIT FISH—it's becoming more and more difficult to avoid the old switcheroo, when fish-processing companies import farmed fish and pawn them off as locally raised. A 2009 investigation by the University of Guelph employing the famous Barcode of Life genetic database revealed that as much as 25 percent of retailed fish has been purposely misidentified—just a plain old swindle perpetrated on a trusting public by greedy conglomerate processors. Tilapia and rockfish are sold as red snapper, farmed salmon is sold as wild, plaice can be flounder or sole, cheap skipjack tuna becomes sushi grade, smoked fish are dyed, the Patagonian tooth fish is sold as Chilean sea bass, haddock and pollock are passed off as cod, threatened Atlantic fish species are commonly labelled as being of Pacific origin, and one fish from a Toronto Chinese market sold as "bluefish" was not even in the database. It's a dangerous trick because while Canadian, U.S. and European fish farmers must adhere to government regulations regarding quality of fish feed, amount of contaminants and bacterial counts, Asian and South American countries have little or no government oversight of their fish farms. Know your fishmonger, but still be wary. *See also* by-catch fish.

CIGUATOXIN

Food fraud is a dangerous game. That supermarket salmon you think is Canadian may be farmed in Chile and contain a nasty surprise called ciguatoxin, which causes a disease called ciguatera, a non-life threatening ailment that affects millions of people in the southern hemisphere but is so rare in the north that doctors have difficulty recognizing the symptoms. Diagnosing ciguatera quickly is essential, for without it victims face decades of pain and debilitating fatigue. Ciguatoxin is produced by tropical plankton consumed by small reef fish, which in turn are consumed by larger fish, some of which are used in the production of farmed fish food.

COUNTRY HAM—a ham that has been rubbed with a dry salt and sugar mixture rather soaked or injected with pickling brine the way a so-called city ham is produced. *See also* city ham.

COWTAILS—a real cream and butter caramel crafted by Barr's Sweet Revenge Confection Company of Saskatoon. Barr's makes a host of Prairie-sourced food products that may be ordered online.

CP RAIL. *See* Canadian Pacific Railway.

CPR STRAWBERRIES—early railway workers' slang for the daily ration of stewed prunes served to keep them working and "regular." In some areas of the West, people still refer to prunes as CPR berries. *See also* Canadian Pacific Railway.

CRAB—the Canadian crab fishery is nearly as robust as the lobster fishery, with exports totalling around $1 billion. It is a foundation fishery, and although Canada is home to many species of crab, the majority of the catch is composed of two species: the Pacific Dungeness (*Metacarcinus magister*) and the Atlantic snow crab, sometimes called queen or spider crab (*Chionoecetes opilio*). Of the nearly 100 crab species found in BC coastal waters, the Dungeness and the red rock (*Cancer productus*) are the most popular owing to their firm, sweet, nutty tasting flesh.

CANADA'S FAVOURITE CRAB SPECIES

Atlantic:

- Atlantic rock crab—a once popular summertime favourite of Maritimers that has been rediscovered by upscale chefs, as the meat is pinkish and wonderfully sweet.

- Jonah crab—prized for its large crusher claws as they make an equally tasty but inexpensive substitute for stone crab claws.

- Red Atlantic king crab (porcupine crab)—there is no commercial fishery for this species, but its similarity to the Pacific king crab has an exploratory fishery underway.

- Red crab—a five-boat Canadian fishery with limited amounts available for distribution.

- Snow crab (queen crab, spider crab)—the predominant catch, which is usually sold in frozen leg clusters.

- Toad crab—extensivly fished for canning during the 1990s, with many areas fished out and now unproductive; often used as filler in canned snow crab meat.

Pacific:

- Dungeness crab—the famous "dungy," a sustainable west coast favourite for boiling, barbecue and cocktails.

- Red rock crab (red crab, rock crab)—similar to the dungy but smaller and meaner; these crabs are prized for their large crusher claws while the body and legs are best used for stock and pasta sauce.

- Pacific snow crab—usually sold in frozen leg clusters; an extensive fishery, but the best of the catch is destined for Japan.

- Tanner crab—not fished commercially, but available locally from divers and an exploratory fishery for the inland species of tanner crab.

- Varanger king crab (red king crab, Alaskan king crab)—outside of by-catch there is little commercial fishing of king crab in BC; however, fishing them for personal consumption is active in northern BC, especially in the Douglas Channel.

Crabby Invasion

- Red king crabs introduced to the North Atlantic by Russian companies hoping to cash in on the species' popularity have so taken to the area that populations have exploded, adversely affecting native fish stocks. The Norwegians are so upset by the crabby invasion that they are thinking of instituting an open season on any size of red king crab.

TIPS ON BUYING AND COOKING CRAB

- Unlike with lobsters, activity in a crab tank is a sure sign of freshness.

- When buying cooked crab, look for ones that are heavy for their size and have legs curled underneath their bodies; uncurled legs indicates the animal was dead when cooked.

- Cooking a fresh crab is as easy as dropping it into salted boiling water, waiting for it to float and allowing an extra 3 minutes, for a total of 10–15 minutes. Drop crabs in one at a time and do not overcrowd the pot.

- Cooked crabs need only be reheated in a steamer until hot, approximately 10–12 minutes.

- Frozen crab legs have been previously cooked, so all they require is steaming until hot, 10–12 minutes if thawed, 18–20 minutes if frozen.

- Already picked (or lump) crab purchased at a fish market can be easily checked for shell remnants by dropping small amounts onto a plate and listening for the click of shell.

RECIPE

Crab Salad

Place 1 cup picked fresh crabmeat, 1 cup diced celery, ¾ cup sliced mushrooms, ½ cup diced green pepper and 3 chopped tomatoes in a large bowl. Mix ¼ cup mayonnaise, 2 tsp vinegar and ¼ tsp sugar and toss with salad. Cover bowl, refrigerate for several hours and serve on a bed of lettuce.

CRAB BOUCHÉES—a BC variation of *bouchées à la reine*, the famous French puff pastry appetizer, with a Dungeness crab–based filling rather than the typical French chicken and mushroom.

CRABAPPLE—from the same genus as the domestic apple but with smaller fruit that is usually far more acidic. Only two species of crabapple are native to Canada, *Malus fusca* and *M. coronaria*, the former native to BC, the latter to Ontario and parts of Québec. Early settlers found the crabapple's high pectin content good for jelly

A
B
C
D
E
F
G
H
I
J
K
L
M
N
O
P
Q
R
S
T
U
V
W
X
Y
Z

making, and its acidic qualities made for excellent vinegar.

CRABAPPLE JELLY—one of the bygone days' national condiments made from native crabapples that have been softened in a hot water bath, sieved, mixed with an equal weight of sugar, laced with a few cloves and a stick of cinnamon, boiled for a half-hour and poured into sterilized jars.

CRABAPPLE PIE—a crusted dessert made with thinly sliced, peeled crabapples sprinkled with sugar, cinnamon and a dredge of flour, dotted with butter and topped with crust.

CRACKLING—the crisp and succulent skin of roast pork that must be prepared properly to become a satisfactory addition to any meal: the skin must be scored with a sharp knife and the pork roasted without larding or basting. An alternative preparation method is simply to remove the skin and roast it in a separate pan. *See also* scrunchions.

CRANACHAN—a toasted mixture of oats, fruit, sugar and rum, topped with whipped cream and traditionally served at Maritime Christmas dinners.

CRANBERRY (*Vaccinium macrocarpon*; also called bogberry, bounceberry)—the cranberry has been part of the great Canadian food experience from the very beginning, starting with the cuisine of the First Nations. The Mi'kmaq harvested cranberries long before John Cabot arrived in 1497 and used them for both food and medicine. A few years after Cabot's visit, French and Basque fishermen began trading with the Mi'kmaq, exchanging trinkets and iron pots for furs, along with some medicinal information thrown in for free, such as, "Listen up, sailor. If you want to keep your teeth from falling out, drink the juice of bogberries." So the fishermen drank lots of juice, dried cranberries went on their trade list and they sailed the ocean blue with toothy smiles. Cranberry juice became every Maritimer's tonic against the dreaded scurvy while the rest of the nautical world suffered and waited years more for lemons and limes.

Cranberries

- Contrary to popular belief, cranberries do not grow in water. Bogs are only flooded from a nearby source to facilitate harvest.

- Cranberries are white until they ripen, and only ripe berries bounce. Modern processing machines drop berries onto a steel plate after washing, and only those that can bounce over a 10-centimetre-high barrier are allowed to proceed.

- The red in cranberries indicates the presence of anthocyanins, flavonoids with antioxidant, antimicrobial and cholesterol-lowering properties.

CRANBERRY CORNBREAD—a Nova Scotia specialty bread that includes cranberries, boiled or canned pumpkin and chopped walnuts. Use a standard recipe with ½ cup milk, then add 1 cup each of cranberries and pumpkin and ½ cup chopped walnuts.

CRANBERRY CURD—lemon curd with a cranberry substitute, and because most Canadians have tried neither, to make it will be a life changer. Try it with raspberries if lemons or cranberries are not your thing.

RECIPE

Cranberry Curd

In a medium saucepan, bring 2 cups cranberries and ¼ cup water to a boil, reduce heat and simmer 2 minutes. Allow to cool slightly, then pour into blender and purée until smooth. Cream together 1 cup sugar and ¼ cup unsalted butter and add 4 eggs, one at time, while beating. Add 1 Tbsp lemon juice and the cranberry purée. Mix well and transfer to a large steel bowl. Place bowl over a pot of simmering water and whisk until thick, about 10 minutes. Remove from heat, cool in a larger bowl of ice water, pour into airtight container and refrigerate.

CRANBERRY KETCHUP—an east coast favourite so good you must try it.

RECIPE

Cranberry Ketchup

Peel 1 lb onions and chop fine; add 4 lbs cranberries and 2 cups water, and boil until soft. Sieve mixture. Add 4 cups sugar, 2 cups vinegar and 1 tsp each of ground cloves, cinnamon, allspice, salt and pepper, and boil until thick. Makes 6 pints.

CRANBERRY PIE—a deep-dish Maritime crusted pie containing fresh cranberries sweetened with molasses and brown sugar.

CRANBERRY SAUCE—a pioneer favourite for game and wild fowl and so good that you will not buy the canned stuff ever again.

RECIPE

Cranberry Sauce

In a medium saucepan bring 1 cup orange juice and ½ cup sugar to a simmer while stirring. Add 2 cups cranberries and bring to a boil while stirring. Reduce heat and simmer for 15 minutes while occasionally stirring gently. Add another ½ cup sugar according to taste and either serve warm or refrigerate.

A
B
C
D
E
F
G
H
I
J
K
L
M
N
O
P
Q
R
S
T
U
V
W
X
Y
Z

CRANBERRY WALNUT SALAD—a pioneer, straight from the land, Sunday dinner salad that remains in vogue even today. In the early days it was a fall salad, made from fresh-picked cranberries, walnuts, beechnut oil and possibly foraged greens.

CRAYFISH—a favourite of Acadians, who took their love of crayfish with them to Louisiana during their forced removal from Nova Scotia. During the initial colonization of Acadia and New France, rivers and streams abounded with crayfish, but by the middle of the 18th century, most were overfished and depleted of crayfish. Down but not out, crayfish numbers have increased in many areas and are just waiting to be caught and popped into a pie. Crayfish are still enjoyed by many Canadian cottagers, who trap the miniature lobsters, keep them in submerged traps for a day to clear their intestines, then boil them in salted water for 3–4 minutes and eat the tails with drawn butter or seafood sauce. There are many species of North American crayfish, with the most common in Canada being *Orconectes virilis*, or Northern crayfish. Not as large as the famed Louisiana red swamp crayfish, it is just as tasty and easily caught.

CRAYFISH BOULETTES—a once popular variation of *ragoût de boulettes*, or meatball stew, using crayfish tails instead of pork or beef and plenty of cayenne pepper or hot sauce. See also *ragoût de boulettes et pattes de cochon*.

CRAYFISH PIE—a favourite Acadian alternative to lobster pie. Acadians living away from the sea

simply had to send their kids to a nearby stream to answer the "what's for dinner" question.

RECIPE

Crayfish Pie

Cook 2 cups chopped crayfish tail meat in ¼ cup butter, and in a separate pan, make a roux with 6 Tbsp butter and ½ Tbsp flour. Add 1½ cups cream, salt and pepper to taste, and cook while stirring until smooth. Add a small amount of sauce to 4 beaten eggs, stir and add to sauce. Add crayfish meat, stir carefully, pour into casserole dish, top with pie crust and bake in a 350°F oven until golden brown.

CRAZY CAKE. *See* wacky cake.

CREAM CAKE—in the early days, most bull calves from dairy cows were slaughtered, providing veal roasts, sausages and plenty of milk and cream from lactating cows for the crafting of butter and baking of cream cakes.

RECIPE

Cream Cake

Mix 1½ cups flour with 1 cup heavy cream, ¾ cup sugar, 2 beaten eggs, 2 tsp baking soda and 1 tsp salt. Pour batter into a square cake pan and bake in a 350°F oven until knife blade comes out clean. Let cool and ice with butter cream of any flavour.

CREAM CHEESE—easy to make, just drain cream through cheesecloth and let it sit a few days until it acquires the consistency of butter. However, if pasteurized cream is used, the end product will lack flavour, so it's best to acquire the finished product at artisanal dairies or farmers' markets. Conglomerate cream cheese produced in Canada is usually a hot-packed coagulated emulsion of 33 percent butterfat, 45 percent milk solids, salt, nitrogen gas (to improve spreadability) and any number of emulsifying, gelling, stabilizing and thickening agents. In Britain, cream cheese must have a minimum butterfat content of 45 percent, while in France that figure is 55 percent, which leaves our Canadian 33 percent looking a bit like highway robbery.

CREAM OF WHEAT PUDDING. *See* mush pudding.

CREAMED CODFISH—an east coast favourite supper dish both then and now.

RECIPE

Creamed Codfish

Soak salt cod at least 24 hours and boil until tender in water containing 1 Tbsp vinegar. Remove any bones while hot, let cool and flake the fish. Prepare a roux from 2 Tbsp each of butter and flour and 1 cup milk; add 2 beaten eggs and mix well. Add flaked fish and a squeeze of lemon juice, and cook for 2 minutes while stirring. Serve with a wedge of lemon and a sprinkle of chopped parsley.

CREAMED CORN—a favourite of pioneer families and easy-peasy to make; your dinner guests will think you are a culinary magician.

RECIPE

Creamed Corn

Slice kernels from 3 fresh-cooked ears of corn into a cooking pot. Add 1 cup heavy cream, 2 Tbsp butter, salt and pepper to taste, and cook for 10 minutes.

A
B

C

D
E
F
G
H
I
J
K
L
M
N
O
P
Q
R
S
T
U
V
W
X
Y
Z

CREAMED CORN SOUP—a popular Depression-era day's starter of canned creamed corn mixed with milk, flour, butter, salt and pepper. A little went a long way and still does, but nowadays this soup is usually made from fresh corn.

CREAMED SALMON ON TOAST—an iconic Depression-era dish made by combining canned salmon, cream of mushroom soup and peas, then heating and serving on toast.

CRETONS (also called gorton)—a spiced onion and pork pâté favoured by Québec habitants.

CRISPY CRUNCH CANDY BAR—a crispy peanut butter centre covered in milk chocolate and sold in a distinctive red-and-white package. Once a handmade Canadian candy, the bar has bounced around from one recipe-tweaking conglomerate to another to become just another mass-produced candy bar.

CROQUE-MATANE—a *croque-monsieur* sandwich peculiar to the Gaspé region of Québec that uses the tiny, flavourful matane shrimp and plenty of local cheese.

CROQUIGNOLE—a twisted fried doughnut dusted with maple sugar popular with French Canadians.

CROSBY'S MOLASSES—the national favourite since 1897, the year Lorenzo George Crosby packed in his Yarmouth, Nova Scotia, grocery store and moved to St. John, New Brunswick,

to open the Crosby Molasses Company. Crosby traded timber and codfish for Caribbean molasses that arrived in 40-kg barrels called puncheons. Still a family-run business, Crosby's clarifies, grades and packs molasses for both retail and industrial use.

CROW'S NEST PUDDING. *See* cobbler.

CROWBERRY SAUCE. *See* mossberry sauce.

CRYSTAL BEACH SUGAR WAFFLES—uniquely Canadian waffles that were hugely popular in the late 19th and early 20th centuries. Made famous by the Crystal Beach Amusement Park in Crystal Beach, Ontario, they are now made by the Crystal Beach Candy Company of Fort Erie and are available at the candy factory, local retail outlets and by ordering online.

CUCUMBER (*Cucumis sativus*)—the edible fruit of a creeping vine with a history that goes back thousands of years to India during the Bronze Age. From India, cucumbers spread to Europe and from there to North America with Christopher Columbus—40 years later, Jacques Cartier found them growing wild in Canada. The English found them good for making soups, salads, teatime sandwiches and the odd commercial pickle (made popular during the Indian

CRYSTAL BEACH AMUSEMENT PARK

During the latter part of the 19th century, travel came into vogue in America, and though few people could afford a shipboard excursion to Europe, almost everyone could manage the cost of a day trip, especially in summer. Summers without air conditioning or electric fans were insufferably hot, and people near water escaped to local beaches, packing them like sardines. Walking about in a soggy woollen swimsuit was not fun, and those day-trippers clamoured for something to get them off the beaches, or at least onto a less crowded beach. Americans living in cities around the Great Lakes—Buffalo, Erie, Toledo, Cleveland and Detroit—cast covetous eyes across Lake Erie to great beaches with far fewer people.

Americans are ingenious people, and where there is a will, there is a way. So was born the excursion ferry, a day-tripper boat to haul folks across the lake to quiet little places like Crystal Beach, Port Dover and Port Stanley, with shallow water that wouldn't wet the wool swimsuits. It was nice, but wading and picnics soon got boring, and the time was ripe for ingenious Canadians to rise up and build Ferris wheels and, heaven forbid, promenade cars. However, pushing your wife or your date around in a buggy also got boring, which led to other amusement rides being installed. Over the years, those rides became more daring until, in 1927, Crystal Beach installed the Cyclone, a roller coaster designed to scare the woollen swimsuit off everyone who dared ride it.

The early 20th century was a heyday for Lake Erie amusement parks. They all had dance halls with big bands, and they all featured thrill rides, but none bettered Crystal Beach, where as many as 20,000 summer day-trippers would descend on the park daily.

Raj), but the cucumber never found its stride until the middle of the 19th century, when glass canning jars made pickling cucumbers a North American tradition.

CANADA'S FAVOURITE CUCUMBER VARIETIES

- Beit Alpha—long, thin-skinned and probably the best-tasting cuke; newer hybrids are more resistant to diseases than their progenitor.

- Boston Pickling—big, short, tasty and a long-time garden standby.

- Long Green Improved—have a thin skin, best for slicing.

- Longfellow—big, with great flavour; they are best for salads.

- Mideast Prolific—thin skin and great for slicing, but a late-season variety.

- Parisian Pickling—one of the best for gherkin pickles.

A
B
C
D
E
F
G
H
I
J
K
L
M
N
O
P
Q
R
S
T
U
V
W
X
Y
Z

RECIPE

Cold Cucumber Soup

Chop 2 medium cucumbers into chunks and buzz in food processor until smooth. Dice another 2 cucumbers and combine with 2 cups plain yogurt, 1 cup sour cream, 1 cup milk, 3 Tbsp olive oil, 1 finely minced garlic clove and 2 Tbsp chopped dill. Add cucumber purée. Cover bowl and refrigerate overnight. Check seasoning and serve in chilled bowls with a topping of toasted walnuts.

CUISINE DU QUÉBEC—book title of the over 30,000 published recipes of a 1980s research project by the Québec government and the Institute de tourisme d'hôtellerie du Québec (ITHQ), wherein old family recipes were searched out, tested and recorded for posterity.

CULBERT'S BAKERY—cream doughnuts are the specialty of Culbert's Bakery in Goderich, Ontario, which has patrons lining up to purchase them. Culbert's is one of those time-warp bakeries that tourists find by accident. Road trippers are prone to seeing a fair amount of the town as they circle back to refill their supply of all things wonderful from the Culbert's ovens, especially the cream puffs and cream doughnuts.

CULLEN SKINK—Scottish immigrants to Canada brought along their appetite for traditional

foods, which included a big breakfast bowl filled with creamy smoked haddock chowder and mashed potatoes mixed up into a kind of soup. It tastes much better than it sounds.

CULTURED BUTTER—a relatively new term to describe a manufacturer's departure from the normal process of separating cream from milk and churning to butter. Before the conglomerates, butter making was less a rush to profits and more a labour of love with some skill required, as the full cream milk was allowed to ripen and develop flavour before pasteurization killed off all flavour-providing bacteria. Today, if butter is cultured, it gets that way through inoculation by a starter culture.

CUMBERLAND CAKE. *See* butter cake.

CUPCAKES. *See* butter cake.

CURD CHEESE. *See* cheese curds.

CURED BEEF—in the days before refrigeration, large cuts of beef were pickled just like hams, and the aromatic and spicy results were much appreciated during festive occasions, especially at Christmas. A saltpeter dry rub was and still is the method of choice, with the flavouring being juniper berries, allspice and cracked peppercorns. *See also* saltpeter.

CURED HAM—pork is quickly surpassing beef consumption in Canada, and to meet demand

into the hams usually by mechanical means. It is nearly impossible to find dry-cured hams in Canada because injecting up to 40 percent water into hams adds weight and represents huge profits for conglomerate processors. A dry-cured ham called prosciutto is available from small Italian meat packers and butchers but is more an appetizer than a main dish.

CURING SALT—a mixture of salt, sodium nitrate and sometimes sugar and flavouring used to preserve and soften meats that is either rubbed on or dissolved in water to make soaking brine. Curing salt is traditionally dyed pink so as not to confuse it with stored table salt. *See also* saltpeter.

CURLY ENDIVE. *See* chicory.

CURRANT—these can be red (*Ribes rubrum*), black (*R. nigrum*) or white (a variation of the red species), with red being the most prominent in the Canadian food experience. English settlers loved their condiments, and there was no Sunday dinner without red currant jelly, a culinary idiosyncrasy that mandated a bush in every yard and required many hands to pick, usually belonging to kids.

there is the battery system, wherein pigs are raised in cramped conditions almost like chickens. Ham is how most pork is consumed, and that can be fresh or cured, with the latter accounting for most retailed consumption. Curing can be dry, with the hams cured in sugar and salt, or it can be wet, wherein a pickling solution is forced

Today, red and black currant jams can be purchased at any supermarket, and while still a cut above cranberry sauce, they lack the ethereal taste of homemade and cannot be used to make an easy but oh so delicious summer pudding.

RECIPE

Currant Jelly

Place 4 lbs fresh currants into a large pot, crush them with a potato masher and add 1 cup water. Bring contents to a boil, then turn down heat and simmer for 10 minutes. Remove from heat and allow to cool a bit, then strain through cheesecloth into another pot and stir in 7 cups sugar. Bring contents to a rapid boil and add in liquid pectin according to instructions. Return contents to a full rolling boil and cook for 1 minute only. Remove from heat, skim off the foam and ladle into jars, allowing a ½-inch top space. Secure jars with sterile rings and tops and simmer in a water bath for 10–15 minutes.

RECIPE

Currant Sauce

Mash currants and set aside in a warm place for 4 days. Strain through a jelly bag (avoid squeezing), and mix in 2 lbs sugar for every pint of juice. Heat juice in a double boiler until clear and pour into sterilized Mason jars. To make a glaze for wild game, add breadcrumbs to sauce along with a few cloves, port wine and a dollop of butter.

CURRANT SAUCE—black, red or white currants cooked down into a sweet, fruity condiment or glaze for fowl and wild game. A favourite of pioneer families, currant sauce is still popular and easily made from commercially raised berries.

CURRY—coriander, cayenne, cardamom seed, turmeric, ginger, mace and saffron are the spice ingredients for curry. In 17th-century India, curry was the culinary choice of officers and employees of the British East India Company, an organization that contributed many settlers to Canada. Those settlers brought family, possessions and a love for curry that became nationalized into the Canadian food experience by the use of game meat. Venison curry, if you have never tried it, is a worthwhile culinary experience.

RECIPE

Curried Venison

Pour 3 Tbsp oil into a heavy cooking pot; when hot, add 1 Tbsp curry powder and cook while stirring until darkened (do not burn). Add 3 lbs cubed venison and brown a bit, then add 1 bunch chopped onions, 3 cloves minced garlic and 1 minced habanero or Scotch bonnet pepper and continue browning. Add 1 tsp fresh thyme, 1 tsp additional curry powder, a few pinches of black pepper and perhaps a bit of seasoning salt. Cover with water and simmer until meat is fork tender and liquid has become thick and sauce-like. Adjust seasoning to taste and serve over rice.

CUSK (*Brosme brosme*)—a cod-like fish species that has suffered the same fate as the cod owing to being passed off as cod, especially in the salt fish trade. Cusk were targeted after the cod moratorium, and they are now also considered threatened. Quotas have been cut to a minimum, and most landings are by-catch. *See also* by-catch fish, counterfeit fish.

CUSTARD APPLE. *See* bakeapple.

D

DAD'S OATMEAL COOKIES—an oatmeal cookie introduced from Scotland via the U.S. by the Christie Brown Company at the beginning of the 20th century. Mr. Christie, you bake good cookies, and in 1928, his company started baking cookies for Nabisco, and in 2000, for Kraft Foods. Aside from the shrinking size, the cookie remains the best milk and coffee dipper in the country.

DAINTIES—a prairie dweller's name for an assortment of baked goods, such as cookies, date squares and jam tarts.

DAIRY PROCESSORS ASSOCIATION OF CANADA (DPAC)—successor to the National Dairy Council and representing not the dairies and responsible stewardship, but the "might is right" attitude of the lawyers and accountants who hammerlock the nation's milk supply.

DALL SHEEP BURGER—a trapper's delight, chopped, fried and stuck into a sliced bannock roll. There are around 20,000 Dall sheep traipsing around BC's Mackenzie Mountain territory, and any Canadian with a spare $7000 to $8000 can shoot one and watch their guide prepare the world's priciest burger.

DAMPER DOGS—scorched balls of dough cooked on stove lids; a Newfoundland specialty and a favourite of children.

DANDELION (*Taraxacum officinale*)—you will think more of your front lawn after trying dandelion greens, either fresh in a salad or cooked. Do not pick flowering dandelions because they will be bitter, and do not pick leaves from places that have even a slight chance of having been sprayed with pesticides. While plucking dandelion plants, keep an eye peeled for another edible weed, the delicious purslane. *See also* purslane.

RECIPE

Dandelion and Pine Nut Salad

Wash the dandelion leaves, spin them dry, tear them into small pieces and place them into a large salad bowl. In a small skillet cook 3 Tbsp pine nuts over medium heat in ¼ cup olive oil and stir until golden. Add oil and nuts to salad, along with 1½ tsp red wine vinegar and salt and pepper to taste. Toss and serve.

A
B
C
D
E
F
G
H
I
J
K
L
M
N
O
P
Q
R
S
T
U
V
W
X
Y
Z

RECIPE

Dandelion Greens Supreme

Melt 1 Tbsp butter in a heavy skillet and stir in 4 cups washed dandelion greens, ¼ cup chopped onion and 2 Tbsp beef broth. Cover and cook for 10 minutes, stirring occasionally. Add 2 Tbsp heavy cream and ¼ cup crumbled bacon and cook uncovered until most of the liquid has evaporated. Season with salt and pepper and top with a pat of butter.

DANDELION COFFEE—much used by early settlers, the roasted and ground-up roots of the common dandelion make a surprisingly good coffee substitute, especially if gathered in fall and mixed with a small amount of ground coffee. Dandy Blend, an American-made dandelion coffee, is available in some Canadian health food stores and online. *See also* chicory, coffee substitutes.

DARE CANDIES—our long-time favourite sweet treats: mints, jujubes, jellybeans and now Real-Fruit gummies, most with natural flavours and all made with the finest ingredients available.

DARE FOODS

Dare Foods, a Kitchener, Ontario, mostly family-owned company with factories all over North America, ships quality baked goods and candy products to over 25 countries. The products are like ambassadors of good taste. Dare is one of Canada's best-run companies, and—except for the tropical oil and cacao-covered Viva Puffs, a cookie dumped on them through acquisition—they mostly eschew artificial flavours, harmful chemicals and peanuts. However, Dare's designation as a family-run business has been somewhat compromised by a partial merger with the Canadian dairy conglomerate Saputo.

DARE COOKIES—consisting of real chocolate Whippets, Grissol Melba Toast, Ruffles, Normandie Fingers, cream-filled cookies with natural flavours, and many more, including the much-anticipated Girl Guide cookies.

DARK TICKLE CHOCOLATES—all the tastes of Newfoundland and Labrador covered in rich, dark or milk chocolate. A "tickle" is a narrow channel of water, and in Griquet, where the Dark Tickle Company is located, the tickle is shadowed by hills. Cranberry-covered chocolates, bakeapple, blueberry and partridgeberry ganache-centred chocolates, as well as screech rum, jams, jellies, juices, teas, pickles and other east coast delights are all lovingly prepared using traditional methods and are available online.

DATE SQUARES. *See* matrimonial cake.

DEER. *See* fallow deer, venison, wild game.

DEPRESSION CAKE. *See* war cake.

DEVIL'S FOOD CAKE—a red-coloured chocolate cake, caused by a culinary oddity in how baking powder turns cocoa red during baking. It is a shared culinary invention, since baking powder was introduced to the U.S. and Canada at about the same time.

A
B
C
D
E
F
G
H
I
J
K
L
M
N
O
P
Q
R
S
T
U
V
W
X
Y
Z

DEWBERRIES AND DUCK—dewberries (*Rubus flagellaris*) are related to blackberries and raspberries and make a fine sauce for wild or domestic duck. A favourite of pioneer families, the sauce is made by adding ½ cup mashed berries to the juices from the roasting pan along with 3 Tbsp brown sugar and a sprig of rosemary.

DIGBY CHICKEN (also called salt herring)—an east coast pet name for salt herring, so named because the fish once served as Christmas dinner for impoverished Maritime families in and around Digby, Nova Scotia.

DIGBY FRIED SCALLOPS—the absolute best way to enjoy the succulent harvest of Digby's scallop fishing fleet, the world's largest.

DILLY BEANS—pickled green beans, made popular across Canada after the invention of the Mason jar. Carrots may also be dilled.

DINE OUT VANCOUVER FESTIVAL—a hugely popular wintertime promotion in Vancouver, where hundreds of restaurants offer three-or-more-course dinners at $18, $28 or $38, with many also offering discounted lunch fare.

A
B
C
D
E
F
G
H
I
J
K
L
M
N
O
P
Q
R
S
T
U
V
W
X
Y
Z

DITCH FISH—a derogatory word used to describe some fish species produced through aquaculture, especially Chinese aquaculture. It takes around 7 kg of wild-caught fish species such as anchovy and alewife to produce 1 kg of the unnatural, or ditch-raised, fish.

DOG BERRY. *See* rowanberry.

DOG SALMON. *See* chum salmon.

DOLLY VARDEN TROUT (*Salvelinus confluentus*; also called bull trout)—not actually a trout but a distant relative; this "trout" is in fact a char native to BC and parts of Alberta. An excellent game and eating fish, the Dolly Varden has unfortunately become rare and is a catch-and-release fish in many areas. It is the provincial fish of Alberta. The bright colours of the fish earned it the name "Dolly Varden" after the fashion of dress worn by characters in Charles Dickens' novel *Barnaby Rudge*.

DOLPHINFISH. *See* mahi-mahi.

DONUT. *See* doughnut.

DORADO. *See* mahi-mahi.

DORÉ. *See* walleye.

DOUGH GODS (also called elephant ears)—flattened bread dough, fried and drizzled with maple syrup or honey. *See also* beaver tails.

DOUGHNUT—the doughnut, or "donut" if you prefer, is simply a sweet leavened or unleavened blob of dough fried in oil and either slathered in a sweet topping, given a dusting of sugar or left plain. Every civilization has munched doughnuts in one form or another—usually square, unleavened and dipped in honey. If your ancestors happened to be tromping around Canada in the early days, they would have undoubtedly eaten clabbered bannock or fried bread dipped in sugar, honey or maple syrup. Doughnuts are an everyman's snack food or dessert: they are easy, quick to make and almost always tasty and satisfying. Canadians eat a lot of doughnuts, more than anyone else on the planet, with over one billion consumed annually. This fried round dough ball has supplanted the entire Canadian food experience

Doughnuts

- The first recorded use of the word "doughnut" was in 1808 in "History of New York," a short story by Washington Irving. In it, he described sweetened bits of dough fried in hog's fat and called doughnuts, or *olykoeks* (a Dutch word meaning oil cakes).

- There are many stories associated with the modern shape of doughnuts, round with a hole in the middle; however, the most accepted and believable tale concerns Hanson Gregory, a 19th-century ship's captain. Captain Gregory's mother, Elisabeth Hanson, a New England baker of Dutch *olykoeks*, changed their shape in 1847 from square to round and called them doughnuts after the word Washington Irving had coined in 1808. To counter the tendency of her round cakes not to cook all the way through, she filled the centres with hazelnut paste. Captain Gregory hated hazelnuts, and so before consuming his mother's specialty, he poked out the centres with a finger. "Hey Mom, why not just leave out the centres altogether?"

A
B
C
D
E
F
G
H
I
J
K
L
M
N
O
P
Q
R
S
T
U
V
W
X
Y
Z

and become Canada's national food. Canada is certainly Doughnut Nation, and if you are what you eat, Canadians—especially Ontarians—are blobs of fried dough of ever-diminishing quality.

DOUGHNUT LASSIES—another army served in World War I, the Salvation Army, and it fielded thousands of volunteers, with probably none being as important to troop morale as the young women known as the Sally Ann Doughnut Lassies. To be served fresh-made doughnuts and a hot cup of tea or coffee by a pretty girl after months of frontline horror caused some of the most battle-hardened men to break down and cry. Try the famous Salvation Army doughnuts; they are yummy, especially when fried in lard.

RECIPE

WWI Salvation Army Doughnuts

Combine 5 cups flour, 2 cups sugar, 5 tsp baking powder, 1 tsp salt, 2 eggs, 1¾ cups whole milk and 1 Tbsp butter or melted lard to make the dough. Thoroughly knead dough, roll smooth to ¼ inch thick, and cut into rings using a round cookie cutter or glass, with a shot glass to cut out the centre. Drop the rings into hot oil or lard, making sure the fat is hot enough to brown the doughnuts gradually (360°F). Turn the doughnuts several times until browned, then remove doughnuts and drain on paper towel. Dust with powdered sugar and let cool before serving.

FREDDIE MAIER'S AMAZING MACHINE

Even Ontarians will not know the name Frederick Maier, but for citizens of Doughnut Nation, it is a name of historical importance. Freddie Maier was the first stone in an avalanche, the instigator of Canada's non-nutritive addition to the doughnut. Freddie, 11 years old and adventurous, arrived in Canada from the Ukraine in 1913. Not wanting to work on a farm, Freddie hit the road and took the only job available to a kid: a baker's boy. He did all the worst jobs in a bakery, including frying doughnuts. Freddie worked his way through southern Ontario into the state of Michigan, picking up doughnut-making skills from German and Mennonite bakers along the way.

As a teenager, Freddie tried starting his own bakery a few times but was unsuccessful, and in 1922, he moved from Michigan to Niagara Falls, New York, for another try. World War I had run its course, people had discovered Henry Ford's Model T automobile and Niagara Falls had become a destination for travellers. Freddie Maier was a big fan of Henry Ford and devoted much thought to how he could emulate Ford's production methods to make doughnuts. In 1924, with his latest bakery on the skids, he moved to Buffalo, New York, prepared to try again, this time Ford style. Bit by bit, Freddie Maier constructed his wonderful doughnut-making machine. To see it in operation was to marvel at the ingenuity of Freddie Maier, but to taste the finished product was to die and go to heaven.

By the time World War II rolled around, Freddie was selling five million doughnuts a year. In the 1950s, that figure rose to 15 million, and in the 1960s to 25 million, making Freddie Maier the undisputed King of Doughnuts. His secret was to use only the finest ingredients, not manhandle the rounds, serve them hot and fresh and have a master baker on site. In 1989, after 65 years of doughnut mastering, Freddie Maier retired and turned off his fabulous machine. North America had lost its signature doughnut, and while today there is no shortage of companies producing the delectable rounds with machines, most are imitations lacking the master's touch.

Today's doughnut shop is a replacement for the ubiquitous jug milk stores that once occupied street corners across the nation. Those stores sold milk and ice cream, while the replacements sell a sweetened fried dough product with the pre-chewed texture of baby food. Ice cream and doughnuts are simply baby foods for grown-ups, our iconic comfort foods, and Canada's appetite for each is boundless, save for price. Milk and ice cream are labour- and capital-intensive and priced accordingly, while doughnuts are simply starchy flour, sugar and fat, inexpensive ingredients perfect for mechanical extrusion and frying on a scale that makes Freddie Maier's fabulous doughnut machine look like a toy.

The Tom Thumb Doughnut Machine

- During the 1950s, a miniaturized version of Freddie Maier's doughnut-making machine began appearing at lunch counters of five-and-dime stores across the United States. Called the Tom Thumb doughnut machine, it proved popular with customers, but the machines were too aromatic for storeowners, who sold them off to carnival and state fair concessionaires. In 1959, the Tom Thumb doughnut machine made its appearance at the Canadian National Exhibition (CNE), and soon thereafter, munching hot, fresh, tiny rounds of scrumptiousness became a CNE tradition.

A
B
C
D
E
F
G
H
I
J
K
L
M
N
O
P
Q
R
S
T
U
V
W
X
Y
Z

DRIED APPLE CAKE—during Canada's early days, settlers helped each other clear fields and erect barns and houses in a trade-off system called the "bee," a system that persevered to become various women's bees including the apple bee, wherein countless apples were peeled, cored and sliced into rings, strung onto twine and hung up to dry. Dried apples had many uses, and chief among them was the apple cake. *See also* drying.

RECIPE

Dried Apple Cake

Soak 3 cups dried apples overnight in water, give them a slight chop and simmer 1½ hours in 2 cups molasses. Cool slightly, then mix in 1 cup sugar, 1 cup milk, 2 eggs, ½ cup melted butter, 1 tsp baking soda and anything else handy, such as jam, raisins or nuts, and enough flour to make a stiff batter, 3½–4 cups. Pour into a well-greased cake pan and bake in a 350°F oven until a toothpick comes out clean, about 35 minutes.

DRIED APPLE PIE—a favourite with early pioneer settlers because drying apples was a major preserving method. Stew dried apples until tender, then add sugar, cinnamon and a dash of lemon juice. Pour into a pie shell, top with pastry and bake.

DRIED PEAS—whole green and yellow, split green and yellow, chickpeas, lentils and beans are called "pulse crops"—crops harvested solely for their dry seed—and except for the chickpeas, we grow more of them than any other country. They arrived here with the very earliest pioneers and became a national crop long before wheat became popular. Nowadays, most pulse crops are grown in the Prairie provinces, especially Saskatchewan, and exported worldwide.

DRUNKEN CHICKEN—in the early days of Canada, every Maritime cook knew how to pair rum and maple syrup, and drunken chicken was, and still is, one of the best applications.

RECIPE

Drunken Chicken

Pound 6 boneless skinless chicken breasts flat, roll up wedges of fresh peaches into the breasts and stick closed with toothpicks. Bake chicken rolls in a 325°F oven for 10 minutes and prepare the sauce. In a small pan combine 1½ cups maple syrup, 3 Tbsp lemon juice, 1 tsp lemon zest, 3 Tbsp dark rum and ¼ cup butter, and simmer until thick. Glaze chicken with sauce and return to oven for another 10–15 minutes of cooking. When done, drizzle each chicken roll with sauce before serving.

DRYING—the simplest and most basic method of food preservation that works by reducing the water content of foods, making them inhospitable to the microbes that cause spoilage. Time is of the essence when drying foods, and salt is a big help in arresting the growth of microbes until the air and sunshine begin doing their work.

Fish and meat drying were the initial engines of commerce that helped create this nation, and they set the stage for an entire gamut of industrially dried foods, including milk, eggs, fruits and vegetables. Nowadays, almost all foods can be freeze-dried and made so free of bacteria-supporting water that the foods are edible for many years with a much fresher taste than canned foods.

DUCK AND WILD RICE DINNER—a favourite on the Prairies, where the combination of duck and wild rice was readily available—where the wild rice grows, you will also find ducks.

DUCK EGGS—they taste like free-range chicken eggs but have a little more fat in the yolk, giving them a deeper orange colour. The whites contain more albumen than chicken eggs, giving them more structure when poached or fried and allowing more loft to cakes.

DUCK FOIE GRAS—produced by a number farmers across Canada, with the most notable being Aux Champs d'Élisé, a Québec initiative started by Marieville dairy farmers Élisé and Annette François in 1988, and who now supply chefs across Canada, Japan and Europe. *See also* foie gras.

DUFF—a word used for pudding in Newfoundland. *See also* figgy duff.

DULSE (*Palmaria palmata*)—an edible seaweed harvested from the northern waters of both the Pacific and Atlantic oceans, with the most prized coming from the Bay of Fundy, especially from around the Dark Harbour area of Grand Manan Island.

DUNGENESS CRAB. *See* crab.

DUROC PIG—an all-red pig originally from Britain but so long raised and bred in Canada that it has become known as the Canadian Duroc. The Ontario Carcass Appraisal Program of 1990–1994 studied 700 swine breeds and judged the Canadian Duroc the best breed for meat quality.

DURUM WHEAT. *See* wheat.

DUTCH MESS (also called hugger-in-buff)— a Lunenburg, Nova Scotia, specialty of boiled salt cod and potatoes often topped with onions fried in pork fat. Many Lunenburg citizens in the 18th and 19th centuries ate salt cod and potatoes out of necessity but made the best of a bad situation with culinary magic. Old habits die hard, and modern-day Lunenburgers are still enjoying the magic at breakfast or dinner, sometimes also calling it a Lunenburg mess. *See also* house bunkin, Lunenburg pudding.

RECIPE

Dutch Mess

Tear ½ lb salt cod into small pieces and soak in cold water for 4 hours. In a large pot boil 6 potatoes, and when half-cooked, toss in the salt fish and cook until potatoes are tender. While the potatoes are cooking, dice an egg-sized piece of salt pork into a frying pan and fry until brown. Add 2 onions cut into rounds and fry until golden. Throw in an egg-sized piece of butter, 1 Tbsp apple vinegar and 3 Tbsp heavy cream. Cook to a boil and pour over the fish and potatoes.

E

EAGLE BRAND SWEETENED CONDENSED MILK—a mix of milk and cane sugar that is vacuum evaporated. Invented by American Gail Borden in 1856 and on the market as Eagle Brand in 1857, the product was first manufactured in Canada at the Ingersoll Dairy in 1899. The sweetened milk had a long shelf life and was great for baking, for whitening coffee and tea, for feeding kids and for military rations, and it could easily be shipped by rail across Canada. Now owned by Smucker's, Eagle Brand is still a fine product and remains a Canadian favourite. *See also* Carnation evaporated milk.

EARTH OVEN—a stone-lined, hole-in-the-ground fire pit universally employed to cook three kinds of foods: bulbs, starchy corms such as taro, and fatty meats. Canadian coastal tribes employed earth ovens to cook camas bulbs. *See also* blue camas.

ECONOMY CAKE (also called poor-man's cake, poverty cake)—a popular ingredient-saving cake of World War I with no milk, no eggs and no butter. Economy cake became popular again during the Depression and World War II rationing.

RECIPE

Economy Cake

In a saucepan, mix 1 cup each of water and brown sugar, 1½ Tbsp each of lard and cinnamon, and a pinch of salt, and bring to a boil. Reduce heat, add ½ lb raisins or dried berries and simmer for 15 minutes. Sift 1½ cups flour with ½ tsp baking powder and stir into cooled wet mix. Pour into a greased 9-inch pan and bake at 350°F for 20–30 minutes.

E.D. SMITH FOODS LTD—established by Ernest D'Israeli Smith in the late-19th century, this pillar of Canadian agricultural processing (making jams, jellies, condiments, etc.) was sold off to a firm of U.S. investment opportunists in 2001 and turned over again in 2007 to TreeHouse Foods, resulting in the loss of hundreds of Canadian jobs and a market for Canadian farm produce.

EDAMAME—immature soybeans (*Glycine max*) popular in Asian cuisines and now available in Canadian markets. Boil the pods in salted water until tender, about 2–3 minutes, then plunge them into ice water to stop the cooking. Drain the

water, sprinkle them liberally with sea salt and serve. To eat, split the pods and release the edible seeds inside. *See also* soybean.

EEL—eel prepared in any manner was a familiar food to our pioneer ancestors. The fish was plentiful in European waters and was served as "food for the masses," but it was also a favourite of landed gentry. Several species are found in Canadian waters, but modern times have seen a marked decrease in the popularity of eel, probably owing to both the fish's resemblance to snakes and the fatty content of the meat. Up to 60 percent of eel meat is fat, and a good percentage of that is artery-clogging saturated fat. Still, a little is not going to hurt, and if you get a chance for a little, make it smoked.

EEL PIE—a casserole topped with pastry. It was a common dish of early settlers along the St. Lawrence River because the slippery, snaky fish could be caught there almost anywhere and at any time of year.

EELS IN CREAM—a favourite Québec habitant dish wherein the plentiful eels of the St. Lawrence River were skinned, chopped into bite-sized pieces and stewed in fresh cream, apple cider, onions and salt pork. Further south in Colonial New England, molluscs were substituted for eel and the dish became known as clam chowder.

EGG CREAM SANDWICH—an Ontario specialty, consisting of chopped hard-boiled eggs mixed with cottage cheese, mayonnaise, chopped pimento and seasoning.

EGG FOO YONG—a fried egg, meat and vegetable omelet dish created by Chinese cooks working on the 19th-century North American railway expansion.

Chinese Railway Cooks

- Chinese railway cooks created a unique stir-fry cuisine that leaned toward meat rather than traditional Chinese vegetable dishes. Chow mein, chop suey and breaded chicken balls are a few examples of that enduring cuisine.

EGGPLANT (*Solanum melongena*; also called aubergine)—a semi-tropical perennial fruit and a member of the Nightshade family, eggplant is a close relative of the tomato and potato. A culinary favourite for its ability to soak up flavours and oils, the fruit has been a staple in the Canadian food experience since early times. Varieties range in shape from small and round to long and slender, and in colour from white to deep purple. One of the best is Black Beauty, grown since 1910.

RECIPE

Eggplant Parmesan

Cut 1 medium eggplant into slices, brush both sides with olive oil and set onto broiler pan rack. Broil until tender, turning once, about 10 minutes. While eggplant slices are cooking, mix ⅓ cup Parmesan cheese with ¼ cup breadcrumbs and fork toss with 2 tsp olive oil. Place cooked eggplant slices into a casserole and top with 1 cup mozzarella cheese. Spoon on the breadcrumb mixture and return to broiler until cheese is melted and breadcrumbs begin to brown, about 1 minute. Remove from broiler and top with heated pasta sauce and shredded mozzarella.

EGGS—poultry eggs are graded A, B and C, with the A quality reserved for retail. In Canada, eggs are weighed individually and packaged according to weight:

- Peewee . . . . less than 42 g
- Small . . . . 42–48 g
- Medium . . . . . . 49–55 g
- Large . . . . 56–62 g
- Extra-large . . . . 63–69 g
- Jumbo . . . . 70 g or more

A
B
C
D
E
F
G
H
I
J
K
L
M
N
O
P
Q
R
S
T
U
V
W
X
Y
Z

BATTERY EGGS

Canadians consume lots of eggs, so many that there is nearly one laying hen for every citizen, but nearly all those hens are confined in tiny wire cages, never see the light of day and are only released from bondage for slaughter. This battery system of egg production does produce a lot of eggs, but they are poor quality. To condition consumers to buy the almost tasteless ovals, supermarkets simply made battery eggs the only game in town, a marketing ploy still popular today. However, many supermarkets are now stocking more humanely produced eggs that are a taste revelation to consumers. Consumers wanting even more of a taste revelation are advised to purchase fresh, free-range eggs at farm gates and farmers' markets. Mmmm, they are good and healthy too, containing more omega-3 fatty acids than battery eggs.

EGGS IN ASHES—fresh eggs holed with a pin and set into the hot ashes of a hearth. Eggs are cooked and ready to serve when a drop of white appears through the pinprick on top. It was a handy trick in pioneer days and still a good one for modern-day campers.

EISWEIN. *See* ice wine.

ELDERBERRY (*Sambucus canadensis*)—the American elderberry tree is a species ubiquitous in southern Ontario and Québec, as well as all through the eastern U.S. Used to treat wounds and respiratory ailments, the berries also made a passable jelly, good wine and an excellent flavouring for bootleg whisky, while the flowers can be used to flavour pancakes.

Elderberries

- Long known to have medicinal qualities, especially for arthritis, the tiny, blue-black berries have been identified as rich in antioxidants and cancer-fighting properties, and they are now a hot property with foragers.

- Oil extracted from elderflowers is one of the flavouring components of the popular Italian liqueur, Sambuca.

ELDERBERRY PANCAKES—a rare treat in early spring when the elderberry tree blooms. The blossoms are picked, the veins and stems removed and the flowers mixed into buttermilk pancake batter that is quickly popped onto a griddle and fried before the blossoms wilt. Elderberry blossoms impart a delicious nutty flavour to pancakes, which are especially good with butter and high-quality maple syrup.

ELDERBERRY PIE—a delectable pie made from the blue-black fruit of the elderberry tree and a favourite dessert of pioneer families. Nowadays, this delight is made even better when served with a big scoop of vanilla ice cream.

ELDERBERRY WINE—a pioneer favourite because the small, blue-black berries grow in clumps and are easily gathered, and both fruit and flowers make a delicious wine.

RECIPE

Elderberry Wine

Soften mashed berries in a covered pan or crock, immerse container in water and turn up the heat. At the simmer, remove berries, sieve and add 1 lb sugar for every 4 cups juice, along with 8 cups water. Boil the liquid while skimming until scum ceases to rise. Cool, then add 2 cups brandy and filter into casks. Set the bung loosely until fermentation stops. Bung tightly and allow 6 months for maturing before clarifying with egg whites.

A
B
C
D
E
F
G
H
I
J
K
L
M
N
O
P
Q
R
S
T
U
V
W
X
Y
Z

ELDERFLOWER CORDIAL—before soda pop, there was elderflower cordial, sumac tea and spruce beer, and the cordial is the best of that lot. You can buy it ready to drink at IKEA or make it yourself if the elderberry trees are in bloom. To make it, prepare a simple syrup of equal parts water and sugar and pour over flower heads with stalks and brown bits removed. Give it a few stirs, then cover and refrigerate for a week, stirring now and then. Filter mixture through cheesecloth into bottles, then cap and refrigerate. *See also* spruce beer, sumac tea.

ELEPHANT EARS. *See* beaver tails, dough gods.

ELEPHANT GARLIC (*Allium ampeloprasum*)—while it might look like a huge garlic bulb, it is more closely related to leeks, though with a milder taste. The bulbs of elephant garlic can reach weights that exceed 500 g (1 lb), and while most are imported from the U.S., limited numbers of fresher, better tasting bulbs are available from local growers and at farmers' markets.

ELK (*Cervus canadensis*; also called wapiti)—once readily available, the elk, like the bison, fell victim to market hunters and was nearly hunted to extinction. Today, because of government protection, elk numbers have increased to a point that many areas of Canada are allowing a limited hunt. The animal is also farm-raised, with steaks and roasts available from butchers specializing in game.

> ### RECIPE
>
> #### *Grilled Elk Steak with Blueberry Sauce*
>
> *In a saucepan, reduce 1 pint blueberries, ¼ cup maple syrup and 2 Tbsp vinegar to about half volume (for sweet and sour, steaks can be marinated in the refrigerator overnight in a bath of balsamic vinegar). Heat barbecue or oven grill to 400°F and cook 8 oz steaks for 1½ minutes per side, repeating once. Meat should be medium rare. Top with sauce before serving.*

ELK BURGERS—a favourite of early pioneers and trappers, the elk meat is chopped, fried and stuck into a sliced bannock roll. There is no commercial hunting of elk, but your chances of biting into an elk burger will improve in BC and the Prairie provinces, where around 80,000 of the giant deer roam, with around 5000 taken annually by hunters.

EMBASSY CAVIAR—extracted from wild-caught freshwater fish from the unpolluted lakes of northern Manitoba by the Freshwater Fish Marketing Corporation, the caviar is available from four fish species: lake whitefish, cisco, pike and carp. *See also* Freshwater Fish Marketing Corporation.

EMPIRE CHEESE—a dairy farmers' cooperative in Campbellford, Ontario, producing a wide range of cheeses with emphasis on aged cow's milk Cheddar. Empire has been crafting cheese since 1876 and is a consistent winner at both the British Empire Cheese Competition and the Royal Agricultural Winter Fair.

EMULSION—a blend of two non-compatible liquids, such as oil and water, where one forms tiny droplets that are evenly dispersed in the other through natural or mechanical means. Heavy cream is a natural emulsion but, having reached fat droplet saturation, is unstable to the point that a little mechanical agitation will cause the droplets to merge and become butter. Light cream, sauces, soups, mayonnaise and many other commercial products are unstable emulsions that without the addition of an emulsifier or binder—usually a gum, alginate or lecithin—will either break or curdle.

ENGLISH MILK PUNCH—a favourite east coast drink of lemons, rum, milk and nutmeg. The mixture is set aside overnight, filtered through a jelly bag and drunk clear and chilled.

ENZYME—a protein that may work in combination with another substance called a coenzyme to alter a specific medium called a substrate. Most enzymes that act on a specific substrate are named for the substance and end with the letters "-ase," so "pectinase" is an enzyme that works on fruit pectin, and "invertase" is an enzyme that puts the caramel into Caramilk candy bars. Unrestricted enzyme action in fruits and vegetables causes ripening and rotting, a condition that may slowed or halted by heat, salt, sugar or pickling chemicals such as vinegar.

ÉPERLANS. See fried smelts.

ESCOFFIER, AUGUSTE (1846–1935)—monumental chef and Parisian restaurateur who, in partnership with César Ritz, opened a string of successful restaurants and streamlined the cooking process with a brigade system wherein the *chef de cuisine* is top flight, followed by the *sous chef de cuisine*, then the *chefs de partie* or line cooks. Of importance to Canada is his designing of kitchens and menus for transatlantic luxury steamships and their adoption by Canadian Pacific ships and hotels. *See also* Canadian Pacific Railway.

ESKIMO PIE—invented in 1920 and introduced to Canadians in the summer of 1921 by the William Neilson Company (now a division of Saputo Inc.), this famous brand name chocolate-coated ice cream bar on a stick was the first ice cream novelty that paved the way for an entire industry. Originally sold out of special countertop thermos buckets in drugstore soda fountains, the bars eventually lost out to dairy-installed ice cream freezers and locally produced novelties. For a time the Eskimo Pie brand was owned by the now defunct Cool Brands, a Canadian franchiser of frozen vegetable gum yogurt, but it is now the property of Dryer's Grand Ice Cream Holdings Inc., a division of Swiss mega-conglomerate Nestlé SA.

ESKIMO POTATO. *See* northern rice-root.

ETHYLENE RIPENING—the process of picking unripe fruits and vegetables and packing them into almost airtight shipping containers and truck trailers with canisters of the ripening gas ethylene for shipment to faraway markets. Canadian supermarket produce sections are filled with fruits and vegetables grown half a world away.

EULACHON (*Thaleichthys pacificus*; also called candlefish, oolichan)—an oily member of the Smelt family and an important food source for First Nations of the Pacific coast. Eulachon are the first fish to make a spawning run into BC rivers, and their arrival was, and still is, awaited patiently by native fishermen, flocks of gulls and hundreds of bald eagles.

Eulachon

- In the early days, oil rendered from eulachon enjoyed such intertribal trade that the trails used to transport the oil became narrow roads called "grease trails" by explorers and pioneer settlers.

- Eulachon contain so much oil that, once dried, an inserted wick will light up the fish like a candle—hence their more common name, candlefish.

EVENING PRIMROSE (*Oenothera biennis*; also called fever plant, large rampion)—a biennial native plant with large, hard roots consumed by First Nations. Exported to Europe during the 17th century by the Hudson's Bay Company, the plant is still extensively cultivated there for its medicinal oil. Evening primrose roots must be boiled to remove their sharp, peppery taste and then seasoned and doused with butter, or they can be served up fried.

F

FABA BEAN. *See* horse bean.

FAD DIETS—both early and modern fad diets have profoundly affected food production in Canada and the U.S., and it's not hard to imagine what happens when a few hundred thousand people either stop or start consuming certain foods. Apples that are thought healthy one year are deemed high-sugar fat producers the next; meats are gobbled up and then put on hold; all manner of vegetables are popular and then not; fat pigs were in then out; grains were good but corn was better, until it wasn't. Keeping up with the fad diets of Canadians has caused widespread confusion in the food-processing industry and for its suppliers, the farmers, who are often caught holding the bag. *See also* Inuit diet, Ruby Red grapefruit.

FAIR-TRADE ORGANIZATIONS—a sensible alternative to the greedy depredation of offshore labour pools and companies by conglomerate public corporations. Fair-trade organizations (FTOs) work with farmers, artisan cooperatives and food processors in foreign countries in an attempt to keep jobs and profits at home.

FALLOW DEER (*Dama dama*)—a Middle Eastern species introduced to Europe and Britain by

early Romans and then to the Americas as park animals during the 19th century. The succesful ranching of fallow deer in New Zealand in the 20th century led to fallow deer ranches in Canada, and they are now ranched in all provinces save Alberta. Gentle, easy to raise, comparatively disease free, and with lean, tasty meat, these animals are the future of cervid game ranching in Canada.

FALSE SAMPHIRE. *See* goose tongue.

FAMEUSE APPLE. *See* snow apple.

FAMINE FOODS—many native shrubs produce nutritious berries not normally consumed owing to bitter or astringent qualities, while the inner bark of several tree species makes for a palatable soup. Animals not normally seen on tables would appear during hard times: skunk, raccoon, groundhog, porcupine and birds such as robins and blackbirds. Both dandelion and purslane are weeds well known to Canadian gardeners, but they can make passable salad greens. *Tripe de roche* (literal translation: rock guts) is an easily found lichen and provides sustenance for the truly desperate. *See also* dandelion, purslane, rock tripe.

FARM HOUSE BUTTER—a superior grade of artisan butter from a mixed herd of Jersey and Swiss Brown cows churned at the Farm House Natural Cheeses dairy farm in BC's lush Fraser Valley. Farm House butter is available at the family-run Farm House dairy store or in Vancouver at the three locations of Les Amis du Fromage.

FARMERS' MARKETS. *See* market squares.

FAST FOOD—a phrase that came into use during the early 1950s drive-in restaurant craze that has now become a blanket term for any food not served at a dinner table.

A
B
C
D
E
F
G
H
I
J
K
L
M
N
O
P
Q
R
S
T
U
V
W
X
Y
Z

FAT ARCHIES (also called boot heels)—a Nova Scotia favourite ginger cookie made either thin and crisp, thick and soft, or cut in squares from a sheet. Ginger was used by fishermen to allay the effects of seasickness and therefore was ubiquitous in the Maritimes, and cookies were the men's preferred way of taking their medicine.

FAT HEN. *See* lamb's quarters.

FATBACK—salt pork, but different in that it contains no streaks of lean meat and is all hard fat from under the skin of the back as opposed to soft or leaf lard found in a hog's abdominal cavity. Fatback may be fried like bacon, used as a sausage ingredient or rendered down to produce lard for baking. *See also* lard.

FAVA BEAN. *See* horse bean.

FECULA—a descriptive term used for starches that have been made pure by washing in water as opposed to normal flour that contains starch but also protein and other substances. Cornstarch and tapioca are feculas, as is potato starch.

FERRER, JÉRÔME (b. 1972)—chef extraordinaire, owner of Restaurant Europea, Birk's Café, Beaver Hall and many others, and provider of some of Montréal's principal gastronomic experiences.

FÊTE DES VENDANGES—held in Magog, Québec, on the first two weekends in September, this harvest festival features around 150 exhibitors of mostly artisanal foods.

FEVER PLANT. *See* evening primrose.

FÈVES AU LARD (also called *les binnes*)—baked navy beans cooked with salt pork and sweetened with maple syrup or sugar. A Québec favourite anytime but prepared religiously at annual sugaring-off feasts and the many Québec syrup-gathering operations that are open to tourists.

FIDDLEHEAD (*Matteuccia struthiopteris*)—the coiled, unfurled and tender shoot of the ostrich fern. Both foraged and commercially cultivated in New Brunswick and Québec, fresh fiddleheads

are available nationally during early spring and in the frozen section of supermarkets year-round. Jiggle them in a brown paper bag to remove the brown bits, then steam and serve buttered.

FIDDLEHEAD CHOWDER—an east coast spring favourite made just like a normal chowder but substituting fiddleheads for clams or fish.

FIELD SALAD. *See* lamb's lettuce.

FIFTH TOWN ARTISAN CHEESE COMPANY—goat and sheep's milk cheeses crafted in Picton, Ontario, at one of the world's most eco-friendly dairies. Fifth Town won first prize for goat cheese at the 2009 British Empire Cheese Competition, and their combination goat/sheep's milk cheese is wonderful as well. Sold only in Ontario for the time being, their cheeses are also available online.

FIGGY DUFF—a Newfoundland pudding made from flour or breadcrumbs, molasses, raisins and spices placed into a muslin pudding bag for a few hours of steaming. Newfoundland figgy duff was, and still is, usually served with coady sauce. *See also* coady sauce.

Figgy Duff

- "Figgy" was a word used by English gentry as a mockery of the fruit used by common folk who couldn't afford figs: namely, raisins.

- In Newfoundland, all pudding desserts are called "duffs"—a word taken from the English pudding plum duff—and raisins provide the figgy.

FILBERT. *See* hazelnut.

FINNAN HADDIE—cold-smoked haddock cooked in butter and milk and borrowed from the Scots as a dinnertime dish rather than for breakfast. Smoked haddock did not ship well and the dish remained mostly a Maritime favourite until the railway came along in the mid-19th century and made it a favourite luncheon dish for businessmen across the country.

FIRE WATER—a translation of the 18th-century Ojibwa word for trade whisky, a horrible concoction created by fur traders as a tool to cheat First Nations out of their furs and into cheap blankets.

FIREWEED (*Chamerion angustifolium*)—a common perennial in Canada's west and north with a proclivity for popping up after wildfires, hence its name. The new shoots taste like asparagus when boiled, and the leaves of mature plants make excellent salad greens with a taste reminiscent of spinach.

FIREWEED HONEY—a fantastic honey derived from flowers of fireweed, a western wildflower. The honey can often be found at farmers' markets in the Prairie provinces and may be ordered online.

FIRST NATIONS FARE—in 1534, when Jacques Cartier and his crew jumped out of their ship's landing boat to claim Canada for France, only a small contingent of its more than one million indigenous residents were on hand to witness the event: a handful of Mi'kmaqs with trade on their minds. Cartier and his men were wary of the traders but soon warmed to the idea, and as was the Mi'kmaq custom, they were treated to lunch while trade ensued. No strangers to trading with Europeans, as both Portugese and Basque fishing boats occasionally landed to take on water, the Mi'kmaqs wanted metal pots and knives and likely treated Cartier and his men to bean soup, oysters on the half shell, lobsters, fish, roast venison and spruce beer while they presented their trade goods, the furs that would start a race to riches by France, England and the Netherlands.

FISH 'N' BREWIS—a traditional Newfoundland and Labrador Sunday morning breakfast dish. Fresh or salt cod was cooked and served with water-softened hardtack biscuits and usually topped with fried bacon bits called scrunchions. *See also* brewis, scrunchions.

FISH 'N' CHIPS—you can take the Brit out of England, but you can't take England out of the Brit, and in Canada, the defining English food of the late-19th century was a culinary phenomenon called fish and chips—salted, with a splash or two of malt vinegar.

Fish 'n' Chips

- During the early part of the 20th century, there were as many as 35,000 fish and chip shops across Britain. Today, there are around 8500 producing 300 million servings annually.

- Only in Canada will you find an order of fish and chips accompanied by a wedge of lemon and a side of coleslaw.

RECIPE

Fish and Chips

Fish: In a bowl, mix some salt and pepper with 1½ cups flour and whisk in a bottle of beer along with 1 tsp baking soda; let batter sit for 20 minutes. Place ½ cup flour on a plate and dredge whatever fish you prefer (fresh walleye is wonderful, but cod is traditional). Dip flour-dredged fish into batter and fry in oil at a temperature of 350°F until golden brown. Serve heaped with chips, a lemon wedge, coleslaw and tartar sauce.

Chips (traditional): Square potatoes (the russet is best) with a knife and cut ½-inch slices lengthwise; turn potato and cut into ¼-inch slices. Rince sliced potatoes in cold running water and place into a bowl of cold water for 2–3 hours (removing every trace of starch so your chips will crisp nicely).

Heat oil in a saucepan to 375°F (keep oil level to one-third of the pot to avoid a conflagration and use a thermometer for the temperature). Dry chips with paper towel, place into a wire frying basket and carefully lower into the hot oil. After the bubbling has ceased, cover the pan, cook for 5–6 minutes and remove basket from oil. Chips should be cooked through, but not brown. Allow the oil to reheat to 390°F (use that thermometer), place wire basket with chips back into oil and cook until brown (about 2 minutes). Remove wire basket, shake out chips onto paper towels and sprinkle with salt. Serve immediately.

FISH LOAF—a ubiquitous loaf pan dish consisting of flaked fish (cod, haddock, etc.) combined with bread crumbs, chopped celery, onions, green pepper and pimentos, held together by egg, milk, salt, pepper and lemon juice. Cod is best, but during trying times—economic depressions or wars—canned salmon or tuna substitutes nicely. Refrigerated overnight, any leftovers will slice easily for sandwiches.

FISH PASTE—Canada's contribution to the Jewish culinary experience is not confined to supplying the Montréal bagel or smoked salmon; it also includes the whitefish paste produced by Winnipeg's Freshwater Fish Marketing Corporation, from which gefilte is crafted. *See also* Freshwater Fish Marketing Corporation, gefilte fish.

FISH SAUCE—every civilization has had its favourite fish sauce, from the Roman obsession with "garum" to the very English Worcestershire sauce, with a few thousand in-between sauces. Most fish sauces are made from the fermented innards of fish, and even though Canada has huge supplies of innards, fish sauces are typically imported because of the unbelievable odour raised by the manufacturing process. That odour long ago prompted sauce makers to replace smelly fish oil with tomato paste and call it ketchup. *See also* ketchup.

FISH STICKS—an easy-to-prepare "fast food" invented in the early 1950s by Newfoundland native Dr. William Forsey Hampton, director of research at General Seafoods.

A B C D E **F** G H I J K L M N O P Q R S T U V W X Y Z

FISH ON FRIDAY

Both the Bible and the Koran prohibit the consumption of pork, but in his letter to the Romans, St. Paul, a founding member of Christianity, declared that all food was a gift from God and should be considered clean (Romans 14:20), a pronouncement that worked like a starter's gun to put sausages on tables and fill barnyards with pigs. Then, in the 9th century, Pope Innocent III became the next monkey wrench in the gears of normal food production when he commanded Catholics to abstain from eating red meat on Fridays.

This well-intentioned Papal edict, meant to support fishermen and their mongers, inadvertently became the first "best before" stamp that has endured for centuries, becoming the impetus for much thought and technological tinkering over how to get the buying public to forget Fridays and consume more fish all week long. There is plenty of fish to be had, but even consumers living close to sources would only buy fish a few days of the week to ensure its freshness. Fish has always been part and parcel of the Canadian food experience, but mostly on Fridays. Then along came Clarence Birdseye, who, in 1925, perfected a way to flash-freeze fish and put it onto dinner tables any day of the week. This fish came squared in a box and was perfect for home freezers.

FISHERMAN'S HASH (*chiard du pêcheur*)—an old-time specialty of the Côte-du-Sud area of Québec prepared by fishermen's wives using salt pork and the hardtack biscuits common to all seafarers' galleys.

RECIPE

Chiard du pêcheur

Layer the bottom of a 2-quart casserole with sliced potatoes, then add a layer of sliced onion, a layer of chopped salt pork and a sprinkle of pepper. Continue layering until almost to the top and carefully add cold water until level with hash. Cook over medium heat until almost boiling, then reduce heat and simmer until potatoes are cooked and liquid has reduced, about 30 minutes. Cover hash with hardtack biscuits and cook another 10 minutes.

FIVE ROSES FLOUR—not bleached or blended and milled from only the finest quality wheat, Five Roses flour made Lake of the Woods Milling Company the largest milling concern in the British Commonwealth. From 1887 to 1967, Five Roses flour shipped worldwide and earned both the company and Canada a reputation as the world's premier supplier of wheat and wheat-based products. Now owned by the U.S. food conglomerate Smucker's, the flour is still one of the best and remains popular with Canadian cooks. *See also* Robin Hood flour.

FIVE ROSES

The Lake of the Woods Milling Company published the *Five Roses Cook Book* in 1913. Over the years, this cookbook succeeded in upgrading the culinary skills of untold thousands of Canadian housewives and produced a Canadian style of cooking. In 1954, the Lake of the Woods Milling Company was acquired by Ogilvie Flour Mills of Winnipeg. Then in 1993, Ogilvie was acquired by the U.S. conglomerate Archer Daniels Midland Company, which a decade or so later sold Canada's favourite flour brand, Five Roses, to Smucker's, the jam people.

Types of Wheat Flour

- All-purpose: a bleached or unbleached mix of hard and soft wheat flours with a gluten content of 9–11 percent.

- Bread: bleached or unbleached flour made from hard, red winter wheat with a gluten content of 12.5–14 percent.

- Cake: bleached soft flour with a gluten content around 8 percent.

- Graham: unbleached whole grain flour with germ and bran removed and bran added back.

- Pastry: a commercial grade flour with a gluten content around 9 percent.

- Self-rising: a mixture of all-purpose flour, salt and baking powder.

- Semolina: course ground durum wheat sifted to remove the fine flour.

- White-wheat: unbleached white flour with bran and germ removed at milling.

- Whole-wheat: unbleached flour with bran and germ left intact during milling.

FLAN AU BLÉ D'INDE—a cornmeal pancake popular in New Brunswick and called johnny-cakes in the United States, a name probably derived from journey cakes.

FLAPPER PIE—a graham-crusted, custard-filled pie and long-time Prairie favourite.

FLAX SEEDS (*Linum usitatissimum*)—an excellent source of omega-3 and omega-6 fatty acids, flax seeds also contain antioxidants with powerful cancer-fighting properties called lignans, and as a bonus, the seeds will keep you regular like nothing else on the planet. Flax seeds are hard as nails and must be milled into a flour for baking bread,

A
B
C
D
E
F
G
H
I
J
K
L
M
N
O
P
Q
R
S
T
U
V
W
X
Y
Z

Flax

- Flax has been growing in Canada since Louis Hébert, Canada's first permanent settler, brought the seeds in 1617, but it did not become an important crop until immigrant farmers took flax seeds west in the early 1800s. Nowadays, Saskatchewan and Manitoba account for almost half the world's total flax production. Nearly all western-grown flax is destined for export as meal, oil and fibre, with a only a tiny amount used by domestic food producers.

- Ever since scientific studies of the early 1990s revealed the many healthy attributes of flax, it has seen a huge increase in demand.

- Linseed oil, a product of flax, is a main constituent of paint and is used to produce linoleum, a common floor covering.

- Flax fibres are used in the manufacture of linen cloth, rope and matting.

but for everything else—smoothies, topping breakfast cereal, etc.—roasting the seeds is best because they develop a rich, buttery flavour.

FLIPPER PIE. *See* seal flipper pie.

FLOP. *See* lobscouse.

FLUMMY DUMM—a quick bread or bannock made by hunters and fur trappers in Newfoundland and Labrador: combine two handfuls of Indian meal (cornmeal), a little soda, salt and water enough to make a dough, knead a bit, spear onto a stick and hold over a fire until baked. *See also* bannock.

FOIE GRAS—enlarged goose livers, an exotic comestible produced in France by force-feeding corn to geese. Never a popular food item with Canadians, this gourmet delight has recently gained popularity as duck foie gras.

SNEAKY FOOD ADDITIVES

In the quest for profits, olive oil importers began to cut their product with sunflower and corn oils, jam manufacturers made strawberry seeds from wood, dairies pumped up the fat content of ice cream with vegetable oil, honey packagers spiked their honey with sugar, and high-fructose corn syrup began replacing expensive cane sugar in almost every processed food. Salmon farmers use food dye to turn their product pink; without that colour, cooked farm-raised salmon bears a marked resemblance to carp. Wild trash fish, anchovies and low-value local catches, have their oils mixed into the food of farmed fish and will provide a hint of flavour, sometimes enough to remind diners what species are being consumed.

Foie Gras

• Animal rights groups around the world have been fighting to have foie gras banned because of the force-feeding nature of its production. Several countries have been persuaded to comply. In the United States, California has instituted a complete ban of the importation, production or sale of foie gras from any source.

FOOD AND WINE ROUTES—almost all Canadian provinces have food and/or wine routes that are either mapped or marked with highway signs. Québec, Ontario and BC have both wine and food routes, while most others have food routes that include vineyards or cider presses. See also *la route des vins*.

FONDA (also called Canadian fonda)—a baked egg omelet consisting of a little flour paste stirred into 1 cup milk, 6 eggs separated and beaten lightly, a spoonful of butter and a dash of salt and mixed together only slightly. Bake for 15 minutes; sprinkle with cinnamon and sugar before serving.

FOOD ADDITIVE DICTIONARY—a dictionary of permitted food additives published by Health Canada for the education of consumers. Besides acquainting consumers with the chemical names, the dictionary also supplies a reason for their use in a section entitled "What Additives Do." The dictionary is available on the Heath Canada website.

A
B
C
D
E

F

G
H
I
J
K
L
M
N
O
P
Q
R
S
T
U
V
W
X
Y
Z

FOOD COLOURS—there are 10 synthetic colours and 25 natural colours permitted as food additives in Canada, the U.S. and Europe, with each agency of oversight having different names or numbers for each permitted colour. While most colours are considered safe with reasonable consumption, processed food manufacturers have grossly exceeded that safe amount, and a few dyes are now suspected disease contributors.

FOOD SAFETY—food safety issues are great disruptors of normal food production, and as big companies bought out small to become conglomerates distributing nationwide, the danger of contamination by human pathogens

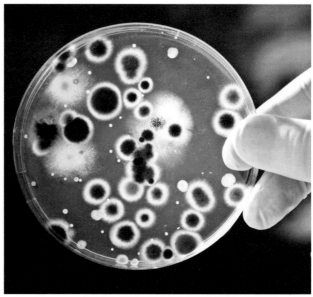

became a national problem. Bad bugs create fear in the populace and can completely derail harvest and distribution of both infected and non-infected produce, and almost every fruit and vegetable has taken a turn. Chickens and livestock are infamous for harbouring bacteria that can transmit to humans through sloppy food processing and packaging. Most of those affected think they have a touch of the flu, while the elderly, the very young and those with compromised immune systems must think

---

PROCESSED FOOD SAFETY

Canada is a nation so inured to the vagaries of processed foods that words such as good fats, transfats, neutral fats and glycosides have become almost meaningless. Canadians read about how margarine rots the liver, genetically modified produce causes allergies and the seaweed in ice cream causes cancer—or maybe not, because for every food safety study, there are reports—most of which are sponsored by the food conglomerates—that contravene unsafe findings.

In the battle for consumer dollars, if conglomerates can convince the buying public that

a competitor's product is unhealthy, they can add serious numbers to their bottom line, and they are not averse to using dirty tricks to bolster those figures. American sugar conglomerates have spent millions of dollars convincing both the public and government food regulators that artificial sweetners saccharin and cyclamate will, rather than might, cause bladder cancer in humans like they do in lab rats fed the equivalent of two 355 mL cans of artificially sweetened soft drinks daily. U.S. food regulators responded by banning cyclamates, while Canadian regulators banned the saccharin.

death is just around the corner. In 2003, bovine spongiform encephalopathy (BSE, or mad cow disease) slammed the brakes on the Canadian beef industry, necessitating the slaughter of over 600,000 beef cows as nobody was buying and ranchers could not afford to keep them. It took the beef industry years to regain consumer confidence, and just when things were looking rosy again, Canada Packers precipitated a total recall in 2008 and XL Foods recalled all their meat products in 2012, with both causing a massive loss in consumer confidence. *See also* Canadian Food Inspection Agency.

FOOL (also called foole)—immigrants to Canada have historically brought along their food taboos, and during the 18th and 19th centuries, some new Canadians believed fruit was an unhealthy food, a belief probably reinforced by the use of arsenic to spray orchards. The rule of thumb to fixing unhealthy foods was to "boil the devil from them" and make fool; in other words, to turn good fruit into sauce. The sauce itself was "fixed" by mixing in a few dollops of whipped cream, sweetened if the fruit was tart and otherwise unsweetened. For those uninitiated to the joys of fool, rhubarb fool is the one to try.

FORESTRY PUDDING—a Canadian settlers' variation of the very English steamed caramel pudding using lard and baking powder to replace eggs and butter, with the cake smothered in butterscotch sauce rather than caramel.

FORFAR DAIRY CHEESE—since 1863, the Forfar Dairy in Portland, Ontario, has produced superb aged Cheddars using a heat process rather than pasteurization and presses curds the old-fashioned way: in wheels. Forfar makes a wide variety of cheeses, including chèvre, and all are available at outlets across Canada and online. Cut from a 40-kg wheel, their five-year-old Cheddar is a memorable experience.

FOX GRAPE (*Vitis labrusca*)—the wild grape that Cartier found growing everywhere made a disgusting wine but was later found useful for hybridizing grape varieties more amenable to viniculture, such as Concord, Catawba and Niagara. Nowadays, except for Passover wines, the hybrids of fox grapes are used for making grape jelly and to supply the table grape market.

FOXBERRY. *See* partridgeberry.

FOXY—a wine-tasting term used to describe the grape jelly flavour of wild grapes and cultivated varieties of fox grapes, such as the Concord grape.

FRAGRANT SUMAC TEA. *See* sumac tea.

FRAISE DES BOIS. *See* alpine strawberry.

FRANKENFOODS—a word invented to describe genetically modified foods. *See also* irradiated foods.

FRANKUM—a Newfoundland word for the resinous sap of spruce trees that is gathered, aged a few days and used for chewing gum. *See also* spruce gum.

FRENCH BREAD—the national loaf of France. Until 1921, when Cousin's Charcutier began baking the bread in Montréal, it was never a product of Canadian bakeries. Nowadays, many artisanal bakers produce French bread, but you have to pick and choose to secure a decent loaf. Fat and dusted with flour does not always equal real French bread. French bread requires more patience from the baker: the right flour and yeast, no additives in the flour, hand kneading and long resting times for the dough.

FRENCH CANADIAN PEA SOUP. *See* pea soup.

FRENCH-FRIED SCALLOPS—one of the dishes that must be tried before you die. Get them from a food truck parked so close to the ocean you can hear the waves.

FRENCH TOAST. See *pain perdu*.

FRESHWATER FISH MARKETING CORPORATION—headquartered in Winnipeg and liking to call themselves simply Freshwater Fish, this company buys, processes and distributes all commercial freshwater fish caught in the provinces of Manitoba and Alberta as well as the Northwest Territories.

FRICÔT—an Acadian word for a meat, fish or poultry stew, as in *Fricôt à la poulet*, or chicken stew. Except for fish, any game meats and poultry should be stewed for a long period

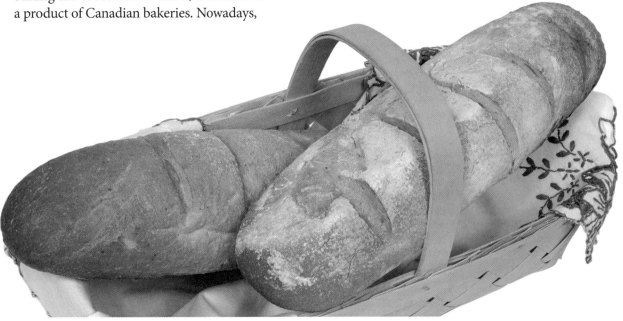

to tenderize the meat. Nowadays, fricôt is still immensely popular in Québec and parts of the Maritimes, but cooking times are considerably shortened owing to the availability of tender meats and poultry.

FRIED BALONEY—a Newfoundland favourite from back in the day and still so popular it can make an appearance at breakfast, lunch or dinner.

FRIED PIG EARS. See *oreilles de crisse*.

FRIED SMELTS (also called *éperlans*)—smelts are a family of small fish found in coastal seas, rivers and lakes. Delicious any way you cook them, but especially tasty fried, purchase them from small stands and chip wagons that dot the roadsides along the St. Lawrence River. *See also* smelts.

FRIED WALLEYE. *See* walleye.

FRIED-OUT PORK—a Maritime method of cooking salt pork to a crisp for a breakfast meat or scrunchions.

FRITTER—an English word meaning a small bit of fish, meat, vegetable or fruit that is battered and fried. All manner of foods have been frittered, with herbs and flowers being a specialty of 14th-century Europe and working up to apples and even just sweetened dough in the 18th and 19th centuries, until fritters burst into the 20th century as crullers and corn dogs.

FROG LEGS—the fried or sautéed back legs of the North American bullfrog (*Rana catesbeiana*). This amphibian is doomed to probable extirpation from its native habitat owing to voracious global demand, with France alone importing over

Froggy Fare

- The American bullfrog was once so common in Canadian wetlands that a few hours of hunting would reap a bounty of hundreds. Tasty, cheap and available almost everywhere, frogs, like crayfish, were hunted almost to extinction in Canada. Today, although frog numbers have recovered enough to allow limited harvesting in some remote wetland areas, most frog legs consumed in Canada are imported.

- Canada is the world's third largest consumer of frog legs, with nearly all of them imported from Indonesia, the world's largest consumer.

- France, the world's second largest consumer, has banned the collecting of frogs for consumption except for a 15-day annual open season, wherein the collected frogs must be consumed on the spot because transportation remains illegal.

- Frog legs became such a craze in 19th-century California that local populations of red-legged frogs were eaten almost to extinction, leading

to the importation of the eastern bullfrog, which quickly became a statewide pest. Oblivious to that danger, the Canadian government promoted frog-farms on Vancouver Island for the employment of returning World War II servicemen. That project failed miserably, but today it has been reinstituted as BC's bullfrog eradication program.

400 million frogs annually. Commercial harvesting in Canada—once a booming enterprise in Ontario, Québec, New Brunswick and Nova Scotia—has waned and is prohibited in some provincial areas. Introduced to BC as a commercial endeavour, the bullfrog has become a pest in that province and is subject to eradication programs.

RECIPE

Crispy Fried Frog Legs

Wash 2 lbs frog legs, pour in ½ cup lemon juice and refrigerate 4 hours (unless you want to see them twitch about). Whisk together 2 egg yolks, ⅓ cup milk and 2 Tbsp oil. Beat 2 egg whites until stiff and fold into yolk and milk mixture. Salt and pepper the legs, dip into egg mixture, dredge in flour and fry in oil.

FROMAGERIE PERRON CHEESE—family run since 1890, this modern cheese plant in Saint-Prime, Québec, produces outstanding cheese with emphasis on Cheddar and some raw milk Cheddar. Fromagerie Perron is a consistent winner at the Royal Agricultural Winter Fair, and its products are available mostly in Québec, with some Ontario and Maritime outlets. For a taste sensation, try its raw milk Cheddar and then write to your MP and ask why unpasteurized milk is not made more readily available to cheese makers across the nation.

FROZEN BABY FOOD—another "why didn't I think of that" product and a Canadian original made by Mother Hen Baby Food Inc., a Montréal producer of homestyle, frozen baby foods.

FRUIT BUTTERS—plums, peaches, berries, apples, etc., mixed with sugar and spices and simmered into a thick, delicious jam spread. Apple and plum butters were popular in Canada's formative years because they made a fair replacement for butter. Nowadays, whizzing the softened fruit in a food processor can reduce the long simmering time.

FRUIT COMPOTES—rhubarb rhizomes and peach pits were brought by 18th-century settlers for the express purpose of making compote, a simple dessert of fresh fruits, sugar and spices.

A B C D E **F** G H I J K L M N O P Q R S T U V W X Y Z

FRUIT LEATHERS—an age-old specialty of First Nations and a kind of byproduct of pemmican production, wherein a portion of pounded berries destined for pemmican was set onto fireside rocks and dried to the consistency of leather.

FRY BREAD—an Ojibwa version of bannock fried in lard. Originally an unleavened cake made with cornmeal, salt and water, fry bread has evolved to include wheat flour and baking soda and has become a favourite of western First Nations and many fast-food outlets in those areas. *See also* bannock.

FUDGE—a "what to do with the kids on a Sunday afternoon" international culinary treat that became a naturalized Canadian confection through the addition of maple sugar. Maple fudge with all-natural ingredients is a candy extraordinaire.

FUDGE BAR—our version of an American creation and the absolute favourite ice cream novelty bar of the 1960s. Perfected by J.B. Jackson Limited, an ice cream manufacturer in Simcoe, Ontario, the creamiest, fudgiest bar in the known universe disappeared in the early 1970s when that company became an acquisition of the mega-conglomerate Unilever.

FUNGY (also called grunt)—a deep-dish pie from Nova Scotia named "fungy" for the way the steam from the cooking juices poked holes in the top pastry, or "grunt" for the sound the steam makes while escaping said pastry. *See also* blueberry grunt.

FUSSELL'S THICK CREAM—a canned sterilized milk and long-time Newfoundland favourite. You had to shake the can to make the cream thicken, and now Newfoundlanders can shake tins of Nestlé Carnation Light Condensed Milk instead, as the Swiss conglomerate now owns the Fussell brand and uses the same formulation.

G

GAI LAN. *See* Chinese kale.

GALETTE—in France, a *galette* is a buckwheat crepe; in French Canadian homes, it is a sugar cookie; and on Québécois restaurant menus, it is a wheat flour pastry disc usually filled with fresh fruit, folded over and baked.

candy and the Delecto brand of quality hand-dipped boxed chocolates. Canada's oldest candy company currently employs 400 people, distributes across the country and exports to the U.S. and Britain.

GARLIC (*Allium sativum*)—a bulbous plant with onion relations around the globe, the culinary strain is thought to be descended from a wild

GALVAUDE—a fries-and-gravy poutine with chunks of turkey or chicken and green peas instead of cheese curds.

GAMMON—originally a butcher's term for the hind leg of a pig, in modern times it has come to mean the cured but uncooked upper portion of the ham. It is sold wet-cured but uncooked to provide for steaks of good thickness called gammon steaks.

GANDY—a Newfoundland pancake fried in pork fat and drizzled with molasses.

GANONG BROS—Ganong's company motto says it all: "Canada's Chocolate Family." The entire family has been devoted to producing fine chocolates and candy since the company's 1873 inception in St. Stephen, New Brunswick. Back then, it produced the world's first chocolate bar, while today it crafts the famous Chicken Bone

A
B
C
D
E
F
G
H
I
J
K
L
M
N
O
P
Q
R
S
T
U
V
W
X
Y
Z

variety found in central Asia. Within this culinary species, there are two subspecies: the hard-neck garlic, such as porcelain, rocambole and purple stripe, and the soft-neck, such as silverskin and artichoke garlic. Wild garlic can be found in many countries; in Canada, it is called *A. canadense*, also known as Canada onion or meadow garlic. Garlic grows well in Canada and enjoyed commercial success until federal politicians allowed cheap Chinese imports to drive garlic off Canadian commercial farms. Down but not out, Canadian garlic is

CHINESE GARLIC

Prior to the mid-1990s, many Canadian farmers grew garlic for supermarkets and commercial canners. Then the Chinese came knocking with an offer nobody could refuse: good-quality garlic at 25 percent of the Canadian market price. Our garlic farmers went ballistic and appealed to the Canadian International Trade Tribunal (CITT) for tariff assistance. The CITT responded by imposing a high Canadian grow-ing season tariff on Chinese garlic, as well as on Vietnamese garlic, because they suspected the Chinese would simply ship from that country. Canadian garlic growers rejoiced, but the Chinese garlic sellers were a wily bunch and simply waited until the Canadian growing season had passed. In 2000, the Canadian growers asked the CITT for a five-year tariff extension to cover the entire year. They got that, and Chinese garlic imports slowed from a raging river to a trickle. Then the Chinese simply started shipping their garlic via the Philippines to avoid the tariff, an act that effectively put an end to commercial garlic sales by most Canadian farmers.

now a niche crop of small produce farmers. Look for lots of garlic varieties at farmers' markets.

RECIPE

Roasted Garlic

Cut the end off each of as many unpeeled garlic bulbs as you want to roast and place them cut end up in a shallow roasting pan or muffin tin. Drizzle each head with olive oil and cover with foil. Bake in a 400°F oven until cloves are soft to the touch, about 35 minutes. Allow to cool slightly before squeezing out the caramelized and scrumptious contents. Can be spread on toast, mixed with sour cream for a baked potato topping or incorporated into almost any pasta sauce.

CANADA'S FAVOURITE GARLIC VARIETIES

- German Red—a hard-neck variety that will zing the taste buds like no other.

- Incelium Red—the best soft-neck variety.

- Northern Québec—a large, hard-neck porcelain variety with great taste.

GASPEREAU. *See* alewife.

GEAI BLEU CHEESE—a raw cow's milk blue cheese crafted at La Bergerie Aux 4 Vents in Champ Doré, New Brunswick. Supply is limited, but the cheese is available across Canada in larger centres.

GEFILTE FISH—a Jewish appetizer consisting of ground poached fish—usually pike, carp, or lake whitefish—that is mixed with finely chopped fried onion, matzo meal, eggs, salt and pepper and a little vegetable oil if the fish is dry, with a few handfuls of chopped parsnip and carrot being optional. Stuffing the fish head and boiling it is the traditional cooking method for gefilte, but it can also be prepared as a terrine or patties and either fried or baked.

GEODUCK (*Panopea generosa*; pronounced gooey-duck)—a very large and tasty clam found in the saltwater tidelands of British Columbia's coastal areas. Geoducks are long-lived bivalves, which enable some to attain a considerable size, up to 7 kg. Sadly, their numbers have dwindled as a result of overfishing, and in most coastal areas of BC, the geoduck clam is a protected species. The geoduck has an Atlantic cousin, the propeller clam (*Cyrtodaria siliqua*), which is not endangered and is a good substitute.

GERMAN TURNIP. *See* kohlrabi.

GHOW—a west coast First Nations word meaning tiny herring eggs or spawn attached to kelp fronds, but to financially hard-pressed BC

fishermen, the word means a lucrative source of income because the Japanese are crazy for ghow. *See also* herring roe.

CRAZY FOR GHOW

Called *komochi konbu* in Japan, ghow is a delicacy much in demand for sushi. It is good for the fisherman and good for the herring, because when BC fishermen capture millions of herring to harvest their roe, the herring are unharmed and released back to the sea. Schools of herring are captured by nets and towed to a bay or inlet that has been hand strung with kelp, and after the herring have attached their spawn to the hanging kelp, nets are lifted and the fish are free to leave. It is a sustainable fishery, and Canada accounts for 80 percent of the annual global harvest of 400–500 tonnes.

GINGER BEEF—invented in Calgary by George Wong, owner of the Silver Inn Chinese restaurant, and originally called "deep-fried shredded beef in chili sauce," ginger beef has become a menu fixture of Chinese restaurants nationwide.

GINGER SPICE CAKE—a moist, butter-rich molasses and ginger cake made with either wheat flour or Indian meal. If early settlers had a cow for the butter, they were set. The molasses and spices to make this cake were kitchen staples thanks to constant trade with Caribbean countries. This delicious cake is enjoyed even today, but nowadays, sugar is more commonly employed as a sweetener.

GINGERBREAD—a molasses, flour and ginger cake made uniquely Canadian by the substitution of maple sugar for molasses.

GINGERSNAP—a crisp ginger and molasses cookie favoured by east coast fishermen to allay the effects of seasickness. Ginger was first a medicine, then a flavouring for breads, drinks

and cookies, with early Canadian settlers being supplied via the Carribbean salt fish trade.

GIRL GUIDE COOKIES—in 1927, Regina housewife and Girl Guide leader Christina Riepsamen was looking for a way to raise money to take her girls camping when she hit upon cookies. Selling cookies worked so well that a few years later her idea was adopted by the national organization, and the rest is scrumptious history. In fact, Canadians like Girl Guide cookies so much that over 7 million boxes are sold every year, with the favourite being Christina Reipsamen's original cream sandwich cookie.

GLASSWORT. *See* goose tongue. *See also* sea asparagus.

RECIPE

Old-fashioned Canadian Gingerbread

Sift together 1¾ cup plus 2 Tbsp flour, ½ tsp each of baking soda and ground cinnamon, ¼ tsp each of ground cloves and ginger, and a pinch of salt. In a mixing bowl, combine 6 Tbsp butter with ⅓ cup maple sugar or cane sugar, and beat until light and fluffy. Add 1 large egg and beat while slowly pouring in ¼ cup dark molasses. Add half the dry ingredients and mix well, then add the other half and slowly incorporate ¼ cup cold water. Pour batter into an 8 x 8 inch pan and bake at 350°F for 30–40 minutes or until a knife inserted into the centre comes out clean. Serve with whipped cream sweetened with maple sugar or syrup.

GLUTEN—a combination protein made up of albumins, globulins, glutelins and prolamins, with albumins and globulins making up the bulk of corn and rice, and glutelins and prolamins the bulk of wheat, rye, spelt, graham, barley, etc. The word *gluten* is a Latin word meaning glue, and that is exactly what the proteins do when joined together by the chemical and physical reaction of kneading and baking them in a dough, causing two groups of molecules in the prolamins—the gliadins and glutenins—to stretch and link together while the heat causes the molecule chains to thicken, a combination that permits bread doughs to hold moisture and the gas produced by working yeast.

GLUTEN ALLERGY—Canada's bakery conglomerates know all about the effects of wheat gluten on the health of Canadians, but because their machines work better using processed high-gluten flours, most carry on baking unhealthy, over-glutenized products, with the worst being the ubiquitous "baker's fog" white loaf. Gluten allergy, also known as celiac disease, is a chronic inflammation of the nutrient-absorbing small intestines, and it affects millions of Canadians. Some celiacs have been medically diagnosed, but the majority attribute their condition to heartburn and seek relief with antacid tablets. Wheat gluten causes celiac disease by triggering the production of zonulin, a gene-modified

version of haptoglobin, a tiny protein that cleans the body of used-up hemoglobin, or red blood cells. Zonulin, or haptoglobin 2, has an additional function: clearing the gut of human pathogens, such as *E. coli*, cholera, salmonella, common tourista (traveller's diarrhea) and others. Zonulin does this by allowing water to leak through the intestinal walls so pathogens can be flushed into the bowel, an uncomfortable process called diarrhea. It is a wonderful, often life-saving gene adaptation with one drawback: zonulin is unable to tell the difference between human pathogens and the proteins called glutens that provide dough its elasticity. Ingesting wheat and other grain gluten stimulates production of zonulin, and according to some scientists, it does this to everyone in varying degrees, with production increasing depending on sensitivity and the amounts of wheat gluten consumed over time. *See also* baker's fog.

GOAT CHEESE (also called chèvre)—some of the world's finest goat cheese comes from the Woolwich Dairy in Orangeville, Ontario, and the Mornington Heritage Cheese and Dairy Co-op in Millbank, Ontario, two companies

that turn milk from hundreds of Ontario goat farms into snowy white, award-winning goodness. However, smaller artisanal chèvre producers abound in Canada: Mariposa Dairy in Lindsay, Ontario, produces a superlative single-herd chèvre, and Ran-Cher Acres in Aylesford, Nova Scotia, crafts a delightful chèvre with a dusting of ash. There is also Forfar Dairy near Kingston, Ontario; Hilary's Artisan Cheese in Cobble Hill, BC; Happy Days Goat Dairy in Salmon Arm, BC; and Fairwinds Farms in Leduc, Alberta. Dozens more across Canada are all making the nation proud.

GOLDEN ROASTED FLAX SEEDS—a roasted, buttery, hulled seed product of CanMar Grain Products Ltd. in Regina, Saskatchewan, and a Canadian original. Available in retail and health food outlets as roasted seeds or milled seeds, plain or milled with blueberries, apple cinnamon, pomegranate or chocolate, the seeds can be used in many different healthy ways. Flax seeds are an excellent source of omega-3 and omega-6 fatty acids and contain significant amounts of lignan, an antioxidant with powerful cancer-fighting properties.

GOLDEN SYRUP—in 1882, Charles Eastick, a chemist working for the London sugar melter Abram Lyle, invented a way to turn waste treacle (i.e., molasses) produced by sugar refining into a product they called golden syrup, and the English breakfast was never the same. Canadian soldiers serving in the Boer War and World War I couldn't get enough of it and were thrilled to find it on the shelves of corner stores when they got home. Lyle's is still found on shelves in most Canadian supermarkets, along with Rogers' Golden Syrup, which is refined in Vancouver. Try some on your pancakes instead of maple syrup.

GOLDEYE. *See* Winnipeg goldeye.

GOOSE BARNACLE. *See* gooseneck barnacle.

GOOSE TONGUE (*Salicornia europaea*; also called false samphire, glasswort, pickle weed, samphire greens)—called goose tongue for the plant shoots' resemblance to that French delight, the shoots have a salty taste of the sea, were a common ingredient in Acadian salads and are still available at farmers' markets. They are commonly used as a nesting salad for fried cod tongues and cheeks. *See also* sea asparagus.

GOOSEBERRY (*Ribes grossularioides*)—loved by the English, this berry-producing thorny shrub arrived in Canada as seeds in immigrants'

baggage and journeyed all the way to BC with the wagon trains. For many years, the Canadian government discouraged growers from planting gooseberries because the plants host a fungus that causes blister rust in white pines. However, new disease-resistant hybrids have become available, and the luscious green berry is fast becoming popular again and making appearances at fall farmers' markets.

GOOSEBERRY CATSUP—a real treat for those who can find the gooseberries, and believe me, quite a pile are needed.

RECIPE

Gooseberry Catsup

Combine 8 lbs berries, 4 lbs brown sugar and 1 pint real farm-crafted vinegar. Boil mixture for 3½ hours. Prepare a muslin bag with 2 oz each of ground cloves and cinnamon. Add spice bag to pot and boil for another 15 minutes, then remove bag and pour catsup into a jar.

GOOSEBERRY CRUNCH—a favourite pioneer summer dessert made with plump, fresh gooseberries, brown sugar and oatmeal.

RECIPE

Gooseberry Crunch

In a bowl, mix until crumbly 1 cup each of flour and brown sugar, ¾ cup rolled oats, ½ cup softened butter and 1 tsp cinnamon. Press half of the crumb mixture into a 9-inch buttered pan. In a saucepan, combine 1 cup each of water and sugar, 2 Tbsp cornstarch and 1 tsp vanilla. Bring to a boil, add 4 cups fresh gooseberries and cool until thick. Pour over pressed crumb, top with remaining crumb and bake at 350°F for 45 minutes. When cooled, cut into squares and serve with whipped cream, maple syrup, ice cream or all three.

GOOSEFOOT. *See* lamb's quarters.

GOOSENECK BARNACLE (*Pollicipes pollicipes*; also called *goose barnacle*)—called *percebes* in

Spain and much sought after at tapa bars, this barnacle with the long neck was until recently a west coast chef's secret. Now the secret is out, and not just chefs are scraping these tasty little molluscs off the rocks. Cook them in salty lemon water until the bases turn pink, about 3–4 minutes. Hold them by the shell and dip the necks into cocktail or aioli sauce.

GORTON. *See* cretons.

GOURGANE—a broad bean specialty of Québec's Saguenay–Lac-Saint-Jean region and the principal ingredient of the iconic *soupe aux gourganes*.

GRAHAM FLOUR—named for its inventor, the Reverend Sylvester Graham, a Presbyterian minister in the U.S. who advocated clean living and the consumption of unprocessed foods, especially bread. Graham flour was originally stone ground once to break the wheat berry, then the component parts—the bran, germ and endosperm—were ground again, with the endosperm ground finer, and the parts were recombined. Today, graham flour is roller milled like whole wheat, but exceptions can be found at health food stores or at most supermarkets in the Bob's Red Mill display. Graham crackers derive their name from the graham flour used in their preperation and from the Reverend Graham, who baked the first ones.

GRAHAM GEMS—these treats were the hit of every Presbyterian Church bake sale in Canada during the latter part of the 19th century.

> ### RECIPE
>
> #### Graham Gems
>
> *Combine 1½ cups each of whole-wheat and graham flour, 1½ tsp each of baking powder and soda, ¾ tsp salt and ¼ cup sugar. In a separate bowl combine 1½ cups buttermilk, ¼ cup vegetable oil and 1 egg. Add wet to dry, mix well, spoon into muffin tins and bake in a 375°F oven for 15 minutes.*

GRAISSE DE RÔTI—congealed pork fat that is quite popular in Québec, where it is refrigerated and served with toast or even used as gravy for poutine.

GRANDFATHERS IN MAPLE SYRUP. See *grand-péres.*

GRAND-PÉRES (also called grandfathers in maple syrup)—a boiled doughnut popular in Québec back then and now.

> ### RECIPE
>
> #### Grand-péres
>
> *Whisk together 1 cup flour, ½ cup milk, a pinch of salt and 2 eggs, and drop spoonfuls of dough into a pot of maple syrup that has boiled and been turned down to a simmer. Cover the pot and simmer for 15 minutes, taking care not to lift the lid.*

GRANELLO CHEESE—a hard cow's milk cheese that is so reminiscent of Asiago and Parmesan it can almost transport you to Italy. It is crafted by the oldest family-operated cheese factory in Ontario, the Paron Cheese Company in Binbrook, a company that makes a wide range of single-herd cheeses.

GRANVILLE ISLAND PUBLIC MARKET—a commercial food and bazaar type market just beyond the periphery of Vancouver's downtown created from abandoned industrial lands during

the early 1970s, emulating the Los Angeles Original Farmers' Market. While Granville does feature a seasonal Thursday farmers' market, it caters mostly to tourists. Locals usually frequent the seasonal Trout Lake, Kitsilano, Main Street Station and West End farmers' markets. *See also* market squares.

GRAPE PIE—a crusted dessert pie popular among pioneers, originally made with wild fox grapes (*Vitis labrusca*). Nowadays it is mostly made from the grape's hybrid, the Concord grape, hybridized at Concord, Massachusetts, in 1849. To make, just pop pulp from grape skins and set the skins aside. Put pulp through a food mill or sieve to separate seeds, combine pulp and skins, pour into a baked piecrust, cover with top crust and bake. Do not ever refuse a piece of wild grape pie—it is heaven on a plate. *See also* fox grape.

GRAYLING. *See* Arctic grayling.

GREAVES JAMS AND MARMALADES—a brilliant selection of jams and jellies made the old-fashioned way at Ontario's picturesque Niagara-on-the-Lake since 1927 and available at specialty stores across Canada or online. Try their raspberry spread, 100 percent fruit and probably the best-tasting jam on the planet.

GREEN ALDER PEPPER—when dried and ground to a powder, catkins from the green alder (*Alnus viridis*) make a passable substitute for black pepper.

GREEN COD. *See* lingcod.

GREEN CORN—a once-common name for sweet corn and found so-named in many old cookbooks. *See also* corn.

GREEN CORN PATTIES—fried sweet corn cakes made by pioneer settlers.

RECIPE

Green Corn Patties

Grate 1 pint of kernels from cobs of corn, mix with 1 teacup flour, 1 spoonful butter, 1 egg, and salt and pepper to taste. Form into cakes and fry in butter until golden brown.

GREEN CORN PUDDING—a harvest-time favourite of pioneer settlers made by heating milk, butter and sugar, adding eggs and kernels of sweet corn and then baking. It was usually served with a sauce made of butter, mild and nutmeg.

GREEN TOMATO CHOW CHOW—a Nova Scotia relish made by combining sliced onions with double the amount of sliced green tomatoes.

Green tomato relishes, sauces and ketchups were popular all across early Canada because of the late-ripening characteristics of older varieties of tomatoes. Chow chow is traditionally served with baked beans.

GREEN TOMATO SOUP—a Québec original made with green tomatoes boiled in water that contains onions, cinnamon, cloves, sugar and pepper, then combined with a roux of butter, flour and milk.

GREENLAND HALIBUT. *See* turbot.

GROATS—cleaned, toasted and hulled whole grains of oats, wheat, barley, rye, etc., crushed or steel-cut into small pieces. Prior to 1877, when the American company Quaker Oats perfected a steam-rolling process, all oatmeal was groat that required soaking and long cooking times to soften kernels. Irish oatmeal is groat, while buckwheat groat is called kasha.

GROSSE SOUP—a hardy Acadian soup resembling English hodgepodge and made with beef shank, onions, beans, peas, green beans, potatoes, cabbage, turnips and corn, and flavoured with herbs. *See also* hodgepodge.

GROUND CHERRY (*Physalis virginiana*; also called cape gooseberry)—a favourite with

A B C D E F **G** H I J K L M N O P Q R S T U V W X Y Z

RECIPE

Ground Cherry Pie

Wash 3 cups ground cherries and lay them into a prebaked pie shell. In a bowl, mix together ⅔ cup brown sugar and 1 Tbsp flour and sprinkle over berries. Wet mixture with 2 Tbsp water, sprinkling evenly. In a bowl, combine 3 Tbsp each of flour, sugar and butter and cut with a pastry cutter until crumbly, then layer onto pie. Bake in a 425°F oven for 15 minutes, then turn heat down to 375°F and bake another 25–30 minutes.

Canadian settlers, the ground cherry is a low-growing perennial commonly found at the edges of clearings and along roadways. It is related to the tomatillo (*P. ixocarpa*); both have a cherry-sized fruit surrounded by a papery covering—the cape. Called *cerises de terre* in Québec, these luscious berries with a taste reminiscent of plums and apples were

and still are prized for making pies, jams and jellies.

GROUND CHERRY PIE—one bite and you will think you've gone to heaven. To get more heaven, you'll just have to find more ground cherries.

GROUND LEMON. *See* mayapple.

GROUNDNUT (*Apios americana*; also called Indian potato, potato bean)—not to be confused with its relative the peanut, the groundnut plant does yield similar-looking tubers that, when dried, have a taste reminiscent of peanuts. A climbing perennial native to North American forests, the tubers were a major food source of First Nations and a lifesaver to many early Canadian settlers. Once dried, the beans can be ground into flour and used to thicken stews, extend wheat flour or make bread. Today, groundnuts are a popular forage food and high on the list of plants with a commercial future.

A
B
C
D
E
F

G

H
I
J
K
L
M
N
O
P
Q
R
S
T
U
V
W
X
Y
Z

GROUSE—the name for various species of game bird closely related to the common chicken and with a similar body structure. Grouse are common to all latitudes in North America and represent a substantial portion of the biomass in sub-arctic and arctic latitudes. They are an important food source for a wide range of predators, including humans. Grouse species indigenous to forests and bush (including Canada grouse, also called spruce grouse, *Falcipennis canadensis*) have maintained their numbers in spite of predation, but open-country species have not fared as well because of habitat loss and have been extirpated from their Canadian range in the Prairie provinces and Ontario. A few North American grouse, the sage and ruffed, are not related to grouse proper but carry the name because they are rasorial, meaning they scratch the ground for food.

RECIPE

Berry-glazed Grouse

In a heavy skillet over medium heat, cook 2 Tbsp diced onions until soft and translucent. Add 1½ cups chokecherries, cranberries or huckleberries and ½ tsp fresh rosemary and bring to a boil for 15 minutes while stirring occasionally. Pour half the glaze over grouse and reserve the remainder for periodic basting. Roast the bird at 350°F for approximately 1½ hours, depending on size.

GUAR GUM—a thickener or stabilizer made from the ground endosperm of the seeds of the guar plant and used extensively in the production of breads, dairy products and sauces.

GUÉDILLES—the base for lobster rolls, but any meat, fish, fowl or egg can replace the lobster. Mix chopped lettuce, tomatoes, green onions, salt and pepper with a good dollop of mayonnaise and your meat selection and serve it on a grilled hot dog bun.

GULF ISLANDS—the many islands in the Strait of Georgia between Vancouver Island and mainland British Columbia that are divided into north and south groups, with the more fertile and lush southern group being a culinary magnet for boutique farms, wineries, fromageries and artisanal food producers.

GUM ARABIC—a thickener and emulsifier made from the sap of a type of acacia tree grown in India and Africa and used extensively in the food-processing industry, especially the confection and soft drink industries.

GUMBOOT CHITON (*Cryptochiton stelleri*)—a large BC mollusc with a flexible plated shell that is easily harvested from shorelines, making it a favourite marine food source for First Nations. The mollusc is large enough to be cut into steaks, and it has become an increasingly popular addition to weekend barbecues. This creature is named for its jointed exoskeleton panels made from chitin, a material common to the exoskeletons of crustaceans and insects.

GUMDROP CAKE—a favourite Maritime cake made by adding chopped gumdrops to a normal white cake recipe. It sounds weird but tastes good, especially with chocolate ice cream.

GUNN'S RYE BREAD—a Winnipeg icon since 1937, Gunn's Bakery somehow instills a sense of place into their glorious rye bread. One bite and you know you are in big sky country.

GUT PUDDING—a Prince Edward Island specialty sausage made by early settlers using a mix of cornmeal, leftover meat scraps and hard beef suet.

G

H

HABITANT PEA SOUP. *See* pea soup.

HABITANT SPLIT PEA SOUP (the brand)—a national favourite since 1938, the year Montréal resident Phillip Morin moved to Manchester, New Hampshire, and canned up a batch of his daughter Marie-Blanche's pea soup and gave away free samples while warning people not to add water. Most Canadians are surprised to learn their favourite pea soup had its beginnings in the U.S., but in 1968, the brand came home when Canadian food giant Catelli bought the company, only to sell it two decades later to the Campbell Soup Company.

HADDOCK (*Melanogrammus aeglefinus*)—a cod relative found in the North Atlantic. Haddock is a popular food fish and is fished commercially in Canadian waters to be sold fresh, smoked, frozen, dried and canned. Populations were depleted owing to overfishing but in recent years have made a comeback.

HADDOCK HASH—an iconic Nova Scotia mixture of haddock, cream, salt pork, potatoes and beets.

HALF-HOUR PUDDING—a simple pioneer dessert made with butter, sugar, eggs and Indian meal.

RECIPE

Half-hour Pudding

Cream 4 Tbsp butter and 2 cups sugar, then add 3 egg yolks and beat well. Add 1 cup cornmeal and fold in the whipped whites of the 3 eggs. Bake in a dish or ramekins and serve with molasses or maple sauce.

HALIBUT (*Hippoglossus* spp.)—these groundfish are the largest members of the right-eye flounder family, and they can be very large indeed, with record catches topping 330 kg. They are also good eats, low in fat with a firm, dense texture and ultra-clean taste. Halibut live in both northern Atlantic and northern Pacific waters, but with Atlantic stocks depleted by overfishing, most retailed fish are of Pacific origin.

HALIBUT BUSINESS

Canadians love to eat halibut, and we like it so much that our government issues over 300,000 recreational licences annually to west coast fishermen and charter boat companies who plumb the depths for mainly salmon and halibut. It is big business, with every kilogram of wild-caught fish generating over $30 of economic value to BC. However, that economic value is countered by restraints. In 2003, the federal government gifted 436 commercial halibut fishermen with "in perpetuity" quotas covering 82 percent of their total allowable catch (TAC), creating a kind of west coast fishing mafia. Called "slipper skippers," these

quota holders rent out their assigned catch limits, while non-quota holders—recreational fishermen and charter operations—must cease fishing for halibut once their meagre 18 percent portion of the TAC is reached. It is hardly fair, especially when commercial fishing contributes only $8 per kilogram of economic value to BC. And it's hardly fair to consumers, given that closing the recreational halibut fishery results in unscrupulous seafood conglomerates passing off plaice and other species of flounder as halibut.

Halibut

- Halibut is the largest of the Atlantic flatfish. Sometimes weighing in at over 100 kilograms, it is normally fished in the 2–3 kilogram range and is called "chicken halibut."

- Fish do not ship well fresh, and Canada is so vast a country that, except for locally caught species, most Canadians dine on the frozen or nearly frozen, as most fish—halibut included—sold "fresh" at inland markets has been chilled to just below freezing and kept on ice. While still a better alternative to fish sticks from the freezer, fresh market fish are a far cry from fresh-caught fish when it comes to taste and texture.

RECIPE

Heavenly Halibut

Mix ½ cup grated Cheddar cheese, ¼ cup butter, 3 Tbsp chopped shallots, 3 Tbsp mayonnaise, 2 Tbsp lemon juice, ¼ tsp salt and a dash of hot sauce in a bowl. Broil 2 lbs skinless halibut fillets for 7–8 minutes. Spread cheese mixture over fish, return to broiler and cook until bubbly and golden brown, about 2 minutes.

HALIBUT LOAF—a Maritimes specialty that uses flaked, leftover halibut as a substitute for ground beef in a standard meatloaf recipe. In Canada's formative years, Maritimers thought cod as commonplace a food as lobster and much preferred halibut.

A
B
C
D
E
F
G

H

I
J
K
L
M
N
O
P
Q
R
S
T
U
V
W
X
Y
Z

HALL'S ORIGINAL SUCKER—a hugely popular lollipop of the late 19th and early 20th centuries. Uniquely Canadian and made at the Crystal Beach Amusement Park in Crystal Beach, Ontario, it has recently been reborn and is now made by the Crystal Beach Candy Company of Fort Erie, Ontario. It is available at the candy company, local retail outlets and online.

HAM IN MAPLE SAP. See *jambon de la cabane à sucre.*

HAM LOAF—a favourite of pioneer-day farmers' wives charged with feeding the harvest help.

> ### RECIPE
>
> #### Ham Loaf
>
> *Combine 9 lbs uncooked ground ham, 6 slightly beaten eggs, 9 cups breadcrumbs, 4½ cups butter-milk and 6 Tbsp brown sugar. Mix well, pack into 3 greased loaf pans and bake in a 350°F oven for 1½ hours, increasing heat to 400°F for last 15 minutes to brown tops.*

HARD-TIMES PUDDING (also called poor man's pudding, *pouding chômeur*)—a hasty raisin pudding, or cake with caramel or maple syrup sauce, popular in Québec, where the translation means "unemployed person's pudding."

HARE (*Lepus* spp.)—a larger relative of the rabbit, of which there are three native species and one introduced species in Canada: Arctic hare (*L. arcticus*), snowshoe hare (*L. americanus*), white-tailed jackrabbit (*L. townsendii*) and the introduced European hare (*L. europaeus*), whose range is confined to southern Ontario. Hares differ from rabbits in both appearance and culinary usefulness; the flesh of hares is darker and stronger flavoured than rabbit. Young hares are usually roasted, while animals with some age are sent to the stew pot for either a simple or a complex preparation.

HASKAP. See honeyberry.

HAW JELLY—a condiment made from berries of various species of hawthorn trees (*Crataegus* spp.), of which there are many. Look for the jelly at farmers' markets, especially in southern Ontario. *See also* hawberry.

HAWAIIAN PIZZA—said to have been invented in Ontario in the 1960s, this pizza features back bacon (called Canadian bacon in most parts of the world) and pineapple. Hawaii used to be the number one producer of pineapple in the world, hence the moniker—at the time this pizza was invented, anything with pineapple in it was considered "Hawaiian."

HAWBERRY (also called thornapple)—the fruits of the hawthorn (*Crataegus* spp.) are found in windbreak hedgerows across Canada. Once popular for jam and jelly making, the berries have mostly slipped into the national dementia with a few exceptions, those being the odd farmers' market and Hawberry Farms.

HAWBERRY FARMS—Manitoulin Island in Lake Superior is paradise in summer and deserted in winter. Elves live there, and though you never see them for the trees, be assured they are out at Hawberry Farms, picking, packing and turning nature's bounty into all manner of jams, jellies, condiments and healthy snacks; in total, around 250 different products. And yes, they pick and turn local hawberries into delicious jelly. Hawberry Farms is online and ready to ship.

HAWKINS CHEEZIES—a popular, extruded fried cornmeal and Cheddar cheese snack food invented and manufactured by the W.T. Hawkins Company in Belleville, Ontario, since 1946.

HAZELNUT (also called beaked hazelnut, filbert)—the sweet nut or seed of the hazel tree (*Corylus cornuta*) and an important food source for First Nations and pioneer families. These days, hazelnuts are used in the confectionary trade, in the manufacture of Nutella and Frangelico liqueur, and can be pressed for cooking and salad oil. Canadian hazelnut production is confined to BC's Fraser Valley, with at least two farms offering U-pick during the month of October.

HAZELNUT BREAD (also called hearth cake)—a fried mixture of hazelnut flour, cornmeal, water and maple syrup; an important food for First Nations and early settlers.

HEARTH CAKE. *See* hazelnut bread.

HEARTNUT (*Juglans ailantifolia*)—the heartnut is the North American variation of the native Japanese walnut (*Juglans cordiformis*). The heart-shaped nuts are easily opened and better tasting than regular walnuts, and the tree takes to our southern areas like fish to water.

HEINZ, HENRY J. (1844–1919)—one of the greatest industrialists of the 19th century and important to Canadians for his promotion of southwestern Ontario as a world leader in tomato and vegetable cultivation. *See also* ketchup.

HEIRLOOM PRODUCE (also called heritage produce)—corn, peas, beans and carrots are the leading seasonal crops grown by Canadian produce farmers, but there are dozens of others, and all are available in heirloom varieties. Vegetables grown for commercial distribution have been so hybridized and gene-fiddled that they are simply called field veggies and are usually lacking the tastes and textures of their heirloom progenitors. Heirloom vegetables have names, and consumers wanting great taste and texture must seek an introduction at their local

greenhouse. The words "heirloom" and "heritage" are interchangeable, but the former is generally used to indicate forgotten plant varieties, the latter for animal breeds.

GROWING AND BUYING HEALTHY PRODUCE

Canadians are turning to vegetable gardening in astounding numbers, so many that retail sales of vegetable seeds have surpassed those of flower seeds. There are gardening handbooks available for turning any size space into a power-house of produce. If space and sunshine are a problem, there are community gardens or garden allotment programs in almost every city and town. Gardening elevates both body and soul. Plant something, big or small—a tomato plant in a pot even. The first bite of harvest will be an epiphany and will create interest in more healthy foods with taste.

Don't have a green thumb? Local farmers selling their produce can be found at farmers' markets or at farm gates across the nation. There are also a few supermarket chains responding to customer demand for healthier, better tasting foods, with some elevating the educational status of section managers and buyers through seminars, field trips and selective hiring. Super-market shoppers are advised to create a rapport with section managers—introduce yourself, show an interest in what he or she is managing and ask questions. If the spuds smell mouldy and the fruits and vegetables are all imports, complain to the section manager. If that doesn't help, write to head offices. Customers are doing that, and while the reaction is slow, the chains are responding.

Lost Fruits and Veggies

- Around 90 percent of the vegetable varieties available to Canadians in 1900 have become extinct: no more Big Mike bananas; Crawford peaches; chestnuts; Pippin and Golden White apples; Clark cherries; etc. Every year, the list grows ever longer.

- Today, industrially farmed produce has been genetically modified for machine picking, packing and shipping; it travels well and is uniform in shape and size, but it is lacking nutritional content and is almost devoid of taste. It is up to home gardeners to grow and propagate the heirloom varieties, before they are all lost.

HEMP HEARTS—hulled seeds of the hemp plant (*Cannabis sativa*) that are a trademarked nutritional supplement of Rocky Mountain Grain Products in Lethbridge, Alberta.

HEMP OIL—exceptionally high in essential fatty acids, hemp oil is not only nutritional but also tastes good and makes a fine salad dressing. Produced near Winnipeg by Hemp Oil Canada, this product is available in some health food stores and online. The company also produces hulled seeds and hemp flour.

HERBES SALÉES—a mixture of salt-preserved herbs from the lower St. Lawrence region of Québec and an important component of early Québec and Acadian dishes. There is no set recipe; *herbes salées* can include almost any herb, but they must be always fresh, never dried.

HERITAGE PRODUCE. *See* heirloom produce.

HERRING. *See* Atlantic herring, Pacific herring.

HERRING ROE—a long-time east coast delicacy, while on the west coast, First Nations harvested and cooked herring roe long before any Europeans arrived. Herring roe are historically a byproduct of the east coast fishery, but on the west coast, herring are trapped explicitly for the roe; the roe are harvested on kelp fronds as a sustainable type of aquaculture.

HICKORY NUTS—early settlers gathered, dried and stored huge quantities of hickory nuts during fall. Sweet and delicious, the nuts were toasted, salted and used for snacks, or chopped and baked into pies, cakes and cookies. They were even used as chicken feed.

Hickory

- Three species of hickory are native to southern areas of Ontario and Québec, but only two—the shag hickory and shellbark hickory—produce edible nuts. The shellbark hickory (*Carya laciniosa*) is the most desirable owing to its larger, sweeter fruit.

- The hickory is a long-lived member of the Walnut family, has hard, durable wood and grows to considerable size, which are traits not missed by early lumbermen. During the first part of the 19th century, most of Canada's hickory trees were turned into tool handles and spokes for wagon wheels.

RECIPE

Hickory Nut Cake

Cream ½ cup butter with 1¾ cups sugar. Blend 3 cups flour, 3 tsp baking powder and a pinch of salt, and slowly add to butter-sugar mixture with 1 cup whole milk. Beat 6 egg whites stiff and fold into mixture along with 1 cup chopped hickory nuts and 2 tsp vanilla. Bake at 350°F for 30 minutes or until an inserted knife comes out clean.

HICKORY STICKS—a fried, hickory-flavoured potato stick that is a favourite Canadian snack food manufactured by Hostess Foods, now a subsidiary of Frito-Lay.

HIGHBUSH CRANBERRY JELLY—a tasty condiment made from berries of the highbush cranberry shrub (*Viburnum trilobum*). Although not particularly pleasing when consumed fresh, the berries take to sweetening nicely and gel easily owing to their high pectin content. The jelly was favourite of early settlers across Canada, and the berries are prized by modern-day foragers who sell their jellies and jams at farmers' markets and through online specialty companies.

HIGHBUSH CRANBERRY WINE—a luscious, deeply flavoured libation made from the orangey-red fruit of the highbush cranberry shrub, native to all Canadian provinces.

HODGEPODGE (also called hotch potch)—a traditional Nova Scotia celebratory harvest stew with a name borrowed from the Scottish mutton stew. However, the Scottish stew pales in comparison; the Nova Scotia version includes every ripe vegetable the family garden has to offer: onions, cauliflower, potatoes, squash, runner beans, peas, carrots, Brussels sprouts, broccoli, beets, turnips and parsnips. Stewed with a bit of salt pork, this mélange of plenty was and still is served alongside beef or fish, or as a meat or fish stew.

HOLLAND MARSH—a reclaimed lake bottom of some 10,000 acres located about 40 km north of Toronto and a virtual cornucopia of produce because of its rich, black muck soil and almost 10-month growing season. Good things grow in Ontario, and 15 percent of all the goodness comes from the Holland Marsh, with about half the production exported to the U.S. Around 135 farming families work the marsh, cultivating over 45 vegetable varieties, with the most prominent being carrots, onions and celery.

HOME FREEZERS—the invention of mechanical, stand-alone home freezers in the 1940s made possible bulk buying of meats and other perishable food items from ever-more popular supermarkets, changing the way Canadians shop for groceries. *See also* Canadian canners, market squares, supermarkets.

HOMINY. *See* lyed corn.

THE EVOLUTION OF REFRIGERATION

European settlers arriving in Canada during its formative years discovered all manner of things not available in the old country: an almost limitless supply of logs, plenty of game and fish, lots of space for building houses and ponds and lakes that froze rock-solid every winter. There was no rocket science in those days, but it took very little brainpower to translate a mix of free lumber and cold into icehouses to store game, fish, dairy products and all manner of perishable produce. As Canada became more urbanized, icehouses became community affairs, with a few families sharing the harvesting of ice from local ponds.

By the early 19th century, industrial concerns were harvesting ponds in almost all urban areas to supply both community and private icehouses, along with a new invention called the icebox. Put together and sold by a Bostonian named Thomas Moore in 1840, the icebox was not well received in the U.S., but in Canada it caught on like wildfire and prompted ice-harvesting companies to begin offering home delivery service. The 1860s and 1870s were boom years because supplying both sides in the U.S. Civil War and its post-war reconstruction with everything from soup to nuts put money in the pockets of Canadians, and iceboxes became a common purchase.

With refrigeration moving inside, many community icehouses became egg storage facilities, and dairies started giving much more thought to advanced mechanical refrigeration. World War I and the Depression years gave rise to the opportunistic bulk-buying of all manner of foods, especially meats. Sensing financial opportunity, local dairies with engine-driven ammonia freezers for the manufacture of ice cream constructed cold-storage facilities and rented out divided units to the general public, with each unit capable of holding the wrapped and frozen carcass of two butchered animals, usually a pig and a side of beef. Public cold-storage facilities became even more popular after they offered butchering services to cut, wrap and even sell whole and half carcasses. Canadian families now had two pantries, with the newest requiring visits for stocking up the home. Refrigerator manufacturers such as General Electric and Frigidaire turned to thinking about those time-consuming stocking-up visits, and in the late 1940s they began to market stand-alone home freezers. Not an instant hit because they were pricey and prone to frosting up, they were still the writing on the wall for public cold-storage facilities, with the last of them disappearing around the mid-1950s.

A
B
C
D
E
F
G
H
I
J
K
L
M
N
O
P
Q
R
S
T
U
V
W
X
Y
Z

HONEY—bee food, 38 percent fructose and 31 percent glucose, with about the same sweetness as granulated sugar. Honey is classified by source, and it can be monofloral, from one type of flower, or polyfloral, from many flowers. To our benefit, Canada has wildflowers in abundance: alfalfa, clover, buckwheat, loosestrife, canola, fireweed, blueberry, cranberry, blackberry, huckleberry, sunflower, basswood, vetch-flower from the foothills of BC's Monashee Mountains and borage from the Prairie provinces. All flowers used by honeybees produce a variety of tastes that make Canadian honey the world's finest. Liquid, creamed or still in the comb, Canadian honey is a national treasure that should be guarded against depredation by foreign conglomerates. Read labels carefully and buy only 100 percent Canadian honey from co-op processors like the Prairies' BeeMaid Company or from farmers' markets; otherwise you may end up with honey cut with a cheap import from Argentina.

Honey

- With over a half-million bee colonies, Canada is a major honey producer and ranks sixth in the world, with an annual harvest of around 30,000 tonnes. Roughly half of that comes from the Prairie provinces.

- Contrary to popular belief, honey was not a foraged food for early settlers because the honeybee is not native to North America. Honeybees were introduced by the French in the early 17th century. The bees soon escaped to the wild and established colonies across the continent. It was a good thing for settlers, as the wild colonies pollinated crops.

- Beekeeping did become widespread, but since it required skill, it progressed across the country slowly. Today, farmers cannot depend on hit-or-miss pollination and employ beekeepers who specialize in providing hives for servicing crops and orchards.

- Disease within honeybee colonies has always been a problem, but in recent years, Colony Collapse Disorder (CCD) has been decimating bee populations. One day the worker bees are busy pollinating and gathering honey, and the next they are gone. Some scientists blame a virus, others blame pesticides and herbicides, and still others say it is a combination. Whatever the reason, it has to be fixed soon or apiarists will begin switching over to unaffected Africanized bees, turning rural areas into dangerous no-go zones.

HONEY BUTTER—a blend of honey and butter popular with early settlers and still available in specialty food stores. Orange, lemon or cinnamon is often added as additional flavouring.

RECIPE

Honey Butter

Combine ½ cup butter, ¾ cup honey, 1 Tbsp orange juice and 1 tsp orange rind. Lemon or cinnamon can be substituted for orange.

HONEYBERRY (*Lonicera caerulea*; also called haskap)—it looks like a big blueberry but tastes like a mix of many berries. Generations of Canadians living in the Prairie provinces have wild-foraged this berry for making jam, jelly and pies, a sometimes dangerous endeavour because the berries are a favourite of bears. But over the last few years, some commercial production has gotten underway and the berries are slowly making their way into markets both local and in other provinces, so be on the lookout for this taste sensation.

HOOLIGAN—another name for the west coast eulachon and also the name of the famous—or infamous—dish prepared from this member of the Smelt family. *See also* eulachon.

RECIPE

Hooligan

Lay 18–20 fish (lake smelt can be used for this dish) in a casserole greased with bacon fat and add 1 finely chopped onion and 1 minced garlic clove, sprinkled evenly over the fish. Salt and pepper to taste and cover with a ¼-inch layer of cracker crumbs. Repeat layering until casserole is full, then pour over 1 cup whole milk and bake in a 350°F oven for 1 hour.

HOOP CHEESE (also called baker's cheese)—originally a soft cheese made by pioneers with skimmed milk and no added salt, having a texture similar to baker's cheese. After being set with rennet, the curd was placed into a wooden hoop draped with cheesecloth and set aside until the whey had dripped out the bottom. In later years when milk became more plentiful, salt was added to the curd for preservation and weights were placed onto the hoops to form a denser, almost-hard cheese with good keeping qualities. Hoops weighing about 20 pounds became so popular on general store counters that a cutter was invented to create cheese wedges; you can sometimes see the device at country auctions or antique shops.

HOPS (*Humulus lupulus* var. *neomexicanus*)—North America's native hop plant produces cones, or strobiles, that were used by First Nations and early pioneers to flavour drinks, baked goods and meat dishes. Fresh, young leaves are a tasty addition to any green salad, and the plant's vine-like growth habit made

wonderful shading for front porches. Most important to early settlers was the hop cones' ability to host yeast and be a readily available bread starter. The pioneers needed only boil a few handfuls in water, pour the still-boiling liquid into some flour, strain, add a bit of old yeast starter when the mixture cooled and place it in a warm spot until fermentation.

HORNE'S BARBECUE SAUCE—an almost perfect barbecue sauce for beef, chicken or pork.

HORNE'S CUSTARD POWDER—Newfoundland's answer to Bird's Custard Powder and preferred by many bakers. It is now made by Select Food Products in Toronto and is distributed across the country. *See also* Bird's Custard Powder.

HORSE BEAN (*Vicia faba*; also called faba or fava bean, Windsor bean)—an ancient broad bean planted by pioneer settlers in maturing apple orchards to suck up excess ground moisture and prevent extraneous wood formation in the trees. Horse beans produce an upright plant with no tendrils. The large pods shell easily and yield five to seven quarter-sized beans. Used extensively by pioneer cooks, the beans lost popularity for a time but have been rediscovered by chefs and heritage food gardeners. *See also* beans.

A
B
C
D
E
F
G
H
I
J
K
L
M
N
O
P
Q
R
S
T
U
V
W
X
Y
Z

RECIPE

Horseradish Vinaigrette

Whisk 2 Tbsp each of freshly grated horseradish and cider vinegar with ¼ tsp each of salt and freshly ground pepper. Whisk continuously while slowly pouring in ½ cup canola or grape seed oil until dressing forms. Before serving, add finely chopped fresh parsley or chives.

HORSERADISH (*Armoracia rusticana*)—a perennial herb related to mustard and cabbage. The sauce, made from the root, is a tasty condiment deemed necessary by the very earliest English settlers, who planted horseradish immediately upon their arrival. Later settlers to Canada were delighted to find an even more potent horseradish growing in the forests; the herb had escaped from gardens and spread into the wild. Young, tender horseradish leaves make a tasty addition to green salads, or they can be cooked like spinach. Grated and mixed with vinegar or lemon juice, horseradish was, and still is, a main condiment for oysters. With the addition of a little fresh mustard and sugar, it becomes an ideal condiment for roast beef and ham. Mix about 1 tsp horseradish into ¼ cup ketchup to make your own seafood sauce.

HORSERADISH VINAIGRETTE—a lively salad dressing and a favourite of Canadian restaurant chefs.

HOT ROCKS CHICKEN—a First Nations method of cooking wild fowl that was adopted by settlers and is now used by campers to prepare a fall-off-the-bone-tender chicken delight. First Nations cooks used clay and hides to wrap the hot rocks, but modern campers use aluminum foil.

Horseradish

- Grated horseradish loses both colour and potency quickly. To counter this loss, manufacturers of bottled supermarket sauce will often formulate it with a bleaching agent, sodium bisulfate, along with a heat source, oil of mustard.

- Horseradish is grown commercially in both Ontario and Manitoba. Most of the crop is used to extract peroxidase, an enzyme used to detect HIV.

- Take care when grating your own horseradish; the fumes are enough to make a grown man cry.

RECIPE

Hot Rocks Chicken

Wrap 4 or 5 rocks in aluminum foil and heat in a campfire for 1 hour. Place seasoned bird on a large sheet of foil with 1 hot rock in the cavity and the remainder around the bird. Wrap entire assembly in foil. Wrap again with 3 layers of newspaper, secure tightly in a black plastic bag and let sit for 5 hours. Scrumptious.

HOT SANDWICH—chicken, turkey or beef on a slice of white bread, topped with hot gravy and served with a side of peas, this dish is thought to have originated in Québec during the early 19th century. Americans will discount our claims to this ubiquitous diner dish, but my grandfather once told me a hot turkey sandwich was the last meal he ate before shipping off to World War I from Halifax in 1915—a long-enough time ago to be part of our national food experience.

HOTCH POTCH. *See* hodgepodge.

HOUSE BUNKIN—a Lunenburg, Nova Scotia, specialty fish stew with salt cod, onions and cream sauce. *See also* Dutch mess, Lunenburg pudding.

HUCKLEBERRY—both black (*Vaccinium membranaceum*) and red (*V. parvifolium*)

varieties grow profusely on the west coast and have a look and taste similar to blueberries, their close relatives. An important food source for coastal First Nations, the berries were quickly adopted by BC settlers and turned into luscious pies, jams, jellies and muffins.

RECIPE

Huckleberry Muffins

Mix 1 cup each of quick rolled oats and milk and set aside. In another bowl, mix 1 cup flour, 1 tsp baking powder, ½ tsp baking soda and ¾ cup brown sugar. In a small bowl, mix 1 beaten egg with ¼ cup melted butter and add to oatmeal along with dry ingredients. Stir only until moist. Fold in 1 cup huckleberries, pour into greased muffin tins and bake at 400°F for 15–20 minutes.

HUGGER-IN-BUFF. *See* Dutch mess.

HURT WINE—a Newfoundland alcoholic beverage made from fermented berries of any plant of the genus *Vaccinium*: blueberries, cranberries, huckleberries, etc. The 16th-century English called these various berries "hurtes" or hurtleberries; the word was changed by American settlers to "huckle," as in huckleberry, but in Newfoundland they kept the word as a catch-all for any dark-coloured berry. Newfoundland has a host of "hurts": hurt pie, hurt pudding, hurt cake, hurt crisps and the infamous hurt wine.

HYDROGENATION—the process of turning liquid oils into solid fats, for example turning vegetable or fish oil into margarine. Liquid oils are heated in a closed container with hydrogen gas and a nickel catalyst, turning healthy unsaturated fatty acids into unhealthy saturated and trans fats. *See also* trans fats.

HYDROMEL (also called *vin de miel*)—a fermented and filtered honey "mead" brewed by the Musée de L'abeille, a honey museum in Château Richer, Québec. The museum brews about 20,000 bottles of hydromel annually and always sells out.

I

ICE CIDER (also called apple ice wine)—the precursor of ice wine, ice cider is the fermented juice pressed from apples that have frozen, intentionally or unintentionally, on the tree. A favourite of New France pioneers, ice cider has maintained a habitant presence through the centuries and nowadays is pressed commercially by a number of Québec artisanal cider producers.

ICE CREAM CONE—thanks to milk, one of New Brunswick's small towns, Sussex Corner, became the site of a world-renowned invention. By the mid-19th century, the introduction of the Holstein breed of milk cows had earned Sussex Corner the title of "Dairy Capital of Canada." Life in this small town revolved so heavily around its dairy products that when a local baker named Walter Donelly forgot to put yeast into his cake dough, the only thing he thought to do with the flat cakes was to roll them up and use them to hold ice cream. Just like that, Walter had invented the ice cream cone. It's true—just ask anybody in Sussex Corner.

ICE WINE (also called eiswein)—an ultra-sweet dessert wine originally made in Germany and later produced in small amounts by wineries in other countries, most famously in Canada.

ICE WINE

The production of ice wine is labour intensive and depends on freezing winter temperatures to concentrate the sugars in the grapes. However, in most wine-producing countries, low temperatures over an extended period are rare, and winter labour is a problem. Canada has the freezing temperatures, but until the 1970s lacked the grape varieties necessary to produce ice wine. Canada is now the world's major producer of ice wines from many new grape varieties.

ÎLE D'ORLÉANS CHEESE—North America's first cheese, produced over 350 years ago on Île d'Orléans, an island in the St. Lawrence River near Québec City. Popular in the 17th and 18th centuries as a dessert accompanied by sliced apples, Île d'Orleans cheese went out of production in the 1970s but has since been reintroduced by Les Fromages de l'isle d'Orléans and is called Le Paillasson. Alas, the cheese is only available in limited quantities in a few Québec cheese shops and on Île d'Orléans. If you happen to visit the island and the fromagerie, be sure to try the wonderful cheese in a galette, a buckwheat crepe prepared on the premises. *See also* galette.

IMPERIAL DRINK—what early 19th-century Canadians prepared to beat the summer heat. In later years, the Imperial drink would have gin added to it and become the Imperial cocktail.

> ### RECIPE
>
> #### Imperial Drink
>
> *Place the following into a 1-gallon container: 2 oz cream of tartar, the juice and peel of 3 lemons and ½ lb sugar, and pour in 2 quarts boiling water. Allow mixture to sit until cool, then fill the container with chipped ice from the icehouse.*

INCA WHEAT. *See* quinoa.

INCONNU (*Stenodus leucichthys*; also called coney, connie, shee fish)—a large, oily game fish found in rivers and streams of northwestern Canada. Touted as a firm-fleshed northern delicacy by outfitters, the meat is actually soft and oily and is best smoked.

INDIAN BREAD—an unleavened flat loaf, the dough being a mixture of Indian meal, dried berries, beans and various nutmeats.

INDIAN BREADROOT. See *pomme-de-prairie*.

INDIAN CANDY—salmon fillets hand-rubbed with maple syrup and salt (kippered), then smoked over alder wood for an extended period.

INDIAN CELERY (*Lomatium nudicaule*; also called lovage, smallage, wild celery)—looks, smells and tastes like cultivated celery, but it is not even a relation. It was a treat for the earliest east coast settlers who foraged Indian celery because it completed their *mirepoix*, the three ingredients intrinsic to French cooking. This carrot, onion and celery base was very important in French cuisine even in early times. Wild celery was also used in western Canada as a medicinal plant by the native people of southern BC. Recently it has caught on with BC chefs as a unique seasoning. Look for it soon at specialty markets in other provinces.

INDIAN CHOCOLATE (*Geum* spp.; also called chocolate root, water avens)—a perennial herb with a root tasting slightly of chocolate. Water avens were gathered and used by First Nations and settlers to make a hot cocoa–like drink.

INDIAN CORN. *See* lyed corn.

INDIAN CORNBREAD—an unleavened, boiled bread made from ground sweet corn and beans.

INDIAN CUCUMBER (*Medeola virginiana*)— a white, crisp, finger-sized root that tastes surprisingly like cucumber.

INDIAN GINGER. *See* wild ginger.

INDIAN ICE CREAM (also called *sxusem*)— buffaloberries are sweetened with sugar, blue camas or the juice of other berries and whipped like egg whites.

INDIAN MEAL (also called cornmeal)—baking flour made from rough ground corn and beans that sometimes contained crushed walnuts, hickory nuts or beechnuts. Created by First Nations and adopted by settlers, the name became synonymous with milled corn, or cornmeal.

Indian meal was a pioneer staple for making bread, cake and pudding and for thickening stews. *See also* lyed corn, nixtamalization.

INDIAN MEAL MUFFINS—in Canada's early days, cheap cornmeal or Indian meal bolstered recipes calling for expensive wheat flour, and these muffins are a breakfast favourite that has lasted the centuries.

RECIPE

Indian Meal Muffins

Mix together 1 cup each of flour and yellow cornmeal, ¾ cup milk, ½ cup each of sugar and butter, 1 Tbsp baking powder, ½ tsp salt and 1 egg. Spoon batter into a well-greased muffin tin and bake in a 375°F oven for 15–20 minutes. Serve hot with plenty of butter.

INDIAN MEAL MUSH—cornmeal boiled until soft, about an hour. It may be eaten hot as a breakfast cereal, or cooled, sliced and served as a meat side.

INDIAN MEAL PANCAKES (also called Indian slapjacks)—pancakes made with cornmeal and fried on a griddle.

INDIAN MEAL PUDDING—a baked cornmeal dessert sweetened with molasses that originated on the east coast and moved west with early settlers.

INDIAN POTATO. *See* groundnut.

INDIAN RICE. *See* northern rice-root, wild rice.

RECIPE

Indian Meal Pudding

Boil 5 cups whole milk. Mix 1 cup Indian meal with 1 cup cold milk, add 4 Tbsp butter and boil while stirring. Beat 4 eggs with 1 cup molasses or powdered sugar, add 1 tsp each of ginger and nutmeg and stir the whole together until thick enough to pour into buttered ramekins. Bake at 350°F for 2 hours.

INDIAN SLAPJACKS. *See* Indian meal pancakes.

INDIAN TEA. *See* Labrador tea.

INDIAN TURNIP. See *pomme-de-prairie*.

INFECTIOUS SALMON ANEMIA—a virus affecting farmed salmon that may or may not be a danger to consumers. As of February 2013, the sale of previously banned infected fish is being allowed in Canada because the Canadian Food Inspection Agency is betting the flu-like virus will not combine with a human flu virus and cause problems. U.S. food safety regulators have refused to gamble and have banned the importation of infected Canadian fish fillets. *See also* aquaculture.

INJECTION CURING—a method of quickly introducing a liquid pickling mixture into meats through machine-mounted syringes. This method is favoured by Canadian meat packing conglomerates owing both to speed and to the amount of profit-generating water that can be deposited into meats—heavier meat means a higher price charged to consumers.

INSTANT MASHED POTATOES—created in 1962 by Edward Asselbergs, a research scientist

at the Canadian Department of Agriculture, and used as military rations, not to mention providing a convenience for campers.

INUIT DIET—in 1906, Vilhjalmur Stefansson, a Harvard University anthropologist, decided to practice what he preached and headed north to live with the Inuit. For 11 years, he ate nothing but fish and fatty meats and returned home a very healthy man—a fact that flew in the face of contemporary nutritional guidelines. This situation gave rise to what is commonly referred to as the "Inuit Paradox": how is it possible for a man to remain healthy on a diet that excludes fruits, vegetables and grains? Thinking he was onto a good thing, Stefansson promoted his fatty all-meat diet and gained a huge following of "waste not, want not" adherents, especially in Canada, where Stefansson's nutritional philosophy added exotic organ meats to the already suffering Canadian food experience. Before Stefansson, organ meat was breakfast kidneys, with all others considered offal and thought to be either poisonous or dog food. But how could you argue with Stefansson, the living proof that this stuff was good for you? Cheap organ meat quickly became every kid's dinnertime horror: tripe, hearts and pork liver meatloaf. Both the Inuit Paradox and its accompanying diet was deflated somewhat after it was discovered the true Inuit diet of high-protein, fatty meats from arctic animals and fish did actually contain many of the nutrients and vitamins found in other foods. *See also* fad diets.

ATKINS AND SCARSDALE

Dimmed but not out, the Inuit diet returned full force in the early 1970s in the guise of the hugely popular Dr. Atkins high-protein diet, causing livestock ranchers to rejoice and produce farmers to cry. Then Dr. Herman Tarnower launched his insanely popular redux of Dr. Atkins' diet called the Scarsdale diet, and it allowed its million or so participants to snack on carrots and celery. To keep Scarsdale dieters supplied, farmers skewed crop production in favour of carrots and celery, causing widespread shortages of other produce and higher prices. A few years later, when the Scarsdale adherents moved on, produce farmers were once again left holding the bag, much to the delight of a certain vegetable juice processor.

IODIZED SALT—in 1949, iodine became a mandatory ingredient in table salt, and the omnipresent goitre emanating from the throats of so many Canadians all but disappeared.

IRISH MOSS BLANCMANGE—a favourite Maritime delight made with milk and thickened with Irish moss (*Chondrus crispus*), a red algae that forms a jelly when boiled. *See also* carrageenan.

RECIPE

Irish Moss Blancmange

Soak ¼ cup Irish moss in 1½ cups water until soft (15–20 minutes). Combine with 1¾ cup milk and a pinch of salt, and cook in double boiler until thick. Strain, add 1 tsp vanilla, pour into jelly moulds and chill. Serve with sliced fruit.

IRON RATIONS—during World War I, "iron rations" was the name given to the standby emergency rations issued to every soldier—a package containing a can of corned beef (known as bully beef) along with a few hardtack biscuits—from which troops concocted all manner of revolting stews and soups. When the odd shipment of canned ham, fish, fruit or vegetables did manage to get to the trenches, it was considered cause for celebration, with plenty of rum to round out the occasion.

IRRADIATED FOODS—foods that have been preserved through exposure to ionizing radiation, a process deemed safe by Health Canada, the World Health Organization and Canada's conglomerate food processors, though this consensus is not shared by independent scientific study. Irradiation destroys vitamins, proteins and fatty acids in foods, creates new and dangerous chemicals and creates mutations and cancers in lab animals. The thought of consuming irradiated Frankenfoods produced and sold by food conglomerates should be cause for revolution and a return to consumer-friendly food production before it's too late.

ISINGLASS—gelatin made from the dried swim bladders of large fish such as sturgeon. A valuable trade product for First Nations, this gelatin was used by early settlers to make aspic and blancmange and to glaze meats for preservation.

ISINGLASS

During the 18th and early 19th centuries, isinglass became a lucrative business for the Hudson's Bay Company because the gelatin was much in demand by English breweries for fining (clarifying) beer. With the rise of the east coast cod fishery, isinglass became a valuable byproduct of that fishery and a much cheaper commodity. Around 1840, an American inventor, Peter Cooper, perfected a powdered gelatin from pigs' feet, but it proved too expensive. Then in 1890, a Jamestown, New York, resident, Charles Knox, perfected a cheaper, granulated gelatin and packaged it for retail sale. Not long after, May Wait, a housewife in Leroy, New York, mixed Knox's gelatin with sugar and powdered flavouring and called her new product Jell-O. May Wait sold her Jell-O brand to American marketing genius Frank Woodward, who in 1926 merged his multi-million–dollar Jell-O empire with Postum Foods, with that company later merging with the J.L. Kraft Company to form the mega-conglomerate General Foods.

J

A
B
C
D
E
F
G
H
I
J
K
L
M
N
O
P
Q
R
S
T
U
V
W
X
Y
Z

JAM BUSTERS—yeast-raised sweet dough formed into balls, fried in lard, slit with a knife and filled with jam.

JAM FOR BRITAIN—a World War II undertaking by the Canadian Red Cross and Women's Institute members to bottle hundreds of thousands of jams, jellies and preserves to assist Canada's war effort and lend food relief to Britain. Participants received extra sugar rations, and local produce farmers were provided a surviving impetus to plant strawberries.

JAMBON À L'ERABLE. See maple-glazed ham.

JAMBON DE LA CABANE À SUCRE (also called ham in maple sap)—a braised ham specialty of Québec habitants since the early days. See also *cabane à sucre*.

> ### RECIPE
>
> #### Ham in Maple Sap
>
> *Braise a whole ham for 3 hours in maple sap. Remove the rind and cover ham with a mixture of raisins, maple sugar, dry mustard, ground cloves and salt, and bake at 300°F for 30 minutes.*

JAM-JAMS—iconic brown sugar and molasses, jam-dabbed cookies very popular with Maritimers.

JEANNE'S CAKES—among the world's tastiest cakes and only available at Jeanne's bakery or at supermarkets in Winnipeg, and that is a crying shame.

JELLY MOULDS—no self-respecting immigrant family would have arrived in 18th-century Canada without at least one copper mould of a fantasy figure to brighten up the dinner table with a shimmering jelly. Made of beaten copper, jelly moulds have become culinary collectibles in modern times but are seldom used in spite of the ease of preparing the jelly.

JELLY SALAD—during World War II, men fought, women worked in armament factories, kids gathered paper and metal, and grannies knitted socks and made weird jelly salads. Ontarians who reside near Lake Erie will know Port Dover and its Erie Beach Hotel and the famous Cove Room restaurant, and anyone unaware of the culinary delights proffered by that establishment

has a treat in store. It's all good, but best are the time-warp salad carts loaded with jelly creations: horseradish jelly salad, coleslaw in lime jelly salad and marshmallow ambrosia jelly salad are just a few of the choices.

JERKY—strips of beef or wild game that have been sun-dried or salt-cured. The name is derived from the Spanish word for a Peruvian process of air drying strips of meat called *charqui*.

Cheaper-to-make jerky took over from pemmican as the trail food of choice for immigrants headed for the Canadian prairies and has maintained prominence right into modern times. The best Canadian jerky naturally comes from where the best beef is: Alberta.

JERSEY MILK BAR—the iconic Canadian candy bar creation of the William Neilson Company. Unfortunately, Jersey Milk bars are no longer

JERSEY MILK: A CANADIAN ORIGINAL

The William Neilson Company was established in 1893 as a back-of-the-house dairy and ice cream operation. As business improved, chocolate products were added as a way of providing winter employment to workers and disposing of unsold milk. Two decades later, the company was producing over 1 million gallons of ice cream and a half-million pounds of chocolate products.

In 1924, William's son Morden decided the time had arrived for a Canadian chocolate bar. Insisting that only the finest ingredients

obtainable be used in its production, he introduced the Jersey Milk chocolate bar to a grateful public. Morden Neilson advertised his product as the best chocolate bar ever made. He was probably right; unlike the Hershey Company in the U.S., Neilson used only high-quality cream from Jersey cows and refrained from adding soured milk to the formulation, which produces a product called "rotten milk chocolate" and the not-disagreeable but slightly off flavour associated with Hershey milk chocolate.

A
B
C
D
E
F
G
H
I
J
K
L
M
N
O
P
Q
R
S
T
U
V
W
X
Y
Z

made with the best Jersey milk, and one can only hope the present owners keep using the best chocolate in Canada's favourite chocolate bar.

JERUSALEM ARTICHOKE (*Helianthus tuberosus*; also called sunchoke, sunroot, topinambour)—not from Jerusalem, nor is it an artichoke, but a North American plant tuber that resembles ginger root, with a taste similar to its namesake artichoke. First introduced to Samuel de Champlain by First Nations in 1605 and called a Canadian potato by the French, the plant was so widely cultivated in France that it became almost an invasive weed. A relative of the sunflower and a staple food of early settlers, the crispy sunchoke makes a delicious addition to salads and stir-fries.

JERUSALEM ARTICHOKE FRITTERS (also called topinambour beignets)—sliced Jerusalem artichokes dipped in batter and fried golden brown. *See also* fritter.

RECIPE

Jerusalem Artichoke Soup

Cook thinly sliced leek, fennel and celeriac in butter until soft. Add 1 lb peeled, thinly sliced Jerusalem artichokes, a bouquet garni and 6 cups chicken stock; simmer until sunchokes are tender. Cool soup, remove bouquet garni, add ¼ cup heavy cream and purée in small batches. Return to pot and reheat.

Jerusalem Artichoke

- Both the Jerusalem artichoke and the sunflower are members of the Daisy family, and mature plants bear similar-looking flowers.

- Introduced to English gardens by way of cultivators in Ter Nuesen, Holland, as *girasole*, the Italian word for sunflower, the sunchoke from France (via Canada) was nicknamed Jerusalem artichoke to differentiate the two species.

JERUSALEM ARTICHOKE SOUP—the iconic Canadian soup: made by the Mi'kmaq, adopted by the earliest French and still enjoyed across the nation.

JEWEL JAM—a berry jam made from pitted cherries, gooseberries, raspberries and red currants. Popular with early settlers, the jam earned its name from the dab of ruby colour it provided to a bowl of mush.

JIGGS DINNER (also called boiled dinner, *bouilli Canadien*, scoff)—a traditional Newfoundland dinner of salt beef or pork and vegetables.

RECIPE

New England Boiled Dinner

Place 3 lbs boneless corned beef brisket in an iron pot, cover with water and boil about 4 hours. Take out the brisket, add 1½ cups yellow split peas, 1 quartered cabbage, 1 cubed turnip, 5–6 roughly chopped carrots and 6 quartered potatoes to the broth and cook until done. Season with 2 Tbsp butter and ½ tsp pepper. Slice meat against the grain and combine with vegetables on a serving platter. Note: a traditional Jigg's dinner includes dumplings, a decadent ingredient omitted by Puritanical-minded New Englanders.

JOE BOURQUE SANDWICH—scrambled eggs and onions with butter and mustard on a grilled hot dog bun, often eaten as a late evening snack. It is reputed to be a New Brunswick favourite.

JOHNNY CAKES. See *flan au blé d'Inde*.

JOLLY BOYS—an old-English method for making pancakes without eggs was made better in Canada by the inclusion of one egg and bacon fat in the preparation.

RECIPE

Jolly Boys

Mix ⅔ cup milk, 2 Tbsp flour, 1 egg and a pinch of salt until the consistency of double cream. Fry bacon in heavy pan and when crisp, remove and drop in a spoonful of batter, coddling with hot fat until cakes are cooked through. Serve with bacon and top with honey or maple syrup.

JOS. LOUIS—a chocolate snack cake with a cream centre invented in Sainte-Marie-de-Beauce, Québec, by bakery owner Rose-Anna Vachon in 1932 and named after her two sons, Joseph (Jos.) and Louis. Over the years, Vachon's little bakery grew into a successful family enterprise, making everything from jams and jellies to Granny's butter tarts, but in 2004, it was bought by the Canadian mega-conglomerate Saputo.

JOSTABERRY (also called mossberry)—crossing black currant (*Ribes nigrum*) and gooseberry (*R. grossularioides*) produces a thornless bush that likes our climate and has large clusters of black-blue berries that are excellent for making jams and jellies. Commercially grown in Alberta, cultivars are available for your garden.

A B C D E F G H I **J** K L M N O P Q R S T U V W X Y Z

A
B
C
D
E
F
G
H
I
J
K
L
M
N
O
P
Q
R
S
T
U
V
W
X
Y
Z

JUMBLES—a naturalized Canadian version (made so by the inclusion of Canadian nuts and berries) of an old-English knot bread, or jumballs.

RECIPE

Jumbles

Mix 1 lb each of cake flour, sugar and ground nut-meats or berries and 1¼ cups each of heavy cream and cooled melted butter. Mix into a stiff batter and fold in 8 beaten egg whites, then add a little cinnamon and fry in butter until golden brown.

JUNIPER BERRY—the berry-like fruit of the common evergreen juniper tree (*Juniperus communis*), native to both Europe and North America, is used to flavour meats and pâtés and as an ingredient in marinades and sauerkraut. Don't be afraid to go outside and pick them off the bush.

JUNIPER BERRY MARINADE—especially great when marinating venison.

RECIPE

Juniper Berry Marinade

Mix 1 Tbsp each of juniper berries and chopped rosemary with 1 tsp each of chopped garlic, mustard seeds and pepper, and 1 cup canola oil.

JUNIPER BERRY SAUCE—pouring this sauce over slices of roast venison loin will instantly turn simple cooks into master chefs.

RECIPE

Juniper Berry Sauce

Place 4 diced shallots and 2 Tbsp butter into the empty roasting pan, and after sweating the onions a bit, pour in ⅔ cup Madeira wine and scrape the bottom of the pan. Add 10 juniper berries and 2 bay leaves and simmer until reduced to half the volume. Add 2 cups beef stock (or venison if possible) and reduce by two-thirds. Add ⅔ cup heavy cream, bring to a boil and immediately strain and serve.

K

KALE (*Brassica oleraea* vars. *acephala* and *fimbriata*)—kale is a form of cabbage introduced to Canada by 19th-century Russian traders. The plant did not become popular until World War I, when the federal government promoted its inclusion in backyard Victory Gardens because of its high nutrient content. The young leaves are best for cooking.

RECIPE

Sautéed Kale

In a pan, heat 3 Tbsp olive oil and 2 cloves minced garlic over medium-high heat until garlic is soft. Turn up heat to high, add ½ cup vegetable stock and 1½ lbs rough-chopped kale, and cook while stirring until all liquid is evaporated. Remove from heat, season with salt and pepper, top with a pat of butter and serve hot.

CANADA'S FAVOURITE KALE VARIETIES

- Dwarf Blue Curled Scotch—an early variety and easy to grow.
- Lacinato—a savoy type with excellent flavour.
- Red Russian—sweet, tender and fast cooking.
- Siberian—the favourite of Canadian growers.

KALE BUDS—flower buds from mature, overwintered kale that are picked just before the flowers open in spring. The buds are tender, sweet tasting and perfect for stir-fry, steaming or a simple sauté with garlic and olive oil. Look for them at farmers' markets in early spring,

A
B
C
D
E
F
G
H
I
J
K
L
M
N
O
P
Q
R
S
T
U
V
W
X
Y
Z

where they are sometimes called kale rabe. To grow your own, you will need to protect mature kale plants from the elements with either a cold frame or a covering of straw.

KAMCHATKA LILY. *See* northern rice-root.

KASHA—an Eastern European word for a range of stiff porridges made with buckwheat groats and cooked in a manner similar to the Italian preparation of risotto. In Russia, kasha is served with all manner of toppings, from Parmesan cheese to bacon, onions and mushrooms; but in Canada, where buckwheat is a major crop in Manitoba, kasha is generally a bulgur wheat–based salad. *See also* buckwheat, groats.

KEDGEREE—originally an Indian spiced rice and lentil dish called *khichri*, it was adopted by the British during the British Raj and adapted as a breakfast dish, with the lentils replaced by flaked salt cod, and the addition of chopped egg and heavy cream. Brought to Canada with the British military, kedgeree underwent other changes, mainly replacing the salt fish with smoked haddock or fresh salmon.

KEEWATIN MEAT AND FISH—located at Rankin Inlet, Nunavut, this company processes and distributes Arctic char and caribou meat sourced from local hunters and fishermen.

KENTUCKY FRIED CHICKEN—although the king of fried chicken, Colonel Harland Sanders, did most certainly develop his secret blend of 11 herbs and spices in the U.S., both he and his secret recipe lived in Mississauga, Ontario, from 1964 until his death in 1980. The Colonel must have thought his "finger licking" chicken belonged in Canada; his charitable fund, the Colonel Harland Sanders Charitable Organization, is still in operation and is based in British Columbia. It's a bit of a stretch to include the Colonel's chicken in the Canadian food experience, but since I once lived near the guy and knew him as a fine Southern gentleman who always had a big smile and a wave for neighbours, I thought I'd include him for old time's sake. Oh, and in one of the few conversations I had with the Colonel while he was out watering his lawn and waiting for the cleaners to deliver his white suits, he told me the most secret ingredients in his mix were lots of white pepper and MSG.

KERR'S BUTTERSCOTCH—a boiled, real butter and brown sugar candy made by Kerr's since 1895. Kerr's started out in St. Thomas, Ontario, moved to Brantford in 1898, and to Toronto in 1904. This all-Canadian family company produces a wide variety of quality candies for consumers.

KETCHUP (also called catsup, catchup)—in the very early days, ketchup was a fish sauce, then a mushroom sauce. It underwent another change around 1770, when American cook James Mease, who immigrated to Nova Scotia in 1782 during the American Revolution, concocted a popular tomato-based sauce. In 1876, an American from Pittsburgh by the name of Henry John Heinz, often called "Jack," began to bottle the ketchup that Canadians learned to love. When H.J. Heinz opened a plant in Leamington, Ontario, in 1909, his cooking vats could barely meet the demand. Today, the Heinz factory is streamlined and processes over 250,000 tonnes of fresh Ontario tomatoes into the ubiquitous red sauce. Heinz ketchup is available in plastic squeeze bottles, but their largest seller is still the skinny glass bottle that Jack made, the one that needs a pounding to get started.

KETCHUP AUX TOMATES ROUGES—a ripe tomato relish traditionally served in French Canada with *cipaille* and tourtière, similar to chili sauce.

KETCHUP-FLAVOURED POTATO CHIPS—first introduced in Canada, ketchup chips are a Canadian favourite rarely found elsewhere. The flavour has been tried and failed in the U.S., but here, they are one of Old Dutch's top two best sellers.

KIAK. *See* alewife.

KING SALMON. *See* Chinook salmon.

KIPPER SNACKS—when the fishing trawlers came and the herring catch exploded, savvy fishermen required some curing techniques to preserve what became known as the "kips," or unsold catch, an event that occurred in 1840 when the newfangled split and smoked herring went on sale in London markets. It created a culinary sensation that was quickly followed up by Canadian fish companies that smoked herring for both domestic use and export. During World War II, it became expedient to can rather than smoke the herrings and add tomato sauce, a product that has survived the years and is known as kipper snacks.

KIPPERED—a curing method wherein the fish, usually herring, is split open, then salted and smoked. Kippering was originally a method for curing salmon, with the word itself originally meaning a spent or line-tired salmon.

KNOB CELERY. *See* celeriac.

KOHLRABI (*Brassica oleracea* var. *gongylodes*; also called German turnip)—another form of cabbage, though confusion reigns when it comes to the name of this vegetable: it is also spelled interchangeably as kolrabi or kohl rabi. Luckily after cooking, it is so good that no one minds the confusion.

CANADA'S FAVOURITE KOHLRABI VARIETIES

- Early Purple Vienna—a purple-skinned, fast-maturing variety with sweet flavour and a tender texture.

- Early White Vienna—similar to Purple Vienna, but white-skinned.

KOSHER—from the Hebrew word *kasher*, meaning "to make fit" and referring to articles of food that have been prepared according to Jewish dietary laws.

RECIPE

Kohlrabi Fries

Peel 2 lbs kohlrabi and cut into finger-sized sticks. Heat 3 Tbsp canola oil over medium-high heat in a heavy skillet. Place 2 Tbsp rice or semolina flour and a bit of salt in a large bowl and toss fries. Fry sticks in oil, browning all sides, about 2–3 minutes each side. Once browned, remove from oil, drain on paper towel and season with chili or curry powder.

KOZLIK'S CANADIAN MUSTARD—in 1948, Toronto resident Anton Kozlik opened a small booth at the St. Lawrence Market to sell his mother's mustard sauce. The booth is still there, but the effusive Kessler family has replaced Anton. They have good reason to be effusive; they craft and sell 38 varieties of mustard from Canadian mustard seeds and all-natural ingredients sourced from Canadian suppliers. Kozlik's Canadian Mustard is available at outlets in major Canadian cities and through online ordering. *See also* mustard.

KRAFT DINNER—known as KD for short, the 1937 macaroni and cheese invention of Kraft Foods was another step toward the complete oblivion of the Canadian food experience.

L

LA ROUTE DES VINS—a 132-km wine tour route in Québec's Eastern Townships that links 18 wineries offering wines for purchase and tasting, some of which are open all year and some only seasonally. Check online for opening times. *See also* food and wine routes.

LA TIRE. See maple taffy.

LA VARENNE, FRANÇOIS PIERRE (1615–1678)—author of *Le Cuisinier françois*, published in 1651 and the founding text of modern French cuisine, comprising 30 editions over 75 years and reprinted as recently as 1983.

LABRADOR TEA (*Ledum groenlandicum*; also called Indian tea, weesukapuka, wishakapuka)—a low-growing, arctic shrub with leathery, furry leaves that, when infused in boiling water, produce a drink tasting of rhubarb. Popular with First Nations and English settlers, Labrador tea leaves are still being gathered from the wilds by people who relish the tea's pleasant taste.

Labrador Tea

- Exported to England by the Hudson's Bay Company during the early part of the 19th century, Weesukapuka tea (the HBC trade name) became a taste-of-Canada sensation after young ladies discovered that an overindulgence of the herb would facilitate a cosmetic dilation of their pupils. However, it also made them sweat—a sales-hampering side effect that soon put an end to exports.

LABRADOR TRAPPER BREAD—risen molasses bread packed with raisins, currants and butter and meant to last for weeks. Baked in quantity by Labrador trappers' wives, the loaves were the main ration of fur trappers making the rounds of their trap lines. *See also* bread.

LAC ST-JEAN SALMON PIE (also called *tourtière à la ouananiche*)—a once-a-week favourite when Lac St-Jean was full of the landlocked Atlantic salmon called ouananiche. Locals may still enjoy the odd pie, but wild ouananiche has become a rare catch; most people have to settle for farmed Atlantic salmon. *See also* ouananiche.

LACOMBE SWINE—a Canadian original breed developed in the early 1950s at the Canadian Department of Agriculture research station in Lacombe, Alberta. Very popular with farmers, the Lacombe pig is second only to the Yorkshire breed in swine production. It's our national porker, and very tasty.

LACTIC ACID—many kinds of bacteria produce acid in their digestion of organic matter and imbue that matter with a sour taste. Lactic acid–producing bacteria found in milk will change the acidity of the milk, causing it to both sour and precipitate proteins, an important process in cheese making.

LAKE ERIE FRIED PERCH—a specialty item of restaurants from Québec to Alberta, but mostly found on menus around Lake Erie, one of the best being the Erie Beach Hotel in Port Dover, Ontario. Yellow perch (*Perca flavescens*) is one of our predominant freshwater fish species and can be found in lakes almost nationwide. *See also* perch.

LAKE HERRING. *See* cisco.

LAKE TROUT (*Salvelinus namaycush*)—once the predominant species of the Great Lakes watershed, the lake trout has been decimated by lamprey infestation, habitat destruction and overfishing. However, the fish maintains predominance in the north, where it is commercially fished and a star attraction for sport fishermen. Frozen lake trout from Saskatchewan, available in supermarkets across the country, is both versatile and tasty fare.

LAMB'S LETTUCE (*Valerianella locusta*; also called corn salad, field salad)—once considered

RECIPE

Weed Soup

Boil 8 cups of only the tips of lamb's quarters in 4 quarts water for 3–4 minutes, then drain and coarsely chop. In a deep pan, fry 1 cup diced salt pork until crisp, then add 1 minced onion and cook until golden. Add 5 cups water, bring to a boil and add 2 diced potatoes and the chopped lamb's quarters. Return to a boil and stir in ½ cup oatmeal (not the rolled or quick variety). Simmer 30–40 minutes, stirring occasionally, and season to taste.

a weed, this plant is slowly making inroads into the modern Canadian food experience and should be looked for at farmers' markets in late winter and early spring. A favourite winter salad green in Europe, it is usually served with beets and walnuts or fried bacon and shallots.

LAMB'S QUARTERS (*Chenopodium berlandieri*; also called fat hen, goosefoot, pigweed, wild spinach)—brought along by some settlers as a garden plant, it promptly escaped into the wild to become a ubiquitous weed from coast to coast. That was bad for farmers but great for foragers, because leaves of this plant cook up to taste just like their relative spinach. Lamb's quarters are delicious and, as the most foraged plant in Canada, are usually available at farmers' markets. The seeds, though tiny, are prolific and can be milled into flour. One day it may occur to people to stop battling this plant and start cooking with it. Try it fried with bacon and apples, and you will be out looking for more. Maritimers make a wonderful soup from lamb's quarters, called weed soup after one of the plant's common names: pigweed.

LARD—pig fat that is usually wet-rendered by boiling and skimming the fat, or dry-rendered where the fat is fried out like bacon fat. Lard is most commonly used for deep-frying and as an ingredient in baking, especially flaky pastry. Lard of the highest grade is obtained from the gut of slaughtered hogs and is called leaf lard, while fat from upper sections is called fatback,

with commercially sold lard being a combination that is usually hydrogenated and may contain bleaching agents, emulsifiers and antioxidant chemicals. In the 19th and early 20th centuries, lard and butter were interchangeable in Canadian kitchens and at dinner tables, with the former gradually replaced by cheaper hydrogenated vegetable fats.

LARDING—the process of sewing long, thin strips of lard called "lardons" into lean pieces of meat. Larding and barding are two methods used to prevent lean meats from drying out during roasting. To lard a roast, one should employ a larding needle to thread thin strips of salt pork through lean cuts of meat, going with the grain. Barding is simply covering a roast of lean meat with thin strips of salt pork or bacon and tying it with string. Either way, lean meats, especially game meats, will benefit and come from the oven juicy and delicious.

LARGE RAMPION. *See* evening primrose.

LASSY BREAD—Newfoundland yeast-raised sweet bread made with raisins, spices and molasses. "Lassy" is the Newfoundlander word for molasses, and it precedes many culinary creations.

LASSY MOGS. *See* mogs.

LASSY PIE. *See* molasses pie.

LAURA SECORD CHOCOLATES—in 1813, an American immigrant to Ontario's Niagara Peninsula named Laura Secord made a monumental 18-hour trek through the wilds to warn British troops of an impending attack by American soldiers. She was our very own heroine, but nobody had a clue she even existed until exactly one century later, when Toronto resident Frank O'Connor began making chocolates and putting her story on the back of every box. Laura Secord chocolates, along with the fame of our heroine, expanded across the country through outlets and drug store installations. In 1960, Ault Foods, owned by John Labatt Limited, bought not only the company but also the Secord homestead and turned the place into a tourist attraction. In 1983, Laura Secord was purchased by the English candy conglomerate Rowntree Mackintosh, and in 1986, the Swiss conglomerate Nestlé bought Rowntree. Then in 1999, Nestlé sold the brand to U.S. candy conglomerate Archibald Candy Corporation of Chicago, the makers of Fanny Farmer brand chocolates. In 2004, a consortium of financial giants, led by the U.S. investment group Gordon Brothers, bought and continues to run the company named for Canada's War of 1812 heroine.

LAVENDER (*Lavandula* spp.)—once a reserved product of southern France and a rare commodity in Canada, fields of the aromatic herb have popped up in almost every province, and its

marvellous aroma is perfuming farmers' markets nationwide. As well as flower buds for deodorizing closets and cupboards, most lavender farmers offer essential oils distilled from the flower buds for cosmetic purposes and honey sourced from their fields.

LAZY CAKE. *See* wacky cake.

LE CANARD LIBÉRÉ—to be in Montréal and not go to Le Canard Libéré to experience all things duck is a crime against sensibility. Foie gras, sausage, pâtés, fat and stock—it's all there, including a duck poutine.

LE CENDRILLON CHEESE—a chèvre (goat cheese) made in Saint-Raymond de Portneuf, Québec, by La Maison Alexis de Portneuf and judged world's best cheese at the 2009 World Cheese Awards.

LE CRU DU CLOCHER—award-winning, raw-milk, aged Cheddar cheese made at the Fromagerie Le Fromage au Village in Lorrainville, Québec.

LE PIED-DE-VENT CHEESE—a well-ripened, semi-hard cheese made by the Fromagerie du Pied-de-Vent, on Québec's Îles-de-la-Madeleine, an island in the middle of the Gulf of St. Lawrence. Le Pied-de-Vent is a raw-milk cheese made from the milk of the original New France cow, the Canadienne. *See also* Canadienne dairy cow.

LE RIOPELLE DE L'ISLE CHEESE—a rich, triple-cream Camembert-style soft cheese made by a cooperative of five dairy farms on Québec's Ile-aux-Grues and named for the famous painter and island resident, Jean-Paul Riopelle.

LEAMINGTON TOMATO FESTIVAL—held every August in Canada's tomato capital, Leamington, Ontario, this three-day extravaganza of all things tomato is a public expansion of the one-time annual H.J. Heinz Company's employees' picnic. It is tonnes of fun and there's something for everybody, even if you don't like tomatoes.

LEAVENING—what occurs after yeast or a chemical such as baking soda or baking powder is added to dough or batter, causing a reaction that produces bubbles of carbon dioxide, which in turn cause the dough or batter to rise.

LECHEVALIER MAILLOUX CHEESE—a soft, raw-milk cheese crafted at La Ferme Piluma in Saint-Basile de Portneuf and judged the finest cheese in Canada by the Dairy Farmers of Canada in 1998.

LECITHIN—a brownish fat-like substance found in plant and animal tissues that, after extraction, is used in all manner of industrial and food processing applications. Food-grade lecithin is usually extracted from soybeans and is used to emulsify and keep packaged foods moist.

A
B
C
D
E
F
G
H
I
J
K
L
M
N
O
P
Q
R
S
T
U
V
W
X
Y
Z

LEEK (*Allium ampeloprasum*)—a close relative of onions and garlic, this vegetable produces a cylindrical leaf sheath that farmers generally blanch by pushing up soil around the sheath. Leeks are subdivided into two types, summer and winter, with the former being smaller while the latter is larger and has a stronger flavour.

RECIPE

Leek and Crab Pasties

Roll out 1 lb puff pastry and use a 7-inch plate to cut out 4 rounds. Set rounds aside in the refrigerator. Soak a pinch of saffron threads in 1 Tbsp water. In a pan, melt 2 Tbsp butter and cook 1 chopped leek over medium heat until soft, about 5 minutes. Add saffron and liquid and cook 1 minute longer. Combine ½ lb crabmeat, ½ cup breadcrumbs, a bit of parsley, zest and juice of 1 lemon and 1 tsp Old Bay seasoning. Stir in leeks and divide mixture among the 4 pastry rounds. Brush edges of rounds with egg and fold, pressing edges together. Brush folded pasties with egg and bake in a 400°F oven until golden brown, about 30 minutes. Allow to cool to room temperature before serving.

CANADA'S FAVOURITE LEEK VARIETIES

- Blue Solaise—a superb winter leek of French origin.

- King Richard—the best short-season or summer leek.

- Musselburg—a very large winter leek of Scottish origin.

LEGUMES—plants in this family bear a simple fruit called a pod, the most well known being beans, peas, lentils and peanuts. Cultivated worldwide, legumes, sometimes called pulses, were among humankind's earliest food crops and are a favourite of gardeners and farmers for the plants' ability to convert airborne nitrogen into ammonia, a process known as nitrogen fixation.

LEMON AND LIME (*Citrus* spp.)—introduced to Spain by the Arabs during the middle of the 13th century, lemon plantations planted by British interests in the Azores were supplying English markets by the 15th century, and by the 18th century the commercial cultivation of lemons was carried on all over the Mediterranean with a brisk trade to England and the Americas, especially to Canada. Limes, however, were late catching on and only made available owing to the efforts of Edmund Sturge, an English manufacturing chemist who, in 1867, began turning the Caribbean island of Montserrat into a lime plantation to facilitate his company's production of citric acid. By the 1870s, Edmund Sturge's Montserrat Lime Juice Company had 150,000 lime trees supplying not only his company but also the entire British navy and every Canadian general store via the railway.

LEMON CURD—an English delight made by settlers whenever the local general store received a barrel of lemons and the farm had an adequate supply of butter and eggs.

RECIPE

Lemon Curd

Juice 4 lemons into a double boiler along with 6 eggs, 2 cups sugar and ½ cup butter. Add the grated rind from 2 lemons, and whisk over boiling water for 20 minutes until thick. Pour into jars, cool and refrigerate. Lemon curd will keep for 3–4 weeks but is usually eaten after only a few days. Spoon it into prebaked tart shells for a treat made in heaven.

LEMON HONEY—a faux honey popular in the early days and made with easily acquired lemons.

RECIPE

Lemon Honey

Mix 4 oz butter with 1 lb sugar and 6 eggs, leaving out 2 whites. Grate in the zest and juice of 3 lemons and simmer until the consistency of honey.

A
B
C
D
E
F
G
H
I
J
K
L
M
N
O
P
Q
R
S
T
U
V
W
X
Y
Z

LEMON PIE—iconic to the Canadian food experience since the early 18th century, when commercial cod shippers began voluntarily supplying their fishermen with citrus rations from the Caribbean. Lemons and limes literally poured into our seaports and found their way into the interior by various routes. Scurvy was well known and dreaded, and to keep their men safe from the disease, pioneer women made sure to bake plenty of lemon pies.

LEMON VERBENA (*Aloysia triphylla*)—a small shrub with yellow and green leaves related to Mexican oregano (*Lippia graveolens*) but smelling and tasting remarkably like lemon. Brought to England from its native Chile around 1840, the shrub wasted no time in getting to Canada and migrating from coast to coast. It was used to make summertime veranda drinks, a custom that died during World War II but has been reborn as patio drinks. A few mashed leaves, a spoonful of simple syrup, a squirt of seltzer and a shot of vodka, and it's off to the races.

LEMONADE BERRY—a name once commonly used for the fruit of the sumac tree (*Rhus* spp.) from which early settlers to Canada, mimicking local First Nations, brewed a refreshing drink with a slight lemon flavour. *See also* sumac tea.

LENTIL (*Lens culinaris*)—Canada is the world's leading exporter of lentils, while India is the world's leading producer and consumer, this latter being the reason for Canada's large exports. Canada grows two varieties, green and red, which can be either whole, dehulled or split.

The red split is the most in demand, with the whole green gaining ground.

LES BINNES. See fèves au lard.

LES TOQUETTES. See maple taffy.

LETTUCE (*Letuca sativa*)—an annual vegetable related to the sunflower that was well known to early Egyptian farmers. Lettuce is a cool crop and well suited to growing in Canadian climates when protected from early frost. There are many modern cultivars, but the tastiest remain the heirlooms.

CANADA'S FAVOURITE LETTUCE VARIETIES

- Black Seeded Simpson—a loose-leaf.

- Cimmaron—a red loose-leaf.

- Crisp Mint—a Romaine type.

- Lily's—a loose-leaf.

- Marvel of Four Seasons—a butterhead and a true marvel in salad.

- Tennis Ball—a butterhead.

- Tom Thumb—a small butterhead for salads.

- White Paris Cos—a Romaine type.

- Yugoslavian Red—a butterhead.

LICORICE ROOT (*Glycyrrhiza lepidota*; also called wild licorice)—grows from BC east to Ontario and was used by First Nations as medicine and sweetener. Pioneer settlers adopted the root to tame the piney flavour of spruce beer and as a flavouring ingredient for chewing tobacco. Wild licorice root is 50 times sweeter than sugar and has been considered by the province of Manitoba as a commercial crop to produce artificial sweeteners.

LIME. *See* lemon and lime.

LIME RICKEY—a sweetened lime juice and seltzer drink extensively advertised by restaurants of the 1950s and '60s as a way to beat summer heat. Almost all restaurants from that era would have a lime rickey sign above the door, but when air conditioning came along, the signs were replaced by ones that read, "It's 20 percent cooler inside."

LIME TREE. *See* basswood.

LIMESTONE ORGANIC CREAMERY—a dairy farm operated by the Groenewegen family in

Elginburg, Ontario, that is helping return sensibility to milk production by specializing in organic dairy products and eggs, including unhomogenized whole milk and artisanal butter. For those living in the Kingston area, Limestone offers once-a-week home delivery of their products, supplemented by the fine yogurts and cheeses of Organic Meadow Products. Go online to order and arrange delivery or for a list of retail stores handling their fine foods.

LINDEN TEA (also called basswood tea)—a therapeutic hot water infusion from the dried blossoms of the linden tree (*Tilia americana*), also called the basswood or lime tree. French settlers were very familiar with the therapeutic qualities of linden tea and were delighted to find the tree growing everywhere.

LINGCOD (*Ophiodon elongatus*; also called blue cod, buffalo cod, green cod)—a west coast ground fish found mainly off the coast of BC and the preferred quarry of scuba divers. Fished commercially but mostly caught accidentally, lingcod is a favourite of chefs because the flesh is yummy, hangs together during cooking and plates pure white.

LINGONBERRY. *See* partridgeberry.

LISTERIA—a food-borne bacteria sometimes found in soft cheeses, hot dogs and luncheon meats that can cause serious illness in pregnant women, the elderly and people with compromised immune systems. Symptoms are flu-like, usually resulting in a misdiagnosis and, in the worst cases, especially among pregnant woman, can lead to bacterial meningitis.

LIVER LOAF—a hard-times, Depression-era meal of chopped liver baked in a bread tin and served with mashed potatoes.

LIVER AS FOOD

Beef or calf liver dishes came into being during the Depression. Before the 1900s, the livers of slaughtered animals were considered toxic, and the organs were either discarded or fed to dogs. Hard times caused both homemakers and restaurant chefs to reconsider the lowly liver; dogs seemed to thrive on it, and the stuff sold for pennies a pound. Liver needed a placebo, a fantasy poison neutralizer, and when some bright chef hit onto soaking it in milk, the word spread through Canada and down into the U.S. like wildfire.

RECIPE

Liver Loaf

Cover 1 lb beef liver with water and simmer 5 minutes. Run liver and 1 chopped medium onion through a meat grinder using a medium blade, then mix in ½ lb pork sausage, 1 cup bread crumbs, 2 beaten eggs, ¼ cup beef stock, 1 Tbsp lemon juice, 1 tsp Worcestershire sauce, 1 tsp salt and a dash of pepper. Press into a loaf pan, top with 4 bacon slices and bake 45–50 minutes at 350°F.

LIVESTOCK—Canadian livestock destined for human consumption and slaughtered by conglomerate meat packers suffer through a gruesome process. Confused, frightened and smelling blood, the animals have only one thought: to flee from danger. They wait for an escape opportunity that never arrives and die with muscle primed for action and loaded with the flight hormones adrenaline and epinephrine. These stress hormones raise the lactic acid content of muscle tissue, imparting an off flavour to and changing the texture of the meat. It is on the consumer to search out farmers and ranchers who care how their livestock is raised and employ humane slaughtering methods, or to find a local butcher who does. Savvy butchers will often attend livestock

Livestock Diversity

- The worldwide elimination of livestock diversity by conglomerate meat packers continues at an astounding rate, with almost 200 breeds becoming extinct over the last 15 years and 1500 more on the brink of extinction. In Canada, around 75 percent of beef cattle are Hereford, Angus or Simmental; 70 percent of the nation's pork comes from three or four breeds; and about 50 percent of lamb comes from a breed called Suffolk.

- Of all the red meat consumed worldwide, about 70 percent is goat. Meat from mature animals is called chevon, while that of young goats, or kids, is called capretto.

auctions that feature championship livestock, such as provincial agricultural expositions or 4-H clubs. These animals often have names, and until the day of the sale have been almost pets; they are being sold to teach sons and daughters that farming is a business. If you find a good butcher, introduce yourself and show an interest; it may get you on the inside track to carnivore heaven.

LOBSCOUSE (also called flop)—a peppery Newfoundland soup made from salt meat, beef stock, shredded cabbage and onion.

LOBSTER (*Homarus americanus*)—absolutely must be tasted fresh from the sea, preferably at dockside. Deepwater lobsters taste better than those hoisted from shallow inland waters, hard-shell taste better than the molted or soft-shell, and any lobster weighing less than 0.5 kg is a waste of both time and money. Today's lobster fishermen navigate by radar, find traps by GPS and use an electric winch to haul them in, allowing lobster so little chance of survival that undersized crustaceans are often caught repeatedly until their main body part, the carapace, attains a length of 82.5 mm, whereas all "berried" lobsters, or females carrying eggs, are returned to the water.

COOKING LOBSTER

Tip: Undercooked lobster is inedible, while overcooked will be rubbery; however, it will take 10–15 minutes of overcooking to arrive at rubbery, so when in doubt, overcooking is better than under. To be really safe, follow the example of top chefs and boil lobster for 5 minutes, then remove all meat from the shell and sauté in butter until cooked through.

RECIPE

Baked Lobster

Separate lobster tails and cut each one in half lengthways. Mix together 1 clove of crushed garlic, ½ cup vegetable oil, ¼ cup brandy and ¼ cup lemon juice. Season tails with salt and cayenne pepper, brush with oil mixture and bake in a 400°F oven until cooked through, about 15–20 minutes.

RECIPE

Boiled Lobster

Not the best method, but the easiest. Fill a large stockpot with enough cold water to cover the lobsters, but do not add the lobsters yet. Instead, add 1 Tbsp salt for each quart of water. Bring water to a boil over high heat, remove rubber bands from lobster claws and toss the lobsters in head first; for a mixed bag of sizes, toss the biggest in first. Once the water is back to a boil, turn down heat to medium and start counting the minutes. Count 10 minutes for the first 1 lb of individual weight and add 3 minutes for every additional 1 lb—a pot of 2-lb lobsters should cook for 13 minutes after water has returned to a boil. (Note: lobsters not consumed immediately should be plunged into cold water to stop the cooking process and prevent them from getting tough and stringy.)

RECIPE

Grilled Lobster

Being low in fat, lobster needs to be parboiled before grilling. Boil lobsters for 6 minutes, cut in half lengthwise with a sharp knife and place halves shell-side down on a preheated, medium temperature grill. Baste meat with butter or oil and sprinkle with salt and pepper. Cook for 10 minutes and check the thickest parts for doneness. (Note: covering halves with an aluminum roasting pan will ensure even cooking, but remember to raise the pan and baste periodically.)

RECIPE

Steamed Lobster

This is the best method to avoid overcooking and waterlogging lobsters. Pour a few inches of water into bottom of a steamer pot and add 1 Tbsp salt for each quart of water along with 1 roughly chopped onion, 2 celery stalks, 1 Tbsp peppercorns, 2 bay leaves and a handful of dill or parsley. Bring water to a boil, insert the basket containing lobsters, cover tightly and steam for 15 minutes, adding more water if necessary.

A
B
C
D
E
F
G
H
I
J
K
L
M
N
O
P
Q
R
S
T
U
V
W
X
Y
Z

BUYING LOBSTER

Consumers who have never been "down east" and partaken of lobster fresh from the sea are lacking a comparison against which to judge the quality of any cooked lobster. The next best thing to tasting the succulent sweetness of fresh-from-the-sea lobster is to dine at a restaurant that specializes in seafood. Those establishments usually have rapid turnover, with some receiving daily air freight shipments

of fish and lobster. Time and stress are the enemies because once plucked from their natural environment, lobsters stop eating, begin to shrink and become tough and stringy.

Shippers such as Clearwater Seafoods maintain a supply of fresh lobsters by storing them in huge, dark holding tanks and do their utmost to alleviate stress by pumping in tonnes of fresh seawater and providing their charges with small compartments for hibernation. They put the crustaceans to sleep, and even though the result is next best to fresh from the sea, they are still using stored body fat to stay alive. Fat equals sweet and succulent, and with lobsters having very little fat to begin with, time is of the essence. In a perfect world, lobsters would be date stamped, but until that happens, buyers must press their noses against the glass of supermarket lobster tanks and gamble.

Activity is no indicator of freshness. Because lobsters arrive from the shipper still in a state of hibernation, activity can mean your dinner has been rudely awakened and is suffering stress. If buying lobsters at a supermarket, it is always better to trust the person behind the counter, but only after dropping a hint that you will take your business elsewhere should the little beasties be tough and stringy. Knowing your fishmonger pays dividends.

All lobster fishermen are licenced and fish to a quota set by the Department of Fisheries and Oceans, with all deepwater (80 km offshore) licences owned by the conglomerate fish processor Clearwater Seafoods Limited, a public company traded on the Toronto Stock Exchange.

LOBSTER BENEDICT—substitute lobster for peameal bacon and you have a scrumptious favourite brunch dish of the Fairmont Algonquin Hotel in St. Andrews by-the-Sea, New Brunswick. Listed on the menu as Lord Selkirk's Lobster

Lobster

- Our Atlantic, or American, lobster is a close relative to insects, in that they have exo-skeletons and a jointed appendage. Lobsters are decapods, like crayfish, shrimp, crabs and prawns, meaning they have 10 legs.

- Once considered a lowly food and a source of cheap fertilizer, the lobster has now risen

to gastronomic stardom by way of good marketing, adventurous chefs and a government that understands resource management.

- Lobster trapped in warm, coastal waters moult their shells twice a year, while those hauled from deeper, colder waters moult only once and have denser, sweeter meat. The best-tasting lobsters in the entire world are hauled from the deep waters around Québec's Magdalen Islands—it's worth going there for that reason alone.

- In 1885, Canadian lobster fishermen hauled in a record 45 million kilograms of the delectable decapods; however, by 1918 the catch had dwindled to around 12 million kilograms. Nowadays, through proper management, the annual catch has increased to around 23 million kilograms.

- Scientists suspect that telomerase, a DNA-repairing enzyme, remains active as lobsters age and gives these crusta-ceans a potentially indefinite lifespan. If size is any indication, the 20.15-kilogram behemoth caught near Shediac, New Brunswick, during the 1977 fishing season is pretty convincing evidence. Rumours abound of even larger lobsters having been spotted by sport divers.

Benedict, the dish honours the memory of Thomas Douglas, Fifth Earl of Selkirk, the Scotsman who brought 800 Scottish Highlanders to New Brunswick in 1803.

LOBSTER BUTTER—the best way to enjoy this delectable crustacean is to dunk it in copious amounts of melted butter. *See also* coral and tomalley butter.

RECIPE

Browned Butter

Cut unsalted butter into pats and cook over medium heat while whisking. Butter will foam up, but continue whisking until colour begins to change. Remove from heat and place pan on a cool surface to stop cooking.

L

RECIPE

Drawn Butter

Place ½ lb unsalted butter in a small saucepan and simmer over medium heat until all water has evaporated and milk solids begin to fry. Remove from heat and pour through dampened cheesecloth into a serving container. Pure butterfat will not adhere to the moist cheesecloth and will be "drawn" through, leaving the milk solids behind.

LOBSTER CHOWDER—a historic Maritime quick supper dish made by adding chopped lobster to a mixture of boiling milk, crushed crackers, butter and seasoning.

LOBSTER FERTILIZER—during both World Wars, the Canadian government deemed components needed to manufacture fertilizer essential to the war effort; so, unable to acquire chemical fertilizer, east coast farmers reverted to using wagonloads of lobster to fortify the land.

LOBSTER OIL—olive oil infused with fresh Atlantic lobster is a tasty drizzle for soups, salads and fish dishes. An inspiration of Vancouver chef Frédéric Couton of the Cannery Restaurant, the oil is sadly only available at that restaurant. You can try making it yourself with the shells gleaned during your next lobster boil.

RECIPE

Lobster Oil

Crush up shells, sans head, into 1-inch bits and dry in a 300°F oven for 10 minutes. Transfer dried shells to a saucepan, along with the coral if possible, cover with olive oil and simmer gently for 3 hours. Strain and bottle the oil, and keep it refrigerated.

LOBSTER PIE—a pastry-topped pie of lobster meat combined with diced potatoes, carrots, green peas and tiny white onions with a cream sauce base. Once an east coast favourite during penurious times, the pie has become the darling of upscale chefs.

LOBSTERS, LOBSTERS EVERYWHERE

In 1867, a New Brunswick lobster packer wrote the following in the *Canadian Naturalist and Quarterly Journal of Science*: "The gales of last August drove more lobsters within five miles of my packing houses than I could make use of during the whole summer. They formed a row one to five feet deep, and I should estimate them at an average of one thousand to every two rods of shore."

Lobsters were such an easy catch for Maritime fishermen that supply always exceeded demand until the late-19th century. Lobster was as cheap as dirt, and that is where much of the catch wound up—in the dirt, as fertilizer. But then the railway and steamships made possible the shipping of live lobsters. Suddenly demand began to exceed supply, and what had been food for the poor was suddenly considered a delicacy. Rising prices lured in more fishermen, causing lobster populations to shrink and forcing fishermen into ever deeper waters. What had been an easy catch turned difficult and dangerous, especially under sail, because not until the late 1920s did lobster fishermen install engines in their fishing boats. Motor power made lobster fishing a less dangerous enterprise, but it remained labour intensive as fishermen navigated by dead reckoning and hauled in traps by hand, providing lobsters a sporting chance at survival.

In 1939 and still recovering from the Great Depression, Canada entered World War II, a conflict that drew much of the remaining rural population into towns and cities. Farmers' sons and labourers enlisted in the military, daughters went to work in the factories and the factories switched production from ammonia nitrate fertilizer to explosives. With no farm help or access to fertilizer, small farmers who had survived World War I and the Depression either abandoned their land or sold to large government contract growers, who had a ration of fertilizer. Farmers who persevered were forced to rely on animal manures or other more exotic fertilizers. It wasn't uncommon to see long lines of farm wagons plodding inland from the coast, piled high with lobsters destined to become fertilizer.

That the humble lobster would be traded on the stock exchange must have been an eye-opener for those older Maritimers who remember them washing up on beaches after storms or used to fertilize fields. The inshore fisheries, while still licenced, are operated as single-boat, entrepreneurial endeavours by around 10,000 fishermen, who set a line of traps and brave weather and high seas to retrieve their catches. Today's lobster fishery is in good shape thanks to government controls. The tasty crustacean is once again so plentiful that Canada is the world's largest shipper of canned, frozen and live lobster.

LOBSTER ROLL—a long-time favourite fast food available almost anywhere on the east coast.

> ## RECIPE
>
> ### Lobster Roll
>
> *Mix 1 lb fresh or frozen lobster meat, chopped into bite-sized pieces, with ¾ cup mayonnaise, 3 Tbsp diced celery, 2 Tbsp minced onion and 2 tsp lemon juice, and serve on a hot dog bun.*

LOBSTER STEW—a very satisfying east coast dish for when the weather turns cold.

> ## RECIPE
>
> ### Down East Lobster Stew
>
> *Dissect 2 cooked lobsters on a baking sheet to save juices. Place all meat and juices in a saucepan with ½ cup melted unsalted butter, stir until all meat is buttered, place lid on pan and let stand 4 hours. Heat 6 cups whole milk or light cream to just below scalding, add buttered lobster and ¼ tsp paprika for colour. Cool mixture and refrigerate at least 24 hours. Reheat just before serving, adding a splash of dry sherry.*

LOCHE ROE—eggs from the burbot (*Lota lota*), a species of freshwater cod. Loche (a local name for burbot) are netted in the small feeder streams of the Mackenzie Delta solely for their delicious roe, which is much prized by Japanese gourmands. *See also* burbot.

LOGANBERRY (*Rubus* x *loganobaccus*)—these berries are a tasty cross between raspberries and blackberries that look like elongated raspberries but have their own flavour and

tartness. Once immensely popular for wine-making and homemade soft drinks, the berries have been relegated to seasonal, serve-with-sugar-and-cream dessert status.

LONG JOHN—a long, fried doughnut specialty of Mennonite cooks and a much-appreciated snack at Mennonite-attended farmers' markets.

LOVAGE. *See* Indian celery.

LUCKY LAGER BEER—brewed by Coast Breweries in Vancouver, New Westminster and Victoria, this beer was west coast Canada's favourite until it was acquired by Labatt and gradually fazed out of production until the brewery was closed down in 1982. Today, Lucky Lager is produced as a budget brand by Labatt in their Edmonton brewery, the same one where they brew Budweiser for all of western Canada. While Budweiser is advertised as the "King of Beers," Lucky Lager's original label proudly bore the words "Peer of Beers."

LUMBERJACK'S BREAKFAST—a huge meal of eggs, ham, bacon, sausages, potatoes, toast and pancakes, in various combinations. Some sources claim its origin dates back to Vancouver in 1870 in response to demand for a hearty start to the workday.

LUNENBURG PUDDING—not a dessert, but a pork sausage with Germanic origins and iconic to Lunenburg, Nova Scotia. *See also* Dutch mess, house bunkin.

LUNENBURG SAUSAGE—salt fish and sausage made this town famous, and though the salt fish has faded into history, Lunenburgers still line up for the sausage.

> ## RECIPE
>
> ### Lunenburg Sausage
>
> *Grind together 4 lbs good pork and 3 lbs good beef. Mix in 2 Tbsp each of ground coriander and ground black pepper, 1½ Tbsp each of salt and allspice and 2 tsp summer savory. Place mixture into a sausage mill and roll into natural casings.*

LUTEIN—a health-providing antioxidant carotenoid plant pigment responsible for the deep green colour of leafy vegetables, such as spinach and kale, and the yellow colour of corn and egg yolks.

LYCOPENE—an antioxidant carotenoid plant pigment responsible for the red and pink colouring in fruits and vegetables such as tomatoes, watermelon, red onions and rhubarb.

LYED CORN (also called hominy, Indian corn, Indian meal)—a rough cornmeal prepared by First Nations, who boiled dried corn in an alkaline solution (water and ash) until the kernels expanded, thus freeing the hard skins. Thick, creamy and called Indian meal by Europeans, the product was dried and often mixed with nutmeats and berries.

LYED CORN

Adopted by Europeans, lyed, or Indian, corn produced in small factories in Montréal was used by voyageurs, fur traders and settlers to prepare mush, a staple food of early Canadians. Fur traders headed west would take only three food items in their canoes: dried peas, salt pork and lyed corn. Settlers with wagons would take along barrels of Indian meal, along with corn seed and instructions on how to make more. When gristmills caught up with western expansion and ground cornmeal became available, settlers abandoned the making of lyed corn. However, old habits die hard and cornmeal was called Indian meal well into the 19th century.

M

MAC AND CHEESE WITH LOBSTER—ordinary American macaroni and cheese with an extraordinary Canadian twist: lobster.

MACKEREL (*Scomber scombrus*; also called Atlantic mackerel)—a small but prolific member of the Tuna family with oily flesh and a taste reminiscent of tuna. Mackerel are best when cooked fresh from the water or brine-cured and smoked like herring. During the early years of the 19th century, Nova Scotia fisheries shipped more than 50,000 barrels of cured mackerel per annum to all points of the globe, but nowadays, mackerel is mostly canned and available in all manner of sauces.

MACKINTOSH TOFFEE—a soft toffee bar invented in 1890 by Englishman John Mackintosh. It became a favourite "in the trenches" candy of Canadian servicemen during World War I, who, on their return home, set in motion a national love affair with the golden bar. In 1969, Mackintosh merged with Rowntree, and the national love affair continued until 1988, when Rowntree-Mackintosh was sold to mega food conglomerate Nestlé. In 2009, in an unfortunate move, Nestlé stopped making the golden bar, replacing it with their poorer quality one-bite, plastic-wrapped toffees.

MACLAREN'S IMPERIAL CHEESE—a sharp, cold-pack cheese food invented in 1892 by Canadian cheese entrepreneur Alexander Ferguson MacLaren and his Imperial Cheese Company. Packed in porcelain containers, his product saw distribution around the world until J.L. Kraft acquired Imperial in 1920 as a vehicle to make and distribute his own patented processed cheese. The porcelain tub cheese went out of production until 1947, when Kraft Foods reintroduced the cheese in a red cardboard container to test the effectiveness of television advertising. The test proved highly successful, and Kraft Foods was hard pressed to meet the sudden demand.

MAHI-MAHI (*Coryphaena hippurus*; also called dolphinfish, dorado)—one of the, if not *the*, best-tasting saltwater species and a very good reason to move to the west coast. Not commercially viable in Canada, the species is much sought after by west coast sports fishermen.

MAIDENHAIR BERRY. *See* snowberry.

MAIDSTONE BAKERIES—the machines at Maidstone Bakeries in Brantford, Ontario—the source of all Tim Hortons "always fresh" doughnuts—operate in a factory perched on a sea of hot oil that more resembles a refinery than a bakery. Maidstone cooks over two million doughnuts every day, flash-freezes them and trucks them off to shops across the country to be thawed and heated. Once half-owned by Tim Hortons (now by a Swiss firm), Maidstone's robotic manufacturing process was adopted after the doughnut company's U.S. owners determined that Canadians prized quick service over quality. Nowadays, Tim Hortons is a touch less foreign-owned—it has become a public company traded on the Toronto Stock Exchange—but it has not abandoned its centralized robotic production system. At least the coffee's always fresh.

MALLARD (*Anas platyrhynchos*)—the most common wild duck and the ancestor of most domesticated ducks. Mallards harvested by

Doughnut Nation

- One jelly doughnut (my favourite), or "jam-buster" in the Prairie provinces, contains a whopping 300 calories, 11 grams of fat, 3 grams of sugar and 580 milligrams of salt.

- According to Statistics Canada, Canadians spend around $14 billion annually at the nation's 90,000 food service establishments (restaurants and fast food), with the most popular food items being coffee, doughnuts and fries.

Duck Breeds

- Heritage breed ducks are either mallard-related or the South American Muscovy breed.

- The Silver Appleyard duck is a 1960s hybrid that trumps all other breeds. It is known as the gourmet's duck, bred for its large, white eggs and its lean, flavourful meat.

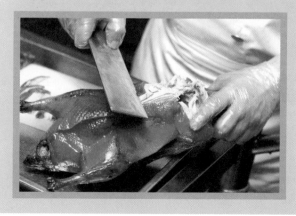

hunters in fall are usually hung for a few days before being roasted. Roasting is the best preparation method for this bird, but be sure to advise all dinner participants of the dangers associated with digging in too heartily—many a tooth has been broken on shot still lodged in the duck.

MALT—barley seeds that have, by various means, been induced to germinate, usually by a method that involves steeping the grain in warm water until it "chits," meaning the rootlets burst from the seed, then killing the seed embryo with heat and kilning the "green malt" to a dryness appropriate to its use. When grains chit, the seed embryo releases amylase, an enzyme that converts the seeds' starch into a sugar called maltose that can be fermented and turned into beer or distilled into spirits. They can also be dry-roasted in a kiln and ground to a fine powder for use as a food additive.

MALT EXTRACT—made by soaking powdered malt in water, then heat-reduced to a syrup for use in the food processing industry where its affinity for water—its hygroscopic nature—helps keep breakfast cereals and brown bread moist.

MALT VINEGAR—vinegar made from malted barley and used extensively for pickling and as a topping for fries.

MALTED MILK—invented by London pharmacist James Horlick in the 1880s, malted milk powder was an evaporated mixture of malted barley, wheat flour and whole milk. Initially sold as a baby food, Horlicks Malted Milk found use and public exposure as a nutritional supplement for long expeditions. Malted milk really took off when it was added to ice cream, creating the famed ice cream soda served by "soda jerks" at "malt shops" across North America during the 1930s and '40s, the main player in Canada being the Borden Company.

MANDRAKE. *See* mayapple.

MAPLE BUTTER—maple syrup cooked to the soft-ball stage (235–245°F, or when a bit of syrup dropped into cold water forms a soft ball), then cooled and beaten until creamy and can easily be spread on bread or toast. Another method is to simply whip ½ cup softened butter with ¼ cup maple syrup.

MAPLE CREAM—a delicious maple spread for toast or sandwiches and a long-time favourite product of the maple sugar industry. Maple cream forms when the temperature of boiling maple syrup reaches 232°F, and you can make your own at home.

RECIPE

Maple Cream

Boil 2 cups fancy grade (or No.1 extra light) maple syrup to 232°F on a candy thermometer. Add ¼ tsp butter to keep the syrup from boiling over.

MAPLE DALE CHEESE—a century-old cheese maker with a brand-new plant in Plainfield, Ontario, Maple Dale produces many varieties of prize-winning cow's milk cheeses. Their special emphasis is on aged Cheddar, with some six years old. Maple Dale's extra-mature Cheddar, a two-year-old variety, came away with the Grand Championship at the 2009 Royal Agricultural Winter Fair in Toronto. The company can ship

cheese through online ordering, including curds made fresh daily.

MAPLE JELLY—an all-Canadian condiment made with maple syrup, cold water and pectin. It was popular with early settlers and is hot with today's trendy chefs. Take note that modern jam-making pectin will not set up with maple syrup unless it's a seaweed-derived (carrageenan) pectin, such as Genugel.

MAPLE LEAF COOKIE—the all-Canadian sandwich cookie, shaped like a maple leaf with a filling flavoured with real maple syrup and baked by almost every commercial cookie company, the Dare brand being immensely popular.

MAPLE MOUSSE—a wonderfully light and fluffy maple dessert made even better with a dollop of whipped cream. It's like eating a sweet, maple-flavoured cloud.

RECIPE

Maple Mousse

(courtesy of Edna Staebler's [Food That Really Schmecks] mom)

Soak 2 tsp plain gelatin in water. Beat 2 eggs, add 1 cup maple syrup and cook in double boiler for about 2 minutes while stirring. Cool mixture slightly, add gelatin and stir. When mixture cools and thickens, fold in 1 cup whipped cream, pour into serving dishes and chill. Serve with a dollop of whipped cream and a dusting of chopped nuts.

MAPLE PUFFS—maple syrup cooked to hard-ball stage (250–270°F, or when a bit of syrup forms a hard ball when dropped into cold water), then cooled slightly, mixed with beaten egg whites and nutmeats and spooned onto wax paper for cooling.

MAPLE SUGAR—maple sap cooked past the syrup stage to a thick molasses, whisked quickly until crystallization begins and poured into moulds. Another type of maple sugar—the type preferred by First Nations and pioneer families—is stirred sugar, wherein the syrup is continuously stirred until granulation. Stirred maple sugar more resembles regular sugar and will keep for longer periods. Prior to the 1860s, when John Redpath's Montréal sugar refinery began shipping to all the settled areas of Canada, the country's residents depended on the forest for sugar for baking, syrup to baste a roast, sweetener for the morning gruel and candy for the kids. *See also* sugar.

MAPLE SUGAR CANDY—a common pioneer sweet made from maple sugar and dried

RECIPE

Maple Sugar Candy

Place 1 cup maple sugar, ½ cup water, a pinch of salt and a dab of butter in a saucepan and boil until brittle, about 300°F. Add 1 cup nuts, pour into a well-buttered tray and allow to set.

Maple Sugar

- There are many types of sugar: brown, burnt, caramelized, castor, coarse, confectioners, demerara, fondant, fruit, golden syrup, golden yellow, granulated, icing, liquid, liquid invert, molasses, muscovado, organic, pearl, plantation, powdered, raw, refined sugar syrup, refiner's syrup, sanding, soft, superfine, turbinado and, you guessed it, maple.

- Canada produces most of the world's maple syrup and sugar, with the province of Québec supplying most of that amount. During the initial decades of the 20th century, Québec's maple sugar production soared to meet the demands of the American tobacco industry because it makes an ideal flavour additive for cigarettes.

nuts, such as walnuts, beechnuts, hazelnuts or chestnuts.

MAPLE SUGAR COOKIES—an iconic pioneer cookie that is still in demand by hungry kids and dads across the nation.

RECIPE

Maple Sugar Cookies

Mix together 1 cup each of flour, maple sugar and maple butter, 2 eggs, 2 Tbsp water, 2 tsp baking soda and, if needed, a little extra flour to make a soft dough. Drop onto a cookie sheet and bake at 350°F for 15–20 minutes.

MAPLE SUGAR RUM—an alcoholic beverage made from fermented and distilled maple sap.

MAPLE SYRUP—from the boiled sap of silver, black and sugar maples, First Nations created an entire maple cuisine that was a huge benefit to early settlers. Wild game infused with maple syrup became a delectable treat, and corn mush sprinkled with maple sugar made that staple food more bearable.

MAPLE SYRUP GLAZE—great for glazing all things pork, especially ribs.

RECIPE

Maple Syrup Glaze

Mix ½ cup maple syrup with ¼ cup apple cider vinegar, 1 Tbsp each of grainy mustard and minced garlic, 1 tsp crushed fennel seeds and ½ tsp pepper.

MAPLE SYRUP GRADES—maple syrup is graded according to translucency; Canada No. 1 is further graded as extra light, light or medium, referring to both colour and taste. The lightest, Canada No. 1 extra light—also called fancy grade—can be almost water clear to amber

colour, has a delicate maple flavour and is the predominant grade for retail, while Canada No. 1 medium is a darker amber with a pronounced maple flavour, the supermarket maple syrup. Canada No. 2 is dark amber with a very pronounced maple flavour. It is usually only sold at the farm gate or at farmers' markets. Ontario also has a No. 2 grade for syrup sold at the farm gate. The federal government mandates that

MAPLE SYRUP TRICKERY

Making the stuff is a cinch, any youngster can do it: drill holes into sugar maples, hammer in the taps, hang buckets and boil the collected contents into syrup. When I was seven or eight, I had a tap into every tree in my neighbourhood and had thoughts of selling the stuff door-to-door. Years later, while returning home for a visit from university, I stopped at a roadside stand advertising new-crop maple syrup. After some price dickering and finger dipping, I purchased a gallon bottle at what I thought was a bargain price. Later, while drizzling syrup over stacks of pancakes, my family discovered that the bargain bottle was only a few inches of syrup floating on almost a gallon of an unidentifiable liquid.

Hoodwinkery is rampant during berry-picking or tree-tapping season, so be leery of roadside stands and inspect their wares carefully. Buy only honey in the comb, use something longer than a finger to sample maple syrup and check for large highbush blueberries mixed into wild-picked lowbush berries. Buyer beware is the rule when foraging roadside stands, but if a good one should be found, it can be a goldmine of produce. If foraging the countryside sounds daunting, there are the local farmers' markets and online suppliers, where buyers can most always be assured of finding produce of exceptional taste and quality.

Maple Syrup

- The Huron people used cold weather to make their maple syrup—they froze the maple sap, causing water to separate from the sugar solids.

- Maple sap is a misnomer; what is tapped from trees is the sugary water that rises in the tree before the sap begins to run. When sap does rise, usually 18 to 20 days into the tapping process, harvesting ceases because the sap smells and tastes like maple buds.

- To maintain optimum flavour, maple syrup should be refrigerated in a glass container. Syrup can also be stored in the freezer, where it will last indefinitely.

- In the old days, 90 percent of Québec's maple sap was boiled down into maple sugar and used as currency at local general stores. The stores accumulated sugar and sold it to local dealers, who in turn sold it to Montréal wholesalers. In those formative years, maple syrup—called maple molasses—consisted of a thick liquid left over from the sugaring process.

- Today, syrup is king and Canada produces 85 percent of the world's supply from over 15 million trees. With each tree tapped by two spigots, that is nearly one spigot for every Canadian. It is big business for rural economies.

Grade 2 and 3 syrups, these being dark with a very pronounced maple flavour, be used in commercial applications. For culinary purposes, chefs want the No. 2 grade, but for your pancakes or ice cream, you'll want the No. 1. The Province of Québec, which produces 70 percent of the world's maple syrup, maintains its own two-category grading standard of extra light, light, medium and amber, with category 1 being for retail and 2 for industrial purposes.

MAPLE SYRUP PIE (also called sugar pie, *tarte au sucre*)—a centuries-old Québec habitant and Acadian dessert pie made with ingredients common to those early days: maple sugar, maple syrup, butter, eggs, cream and flour.

MAPLE SYRUP SWEETIES—a once-popular children's candy made during the annual sugaring off. Mix the thickest syrup with fine flour, butter and a flavouring such as lemon or peppermint and, when hardened, cut into small squares.

MAPLE TAFFY (also called *la tire*, *les toquettes*, snow taffy)—a taffy candy made by pouring

boiling syrup onto snow and twirling the sweet onto a stick as it cools. In early Québec, taffy pulls were attended by entire villages and were especially popular with boys trying to meet girls.

MAPLE VINEGAR—vinegar produced by boiling five pails of sap down to one, adding yeast and fermenting the liquid in a cask. Several brands are available today, all from the province of Québec and indispensable in the kitchens of upscale restaurant chefs.

MAPLE WALNUT ICE CREAM—one of our favourite flavours of ice cream enjoyed then and now and made with our most plentiful ingredients. Before the hand-cranked ice cream freezer came along, there was *crème anglaise* poured into metal trays and set on windowsills in winter, or onto a block of ice in icehouses during summer. Canadian cooks still make this frozen delight, now called icebox ice cream. Or try the flavour as a pie!

M

> ### RECIPE
>
> #### *Maple Walnut Pie*
>
> *Melt 2 Tbsp butter in a saucepan, add ¼ cup flour and stir constantly until golden brown. Add 1 cup maple syrup and ½ cup maple sap (or water), stirring constantly until thick. Add ¾ cup halved walnuts, stir and allow to cool until just warm. Pour into prepared pie crust and bake in a 350°F oven until filling sets and top is golden brown, about 35–40 minutes.*

MAPLE-GLAZED HAM (also called *jambon à l'erable*)—a Québec habitant ham that once featured a glaze of only maple syrup and sugar, but is now made with maple syrup, mustard and brown sugar. It has become a nationwide favourite. See also *jambon de la cabane à sucre*.

MARCHÉ ATWATER—the premier market among Montréal's many fabulous farmers' markets, the Atwater is open all seasons and, while touristy, still manages to attract serious foodies with a periphery of seasonal farmers'

stalls and a main building filled with bakeries, restaurants, produce and commercial sellers. *See also* market squares.

MARCHÉ JEAN-TALON—slightly less touristy than the Atwater, the Jean-Talon is open year-round and caters more to serious foodies. It's all here and it's really big, so come early, armed with a map. It is a gourmet's heaven. Do not miss Marché des Saveurs, a store full of artisanal foods from all over Québec. In the last few years dozens of farmers' markets have opened up in and around the city; for a complete listing go online to the Marchés de Quartiers website. *See also* market squares.

MARGARINE—invented in France in 1869 as "butter for the poor," margarine quickly caught on. By 1883, Dutch butter dealer Jurgens, the largest in Europe, was shipping 40,000 tonnes of margarine to England, a situation that prompted that company's merger with the English soap maker Lever Brothers, forming the conglomerate Unilever. In North America before World War I, strong lobbying by dairy interests prevented the sale of coloured margarines, usually buttery yellow, thereby forcing manufacturers to supply tiny dye capsules that required kneading into the lard-white margarine—a situation that persisted in Québec, a province with a very strong dairy lobby, until 2008.

MARIONBERRY—a cross between two varieties of blackberries, marionberries are still black-berries but are slightly different in taste and size and are easier to cultivate. West coasters purchasing blackberries are probably buying marionberries, which account for about 60 percent of commercial production. *See also* blackberry.

MARITIME BROWN BREAD—iconic, down east leavened bread made with three flours (whole wheat, rye and corn) combined with buttermilk, molasses, salt and unsweetened applesauce. Traditionally served with baked beans, it is good anytime. *See also* bread.

MARKET SQUARES—during Canada's formative years, Saturday was market day, a time for rural populations to make the journey into towns and villages to exchange farm produce for cash at market squares. Farmers arrived with the dawn and sold from their wagon tailgates, rain or shine, then made the long journey home. Sensing oppor-tunity, a few savvy individuals set up covered stalls and bought farmers' produce at a dis-count, allowing farmers a quick turnaround. Over time, market day in Canada's larger towns began to resemble Middle Eastern bazaars, with stall owners diversifying into all manner of foods and consumer goods. Every town in Canada had

THE END OF THE MARKET SQUARE

Market squares were early-day precursors to brick-and-mortar mercantile/food operations, such as Toronto's great T. Eaton Company, an entrepreneurial endeavour with a long reach thanks to Canada's excellent system of railways. Where the trains went, so went the settlers to farm the land, and the trains' frequent fuel and watering stops became villages and a market for farmers' produce. It was a most satisfactory arrangement for both farmers and consumers, but in 1914, the equilibrium began to quickly unravel.

World War I extracted a heavy toll on Canada's servicemen and women: almost 10 percent were killed or missing in action, while another 25 per-cent suffered grievous wounds. Because Canada was largely an agrarian nation, farming families were the most affected. Many abandoned rural life for the towns and cities and work in the new factories. World War I created a farm labour crisis that lingered for years, and a countless number of Canadian farms began coalescing into larger entities, as did the food canneries. Facilitated by the tractor, modern-ized steel plows and mechanical harvesters, these larger farms kept the huge canneries

supplied and profitable. It was a sad end to many small produce farms, but fortuitous for consumers as the great factories were able to keep Canada's impoverished citizenery in beans and wieners until better times returned.

The Great Depression deconstructed Canada's economy much earlier than in the U.S., with unemployment soaring to over 60 percent of the labour force even before the U.S. stock-market crash of 1929. With little money to spend at the traditional market square, the Canadian housewife had to abandon the local suppliers and endured the tough economic times by continuing to produce meals from cans and backyard gardens. A few small markets tucked away behind railway stations and in rural areas survived by selling flowers, root vegetables and pork on Saturday morn-ings, but most gave way to corner stores stock-ing cheap staples and canned goods. The traditional Saturday market square that bustled with frenzied activity for an entire day had become an historical footnote and was replaced by a sometimes-stop Saturday morning shopping convenience still called the "farmers' market."

A
B
C
D
E
F
G
H
I
J
K
L
M
N
O
P
Q
R
S
T
U
V
W
X
Y
Z

a market square, and if people wanted to eat, it is where they shopped. As towns became cities, a few of these market bazaars survived and are still in operation in spite of some relocations, the most notable being the Halifax Seaport Farmers' Market, St. John City Market, Ottawa's ByWard Market, Toronto's St. Lawrence Market, the Kingston Farmers' Market and Montréal's Marché Atwater. *See also* Canadian canners, home freezers, supermarkets.

MASON JAR—invented in the U.S. by John L. Mason and patented in 1858, the zinc-topped glass canning jar revolutionized and popularized home canning until rural populations emigrating to cities and towns discovered corner stores and cheap canned goods. Almost gone but not out,

home canning is making a comeback in response to health scares and the uncaring attitudes of conglomerate canners.

MAST—the collection of nuts on forest floors, shaken from nut-bearing trees by strong winds, that in days gone by was an important source of food for livestock and swine.

MATANE SHRIMP CHOWDER—a favourite of people from the Gaspé region of Québec and made from the famous Matane shrimp harvested from the Gulf of St. Lawrence.

MATRIMONIAL CAKE (also called date squares)—a traditional Mennonite butter and brown sugar cake with a date filling, customarily handed out at weddings and a favourite of all Prairie residents.

MAYAPPLE (*Podophyllum peltatum*; also called ground lemon, mandrake, wild citron, wild jalap)—the fruit looks like a small lemon and tastes like a fig, but one bite of the root can kill you. This delicious fruit was cultivated by settlers but has been completely passed over

by modern growers. Mayapples make an excellent jam and are much sought after by foragers.

MCINTOSH APPLE—the world's favourite apple was discovered by accident by a Canadian in 1811. The accidental discoverer was John McIntosh, an Ontario farmer who, legend has it, found the tree growing wild and put it on course to being the world's most famous apple tree. Truth is, John McIntosh's fabulous tree went completely ignored for the next 60 years. McIntosh's son, Allen, actually deserves the credit for its discovery, as he was the first to recognize the apple's potential and the first to make grafts available to neighbours and eventually the whole world. "Mac" apples have ideal skin colouring, a tart flavour and crisp, white flesh. They are perfect for making apple sauce or cider or just as a healthy snack. Plant scientists are pretty sure that it was the magnificent Snow (Fameuse) variety that created the McIntosh strain. The McIntosh, in turn, has been crossbred to produce many additional popular apple varieties, such as Spartan, Empire and Cortland. *See also* apple.

MEAT CAKES—a dinner mainly composed of meat chopped very fine, seasoned, mixed with egg and celery salt, pressed into cakes and fried in butter until crisp. Meat cakes are an early version of Spam, but delicious and still popular in western provinces.

MEAT PIE (also called *pâté à la viande*)—an Acadian meat pie traditionally served at Christmas but now popular throughout the year. Originally a mixed game pie, *pâté à la viande* has evolved to include chicken, pork, domestic rabbit and sometimes beef.

MEATBALL AND PIGS FEET STEW. See *ragoût de boulettes et pattes de cochon*.

MEATBALL STEW. See *ragoût de boulettes*.

MEATLOAF—an Acadian casserole dish that evolved through wars and hard times to become a classic family favourite nationwide.

> ### RECIPE
>
> #### Meatloaf
>
> *Mix 2 lbs ground beef with 1 minced onion, 2 eggs, 1 cup quick rolled oats or bread crumbs, ½ cup ketchup, 2 Tbsp Worcestershire sauce, 1 tsp grated fresh horseradish, 1½ tsp salt and ½ tsp pepper. Press into a loaf pan, cover with aluminum foil and bake at 350°F for 1½–2 hours or until the edges pull away from the pan. Remove foil for the last 30 minutes and brush with ketchup or barbecue sauce. Serve with mashed potatoes and green peas.*

MEDICINAL PLANTS—hundreds of different plant species were used by First Nations for medicinal purposes prior to the arrival of Europeans, and though a few were adapted to farm culture, most remain a mystery even to modern-day First Nations. The most successful commercially raised medicinal plants in Canada are ginseng, echinacea and licorice.

MENNONITES—Reformist Christians or Anabaptists who adhere to a form of Christianity unfettered by dogma. Chased around Europe for most of the 16th century, they headed for North America in the 17th century. Some fared badly during the Revolutionary War and joined the exodus of United Empire Loyalists to Canada.

Today there are around 200,000 Mennonites of various sects in Canada, mostly in and around Waterloo County, with the most visible sect being "Old Order," whose members hold to old-fashioned traditions in all aspects of life, including farming and food preparation. Graduates of Canada's agricultural schools should be required to spend time on Mennonite farms to learn natural farming methods, while all Canadians could benefit from a few days in a Mennonite kitchen.

MICE COOKIES—a favourite Newfoundland snowball-type cookie made with butter, peanut butter, coconut, rice crispies, icing sugar and chocolate chips.

MICROBREWERY—any brewery that produces less than 15,000 barrels of beer annually—a craft or artisanal brewery. Small breweries usually make good beer, and most artisanal beer buyers look on every bottle consumed as a vote for sensibility, believing that beer should be made by local brewers and incorporate local flavours.

Breweries

- There are approximately 200 licenced breweries in Canada (about half located in Ontario) and around 800 licenced wineries and cider presses.

MIGNERON DE CHARLEVOIX CHEESE—this washed-rind, creamy, unpasteurized sensation is crafted by Laiterie Charlevoix of Baie-Saint-Paul, Québec, from the milk of a single herd of Canadienne cows and aged to a finish by master cheese maker Maurice Dufor. Laiterie Charlevoix crafts a wide variety of single-herd cheeses available at specialty cheese shops; check online for sources.

MIKKU—caribou meat cut into thin strips and air-dried; a historically important food for indigenous people in our Far North. *See also* caribou.

MILK—that so few Canadians know the taste of whole, unprocessed milk flies in the face of sensibility. The average Canadian consumes 220 kg of milk products annually, and almost every drop is subjected to violent processing methods that alter both its taste and texture, producing a fluid that so faintly resembles the original that it should be called dead milk. Drinking a glass of unprocessed milk is a revelation to the senses that should be experienced by everyone. Guernsey or Jersey milk is best, and served full fat and ice cold it is an unforgettable wonder. Jersey cows produce a rich, buttery milk that tastes like summer. Cheddered Guernsey is the stuff of dreams for cheese lovers. Ask around at a farmers' market; there will be somebody to point the way to market dealers selling cream cheese, sour cream and double cream *au naturel*, without the ubiquitous vegetable gum thickeners.

UNPROCESSED MILK

Dairy conglomerates and government agencies call unprocessed milk "raw"—as in raw material unfit for human consumption—and though historically valid, today's dairy cow is thoroughly vetted for human pathogens. Large dairy processors buy milk in tanker loads and test each one for pathogens, antibiotics and hormones before they accept a single drop. If they only buy milk that is safe for human consumption, then why not sell some that is unprocessed? It is because the law insists it be pasteurized to protect consumers from pathogens that used to be there, are not there now, but might be there again. Okay, then how about semi-processed milk? Why can't consumers buy unhomogenized milk, as studies indicate that the homogenization of milk fractures fat molecules and may contribute to the build up of arterial plaque? The conglomerate dairies can do that, as there is no law preventing it, but that would cause a blip in their lucrative butterfat removal process, so they will not go there.

How about making cheese from unprocessed milk? That is permitted under law if the cheese is aged 60 days, as aging kills all pathogens and makes for a superior product. While many small Canadian cheese makers do that and win awards, the conglomerate dairy operations producing brand name cheeses—with the exception of Québec's huge Agropur dairy co-op—will not go there for fear of listeria contamination and a repeat of the 2008 Maple Leaf Foods recall that cost that conglomerate and its insurance company over $50 million. Why should they chance it? Canadian consumers have been conditioned to buy the ubiquitous tasteless rubbery stuff called process cheese, and $50 million is a lot of money.

But the risk is there regardless. The listeria contamination at Maple Leaf Foods came not from the cooked meats being processed but from a packaging line, and most probably from a human carrier. Human bacterial pathogens such as listeria and salmonella are as common as dirt, which is how they get into the food chain, from soil to food or from dirty hands to food, be it fruit, meat or dairy. Most people are either unaffected or suffer a bit of tummy upset. If not for Maple Leaf Foods' nationwide distribution skewing the number of cases of listeriosis, the bacteria would be considered only a bit more threatening to health than salmonella, would still be called simple food poisoning and would not be a barrier to the consumption of unprocessed milk and cheese.

Processed Foods

- Conglomerate processors routinely strip raw foods into constituent parts and reconstitute them into finished products: milk is completely skimmed of butterfat and reconstituted into 1 and 2 percent or whole milk; flour mills remove bran before grinding and add it to bleached white flour to make whole-wheat flour; and sugar refineries turn bleached white sugar into various brown and turbinado sugars by adding molasses.

Milkweed

- Milkweed is the preferred host plant of the monarch butterfly.

- Silk from mature milkweed pods is too short for spinning into cloth, but when mixed with wool or flax it produces a light, serviceable material. During the early 1800s, Canadian milkweed plantations provided material for lightweight hats. During World War II, milkweed silk, or floss, gathered by thousands of schoolchildren made a passable substitute for kapok fibre in military clothing and floatation gear.

- An infusion of roots and leaves was used by First Nations and early settlers to treat coughs, ague, typhus and asthma.

- Of the 20 or so species of milkweed, around half are native to Canada. Most are edible, but plants with white leaves are poisonous and should be avoided. Before consuming any parts of milkweed, be absolutely sure the species is safe.

MILK PUDDING—during the 18th and early 19th centuries, most Canadians lived on farms where at least one milk cow provided the family with about 20 L of milk daily during its lactation period. Aside from 4 L reserved for churning butter, the milk was used for milk cake, porridge and pudding, with surpluses going to feed the pigs. Pudding was an especially favoured use for milk; it could be baked, boiled, turned into pie, served hot or cold and be flavoured with whatever was at hand, and all that was needed besides the flavouring and milk was egg yolks and sugar, with starches augmenting or replacing eggs beginning in the 19th century.

MILKWEED (*Asclepias syriaca*; also called silky swallow wort, wild asparagus, wild cotton)—cultivated by First Nations and gathered wild by legions of settlers, milkweed is a total utility plant, in that every part is used: flowers, leaves, pods and roots. If enough flowers are gathered, sugar syrup can be pressed out; the young leaves boil down like spinach and taste like okra; and young pods are excellent as vegetable sides and make great pickles. In early spring, the roots are safe to eat and are reminiscent of asparagus, but they are used mostly for their various medicinal qualities.

MILLHOUSE BARLEY—a newer Canadian hybridized barley with grains that contain starch compatible with wheat in the flour milling process. Barley is more nutritious than wheat, and combination flours will increase the food value of commercial and home-baked goods. *See also* barley.

MILLION DOLLAR HAMBURGER—the burger specialty of Morton's Steakhouse, created in the 1970s by Arnie Morton's partner, Klaus Fritsch, while he was a chef at the Montréal Playboy Club. One of the—if not *the*—world's best-tasting hamburgers, its secret lies in the quality of the ground sirloin and the hand mixing with raw egg, tomato juice, salt and pepper. Grilled to perfection, the burgers arrive with lettuce and sliced tomato on buttered, grilled buns—cheese or mushrooms are available on request.

MILSEAN CANDIES—superlative butter and demerara sugar toffees covered with Belgian chocolate and crafted by Sterling Rose Creations of Aldergrove, BC.

MINER'S LETTUCE (*Montia sibirica, M. perfoliata*)—two low-growing annuals or short-lived perennials native to BC and much used by coastal First Nations, settlers and, yes, miners as salad greens. Still widely foraged, the greens are available at BC and Alberta farmers' markets.

MINT (*Mentha* spp.)—First Nations across the country used the native variety both as medicine and for culinary purposes. However, pioneer settlers from Britain, fearful of being without adequate supplies of mint (including peppermint and spearmint) for sauce, tea and candy, brought along seeds to grow plants that

promptly escaped into the wild, so nowadays most wilderness areas of southern Canada are awash in many varieties of mint. European mint varieties are grown commercially in almost every province for making jam, jelly and candy and for retailing in supermarkets. Wild mint is a treat, as the flavour is very pronounced; to find it, look for square stems.

MOCK CHERRY PIE—a prairie specialty, made before the railway enabled the purchase of fresh or canned cherries. Prairie cooks used cranberries and raisins to replace cherries and made respectable cherry pies.

MOCK OYSTER. *See* corn oyster.

MOGS—Newfoundland specialty cakes made with white flour, butter, sugar, baking powder and salt. If molasses is used instead of sugar, the cakes are called lassy mogs.

MOLASSES BREAD—a long-time east coast favourite. During the early 18th century, it used three readily available ingredients: cornmeal, butter and molasses. *See also* bread.

MOLASSES CAKE—a molasses spice cake popular on the east coast.

> ### RECIPE
>
> #### *Molasses Cake*
>
> *Combine 1 cup molasses, 1 cup sugar, 2 cups raisins, ⅔ cup shortening and 2 cups cold water and cook until thick, stirring constantly. Sift together 3 cups flour, ½ tsp salt, 1 tsp baking powder and 4 tsp cinnamon, and combine with wet ingredients. Bake at 350°F for 45 minutes, or until a knife comes out clean.*

MOLASSES COADY. *See* coady sauce.

MOLASSES COOKIES—an east coast favourite that spread across the continent in dozens of variations. They made them big, flat, small and fat, with some as big as your head with icing. Initially made only with molasses, this still-popular cookie now includes light

TRIANGULAR TRADE

Until the middle of the 19th century, molasses, muscovado and maple sugar were the ubiquitous sweeteners in Canada, muscovado being an unrefined and sometimes half-fermented crystalline molasses used to distil rum. Canadian pioneer settlers enjoyed a plentiful supply of molasses and muscovado as a result of triangular trade, including the odious trade in human beings. Molasses and muscovado from the Caribbean were sent to New England ports to be distilled into rum. A portion of the rum, along with molasses, muscovado and citrus, was sent on to Newfoundland to exchange for salt cod. Salt cod was then shipped to Africa in exchange for slaves, who were transported back to the Caribbean to trade for sugars to make more rum.

brown sugar to temper the strong-tasting molasses.

RECIPE

Molasses Cookies

Cream 1 cup shortening and ½ lb light brown sugar and mix with 1 pint each of molasses and buttermilk. Stir in 6 cups flour and 1 Tbsp baking soda. Spoon onto baking sheets and bake in a 375°F oven for 8–10 minutes.

MOLASSES PIE (*tarte à la farlouche*; also called lassy pie)—the fabled precursor to the butter tart. It is similar to brown sugar pie but more buttery. *See also* brown sugar pie.

RECIPE

Molasses Pie

Combine ½ cup flour with 1 cup each of molasses and water and cook over medium heat while stirring until thick and transparent. Stir in ½ cup raisins or walnuts, 1 Tbsp butter and ¼ tsp almond extract. Cover and allow to cool slightly before pouring into a prebaked pie crust.

MONT SAINT-BENOÎT CHEESE—a mild, semi-soft Gruyère-type cheese produced at the Fromagerie de L'Abbaye Saint-Benoît, a dairy owned and operated by Benedictine monks in Saint-Benoît-du-Lac, Québec. An aged, stronger-tasting version called Le Moine is also available.

MONTRÉAL MELON (also called Montréal market muskmelon)—a cultivar of *Cucumis melo*, the muskmelon, which in the 19th century was a huge export crop for Québec farmers.

Montréal melons have a green flesh with a taste reminiscent of nutmeg, but it was their green flesh that almost caused their complete extinction when 20th-century demand for green-fleshed melons waned in favour of the pinks and reds of watermelon. Now an heirloom crop, Montréal melons are grown by small farmers and are enjoying a comeback.

MONTRÉAL SMOKED MEAT—the specialty of Schwartz's, Dunn's and Lester's, all world-famous Montréal delicatessens. Melt-in-your-mouth, chemical free and every bite will make you wish you lived in Montréal.

MONTRÉAL STEAK SPICE—the flavour of old Montréal, blended and bottled by Club House Foods in London, Ontario, since 1990. For the answer to the question "why not London steak spice," you will have to ask the American owners, because the U.S. spice and flavour conglomerate McCormick & Company bought Club House in 1959. A popular spice mix, Montréal steak spice is shaken onto barbecuing steaks and roasts across the country.

MONTRÉAL-STYLE BAGEL—Fairmount and St-Viateur are the Montréal bagel shops customers rave about, and for good reason. Both use wood-fired ovens to produce an extra crispy outside while maintaining a melt-in-your-mouth centre.

Montréal-style Bagels

• American astronaut Greg Chamitoff took along Fairmount bagels for his six-month stay on the space station. He picked sesame seed bagels and, although there is no report, a few seeds must have floated around and probably accounted for a few Marx Brothers antics.

MOOSE BURGER—an old-time favourite of pioneers and trappers, moose meat was chopped, fried and stuck into a sliced bannock roll. While the commercial sale of moose meat is prohibited by law, more than a million of the beasts (*Alces alces*) wander around Canadian forests and many thousands are harvested by hunters. If you want to try a moose burger, get to know a hunter.

A
B
C
D
E
F
G
H
I
J
K
L
M
N
O
P
Q
R
S
T
U
V
W
X
Y
Z

MOOSE STEAK—too large for roasting except for the loin, moose meat is historically cut into steaks or cubed for stewing. Steaks should be dredged in flour, pan browned on both sides, topped with onion and garlic sauce and simmered for two hours, or until tender. In 17th-century New France, moose steaks were most often grilled and served with red wine sauce, the wine most probably Spanish, brought as ship ballast by Basque and Spanish fishing fleets.

MOOSEBERRY JAM—a specialty of the northern Cree made from the bright red fruit of the lowbush cranberry (*Viburnum edule*). Sometimes an ingredient in pemmican, the berries were an all-time favourite of early pioneers. Gathered and dried into loaves, the berries sweetened corn mush, glazed wild game and made wonderful pies, cakes and jams.

MOOSEHUNTERS DELIGHT—a favourite Newfoundland molasses cookie. *See also* molasses cookies.

MORDENS' RUSSIAN MINT CHOCOLATES—a made-in-Winnipeg delight and the best chocolate mint in the world, Mordens' has been a part of our Canadian food experience since 1959.

MOSSBERRY SAUCE (also called crowberry sauce)—a wild game condiment popular in Canada's northwest. Big, blue-black and juicy, the berries (*Empetrum nigrum*) are too bitter to be eaten fresh but are much used in sauces, jellies and pies.

MOULD—a type of fungus that is usually undesirable during food preparation, with some exceptions such as in cheese production, with inside and outside moulds contributing to the taste and texture of cheeses.

MOUNTAIN SORREL (*Oxyria digyna*)—a wild, tender-leaved herb used extensively by western First Nations and early pioneers as a soup ingredient, flavouring agent and stew thickener. Young leaves have a pleasant citrus taste and have become a popular ingredient with chefs.

MOZZARELLA DI BUFALA—authentic mozzarella cheese made from water buffalo milk by Natural Pastures Cheese Company in Courtenay, BC. *See also* Natural Pastures soft cheeses.

MUFFIN—an English word that, until the early 20th century, meant any bread or roll baked in a pan other than a loaf pan. It was also, along with crumpet, a 19th-century slang word for a woman.

MUGWUMPS—mashed carrots and potatoes mixed with fried chopped onions and bacon. Derived from an Algonquin word for important person, the dish was an important presence at dinner tables of early settlers. The word would later be borrowed by 19th-century U.S. politicians to mean a fence sitter, or anyone in a stew over what political party to support.

MUKTUK—narwhal blubber and skin; discerning gourmands may purchase a supply from Iqaluit Enterprises, in Nunavut.

MULBERRY (*Morus* spp.)—cherry growers planted mulberry trees to divert the attention of birds, but over the years the birds wised up and went back to cherries, creating a mulberry boon for those frequenting farmers' markets. They look like big blackberries, but with a taste all their own.

When spotted at farmers' markets, buy lots because you have not lived until you have tried mulberry pie.

RECIPE

Mulberry Pie

Mix together 4 cups washed and stemmed mulberries, 1 cup sugar and ½ cup flour, being careful not to break up the berries. Spoon mixture onto bottom pie crust, top with pastry (lattice or not) and bake in a 400°F oven for 15 minutes. Reduce temperature to 350°F and bake another 45 minutes. Cool to room temperature before cutting into it to keep the filling from running.

MULTI MILK—a concentrated milk for home consumption produced by Canada Dairies Corporation in Ontario during the 1970s. It was a favourite of northern communities and Canada's military, but production ceased when Ontario fluid milk quotas pushed milk prices into the stratosphere. This company also produced a canned chocolate drink called Jocko that was out-of-this-world good.

MUSH—a thick, Indian or cornmeal porridge ubiquitous in the diet of early Canadian settlers. Settlers brought along barrels of lyed corn for making mush and seeds to grow more corn. For many Canadian pioneers, stewed rabbit and mush was an everyday meal for many years. Allowed to cool, mush can be sliced, fried in butter and served with meat drippings or gravy—a welcome change to a gruelling diet. For breakfast, mush was cooked in milk or water and sweetened with sugar, molasses or maple sugar. *See also* Indian meal mush.

MUSH PUDDING (also called Cream of Wheat pudding)—another "we have nothing else in the pantry" dessert common on the tables of early settlers. Made with cornmeal, or Cream of Wheat, thickened in heated milk and beaten with eggs, sugar and spices.

MUSHROOMS—during spring and fall, our forests are a cornucopia of wild mushrooms: chanterelle, king bolete, morel, oyster and pine mushrooms abound. Pioneer settlers hunted wild mushrooms vigorously because they made wonderful soups and were a welcome addition to game meat stews. Nowadays, consumers

CANADA'S FAVOURITE MUSHROOM VARIETIES

- Button—the common supermarket mushroom.

- Chicken of the Woods—a real delicacy and a good beginner mushroom.

- Giant Puffball—can be small or as big as basketballs.

- Golden Chanterelle—one of the best-tasting mushrooms.

- King Bolete (also called Cepe or Porcini)— easily identifiable in the wild by its robust form.

- Morel—black, white or yellow and hands down the best-tasting native mushroom.

- Oyster—available in most supermarkets; named for its taste, which is a bit like oyster.

- Pine—delicious and with medicinal benefits that are causing it to be overpicked from the wild.

- Truffles—white or black and imported mostly from Italy, these are the ultimate in mushroom flavour and must be tried at least once; several boutique farms on Vancouver Island are experimenting with black truffles, and local chefs have their fingers crossed.

are more likely to forage their mushrooms from supermarket shelves, where the button mushroom is king. Canada produces around 110 million kg of these treats annually, with a quarter of that production shipped to U.S. markets. Better safe than sorry, so unless you are willing to undertake a course in mushroom identification, never eat mushrooms harvested from the wild unless a mushroom expert attests to their safety. It is probably wisest to purchase wild mushrooms from knowledgable purveyors at farmers' markets.

MUSKOX (*Ovibos moschatus*)—wild game meat from Canada's most northern communities of Nunavut and the Northwest Territories. The meat has a taste and texture similar to beef or bison and is prepared in a like manner.

MUSKOX MIPKUZOLA—air-dried muskox meat sliced thin like Italian prosciutto; a wild-game specialty product of Canada's most northern communities.

MUSKRAT (*Ondatra zibethicus*)—a ubiquitous rodent during the 18th century and a favourite

of both First Nations and Canadian bush settlers, and while the former preferred to stew the meat, the latter favoured a cornmeal breading and stick roasting—much like a corndog.

RECIPE

Muskrat Stew

Cook in an iron kettle. Cut up 1 plump muskrat, removing all fat and the musk sac, and soak overnight in cold water. Melt ½ lb fatty salt pork in a pot, sear meat on all sides, cover with 2 cups water and simmer 30 minutes. Place 4 halved potatoes on top, add salt and pepper to taste and cook until potatoes are almost done. Remove lid, and when liquid is evaporated, serve muskrat along with the spuds.

MUSSEL SOUP—steamed mussels in a broth made with butter, leek, celery, cider vinegar and seasoning.

MUSSELS—Canada's native east coast mussel is the blue mussel (*Mytilus edulis*), the bivalve found in net bags at local fishmongers and in supermarket display coolers and the species raised by our Maritime aquaculture industry by the millions. Blue mussels are native to both Atlantic and Pacific coasts, with the latter having only been recently recognized as a separate species. Mussels were once harvested from the wild but are now raised in long nylon mesh "socks" suspended from float lines and hung out to grow for two years by

aquaculturists; they receive all the benefits of a wild life without ever touching the sandy bottom. There is no grit in cultured mussels, the meat is plumper and the shell thinner, and they come clean and ready for the pot. These delectable farm-raised bivalves are good eats. Even though British Columbia is not a big player in the mussel industry, mussel aquaculture is a growing concern in bays and esturaries, producing not only the blue mussel, but also the Mediterranean species (*Mytilus galloprovincialis*).

RECIPE

Fried Mussels

In a large pot, mix ½ cup each of dry white wine and diced onion with 2 Tbsp minced garlic and bring to a simmer. Add 4 lbs mussels and cook until all shells are open, about 5 minutes. Remove mussels from pot, allow to cool and remove meat from shells. Prepare an egg dip by beating together 4 eggs and 4 Tbsp milk. Combine ½ cup flour, 1 tsp garlic powder, ½ tsp salt and a pinch of cayenne pepper in a bowl and toss mussels until lightly coated. Dip mussels into egg mixture and then toss them in 2 cups breadcrumbs and repeat once, making sure mussels are well coated. Fry mussels in canola oil preheated to 365°F until golden brown, about 4–5 minutes. Drain on paper towel and season with salt and pepper to taste. Serve with mayonnaise, ketchup or seafood sauce.

MUSSEL AQUACULTURE

If any segment of the Canadian east coast aquaculture industry can be called a success, it is the mussel fishery. Mussels require no feeding, are fairly disease resistant, offer no threat to wild populations and are so sensitive to water pollution that musselmen are constantly monitoring water quality. It is an all-around good business, especially for PEI, given that the province raises about three-quarters of the Canadian harvest, most of which is sacked and shipped live to Canadian and U.S. markets.

MUSTARD—Canada is the world's largest exporter of mustard seed, supplying 90 percent of world demand. The Prairie provinces grow three types of mustard seed: white, for making yellow ballpark mustard; brown, an extra-strong variety for making Dijon mustard; and yellow for making Oriental-style mustard. In Europe, farmers grow a variety of brown seed called black mustard that is used for making strong-tasting European-style sauce. *See also* charlock.

Mustard

- Mustard was originally the name of the condiment; the plant was called sinapis.

- Mustard oil is extracted from ground brown mustard seeds.

RECIPE

Mustard Pickles

Sprinkle 2 Tbsp pickling salt over 8 thinly sliced, large cucumbers and 4 cups thinly sliced onions, and allow to stand overnight. In the morning, drain the mixture and pop it into a large pot, cover with water and boil for 3 minutes; drain. Mix together 2 cups each of vinegar and sugar, and add 1 Tbsp turmeric, 1 Tbsp dry mustard and ½ tsp celery seeds. Mix a bit of vinegar with 2 Tbsp flour to make a paste. Add the paste to the liquid mixture, then pour it over the cucumbers and onions, bring to a boil and fill sterilized Mason jars.

MUSTARD PICKLES—a national favourite since pioneer days.

MUSTARD POWDER—King George I's preference for hot, smooth mustard turned that style into the iconic condiment known the world over as English mustard. The two oldest and most famous brands are Colman's and Keen's. Although Colman's bought out Keen's, it continued the Keen's brand outside of Britain, and today Canadians have their choice of either yellow tin.

MYCOPROTEIN—an imitation meat substance developed by the last remnant of the once socially responsible Rank Hovis McDougall company and Imperial Chemical Industries, both based in Britian, from a fusarium mould found growing in a Buckinghamshire backyard compost pile. The product, called Quorn, is sold as a mushroom product but is definitely not that. Companies producing real mushroom-based foods have protested loudly while pointing out to government food agencies that the product they call frankenfungus causes an allergic reation in about 5 percent of the population—not reason enough for most countries to ban its sale, but good enough for Canada, whose regulators want more information. Surely the okay will come eventually because the stuff is the perfect product for food conglomerates: with it, they will no longer need farmers. In 2010, Imperial Chemical's patent expired and the Chinese announced plans to build a mega mycoprotein factory to manufacture pig food, so Canadians should be prepared for Chinese food foolery on a grand scale.

N

NABOB COFFEE—a branded product of wholesale grocers Kelly Douglas and Company—a Vancouver-based tea, coffee and spice company—with that company acquired by George Weston's Loblaw Company and the Nabob brand winding up with mighty Kraft Foods in 1994.

NAGOONBERRY (*Rubus arcticus*; also called arctic raspberry)—these berries look like tiny versions of raspberries and have similar uses, such as jams, jellies, and flavouring for liquors. Not cultivated in Canada, but a favourite of foragers in the Pacific Northwest.

NANAIMO BAR—an iconic, three-layer, diet-busting confection consisting of a bottom layer of butter-soaked graham crackers with a creamed pudding centre topped by a thick layer of chocolate. Invention claims abound, with most crediting the BC city of Nanaimo, while only a few concede that it may have been from a 1950s-era New York City café called the Nanaimo.

NANNYBERRY (*Viburnum lentago*; also called sheepberry, sweet viburnum, wild raisin)—edible drupes of the shrubby nannyberry tree were used extensively by First Nations to flavour pemmican and as a snack food. Dried berries make a passable substitute for raisins and were often used by pioneer settlers for baking, jelly making and snacking.

NANOPARTICLES—they are 1/100,000 the width of a human hair, almost as hard as diamonds, and since the early 1990s have been working their way into hundreds of consumer products without any regulations or foresight. They make toothpaste white, are used in sunscreen, cosmetics, paint, paper, as a bulking agent for prescription drugs and vitamins, to reduce fat content in foods, and as a brightener in confection coatings, cheese and various canned products.

Once considered benign, nanoparticles are now cause for concern over their ability to work their way into the lung and kidney cells of mice, where they become carcinogenic. A 1996 Canadian survey found 1600 consumer products containing nanoparticles, and experts predict in a few years that number will encompass almost 25 percent of all consumer products. In July 2012, the Canadian government banned nanoparticle use in organic food production, and though that is comforting to consumers of fresh produce, the ban has no effect on food products imported from the U.S., where Big Food has derailed a proposed ban. Both the homogenizing of milk and the milling of flour create nanoparticles, and while some scientists suspect a health risk, little study has been done.

NASTURTIUM (*Tropaeolum majus*)—this popular flowering garden annual is edible; it has a peppery watercress taste that works well in salads. Use the leaves as salad greens and the flowers as garnish. *See also* watercress.

NATURAL PASTURES SOFT CHEESES—makers of Brie, Camembert and triple cream Camembert to die for, made from only the finest cow's milk in Courtenay, BC. Natural Pastures also makes farmer's cheese, water buffalo mozzarella and specialty cheeses. Look online for sources.

(*Urtica dioica*). It is popular with foragers of wild food and simple to make, unless you forget to wear gloves while picking the tips.

> ### RECIPE
>
> #### Nettle Soup
>
> *Blanch a few handfuls of stinging nettles in a small amount of water, then strain out the nettles and add the blanching water to a roux. Purée the nettles in a food processor and add back to the pot along with some chives or garlic. Serve hot with sliced hard-boiled eggs and some crusty bread spread with good butter or goat cheese.*

NECTARINE—while considered different from peaches by most consumers, the nectarine is botanically the same as the peach but without skin fuzz. *See also* peach.

NEEPS—a common Scottish word for the turnip relatives that originated in Sweden and are called "swedes" by the rest of the world. Swedes and turnips may look similar, but they taste different, with the former having a milder flavour. Scottish immigrants to Canada brought along both turnips and swedes, a fortuitous event for civilization and Canada's farmers as it led to hybridizing the rutabaga, a turnip look-alike with an even milder taste. *See also* rutabaga, turnip.

NETTLE SOUP—a surprisingly tasty and richly flavoured soup made from the tender tips and first two leaves of the stinging nettle plant

NEW HAMBURG MENNONITE RELIEF SALE—all that really *schmecks* is here at the New Hamburg sale event to assist the Mennonite Central Committee in its charitable work. Quilts are the main attraction, but there's also furniture and lots of food: Russian Mennonite food, Swiss Mennonite food, Amish food, Spanish Mennonite food, even Asian Mennonite food. Stuff yourself and take home lots because the cause is so worthy that the calories don't count.

NEWFOUNDLAND BLOOD PUDDING— a favourite anytime sausage made to a European recipe, but with added oatmeal, onions and spices.

NEWFOUNDLAND PEA SOUP—similar to the French Canadian preparation of yellow peas and salt pork but with chunks of vegetables, potatoes, turnips and doughboys (dumplings).

NEWMAN'S PORT WINE—Newman's, an early English trading company engaged in the lucrative codfish trade, discovered quite by accident in 1679 that Newfoundland's pea soup weather was good for maturing port wine. They built extensive aging vaults under the city of Saint John's, and until 1914, the city was a major hub in Newman's port wine business. Newfoundlanders came to love Newman's port and not only drank it but also used it for culinary purposes. Today, Newman's port wine still portrays a picture of Newfoundland on labels, but as of 1996, EU regulations forced them to remove the words "Matured in Newfoundland." However, the vaults still remain and have become a tourist attraction.

NEWPORT FLUFFS—a once hugely popular puffed wheat cereal that is still produced and distributed by Associated Brands of Manitoba.

NITRATES AND NITRITES—chemicals used in the preserving of processed meats such as ham, bacon, sausages, corned beef, etc., for which the

NITRATE OVERLOAD

Nitrates and nitrites form nitrosamine, a proven carcinogen, during the meat-cooking process, and though some conglomerate food processors have switched to methods other than nitrate corning, most are still adding it to bacon, hot dogs and processed meats. They say it helps to preserve colour and shelf life and also claims it protects consumers from pathogens, even though the products are refrigerated or frozen.

Leafy vegetables such as lettuce and spinach are so pumped with nitrates from fertilizer that they convert to sodium nitrite during digestion and may become poisonous to consumers, especially to infants, who may develop "blue baby" syndrome as the nitrites restrict the oxygen pickup of blood hemoglobin.

chemical compound is usually potassium nitrate (saltpeter) or sodium nitrate. Saltpeter slows the progress of bacteria in meats and provides an appealing red colour, but the bacteria will eventually convert some of the preserving nitrates to nitrites, and nitrites are a concern because they are known to cause cancer.

NIXTAMALIZATION—the process, discovered by the Aztecs, of removing the hard outer surface (pericarp) of corn kernels by cooking them in a mixture of water and lime derived from wood ash. Not only do the corn kernels grind into meal easier, but the process also enhances the protein content of the corn. Indian meal (cornmeal) is the end product of nixtamalization and was the milled grain widely available to early Canadian settlers. *See also* Indian meal.

NODDING ONION (*Allium cernuum*)—a strong garlic-flavoured wild onion native to western Canada and used by First Nations in various cooked dishes. Now mostly relegated to flower gardens and appreciated for its pink flowers, nodding onion is slowly making a comeback and should be looked for at western farmers' markets.

NORTH GOWER CHEESE—produced by a marvellous little dairy farm in North Gower, Ontario. Cheeses are made from milk taken from their own Brown Swiss cows, which produce better milk than the common Holstein. Alas, the cheesy wonders from the Swiss cows are only available at the farm's store.

NORTHERN DELIGHTS HERBAL TEAS—a fantastic selection of Inuit-gathered herbs that are tea-bagged and ready to brew. Check online for retail outlets in your city.

NORTHERN PRAWN. *See* prawns.

NORTHERN RICE-ROOT (*Fritillaria camschatcensis*; also called Eskimo potato, Indian rice, Kamchatka lily)—a wet meadow plant once extensively cultivated by BC First Nations for its tuber. Eaten raw, the tubers taste like hazelnuts.

NOUGABRICOT—a preserve of apricots, almonds and pistachios that is popular in Québec.

NOVA LOX. *See* Nova Scotia lox.

NOVA SALMON. *See* Nova Scotia smoked salmon.

NOVA SCOTIA LOX (also called Nova lox)—a filleted salmon lightly cured in a mixture of salt, sugar and spices and not smoked.

NOVA SCOTIA SEA PARSLEY. *See* sea parsley.

NOVA SCOTIA SMOKED SALMON (also called Nova salmon)—a filleted salmon cured in a mixture of salt, sugar and spices and either hot or cold smoked. Cold smoking does not cook the fish; it only adds flavour and is the usual preparation method.

NUNS' FARTS. See *pets de soeur*.

NUT BREAD—a "chock-full of nuts" delicious wheat or Indian meal bread that uses molasses as a sweetener. Popular with early settlers, nut bread

was baked during the autumn months when the forests became a cornucopia of sweet nutmeats. It is made with a normal bread recipe but with a tad less flour, which is replaced with crushed and floured nutmeats. Today, nut bread is still a delicious treat, especially if honey is used in place of molasses. *See also* bread.

NUT TREES

Nut trees were once plentiful in Canadian forests: beech, chestnut, hazel, hickory and walnut (black and white) abounded, with most being cut down for their hard wood. If you have the space and admire both the majesty and giving nature of native nut trees, why not plant a few? For planting and species information, go online or visit Grimo Nut Nursery or Rhora's Nut Farm and Nursery, both in Ontario's Niagara Peninsula, or the Gellatly Nut Farm in West Kelowna, BC. Native or hybrid, your choice—there is even a pecan hybrid that will grow in southern areas of Canada.

NUT BUTTER—dried nutmeats ground to a fine paste using a mortar and pestle, blender or food processor. Sweeten with honey or maple syrup, season and store in the refrigerator or a cool place.

NUT CANDY—a sinfully delicious brittle, or brickle, popular then and now. It is one of our most historical sweets.

NUT OIL—an important source of cooking oil for settlers. Walnuts, acorns, beechnuts and hazelnuts were gathered, dried, cracked and pressed in such quantities that they provided settlers with much-needed income because the oils could be traded for goods at general stores.

O

OATCAKES—classic Scottish pancakes made with steel-cut Scottish oatmeal, flour, water, salt and yeast. They became a Canadian classic by the substitution of rolled oats and the addition of baking powder and sugar.

OATMEAL—a term used to mean both rolled oats and the porridge made from them. Early settlers

brought oats (*Avena sativa*) along with them to plant, both for themselves to make porridge and various baked goods, and for animal feed.

OATMEAL BOUCHIES—leftover porridge pressed into ramekins and turned out when cooled. Scoop out the centres, fill with berries or fruit and serve with cream.

OATMEAL BREAD. *See* porridge bread.

OCTOPUS—in Canada, octopus on the plate is a by-catch of the crab fishery or a singular endeavour of sport divers, who, by law, must use only a knife to subdue and kill the animal, several species of which inhabit Canadian waters. During the early part of the 20th century, wrestling giant octopus was a popular sport. That this pastime has not made a comeback as a reality television show is a baffling mystery.

OILNUT. *See* butternut.

OKA CHEESE—a semi-soft, cow's milk cheese manufactured at the Fromagerie de L'Abbaye Saint-Benoît, a dairy owned and operated by Trappist monks in Saint-Benoît-du-Lac, Québec. The flavour and texture of Oka is reminiscent of Port-du-Salut cheese, an equally famous cheese made in France by monks of the same religious order. Oka-style cheese is also a product of the Trappist monastery in Holland, Manitoba.

OKA MELON—an orange-fleshed cross between the green-fleshed Montréal melon and the yellow banana melon and released to the public in 1912 by its breeder, Father Athanase of the Trappist Monastery at La Trappe, Québec. A Canadian original thought abandoned by growers for more convential melons until recently rediscovered on an island in the St. Lawrence. *See also* Montréal melon.

ONION (*Allium cepa*)—also called bulb, common, paper or cooking onion, it is the onion that is known, grown and loved worldwide. Although usually bought by the bag at supermarkets, try the taste of heirloom onions at farmers' markets.

ONION SHORTCAKE—an Acadian onion and cheese dinner cake popular in the Maritimes and the U.S. state of Louisiana.

CANADA'S FAVOURITE ONION VARIETIES

- Ailsa Craig—large bulbs with great taste, but not good for storage.

- Australian Brown—a large orange-coloured bulb with strong taste and good storage qualities.

- Early Yellow Globe—a midsized heirloom onion with great taste and good keeping qualities.

- Red of Florence—not good for storage, but very sweet and tasty.

- Southport Red Globe—a large, red-skinned heirloom with big taste and excellent keeping qualities.

- Yellow of Parma—a large, golden, globe-shaped heirloom bulb and probably the all-time best storage onion.

RECIPE

Onion, Apple and Cheddar Cheese Pie

Warm 1¼ cups buttermilk and combine with 2 Tbsp honey and 2 tsp dry yeast in a large bowl. Allow mixture to stand for 15 minutes and stir in 1½ cups rye flour and ¾ cup whole-wheat flour to form sticky dough. Sprinkle work surface with whole-wheat flour and knead dough, using more flour until a smooth but still sticky dough ball is formed. Place dough ball in greased bowl, cover and let rise for 2 hours. Punch down dough, knead a few times and roll out to fit a baking sheet. Sprinkle baking sheet with flour, lay on the dough, cover with a cloth and let rise for 1 hour.

In a large skillet, cook 1 lb chopped onion in butter until golden, adding 1 tsp each of caraway seeds and salt during the last few minutes. Add 2 lbs sliced apples and 1 cup cider, raise heat to high and stir until liquid is boiled out and apples are tender. Transfer mixture to a bowl and allow to cool slightly. Stir in ⅓ cup chopped dry-cured ham, spread mixture over dough and spinkle with grated Cheddar cheese. Bake in a 425°F oven until bottom crust is golden brown, about 25 minutes. Serve warm or at room temperature.

ONION SOUP—a simple onion and meat stock soup of French origin, but made Canadian by the addition of croutons and cheese.

ONTARIO CHEDDAR SOUP—before cheese making became big business, Cheddar was an Ontario speciality crafted by over 1200 small producers and exported to countries around the world. Ontario Cheddar could be found on hotel, restaurant, steamship and railway menus worldwide, and when not featured with the desserts it was in sauces and soups. Cheddar cheese soup became so popular a dish that it started many a Canadian ambassadorial dinner and has survived the years to become the featured soup at the Canada pavillion at Epcot Disney World, albeit with a name change to Canadian Cheddar soup.

RECIPE

Ontario Cheddar Soup

Melt 3 Tbsp butter in pan and add in 2 grated carrots, ½ cup diced celery, 1 minced onion and 1 small peeled and grated parsnip. Cover pot and cook over low heat for 10–15 minutes. Make a roux using 2 Tbsp butter and 4 Tbsp flour and whisk into 4 cups beef consommé. Add to vegetables and cook over low heat for 10 minutes while stirring. Add in 3 cups grated Cheddar cheese and stir until melted. Add 2 cups whole milk a bit at a time and cook for another 10 minutes, but do not allow to boil. Season to taste and garnish with chopped parsley before serving.

ONTARIO MINAMATA DISEASE—Minamata is a small fishing village in Japan where residents suffered from severe mercury poisoning in 1956, resulting from the release of methyl mercury into the water supply by local industrial chemical producer Chisso Corporation. For many years, Japanese big business and government conspired to camouflage the effects of methyl mercury, allowing the extremely toxic substance to pollute vast areas of prime fishing grounds and poison thousands of local seafood consumers. In Ontario, big business was also dumping methyl mercury into areas fished by various First Nation bands, who began to show symptoms of mercury poisoning in the late 1960s. The government

A B C D E F G H I J K L M N **O** P Q R S T U V W X Y Z

banned the dumping of mercury into river and lake systems, but not the air. The release of toxic mercury into the atmosphere continued for almost a decade, resulting in such a widespread dispersal of the pollutant that it continues to show up in Ontario's fish and game.

OOLICHAN. *See* eulachon. *See also* hooligan.

OREILLES DE CRISSE (also called fried pig ears, smoked pork jowls)—deep-fried pork jowls with maple syrup. They are a common menu item of Québec maple sugar shack tours, but tourists usually receive pork cracklings called scrunchions. *See also* scrunchions.

ORGANIC FOODS—a term used to describe foods produced using traditional farming methods that prohibit the use of synthetic fertilizers, pesticides, industrial solvents, irradiation, chemical additives and genetically modified organisms (GMOs), and also the breeding and rearing of animals with due regard to their welfare and by methods best described as natural, humane and traditional. Most countries, including Canada, have taken to regulating what has become an extremely popular segment of agricultural production, requiring producers to obtain certification in order to market their foods as organic, even providing an identifiable logo. To be labelled organic in Canada, a food product must contain 95 percent organic ingredients.

ORGANIC FOODS CERTIFICATION LOGO

As of June 30, 2009, all Canadian food products claiming to be the result of organic production that are traded internationally or interprovincially must meet the requirements of the Canadian Organic Products Regulations and be certified by the Canadian Food Inspection Agency (CFIA). Use of the "Biologique Canada Organic" designation and logo will be permitted on labelling of those food products certified as meeting the requirements of the National Organic Standards Board (Canadian Organic Production Systems General Principles and Management Standards CAN/CGSB 32.310 and Permitted Substances Lists CAN/CGSB 32.311).

OUANANICHE (*Salmo salar ouananiche*)—a small, landlocked form of Atlantic salmon found in Québec's Saguenay River and Lac St-Jean as well as in Trout Lake near North Bay, Ontario, and a few Maritime lakes. *See also* Atlantic salmon, salmon.

OVEN HEAD SMOKED SALMON—Bay of Fundy salmon cold-smoked 40 hours using maple chips brought in from Québec. Owners Joe and Debbie Thorne have followed this recipe for success religiously—you will have a divine experience when you taste their scrumptious products. Order online or, better still, take a trip to Bethel, New Brunswick, and buy right from their shop.

That way, you can then drive around the corner to Ossie's Lunch and partake of Rose Anna Waite's to-die-for fried clams and lobster rolls.

OVERSEAS FUDGE—a 1940s-era trick dessert made by boiling unopened cans of sweetened condensed milk for a few hours until the contents turned brown and fudge-like. Caution: If attempting to duplicate this treat, be aware that modern cans with quick-open tops are sometimes unable to withstand the internal pressure created during the extended boiling process.

RECIPE

Oxtail Soup, a heritage recipe

Fry a cut-up oxtail and 2 lbs cut-up lean stewing beef in butter until browned, then remove to a bowl. In the pan, cook 4 sliced carrots and 3 chopped onions until browned. Remove vegetables and tie them into a piece of cheesecloth with a bunch of thyme, and drop into a large soup pot. Add in the meat and pour in 2 quarts cold water. Bring to a boil and then simmer for 4–6 hours, depending on size of tail. Strain soup, thicken with 2 Tbsp flour and boil for 10 minutes. Serve.

OXEYE CAPERS—pickled unopened flower buds of the oxeye daisy (*Leucanthemum vulgare*) that resemble true capers but have a milder flavour. Introduced from Europe in the 18th century, the oxeye daisy has spread across Canada and is now considered an invasive weed.

OXTAIL SOUP—once common but now confined to the Kitchener, Ontario, area, where is seems almost every restaurant has it on its menu.

OYSTER—these bivalves can be either Atlantic or Pacific, farmed or wild caught, big or small, and can vary in taste and texture depending on the area of water from which they are harvested. Although there are hundreds of varieties of oysters, there are only five species in Canada: Atlantic (*Crassostrea virginica*), European flat (*Ostrea edulis*), Pacific (*Crassostrea gigas*), Kumamoto (*Crassostrea sikamea*) and North America's own native species, the Olympia (*Ostrea conchaphila*).

OYSTER PLANT. *See* salsify.

OYSTER SOUP—a special-occasion dish for pioneer families, usually reserved for New Year's or Christmas suppers. In recent times, this tasty dish has been revived by some chefs.

OYSTERS IN CANADA

During the early days of the 19th century, oyster-packing companies sprang up in PEI and Nova Scotia. When the Rideau Canal opened in 1832, oysters made the trip all the way from the east coast to Toronto on a regular basis. With the advance of railways, inexpensive oysters became a regular item with fishmongers nationwide. By 1870, the best Maritime oyster beds had been worked to exhaustion and prices for the tasty bivalve skyrocketed, causing restaurants to stop offering oysters by the quarter- or half-barrel (200 in a barrel). However, demand remained high, and by 1890, the packing companies were shipping out 35,000 barrels annually of the soon-to-be famous Malpeque oysters. Then, in 1898, judges at the Paris Exposition declared Canada's Malpeque oyster the finest in the world and demand soared to over 100,000 barrels annually.

In 1913, disaster struck when the remaining Malpeque populations were devastated by a virus dubbed the Malpeque oyster disease, putting our oystermen out of business. But, in the 1930s, the federal Fisheries Department hired Dr. A.W.H. Needler, a zoologist, to study the problem and find a fix. Although he never found a cure for the disease, he did save the oysters for future aficionados by searching out resistant oysters, re-establishing beds and plotting a course for aquaculture, a process that today yields almost 10 million kilograms of oysters annually from both east and west coast fisheries.

CANADA'S FAVOURITE OYSTER VARIETIES

- Beausoleil oysters—hail from New Brunswick, have a small shell and taste very delicately of the sea.

- Belon oysters—imported from France and raised by aquaculture in Nova Scotia waters, they are flat shelled with a nutty taste.

- Bras d'Or oysters—farmed in the salty water of Bras d'Or Lake in Nova Scotia, they are plump and slightly salty but sometimes a rarity in oyster bars because of their susceptibility to disease.

- Caraquet oysters—also from New Brunswick waters, they are small and round and taste similar to Malpeques, but they are slightly less salty.

- Kumamoto oysters—farm-raised in comparatively warmer water, they have a fluted shell and firm, sweet meat.

- Malpeque oysters—derive their name from Malpeque Bay on the north shore of Prince Edward Island; after being judged the world's best oyster at the 1898 Royal Exposition in Paris, all PEI oysters, farmed or wild, are called Malpeques; Malpeques are round shelled and juicy, and have a delicate texture.

- Olympia oysters—North America's only native oysters, they are too small and slow-growing for aquaculture; gathered from the wild, they are much in demand for their crisp, sweet taste.

- Pacific (also called Kusshi or Miyagi) oysters—Japanese imports, they are line-suspended or tray-farmed in the various bays of Vancouver Island.

- Raspberry Point oysters—another famous PEI oyster, smallish with a salty flavour and sweet aftertaste.

- Shediac oysters—harvested from Shediac Bay in Northumberland Strait and all but wiped out by disease, they are thankfully making a slow comeback.

- Village Bay oysters—farmed in Bedec Bay, New Brunswick, they are an easy-open bivalve with a well-balanced, salty taste.

A
B
C
D
E
F
G
H
I
J
K
L
M
N
O
P
Q
R
S
T
U
V
W
X
Y
Z

Oysters

- Our east coast oysters (*Crassostrea virginica*) not only carry famous names of origin but also are marketed with boutique names. For example, a Malpeque oyster farmed in Colville Bay, PEI, will be called a "Colville Bay" at oyster bars. Not to be outdone, BC oysters have also been given boutique names, such as Metcalfe Bay, Pearl Bay and Sinku.

- British Columbia accounts for over 60 percent of Canada's oyster production. All except the tiny Olympia oyster (*Ostrea conchaphila*) are species imported specifically for aquaculture from Japan, most notably the Pacific oyster (*Crassostrea gigas*), the most favoured being the succulent, briny-flavoured Kusshi oyster.

OYSTERS ON THE HALF-SHELL—fresh, plump oysters served on their shells with a squirt of lemon or a dab of grated horseradish are a gourmet delight more Canadian than butter tarts. John Cabot's triumphant 1497 round-trip to the New World and his report of fish so plentiful you could haul them out with baskets caused French, Basque and Portuguese fishing fleets to beeline across the pond and cast their nets. Almost 100 years later, Champlain made a note in his log on the number of fishing boats

RECIPE

Oysters Rockefeller, Canadian-style

Shuck 24 good-quality oysters, such as Malpeques, reserving the liquid. Use rock salt or crinkle aluminum foil onto a baking sheet to support half-shells. Cook 1 Tbsp minced shallots and 1½ tsp minced garlic in 1 Tbsp olive oil until translucent. Deglaze with 1 oz white wine, add oyster liquor and 12 oz spinach greens, stems removed, and steam for 1 minute. Place a spoonful of greens on each half-shell and top with an oyster. Reduce juice in saucepan by half, add 3 cups heavy cream and stir until thickened. Add 4 Tbsp grated Cheddar cheese, 1 Tbsp each of parsley, thyme and dill, and salt and pepper to taste. Top each oyster with some sauce, bacon bits and bread crumbs and bake in a 375°F oven until golden brown, about 5–6 minutes.

he encountered at the mouth of the St. Lawrence River—a thousand, he wrote, but he was prone to exaggeration. Many fishermen dried fish on the shore and had friendly relations with the Mi'kmaq, the indigenous people of the area who loved to trade for European beads, mirrors and iron pots. Fascinating people, the Mi'kmaq: accomplished fishermen and good at getting the best deal, they hosted banquets for their European friends and stuffed them full of baked fish, tender moose fillets, seafood chowders and fresh oysters on the half-shell while dickering for trade goods.

RECIPE

Oysters on the Half-shell with Mignonette Sauce

For the mignonette sauce, combine 1 Tbsp coarsely ground pepper, ½ cup red or white wine vinegar, 2 Tbsp finely chopped shallots and salt to taste and refrigerate several hours. Arrange shucked oyster bottom shells onto a bed of crushed ice and serve with a bevy of condiments: lemon wedges, mignonette sauce, various hot sauces, chilli sauce, freshly grated horseradish, flavoured vinegars, sherry, gin, etc.

SHUCKING OYSTERS

Opening bivalves is like the game of golf: only a few players have any talent, and the majority simply fumble along. Unfortunately, fumbling an oyster with the infamous stubby oyster knife can inflict serious injury, so it is advisable to invest in a protective glove. To open, pick up oyster in your glove (or a tea towel), place point of stubby oyster knife into the hinge (the pointy end) and bore in, making small turns with the knife. When the hinge pops, open the shell carefully so as not to spill the liquor, then run the knife under and around, freeing the meat from the bottom shell.

A
B
C
D
E
F
G
H
I
J
K
L
M
N
O
P
Q
R
S
T
U
V
W
X
Y
Z

P

PABLUM—a popular baby cereal invented in 1930 at Toronto's Hospital for Sick Children by doctors Alan Brown, Teddy Drake and Frederick Tisdall as a preventive for rickets by ensuring children had enough vitamin D in their diets. Good for kids, and moms soon found Pablum a useful ingredient for breads and muffins as well.

RECIPE

Pablum Muffins

Sift together ¾ cup flour, 2 tsp baking powder, ¼ tsp baking soda and ½ tsp salt, and mix with 1½ cups Pablum. Cream 1 Tbsp each of sugar and corn syrup with 2 Tbsp butter. In a medium bowl, beat 1 egg into 1 cup milk and add creamed mixture, then stir in the Pablum mixture. Pour into muffin tins and bake at 375°F for 25–30 minutes.

PACIFIC HERRING (*Clupea pallasii*; also called sardine)—once the cornerstone species of the west coast fishery, this species has suffered massive decline from overfishing and roe harvest.

Pacific Herring

• It is interesting to compare the average size of today's Pacific herring to measurements recorded during the mid-20th century: today's fish are half the size, a phenomenon attributed to the removal of large fish from herring populations.

PACIFIC HERRING

Until 1967, Pacific herring were the main component in the odious reduction fishery, where most of the harvest was for processing, or reduction, into fishmeal, oil and fertilizer. In the 1960s, the herring fishery turned to using purse seine nets that enabled quarter-million–tonne catches and led to inevitable consequences. In 1967, the Pacific herring fishery collapsed, and our government declared a four-year moratorium on commercial herring fishing. While the moratorium ran its course, herring fishermen turned to catching other species, and after four years, only the big-money fishing conglomerates, eager to capitalize on our Atlantic fisheries' successes with herring roe, were able to reestablish the reduction fishery.

Nowadays, Pacific herring are caught for their eggs (the roe), while the fish sees reduction into meal to feed farmed salmon. BC Packers, owned by George Weston, and the Canadian Fishing Company (Canfisco), owned by advertising mogul Jim Pattison, are the major players in the west coast roe fishery, with each company raking in huge profits from the sale of salted roe to Japanese distributors.

Ovens for All

- In 17th-century Québec, home bake ovens were a symbol of freedom, since back in France, citizens had to pay to use communal ovens.

PACIFIC SALMON (*Oncorhynchus* spp.)—this genus contains several west coast anadromous species that are semelparous, meaning the fish die after spawning. While Pacific salmon are under constant threat from overfishing, habitat destruction and pollution, their numbers are still high when compared to the Atlantic species, and in some cases, populations are rebounding as a result of remedial action by authorities. The most important commercial Pacific salmon species are sockeye, coho, chinook, chum and pink salmon. *See also* salmon.

PACIFIC SARDINE. *See* pilchard.

PAIN D'HABITANT—iconic Québécois white bread baked in brick or stone ovens well into the 19th century. During the 18th and 19th centuries, bread made from white flour instead of Indian meal became a coveted status symbol. *See also* bread.

PAIN PERDU (also called French toast)—thick slices of bread soaked in milk and egg by French cooks as a way to use up stale bread—hence the name, which translates as "lost bread." This rather blasé breakfast dish and sometimes dessert underwent a culinary transformation in the New World when it met up with maple syrup for a match made in heaven.

PAL-O-MINE BAR—a fudge and coconut chocolate bar made by Ganong Bros. of New Brunswick and a Canadian favourite since 1920. *See also* Ganong Bros.

PAN DADDLINGS—fried cakes similar to Newfoundland damper dogs, but deep-fried.

> ### RECIPE
>
> #### Pan Daddlings
>
> *Mix 2 parts rough milled rye flour, 1 part Indian meal, suet and a touch of allspice. Add milk to thin and sweeten with 1 cup molasses. Deep-fry in hot oil.*

PANCAKE BALLS—an east coast favourite and sometimes rolled in icing sugar.

> ### RECIPE
>
> #### Pancake Balls
>
> *Mix 2 cups each of flour and milk with 3 egg yolks, 3 tsp sugar and ½ tsp salt. Beat the egg whites and fold into the batter. Place a bit of fat in each depression of a muffin tin and fill to ¾ full with batter. Top each with cranberry sauce or jam, bake at 350°F until bubbles form, then turn and cook on the other side.*

PANDOWDY—a Maritime fruit dessert similar to a deep-dish cobbler except for the crust being "dowdied," or crushed up halfway through the baking so it soaks up juices and becomes extra crispy. Pandowdies were traditionally served with hard sauce or double cream, but a more modern accompaniment is vanilla ice cream.

PAPER BREAD—a thin cornbread made by rubbing a handful of cooked cornmeal gruel across a hot rock or frypan.

PAPS—a traditional stiff and crumbly breakfast porridge of Scottish origin named after the hills that those bowlfuls resembled and made by replacing oatmeal with nutmeal. In Scotland, the nutmeal was usually acorn, but in Canada, it was usually a mixture of plentiful nuts.

PARKIN—an English molasses and ginger cake, but naturalized into east coast cuisine by the substitution of rolled oats for cut oats, no ginger and more egg and butter, turning it into an oatmeal cake, sometimes sweetened with maple sugar.

PARMA HAM (*prosciutto di Parma*)—the most famous of Italy's dry cured hams, produced in the area of Parma. All the essential ingredients to produce ham of equal quality are present in Canada, and even though Canadian hog farmers produce an enormous number of pigs, with some being of exceptional quality, unfortunately, all Canadian hams are wet cured and pumped full of brine to maximize profits.

CANADA'S FAVOURITE PARSNIP VARIETIES

- Albion—a sweet hybrid with a good texture and resistance to disease.

- Countess—a sweet, late-crop hybrid with excellent colour and keeping qualities.

- Hollow Crown—so good even kids like it.

- Tender and True—a hybrid that is very sweet and almost coreless.

PARSLEY SAUCE—an indispensable sauce for fish dishes, especially those with firm, white flesh.

RECIPE

Parsley Sauce

Whisk 1 Tbsp each of unsalted butter and flour in 1¼ cups whole milk over medium heat until thick. Add 2–3 Tbsp fresh chopped parsley and salt and pepper to taste.

PARSNIP (*Pastinaca sativa*)—a close relative of the common carrot and not so far removed from the wild version of parsnip that it will sometimes drive gardeners crazy with its tendency to cross-pollinate. Parsnips contain about 5 percent sugar, and before the discovery of cane and beet sugars were, along with honey, a main source of processed sugar. Parsnips also served as the prime side for meat dishes before the potato was introduced into European cuisine.

RECIPE

Parsnip Purée

Peel and dice ½ lb parsnips, then boil until very soft, about 25–30 minutes. Drain water and add ½ cup heavy cream and 2 Tbsp butter and heat. Remove from heat, purée in blender and season to taste. Top with a pat of butter, a pinch of chopped parsley and serve aside any meat dish just like mashed potatoes.

PARSNIP FRITTERS—boiled and mashed parsnips mixed with flour, butter and seasonings and fried by the spoonful. The parsnip was a recommended "bring with you" crop for early settlers and was used in dozens of recipes.

PARTRIDGE AND CABBAGE PIE—a game bird casserole or crusted pie with the main ingredient being spruce partridge, ruffed grouse or ptarmigan, all common game birds along the entire length of the St. Lawrence River. French explorer Jacques Cartier brought the minor ingredient, cabbage, to the New World in 1540, where it soon became as ubiquitous as the game birds.

PARTRIDGE IN GRAPE SAUCE—sautéed pieces of small game birds simmered in a white sauce with the wild grapes that grow on the east coast and along the St. Lawrence River.

RECIPE

Partridge in Hard Cider Sauce

Skin, debone and cut up 2–4 partridges. Season with salt and pepper, brown in a hot skillet and transfer to a roasting pan. To the skillet, add 2 Tbsp butter and ½ cup chopped white onion and cook over medium heat until soft and slightly brown at the edges. Add 1 cup hard cider and boil 4–5 minutes, making sure to scrape the bottom. Pour ⅔ of the sauce over partridges and roast in hot oven until juices run clear. Heat remaining sauce and pour over meat before serving.

PARTRIDGEBERRY (*Vaccinium vitis-idaea*; also called foxberry, lingonberry, squash-berry)—a close relative of the cranberry but found on much taller bushes. The brilliant red berries are widely foraged on the east coast to make jams, jellies, puddings and wines that are often mixed with bakeapples. *See also* wintergreen.

PARTRIDGEBERRY PUDDING. *See* squashberry pudding.

PARTRIDGEBERRY WINE. *See* squashberry wine.

PASTA—of Chinese origin, improved by Italians and made perfect by the inclusion of semolina flour made from Canadian durum wheat in the recipe. The finest pasta wheat in the world grows on our prairies, and we plant over five million acres to satisfy world demand. Even the Italians buy our durum wheat to make pasta; in fact, they are our best customers.

RECIPE

Pasta

Break 7 eggs into a large bowl and whisk. Continue whisking while adding 4½ cups durum semolina flour and 2 tsp salt. When too stiff to whisk, turn out onto a floured surface and knead dough for 4–5 minutes. Cover dough with a damp towel, and let it rest for 1–2 hours. Cut into four parcels and run through pasta machine.

PÂTÉ À LA RAPURE. *See* rappie pie.

PÂTÉ À LA VIANDE. *See* meat pie.

PÂTÉ AUX BUCARDES. *See* clam pie.

PÂTÉ AUX MOUQUES—an Acadian mussel and potato pie still popular in parts of the Maritimes and Québec.

PÂTÉ CHINOIS (also called Chinese pie, shepherd's pie)—ground beef, corn and whatever vegetables seem apropos, topped with mashed potatoes and baked. It's called Chinese pie because during the late 19th century, many Québécois men travelled to the U.S. state of Maine to work in the mills, and at one mill town called China, they discovered shepherd's pie and returned home with the recipe. While not an original part of the Canadian food experience, *pâté chinois* has existed in Québec so long and in so many variations that it must be included. *See also* cottage pie.

PÂTÉ CROCHES—a pork turnover or pasty specialty of L'Isle-aux-Coudres, an island off Baie-St-Paul in the Charlevoix area of Québec. Originally containing a game filling, this meat pasty is now made with ground pork but has lost very little of its appeal.

RECIPE

Pork Turnovers

Brown 1½ lbs ground pork in a heavy skillet, drain the fat and set meat aside. Add some butter to the pan and cook ½ cup chopped onion until soft. Stir in the meat, season with salt and pepper, add a few teaspoons of water and cook until hot. Roll out 6 circles of pastry dough, each about 8 inches in diameter. Divide the meat filling equally, placing it off centre on each circle. Moisten pastry edges with water and fold over the meat filling to make a crescent shape. Place turnovers on a greased cookie sheet and bake at 350°F until golden brown, about 1 hour.

PÂTISSERIE—the French word for a bakeshop that, in the province of Québec, will be on the sign hanging over some exceptional establishments. Among the best in Montréal are G&G Pâtisserie Gourmande, where chef Géraldine Paumier conjures up all manner of amazing mouthwatering confections, and Pâtisserie Rhubarbe, a tiny shop that is out-of-this-world good.

PAWPAW (*Asimina triloba*)—a tree native to North America and once common to the north shores of Lake Ontario and Lake Erie. It produces the largest fruit on the continent, and the fruit was commercially harvested during the early 18th century. A relative of the more southern custard apple and tropical cherimoya, pawpaw has a creamy texture with a taste reminiscent of banana, pineapple and mango.

PEA (*Pisum sativum*)—peas are either shelling varieties (where the pod is opened and peas stripped out); hybridized snaps (snow or sugar snap peas) and consumed whole, either cooked or raw; or they are left on the vine to dry or picked and dried mechanically and called field peas, which can be yellow, green, maple, green marrowfat or Austrian winter peas. Fresh peas are a farmers' market treasure because of the plants' susceptibility to pea enation mosaic virus (PEMV), a disease spread by aphids. Only brave and caring farmers will grow heirloom pea varieties, and they are truly a taste revelation. It is a sad fact, but most Canadians have never tasted garden fresh peas, preferring instead the convenience of frozen or canned peas, both of which lack flavour and texture.

CANADA'S FAVOURITE PEA VARIETIES

- Alderman—a shelling pea with a huge pod that is hard to beat for flavour.

- Amish Snaps—find or grow them and be a hero to your family.

- Carouby de Mausane—one of the best tasting shelling pea varieties.

- Champion of England—one of the sweetest old English pea varieties.

- Dwarf Gray Sugar Pea—a very sweet English snow pea with huge flavour.

- Harrison's Glory—a hard-to-find wrinkled pea and one of the best tasting.

- Lincoln—a shelling pea with a small pod, and the ultimate benchmark.

- Margaret McKee's Baking Pea—a BC hybrid wrinkled pea with great taste.

- Prince Albert—a sweet shelling pea with a small pod, and a 19th-century garden icon.

- St. Hubert Soup—excellent for pea soup.

- Tom Thumb—one of the best hybrids for growing in pots, and very tasty.

Peas

- Adding sugar to the water before boiling peas will prevent the boiling water from leaching the peas' natural sugars.

- During Champlain's fourth voyage up the Ottawa River, he was much surprised to find the local Iroquois growing French peas. He was even more surprised to find that the peas grew larger and had superior taste to the peas he was used to. French garden peas had found their paradise in Canada.

Pea Soup

- Contrary to popular belief, pea soup did not originate in Québec; it emigrated to that province from Europe through foggy ("a pea soup day") Newfoundland. "It's the devil's birthday again," was a Newfoundlander's greeting to another day of pea soup.

- Basque fishing fleets plied the Newfoundland coast for years before Champlain made his historical visits, and the fishermen consumed large quantities of soup made from easily transported dried peas and salt pork.

PEA SOUP (also called French Canadian pea soup, habitant pea soup)—an historic Québécois soup made from dried green or yellow split peas and a ham bone. Originally an Acadian soup with salt pork, it now has many recipe variations, but most include a ham bone.

RECIPE

Pea Soup

Start with a meaty ham bone in a stockpot and cover with water, throw in 1 chopped onion, some dill, chives and parsley, bring to a boil and then turn down to medium. Place 1½ cups dried split peas in a bowl, add boiling water to cover the peas, then cover the bowl with a lid and allow to stand for softening. When the water in the stockpot is down by one-third, remove bones and fat. Cube 3 potatoes and add to soup along with extra ham, salt and pepper, and simmer until potatoes are soft.

PEACH (*Prunus persica*)—there are hundreds of peach cultivars, but all of them are either cling or freestone depending on how easily the flesh separates from the pit or stone. These can be divided into yellow- and white-fleshed fruits, the white being sweetest and the yellow having more peach flavour, while nectarines are simply fuzzless varieties of either.

PEACH CHUTNEY—a condiment originating in British-ruled India but nationalized by substituting fresh peaches for mangos.

PEACH JAM—once ubiquitous on Canadian breakfast tables, this jam disappeared in the late 19th century when a virus started killing off the trees.

RECIPE

Peach Jam (Traditional)

Peel, pit and chop 12 fully ripe peaches and place into large saucepot along with 6 cups white sugar and a few chopped up lemons and oranges. Bring to a simmer over low heat and cook for 3 hours. Divide into jars.

CANADA'S FAVOURITE PEACH VARIETIES

- Baby Crawford—a rediscovered Crawford hybrid of diminutive size but huge flavour.

- Early and Late Crawfords—hybridized by William Crawford of New Jersey and distributed in Canada by the C.E. Woolverton plant nursery near Grimsby, Ontario, in the early 19th century; the fruits of both varieties were deemed the world's finest eating peaches until they were decimated by diseases and abandoned by growers.

- Harrow Diamond—a freestone hybridized at Agriculture Canada's research station at Harrow, Ontario, it is the third most common peach grown in Canada after Red Haven and Garnet Beauty.

- Peregrine—what Cox's Orange Pippin is to apples, the heirloom Peregrine is to peaches: a flavour bomb.

- Red Haven—the rosy-skinned, semi-freestone hybrid and a favourite of canners and snackers alike.

Peaches

- Starting around 1870, farmers around the western shore of Lake Ontario were harvesting and shipping over 100,000 bushel baskets of peaches from 6 million trees. Around 1880, the peach trees were struck by a virus that wiped out half their number, and the unusually hard winter of 1898–1899 wiped out almost all that remained, so many farmers turned to growing other fruits.

- Today's commercial peach crop is from hybrid trees better able to withstand disease and weather, and the peach is once again a main crop of Ontario and BC's Okanagan Valley fruit growers.

A
B
C
D
E
F
G
H
I
J
K
L
M
N
O
P
Q
R
S
T
U
V
W
X
Y
Z

PEAMEAL (also called peasmeal)—flour made from roasted yellow field peas and favoured by immigrant Scots as an ingredient in bannock and also brose, a solidified oatmeal porridge that is eaten with milk and butter or as a side mixed with kale or turnip.

PEAMEAL BACON (also called Canadian bacon)—an iconic slab of lean, cut-from-the-loin and cooked bacon coated with yellow cornmeal. The baked or boiled peameal bacon supper was a settler's dish during early fall when hogs were butchered and the bacon was plentiful. Peameal bacon derives its name from the traditional practice of rolling cured pork loins in peameal as an aid to preservation—a practice supplanted by cornmeal when difficult-to-mill peameal slipped out of vogue. Often confused with cured and smoked back bacon, peameal bacon is brine-cured and more resembles ham.

RECIPE

Canadian Baked Eggs

Lay slices of peameal bacon in buttered ramekins. Break 2 eggs side by side in each ramekin and sprinkle with grated Cheddar cheese. Bake at 325°F until the whites are set, then sprinkle with parsley before serving.

PEANUT BUTTER—a ubiquitous paste made from macerated roasted peanuts, an invention wrongly attributed to American food scientist George Washington Carver. Peanut butter was actually invented and patented in 1884 by Montréal resident and physician Marcellus Gilmore Edson a full five years before Carver entered Iowa State College at Ames to study botany.

PEANUT BUTTER COOKIES—invented by Marcellus Gilmore Edson to supply sustenance to his patients with bad teeth.

RECIPE

The Best Peanut Butter Cookies

In a bowl mix ½ cup each of peanut butter, shortening, white sugar and brown sugar with 1 beaten egg and 1 tsp vanilla. In another bowl mix 1½ cups flour, 1 tsp baking soda and ½ tsp salt. Add dry ingredients to wet, and mix. Roll into balls, place onto a greased cookie sheet and bake at 375°F for 10 minutes or until golden brown.

PEAR (*Pyrus* spp.)—native to China and Eastern Europe, pears have evolved into a group of 20 primary species, each one having a great many varieties. Pears can be found in all manner of shapes and sizes but have a common denominator: great taste. Heritage varieties abound in BC and Ontario, but the commercial successes

Peanuts

- Native to South America, peanut plants taken from Brazil to Africa by early 18th-century Portuguese traders came to North America in the pockets of slaves. Slaves planted them and ate them, and although some white farmers grew them for pig food, the peanut was mostly ignored until the Civil War, when soldiers found it a handy battlefield snack. After the war, the peanut reverted to relative obscurity until the beginning of the 20th century, when new machinery became available for harvesting. In 1901, peanut vending machines began to pop up, and the snack became popular at baseball games. A few years later, World War I created a huge demand for both peanuts and peanut oil. Today, the U.S. has around one million acres devoted to peanut cultivation, with a good percentage of that acreage becoming the Canadian invention: peanut butter.

- U.S. farmers cultivate four varieties of peanuts: runners, used mostly for peanut butter and accounting for 74 percent of production and most of Canada's imports; Virginia, used for in-shell snacking and accounting for 21 percent of production; Spanish, used for snacks, candy and some peanut butter and accounting for 4 percent of production; and Valencia, used for in-shell snacking and boiling and accounting for 1 percent of production.

- A few southern Ontario farmers grow peanuts in lieu of tobacco, but their production is one drop in a very large bucket and usually supplies value-added products such as candy or snacks sold in local retail outlets and farmland specialty stores.

- The peanut is a legume, a relative of the bean, and while it might be considered a pea, it is definitely not a nut.

are the European species, especially the Bartlett, a summer-ripening variety that is iconic and unsurpassed since 1765. Other popular varieties of European pears are the winter-ripening Comice, d'Anjou and Bosc varieties that ripen only after exposure to cold. Note: pears ripen from the inside out, so it is often difficult to determine ripeness. To check for ripeness, gently squeeze the neck of the pear. If it gives slightly then the pear is ripe and juicy; if not, the pear requires some extra time, possibly in a bowl next to an ethylene-producing banana.

A
B
C
D
E
F
G
H
I
J
K
L
M
N
O
P
Q
R
S
T
U
V
W
X
Y
Z

CANADA'S FAVOURITE PEAR VARIETIES

- Bartlett—iconic and unsurpassed since 1765 and a favourite of snackers and canners alike.

- Bosc—a European import that is great for snacking and able to hold its shape during cooking.

- Comice—the sweetest and juiciest of all the pears and the one usually found in gifted fruit baskets.

- d'Anjou—can be either yellow-green or red skinned but will always have a rich, sweet classic pear flavour and is best consumed fresh.

- Forelle—a small, sweet dessert pear of Germanic origin and the best selection to pack in school lunches.

- Harovin Sundown—a newly released culitvar that was 35 years in the making and worth the wait. Look for it at farmers' markets.

PEAR CIDER (also called pear wine, perry)— an easy-to-make alcoholic beverage produced by fermenting pear juice in a closed container equipped with a one-way valve. No sugar or yeasts are needed, and after a few weeks of fermentation, the party can start. Pear cider has been a Canadian treat since the 16th century and is traditionally pressed from ripe, tree-picked fruit. Pear cider is brewed by artisanal cider presses in most Canadian provinces, and the largest—Growers Cider Company in Victoria, BC—markets cider across the country.

RECIPE

Pear Pie

Sprinkle 6 cups sliced fresh pears with 3 Tbsp lemon juice (to keep them from browning). Sift together ½ cup sugar, 2 Tbsp flour, ½ tsp cinnamon, ¼ tsp nutmeg and mix with pears. Pour into a well-greased baking dish and cover with a top pastry. Bake at 425°F until pears are soft and crust is brown and bubbling, about 30 minutes.

PEASE PORRIDGE—pea soup allowed to cool and thicken into a paste and used as a breakfast gruel or a side dish for evening meals. A traditional British food, but widely adopted by French habitants as a way to turn the dregs of a soup cauldron into pig chow.

PEASMEAL. *See* peameal.

PECTIN—a carbohydrate found in the cell walls of fruits and vegetables that causes jams and jellies to set. Fruits vary in the amount of pectin they contain, with apples and citrus fruits containing lots and cherries, peaches, pears and rhubarb having minimal amounts, while strawberries, raspberries and some other berries contain an inferior type of pectin that usually requires additional pectin to set jam or jelly made from those fruits. Liquid or granulated pectin is made from apple and citrus peels, with apple peels producing a superior product.

PEMMICAN—a high-energy food ration developed by First Nations and adopted by the earliest settlers and Hudson's Bay Company voyageurs. Meat, mostly bison, was dried and pounded almost to a flour, mixed with animal fat and berries and packed into skin bags. The HBC manufactured pemmican in Montréal and packed the product in 40-kg sacks.

RECIPE

Traditional Pemmican

Pass 1 lb dried beef or venison, ½ lb chopped beef suet and ¾ lb dried berries (blueberries, cranberries, currants, etc.) through a meat grinder. Add ½ cup light brown sugar, mix well, pack into a bowl, cover and keep refrigerated.

PEPPERMINT NOBS CANDY—handmade in Newfoundland by Purity Factories Ltd. since 1924, these hard candies with a soft, chewy centre are a sweet treat no one on the east coast can live without. Purity creates other east coast necessities, such as hard biscuits or brewis, candy kisses and fruit syrups. *See also* pilot biscuits.

PEPPERS (*Capsicum annuum*)—while indigenous to the Americas, sweet peppers (also called bell peppers) were brought to Canada by European colonists. The most popular sweet pepper is the green, an immature pepper that if allowed to ripen will become red, yellow or orange. Chili peppers are hot varieties of the same species.

CANADA'S FAVOURITE PEPPER VARIETIES

- Bull Nose—an early-maturing bell pepper and a favourite of 19th-century Canadians.

- California Wonder—a sweet, blocky heirloom bell pepper introduced in 1928 and still going strong.

- Cayenne—a thin, hot chili pepper sometimes called a bird pepper, it has become a popuar farmers' market offering in BC.

- Doe Hill—a sweet, golden bell pepper that is excellent for stuffing.

- King of the North—a short-season, sweet bell pepper that should be looked for at farmers' markets.

- Orange Bell—a sweet heirloom bell pepper that has recently regained some popularity and a prominent place at food and farmers' markets.

- Super Chili—about as hot as tabasco peppers but easier to grow and often found at farmers' markets.

- Weaver's Mennonite Stuffing—perfect for stuffing with a cabbage roll meat sauce.

A B C D E F G H I J K L M N O **P** Q R S T U V W X Y Z

RECIPE

Roasted Red Peppers

Char peppers under broiler and pop into a paper bag or wrap in aluminum foil until cool. Clean char from peppers, cut into strips and toss with favoured ingredients. Allow to stand for at least 1 hour so flavours can mingle, then check seasoning and serve with a cold meat or cheese.

PERCH (*Perca flavescens*; also called yellow perch)—one of the sportiest and best eating fish found in Canadian lakes and rivers, and a fully sustainable fishery. They are caught year-round, but summer is best because what would summer be without a feed of fried perch?

RECIPE

Fried Perch

In a bowl, whisk together 2 eggs and ½ cup milk. In another shallow bowl, mix together 2 cups cracker crumbs, ½ tsp garlic salt and ¼ tsp each of dried oregano, tarragon, salt and pepper. Dip perch fillets in egg mixture, then roll in cracker mixture and fry in hot oil on both sides until fish flakes with a fork, just a few minutes each side.

PERIWINKLE (*Littorina littorea*)—marine snails introduced to North America in the mid-19th century, now common to the entire eastern seaboard. Gathered at low tide, the tasty rock crawlers are turned into soup or served up like escargot.

PEROGY—a meat- or cheese-filled dumpling that was originally a culinary creation of Eastern Europeans, and brought to Canada by immigrants at the end of the 19th century. Perogies are naturalized into our great food experience by the addition of our Cheddar, cottage cheese, potatoes, beef, flour, mushrooms and canola oil.

PERRY. *See* pear cider.

PESTICIDES—nutrient-depleted soils produce food crops lacking life-sustaining nutrients, taste and the ability to resist disease and weed infestation. To counter various infestations, North American factory farms rely on an arsenal of thousands of permitted pesticides, and they apply around 1 billion tonnes of these poisons annually. As if to add insult to injury, the factory farms—and let's not forget the conglomerate

YOU ARE WHAT YOU EAT

In 1923, the Bridgeport, Connecticut, *Times* wrote: "Ninety percent of the diseases known to man are caused by cheap foodstuffs. You are what you eat." This now-famous declaration was part of an advertisement placed by a local food store and was the first use of the phrase "you are what you eat." A memorable coinage, it quickly became the iconic banner of thinkers concerned with the increasing degradation of public health caused by overuse of synthetic fertilizers and pesticides and the consumption of processed foods. In 1940, Dr. Victor Lindlar, a U.S. health and nutrition advocate, wrote a book entitled *You Are What You Eat* and sold a half-million copies in the U.S. and Canada.

In that same year, U.S. organic food advocate and publisher J.I. Rodale began pumping out a magazine called *Organic Farming and Gardening* (later shortened to *Organic Gardening*) that crossed international borders to become the most widely read gardening periodical both then and now. Rodale's magazine was instrumental in changing public perception of food production and created demand and markets for smaller farms and organic produce. While a few readers will remember J.I. Rodale as the nutrition advocate who died of a heart attack while being interviewed on the *Dick Cavett Show*, most people know him for his *Prevention* magazine, one of the most widely read periodicals with a worldwide readership of over 10 million. For the record, his heart failure was the result of a hectic work schedule, too much stress and not enough sleep.

In 1962, Rachel Carson wrote a book entitled *Silent Spring* that caused people to step back and have a good look at what the uncontrolled application of pesticides was doing not only to their health, but also to the environment. Her book scared a lot of people and spawned environmental protection movements around the globe. Her book also helped to reinforce the public awareness of the phrase made famous by that Bridgeport, Connecticut, food store: "You are what you eat."

partnered livestock operations—dump this humungous amount of poison onto crop plants that bioscientists jokingly call "Frankensteins," genetically modified plants with a built-in ability to withstand applications of those concentrated poisons. Sunshine will eventually dissipate most of the chemicals, and factory farms do not apply pesticides when rain threatens or during crop irrigation. But when rain catches the farmers by surprise, it costs them big because pesticides are expensive and a run-off requires reapplication. The initial application runs off into the soil with

the rainwater and is taken up by always-thirsty crops. It is hit or miss, but common sense dictates caution; that imported Frankenstein lettuce in the supermarket produce section may contain more poison than Snow White's apple. Factory farms in other countries are seldom constrained by pesticide permits, and their arsenal often includes extremely toxic poisons not permitted for use in Canada.

PETS DE SOEUR (also called nuns' farts)—originally a French pastry fritter, it was adapted by Acadians as a cinnamon pastry made with leftover pie dough and is still a favourite in Québec and northern Ontario…think cinnamon rolls with attitude. Called *pets de putain*, or tart farts, in the 18th century, the name underwent a spontaneous public change as a way to poke fun at nuns, with the largest fritter in the batch always called the Mother Superior.

PFRA. *See* Prairie Farm Rehabilitation Administration.

PHEASANT (*Phasianus colchicus*)—the common or ring-necked pheasant is a game bird of Asian origin introduced to Europe by the Romans and

Poisoned Produce

- The story of Snow White and the Seven Dwarfs was a bedtime story told to Eastern European children long before the Brothers Grimm wrote down their version in 1812. In the ancient version, Snow White was put to sleep by a poisoned ring; the Brothers Grimm creatively changed it to an apple, as people of that time were beginning to suspect that the lead arsenate used to spray apple trees was somehow migrating into the fruit and causing health problems, including stomach cancer. The poisoned apple assumption proved correct, but lead arsenate was used in southern Ontario apple orchards until 1976 and is still used by many overseas growers.

- Less than 10 percent of Canada's imported foods are inspected, and there is no requirement for those foods to meet Health Canada Guidelines for food production.

to North America by new settlers in 1881. It is the world's most hunted bird, and each year many millions are plucked and turned into dinner, with the young ones (they have short claws) larded and roasted and the old birds (they have long, sharp claws) stewed or braised.

PICKEREL. *See* walleye.

PICKLE WEED. *See* goose tongue.

PICKLED BABY CORN—a central Ontario specialty made from boiled immature field corn cobs soaked in pickling brine.

PICKLED CRABAPPLES—native crabapples boiled until soft and soaked in pickling brine syrup, made by adding extra sugar to normal brine.

PICKLED EGGS—a Pennsylvania Dutch food phenomenon that arrived in Canada with the first Mennonite immigrants in the early 19th century and widely adopted as a saloon and beer parlour snack.

PICKLED WALNUTS—crafted from unripe green Persian walnuts on Vancouver Island and from unripe black walnuts in eastern parts of the country, none are packed commercially and must be sourced from farmers' markets.

PIE BIRD—a whimsical, hollow ceramic figure stuck into the centre of a pie to release steam, often shaped like a bird with an open mouth.

PIE PLANT. *See* rhubarb.

PIG BERRY. *See* rowanberry.

PIGEON PIE—a common pre-20th century dish incorporating what was then the most common bird in North America, the wild pigeon (*Ectopistes migratorius*), also called the passenger pigeon, now extinct.

RECIPE

Pigeon Pie

Prepare a shortcrust or puff pastry and border a baking dish. Line the bottom with a slice of tender beefsteak, and season with salt, cayenne pepper and mace. Lay in as many dressed pigeons as the dish will hold after placing a pat of butter in each cavity. Season birds with salt and pepper, lay in 6 sliced, hard-boiled eggs, more butter, some veal stock or beef stock and cover with slitted pastry. Bake at 300°F for 1½ hours. For a traditional touch, stick two pigeon feet into the top crust.

Pigeons

- The wild pigeon (*Ectopistes migratorius*; also called passenger pigeon) was once the most common bird in North America. A migratory bird that loved company, wild pigeon flights could number in the millions and darken the sky for hours.

- The commercial harvest of wild pigeons began in earnest during the early 1800s and continued until the latter part of that century, resulting in the wholesale decimation of the flocks. Hunters filled railcars, farmers blew up their roosts with black powder, and in Montréal and New York City, the birds sold for 2 cents each.

- Estimates of pigeon numbers at the turn of the 18th century run as high as five billion; two centuries later, there were none. Martha, the last of the wild pigeons, died at the Cincinnati Zoo on September 1, 1914.

PIGGLY WIGGLY—the first self-service grocery store was founded in the U.S. in 1906 by Clarence Saunders, who franchised the concept across the U.S. and in the 1920s into western Canada. Piggly Wiggly stores were the go-to markets in western Canada until the 1930s, when the name and stores were taken over by Safeway, an L.A.-based conglomerate. *See also* supermarkets.

PIGJEREE—a supper dish popular with west coast pioneer settlers and miners, consisting of chopped boiled bacon and rice fried until golden brown.

PIGS IN CORN—a much-loved Maritime dinner casserole made to celebrate the seasonal arrival of sweet corn.

PIGS PUDDING—a Lunenburg, Nova Scotia, waste-not, want-not sausage made with the entrails of butchered hogs.

PIGWEED. *See* lamb's quarters.

PILCHARD (*Sardinops sagax*; also called Pacific sardine)—a small, oily fish related to herrings and an important canned food item during Depression days and World War II, pilchards are now mostly used for the production of fish oil and meal. During the early 20th century, pilchard canneries dotted the west coast from

RECIPE

Pigs in Corn

Scrape 1 lb sweet corn into a bowl and add ¼ cup light cream or whole milk, 2 beaten eggs, ⅔ cup cracker crumbs, 3 Tbsp minced parsley and ¼ tsp sage. Season with salt and pepper according to taste, pour into a well-buttered casserole, lay on top 1 lb sausages (preferably Lunenburgs) and bake in 350°F oven until corn mixture is set.

California to Alaska and inspired American writer John Steinbeck to pen *Cannery Row*, a series of vignettes about life in California cannery towns during the 1930s. *See also* Atlantic herring.

PILOT BISCUITS—a brand of hard biscuit or hardtack baked by the Purity Factories Ltd. in Newfoundland and sold in the Far North and in some U.S. states.

PIN CHERRY (*Prunus pensylvanica*; also called bird cherry)—known for its ability to attract birds, this tree can grow very tall in full sunshine but is more shrub-like when shaded. Common across Canada's southern areas, the pin cherry produces bright red drupes or berries that are too sour for fresh consumption but are good for jams, jellies, puddings, pies and homemade wines. Look for pin cherries at farmers' markets and at some Pick-Your-Own operations in the Prairie provinces.

RECIPE

Pin Cherry Jelly

Place 6 cups washed and stemmed pin cherries into a saucepan with 1 cup water and bring to a boil. Reduce heat and simmer until soft, about 15 minutes. Mash fruit well and strain out the juice. In a fresh pot, combine juice and pectin according to instructions and over high heat, stir until boiling. Add 4½ cups sugar and boil for 1 minute. Pour into sterilized jars and either seal with paraffin wax or refrigerate.

PINE NUTS—the edible seeds traditionally gathered by First Nations from the limber pine (*Pinus flexilis*), found in the Rocky Mountains of southwestern Alberta. Many pine trees have edible seeds, and pine nuts have exploded in popularity.

PINE NUT SYNDROME

Pine nut syndrome is a condition caused by ingesting cheap imported pine nuts from the Chinese white pine (*Pinus armandii*). Also called "pine mouth," the metallic taste disturbance known as metallogeusia is usually encountered two to three days after ingesting the nuts and can continue for weeks. It is extremely unpleasant, so be sure to buy your pine nuts from a reputable source.

PINE RIVER CHEESE—a dairymen's cheese cooperative in Ripley, Ontario, producing outstanding Cheddar cheeses since 1885 and now doing it in a modern facility. Pine River is a consistent prize-winner at both the British Empire Cheese Competition and the Royal Agricultural Winter Fair. Their products are available at over 800 retail locations in Ontario and online.

PINK SALMON (*Oncorhynchus gorbuscha*)—the smallest of the Pacific salmons, averaging 1–3 kg, but the species is also the most plentiful. Pinks leave spawning rivers soon after hatching, spend two years at sea and return to the same river to spawn and die, and they do this in huge migrations numbering many millions of fish. Short-lived and not far-reaching as a spawner, the pink salmon has no need for fat stores and possesses a lean flesh best cooked by steaming or poaching. Most of the pink salmon catch is canned or processed into great blocks of frozen fillets for the meat-packing conglomerates to add into their tube meat concoctions, such as hot dogs and sausages. *See also* Pacific salmon, salmon.

PIPSI—air-dried and smoked arctic char, a specialty of the Kivalliq region of Nunavut. *See also* arctic char.

PLANKED FISH—a method of cooking fish common to west coast native peoples and best used for thicker species of fish, such as salmon and halibut.

A cleaned and split fish is tacked to a cedar plank skin-side down, brushed with oil and is set upright next to a fire or leaned over hot coals.

> **RECIPE**
>
> *Planked Fish*
>
> *To make planked fish in a home oven, place fish fillet skin-side down on a cedar plank, brush with butter and bake at 350°F for 20–25 minutes. Make sure your plank hasn't been treated with anything or your dinner will end in disaster.*

PLORINE—the French word for "prostitute," but in early Québec it came to mean a mushroom cap stuffed with sausage.

PLOYE—a Québécois buckwheat pancake cooked on one side only and used to wrap fruit or sausage.

PLUOT—a tasty cross between an apricot and plum that looks like a plum but tastes more like an apricot. Excellent for tart making or sauced and served over vanilla ice cream. Can also be called an apriplum, plumcot or aprium.

POMME BLANCHE. See *pomme-de-prairie*.

POMME PAILLASSON—the French name for a fried potato pancake, so-called because the grated potatoes are said to look like woven straw. *See also* potato pancakes.

POMME-DE-PRAIRIE (*Psoralea esculenta*; also called breadroot, Indian breadroot, Indian turnip, *pomme blanche*, prairie potato, prairie turnip, timpsula, wild turnip)—a staple food of First Nations and a welcome adjunct to the diet of early settlers. Roasted or boiled, the potato-like tubers taste of slightly sweet turnip and grow from Ontario to BC. Dried, the tubers were often ground into flour by settlers and used as an ingredient in Indian meal or to extend wheat flour. The tubers are still popular with foragers and are often found for sale at farmers' markets in the Prairie provinces. Now and then there have been attempts to cultivate the plant for commercial purposes, but all efforts have either failed or met with only limited success.

POOR-MAN'S CAKE. *See* economy cake.

POOR-MAN'S PUDDING—a traditional English bread pudding popular with pioneer settlers across the nation. In the 19th century, rice was substituted for bread and the dessert became synonymous with rice pudding. *See also* hard-times pudding.

POP WINE—a flavoured wine introduced in the mid-1960s that proved immensely popular. One in 20 bottles of wine sold in Canada during the 1970s was a pop variety, now called a "refreshment beverage."

Pop Wine

- In 1952, Brights, an Ontario winemaker, introduced Winette, a sparkling emulation of a hugely popular British product called Babycham, a sparkling pear wine.

- In the mid-1960s, Andrew Peller of Andrés Wines introduced the country to Cold Duck, a pop-sweet, foxy-tasting sparkling wine made from the ubiquitous and cheap Concord and Bath grapes.

- In 1971, Cold Duck was replaced by the astronomically successful Baby Duck, a sweet sparkling wine made from a mixture of white and red Chanté grapes.

POPCORN—an ancient variety of Indian corn with hard kernels that explode and puff up when heated in oil. Today, all popcorn is hybridized, and while there are many varieties, all popped kernels are judged to be white mushroom, butterfly or yellow butterfly according to their

puffy appearance, with yellow butterfly being most popular.

PORCUPINE—any baked pudding studded with nuts that, after browning, cause the dessert to resemble a porcupine.

PORK PIE—a British culinary invention wherein the piecrust is hard baked (coffin pastry) and the filling is added through a hole in the top crust. Once popular in Canada as travelling food, the pies are now relegated to supermarket deli cases, where they are called Melton Mowbrays after the town in Leicestershire, England, that perfected their production. Served cold with plenty of good mustard and a tall beer, they stand a body well for lunch.

PORRIDGE BREAD (also called oatmeal bread)— Scottish immigrants to Canada brought along their love of all things oatmeal and added many fine food items to the Canadian food experience. Although bannock is probably prime, this bread finishes a close second. Porridge bread is a waste-not, want-not pioneer bread incorporating leftover porridge into the dough, but a bread that held its own and became something of an east coast favourite, even into modern times. *See also* bread.

> ### RECIPE
>
> #### *Porridge Bread*
>
> *Dissolve a little sugar in warm water, add some yeast and let it rise until foamy. Cook up 1⅓ cups rolled oats or use leftover breakfast porridge, and in a large bowl, combine with ½ cup brown sugar, ¾ cup vegetable oil and ½ cup molasses. Add yeast to porridge mixture and stir well. Now add 7 cups flour, 1 cup at a time, until dough comes clean from side of bowl. Turn onto a floured surface and knead until smooth and elastic. Form a ball and cover with linen cloth and let rise until doubled in volume, about 90 minutes. Punch down risen dough and divide into 6 equal parts. Form into loaves and place into well-greased bread pans. Once again, cover with linen and let rise in a warm spot until doubled in volume, about 1 hour. Bake in 325°F oven until golden brown, about 30–40 minutes.*

PORT HOPE BISCUITS—baking soda crackers made famous by Port Hope baker W.J.B. Davison at the beginning of the 20th century.

PORT STANLEY ORANGEADE—called "The Drink That Made Port Stanley Famous," orangeade was the 1911 patented creation of Mackie's, a family-run beach food concession still in operation and equally famous for its French fries.

PORTABLE SOUP—a dehydrated meat and vegetable soup made by cooking defatted stock into a jelly and drying it into a hard slab, a process invented in 1755 by a London tradeswoman named Dubois who turned to manufacturing the product for the Royal Navy and commercial ship owners in 1756. No self-respecting New World explorer would venture far without a supply of portable soup, and for some Hudson's Bay employees headed for their remote factories, the supply was enormous. To make this soup, a mix of meat and water was boiled for many hours until only a jelly remained. After the jelly cooled it was put in the sun to dry and then packaged in leather pouches like pemmican. When soup was required, one simply reconstituted the hard pellet in boiling water.

PORTULACA. *See* famine foods.

POT BREAD—a bread-baking method wherein a leavened or unleavened loaf is placed on a flat rock, deposited in the coals of a fire, covered with a metal pot and heaped over with hot coals.

POT DE CRÈME—we all love chocolate pudding with whipped cream, but you'll never know how good that dessert can be until you try this old favourite that arrived with early French explorers.

RECIPE

Pot de Crème

In a steel bowl fitted into a pot of hot water, combine 6 oz fine dark chocolate and ⅓ cup best quality cocoa powder. In a large bowl, whisk together 2 large egg yolks and ⅓ cup sugar and set aside. In a large saucepan, heat 1 cup each of heavy cream and milk until almost at a boil and whisk in the egg and sugar mixture, making sure to temper to prevent scrambling. Bring mixture to a simmer while constantly stirring with a wooden spoon and cook until back of spoon is coated, about 5 minutes. Slowly whisk custard mixture into chocolate and pour into individual serving dishes or glasses (4 large or 6 small). Cover with plastic wrap and refrigerate for at least 1 hour. Top with whipped cream and a few chocolate shavings.

POT ROAST—a form of braising wherein the hearth pot containing the fowl or meat was suspended over hot coals with a considerable amount of coals placed onto the pot's lid for all-around heating. Today, pot roasting is synonymous with braising.

POT-EN-POT "TANTE YVONNE"—a lobster and fish pot pie made famous by Îles-de-la-Madeleine chef Aunt Yvonne and a good enough reason to visit that island paradise.

POTATO (*Solanum tuberosum*)—introduced to Europe in 1570, the Andean potato saw only limited cultivation by poor farmers. The potato is a member of the deadly Nightshade family,

A
B
C
D
E
F
G
H
I
J
K
L
M
N
O
P
Q
R
S
T
U
V
W
X
Y
Z

RECIPE

Redskin Potato Salad

Boil 3 lbs new redskin potatoes until tender but firm. Drain and cut into fours. In a medium bowl whisk together 1½ cups mayonnaise, 2 Tbsp white vinegar, 2 Tbsp milk and ½ cup chopped green onions. Pour mixture over potatoes and mix in 4 diced hard-boiled eggs and 1 cup chopped celery, adding salt and pepper to taste. Cover and refrigerate at least 3 hours before serving.

CANADA'S FAVOURITE POTATO VARIETIES

- All Blue—a blue potato of Peruvian descent that is best for roasting.

- Arran Victory—medium-sized with purple skin, and the best tasting ever.

- Bliss's Triumph—a red-skinned seed potato great for boiling.

- Catriona—has purple-blotched skin and is great for roasting.

- German Butterball—a buttery flavoured, yellow-fleshed seed potato for boiling or mashing.

- Heirloom Russets—high starch content makes them great for soups or baking.

- La Ratte d'Ardeche—a fingerling type good for boiling.

Potatoes

- Pioneers heading west from Montréal stocked up on mainly Indian meal (lyed corn) and pemmican, but the smart ones also took along seed potatoes, rhubarb rhizomes and various fruit and vegetable seeds to supplement those brought from home. Potatoes planted into virgin soil produced bumper crops that were often a lifesaver for destitute families. A good supply of potatoes instilled confidence in farmers and supplied their wives with yeast to make bread, starch to iron clothes and pocket warmers for milking cows on cold mornings.

- Canadians annually consume about 75 kilograms of potatoes per person, and spuds account for around 65 percent of vegetables consumed. Total potato production in Canada is around 4.5 million tonnes, with the provinces of PEI, New Brunswick, Manitoba, Alberta and Ontario being the leading producers.

- Florenceville, New Brunswick, is the home of mega-conglomerate McCain Foods, a company that supplies the world with frozen French fries. And yes, there really is a Mister Potato Head—he lives in Florenceville.

- New potatoes are any variety harvested before maturity, except for red new potatoes, which are fully mature but small. New potatoes are high in sugar and not great for storing, but they do hold their shape and work great in potato salads.

and as such was considered a risky nosh for the wealthy. When French farmers enlisted to establish subsistence gardens for New World settlements in the 17th century, they took along the potato, a fortuitous inclusion for settlers of the 18th century.

POTATO BEAN. *See* groundnut.

POTATO BREAD—common in settler days and usually started with hop barm, this bread is still baked and enjoyed today, although the "rise" is now provided by modern yeast. *See also* bread.

A
B
C
D
E
F
G
H
I
J
K
L
M
N
O

P

Q
R
S
T
U
V
W
X
Y
Z

POTATO CAKES—when tired of plain mashed potatoes, do what the Maritimers do: turn them into a dough and fry them up.

RECIPE

Potato Cakes

Mix 6–8 mashed spuds with 2 tsp salt and 1 tsp baking powder. Then add 4 Tbsp melted butter and ½ cup milk and knead until the dough can be rolled out ½ inch thick on a floured surface. Cut dough into rounds and fry to brown on a cast iron skillet.

POTATO DUMPLINGS—wonderful with tomato sauce or as side for barbecued meats.

RECIPE

Potato Dumplings

Cook and mash 1 lb Yukon Gold potatoes. Stir in 1 egg, 1½ cups flour, 2 Tbsp basil or thyme and 1 tsp salt. Roll dough into a log and cut off ¾-inch sections, then boil in salted water until they float, about 5 minutes. Once they have cooled, fry them golden brown in a mix of canola oil, butter and chopped garlic.

POTATO PANCAKES—a culinary commonality in every pioneer kitchen and a welcome change from congealed cornmeal cakes. For something a little different, add canned salmon to the preparation.

RECIPE

Potato Pancakes

Shred 2 potatoes and wring out well in a dish towel. Mix with 2 eggs, some salt and pepper and a little diced green onion or parsley. Form into cakes and fry until golden brown.

POTATO PIE—a PEI and Acadian layered casserole of thinly sliced potatoes with bacon and Cheddar cheese.

RECIPE

Potato Pie

Layer a casserole dish with bacon, followed by a layer of thinly sliced potatoes, followed by a layer of grated Cheddar cheese. Repeat the layers to the top of the dish, making sure the last layer is cheese. Bake at 375°F until bubbly and toasty brown.

POTATO PUDDING—a waste-not, want-not dish that relieved pioneer cooks of leftover mashed potatoes. Mixed with egg, butter, sugar and nutmeg, leftover mashed potatoes could make a dessert, while more mashed potatoes mixed without sweetener and baked in a crust could be a dinner side for a haunch of venison.

POTATO SOUP—a mainstay meal for many early settlers in the home country, the soup took on a Canadian flavour through ingredient substitutions like venison bones instead of beef, and onions fried in venison fat. In later years, the beef bone returned, but a great dollop of butter or some grated Cheddar cheese helped the soup retain its Canadian flavour.

RECIPE

Potato Soup

Boil a shank of beef or venison and allow the broth to stand for fat skimming. Fry 4 chopped onions in the fat and add to the broth. Mash boiled potatoes and add to the broth until it reaches the consistency of heavy cream. Season with salt and pepper, top with grated Cheddar cheese and enjoy.

POTEEN—potato whisky produced in illegal stills by Irish immigrants. Similar to vodka but much stronger, the liquor has gone out of style in Canada but is still popular in Ireland.

POTLUCK—originally meant to signify a meal from whatever happened to be in the cooking pot, the word has come to mean a meal where each participant contributes something to the whole.

POUDING CHÔMEUR. See hard-times pudding.

POUND CAKE—named for the ingredients, a pound each of butter, flour and sugar, the cake could also include lemon for flavour and eggs that were often divided, with the whites whipped to supply leavening.

POUTINE—Acadian dumplings that evolved to become French-fried potatoes mixed with cheese curds and smothered in hot gravy or sauce. This artery-clogging Québécois culinary invention now has all manner of preparation techniques and toppings.

POUTINE À TROU—an Acadian fried pie with a diced salt pork and apple filling usually topped with syrup or molasses.

POVERTY CAKE. *See* economy cake.

POUTINE HISTORY

The word "poutine" is an Acadian borrowing of the English word "pudding" at a time when it meant chopped meat and spices jammed into a sock and boiled. The Acadians used the word to describe any chopped and mixed food preparation, sweet or savoury, in a sock, pie or pot.

Then one day in 1957, at a roadside café in Warwick, Québec, called Le Café Ideal, a truck driver named Eddy Lainesse sat at the counter contemplating a plate of savoury French fries. Eddy liked his fries with ketchup but had lately found the combination boring. Eddy thought of having gravy, but he hated soggy fries. Then he thought, "If only there was something between the fries and gravy," and his eyes suddenly focused on something.

Fernand Lachance, the proprietor of Le Café Ideal, also sold bait boxes filled with fresh cheese curds procured from a local dairy and was busily tucking a fresh shipment into the little boxes. Fernand glanced over at Eddy and read his mind. He pointed to his cheese scoop and said, "You want some of these curds on your fries, Eddy? You want them mixed in like—like a poutine?"

"Avec gravy, s'il vous plâit," replied Eddy, smiling. The rest, as they say, is history.

POWDERED MUSHROOMS. See *tabac des bois*.

PRAIRIE CHICKEN (*Tympanuchus cupido*)—
a mid-sized grouse once common to the Canadian prairies. Apparently it tastes better than chicken and was much appreciated by early settlers. Modern-day sportsmen are appreciating the bird almost to extinction.

PRAIRIE FARM REHABILITATION ADMINIS-TRATION (PFRA)—an agency of the federal government established in 1939 to counter the effects of the Dust Bowl through systems of farm practice, tree culture, water supply and the rehabilitation of drought-devastated fields. Hugely successful at mitigating the effects of drought erosion, the agency turned to water supply and was involved in thousands of water projects including dam and reservoir construction. Today, the agency is still active in water and land management and oversees almost a million acres of prairie pasturelands. *See also* Dust Bowl.

PRAIRIE OYSTERS—the fried testicles of male beef cattle and a culinary thrill at dude ranches and the Calgary Stampede. Beef testicles are readily available in Alberta because male beef cattle are usually castrated before reaching sexual maturity, turning them into steers.

PRAIRIE POTATO. See *pomme-de-prairie*.

PRAIRIE TURNIP. See *pomme-de-prairie*.

PRAWNS (northern prawn, *Pandalus borealis*; spot prawn, *P. platyceros*)—both are shrimp and both are scrumptious, especially the large west coast spot prawns when breaded with Japanese panko-style breadcrumbs and fried. Northern prawns,

also called pink shrimps, are smaller, harvested in larger quantities and are generally used in salads. *See also* shrimp.

Prawns

- A rose is a rose, but a prawn is a shrimp, except in Europe where it can be a langoustine or scampi. In North America, scampi are large shrimp cooked in butter and garlic, and prawns are big shrimp. Confused? You would be more so in Ireland, where prawns are still shrimp, but have tiny claws like lobsters.

RECIPE

Shrimp Fritters

In a pot, bring 6 cups water to a boil and add 1 lb medium shrimp, cooking until they turn pink, about 4 minutes. Drain and rinse with cold water. Peel, devein and coarsely chop shrimp. In a bowl combine 1 cup flour, 1 tsp each of baking powder, salt and pepper, 2 large eggs and mix until smooth. Stir in 1 minced onion, 1 minced jalapeno pepper, 4 minced garlic cloves, ½ tsp dried thyme and the shrimp. Cover and refrigerate for 3 hours. Pour canola oil in a deep pot to a depth of 3 inches and heat to 375°F. Drop in batter by the rounded tablespoon and fry in small batches until golden, about 5 minutes. Drain on paper towel, check for seasoning and serve them hot.

PRESERVES AND CONSERVES—while considered pretentious today, both words were used to describe various jam preparations long before the word "jam" entered the English vocabulary. From having the same meaning back then, the words have undergone a change over time, becoming more apropos for describing expensive jams made with chunks of fruit.

PRESSURE COOKING—a healthy method of cooking with steam that is produced in a pot with a tight-fitting lid and a pressure release valve. Popular from the 1950s to the late '70s, pressure cooking has become an almost lost cooking technique because of a culinary dumbing down of the population.

PROCESSED CHEESE—raised on a dairy farm in Stevensville, Ontario, James Lewis Kraft, called J.L. by everyone, saw a great future in cheese. In 1903, he moved to Chicago to enter the wholesale cheese business. Struck by the waste incurred while cutting large wheels of Cheddar, he went to work on a stovetop and developed a process that incorporated wastage into a semi-solid block he called processed cheese. In 1920, flush with cash from supplying the U.S. military during World War I, J.L. entered the Canadian food market when he purchased MacLaren's Imperial Cheese Company of Montréal.

PRODUCT OF CANADA—food conglomerates, especially the giant fish processors, will often have "Product of Canada" on their packaging even though 100 percent of the contents are imported. Canadian food labelling laws permit these companies to claim "Product of Canada" status so long as at least 51 percent of the production costs are incurred in Canada.

PRONGHORN (*Antilocapra americana*)—looks like an antelope, but is no relation and until recently was in danger of following the prairie chicken to extirpation in Canada. However, with help from prairie farmers, government and hunting organizations, the species has recovered to the point where some limited hunting is allowed. Today's population is a far cry from the millions of pronghorns that once wandered the prairies with the equally abused bison, but it's better than none.

PTARMIGAN (*Lagopus* spp.)—these birds are hardy members of the Grouse family, and three species call Canada home: the willow (*L. lagopus*), rock (*L. mutus*) and white-tailed (*L. leucurus*) ptarmigans, with each having a white winter moult and two additional seasonal moults of differing colours. The birds also keep different habitats: the willows prefer the tree line and high valleys; the rocks inhabit dry, shrubby lands; and the white-tails stick to mountainsides. One thing that's not different is their suitability for the grill or stew pot, and they are much valued by northern peoples.

PUFFBALLS—easily identifiable ball-shaped fungi that range in size from small buttons to huge specimens the size of basketballs, the *Langermannia gigantea*. To be edible, puffballs must be young, and when sliced open they must be snowy white and fresh smelling. For culinary purposes, puffballs can be cooked like commercial mushrooms or sliced, egg dipped and breaded. *See also* mushrooms.

PUMPKIN (*Cucurbita pepo*)—native to North America, pumpkin is a squash with a thick orange or yellow shell to contain seeds and pulp. Pumpkins are mainly cultivated for various baked goods including pie and muffins, and for recreational use such as Halloween carving. *See also* squash.

PUMPKIN LOAF—ground corn and pumpkin baked in a loaf and served warm with butter and maple syrup. An 18th-century United Empire Loyalists' delight, it is still going strong today.

PUMPKIN PIE (also called squash pie)—an Acadian one-crust pie with a boiled pumpkin, egg, sugar, cream and spice filling. Perfected in the 17th century and sweetened with maple sugar, then molasses and finally cane sugar, the pie was sometimes flavoured with brandy, a wonderful addition and a custom that survives to this day as the ever-delicious maple and brandy pumpkin pie.

Pumpkin Pie

- Americans like to claim pumpkin pie as their own—part of their Pilgrim cuisine—but what the Pilgrims called pie was actually a pumpkin filled with sugar and spice and baked, what we might today call pumpkin pudding. Our 17th-century Acadians loved their crusted pies and gave us not only the pumpkin pie but also the pork pie called tourtière.

PUMPKIN SOUP—autumn in a bowl, perfected by 17th-century Acadians and enjoyed by Canadians for over four centuries.

RECIPE

Pumpkin Soup

Rub the cleaned halves of a small pumpkin with olive oil, season with salt and roast in a 375°F oven until fork tender, about 70 minutes. Allow halves to cool, then scoop out flesh into a medium bowl; there should be about 3 cups. Fry 3 slices bacon in a heavy skillet or Dutch oven until crispy and set aside. Add 2 diced shallots to the bacon fat, season with salt and pepper and cook until soft and translucent, about 5 minutes. Add ¼ cup dry sherry and reduce by half, about 2–3 minutes. Add 2 cups chicken stock, 2 cups water, 1½ tsp fresh thyme and the pumpkin. Cook to a simmer while stirring and let simmer for another 10 minutes. Remove contents to a blender or food processor and purée in batches; pour into a fresh pot. Add ¼ cup heavy cream while stirring, check seasoning, and serve topped with chopped parsley and croutons.

PURSLANE (*Portulaca oleracea*)—a common lawn weed in Canada, but in Europe it has attained almost vegetable status and is found alongside other salad greens in produce markets. Purslane has a pleasant lemony flavour and can be eaten raw or cooked, alone or in combination with other greens such as kale. Low growing, with spatula-shaped leaves and rose-coloured stems, tasty purslane is the most nutritious green on the planet and is just waiting to be chopped up and tossed into any salad. While it may be tempting to pick some from the front yard, avoid doing so if any pesticides have been used during the last two years. *See also* famine foods.

Q

QUAHOG (*Mercenaria mercenaria*)—favourite PEI molluscs that, when small, wind up on the tables of restaurants as cherrystone clams, with the meat from larger ones either cut up for chowder or ground up and made into clam patties that are baked in their half shells. Not to be confused with the deep-water ocean quahog (*Arctica islandica*), hard-shell quahogs are found in shallow water between the high and low tidal zones.

QUAIL. *See* bobwhite quail.

QUAIL PIE—a crusted pie with the main ingredient being small game birds such as bobwhite quail, snipe or woodcock.

QUAKER OATS—a 1901 merger, or trust, of three oat mills spearheaded by Cleveland grain merchant Henry Crowell, owner of the Quaker Mills, succeeded in cornering the market for oats. The new enterprise, initially called the American Cereal Company, dropped a word from a Quaker Mills brand, Quaker Man, and called both their company and cereal Quaker Oats. Two years later, the Quaker Oats Company entered the Canadian market through a mill purchase in Peterborough, Ontario, and in 1912, built another mill in Saskatoon, Saskatchewan. Historically called the "oatmeal trust," the Quaker Oats Company controlled the North American oat business from farm to mill to consumers.

In 1983, the company bought the pork and bean canner Stokely-Van Camp, which also produces the sports drink Gatorade, a fortuitous acquisition that enabled the conglomerate to avoid takeover overtures from predatory conglomerates.

QUÉBEC FÉDÉRATION DES AGRICOTOURS. *See* Association de l'Agrotourisme et du Tourisme Gourmand.

QUÉBEC FRICASSÉE—a French-Canadian heritage dish consisting of finely diced cooked meat fried up with left-over gravy fat, chopped onions and diced potatoes and laced with fresh or dried savory.

QUÉBEC SMOKED MEAT HOT DOG—while the entire city of Montréal is famous for its smoked meat, there are spots that offer variations. Québec Smoked Meat is one of those, a restaurant in the Pointe-Sainte-Charles area that whips up a smoked meat hot dog that is amazing.

QUEEN CAKE. *See* butter cake.

QUEEN ELIZABETH CAKE (also called Queen Elizabeth squares)—a cake named after Queen Elizabeth, the late Queen Mother, and baked by Canadian women's fundraising groups during World War II. Sold by the square in munitions factories, ration queues and anywhere people gathered, the squares raised considerable monies for the war effort. The cake is moist, delicious, chock full of nuts and dates and easy to make.

RECIPE

Queen Elizabeth Cake

Soak 1 cup chopped dates and ½ cup walnuts in 1 cup boiling water and let stand. Cream 1 cup sugar and ½ cup butter, adding 1 egg and 1 tsp vanilla while beating. Add 1½ cups flour, 1 tsp baking powder and ¼ tsp salt and mix well. Mix in dates and nuts. Pour batter into greased cake pan and bake at 350°F until top is golden brown, 25–30 minutes.

RECIPE

Quince Preserves

Wash, peel and core 4 lbs quince fruit and chop into ½-inch cubes. Add cold water to cover and boil until soft. Drain the juice into another pot and add ¼ cup sugar for each cup juice and boil 5 minutes. Add fruit to juice and boil until clear and a deep red colour. Pour into sterilized jars and seal tightly.

QUEUES DE CASTOR. *See* beaver tails.

QUINCE (*Cydonia oblonga*)—large, yellow and sour, they look similar to a pear and were an early Canadian backyard staple for jelly making, desserts and pickling, while in modern times the fruiting variety has given way to a hybridized ornamental flowering tree. Look for the fruit at farmers' markets and the fruiting bush (which can be pruned to a tree) at plant nurseries; the desired fruiting cultivar is Boyne's Choice.

QUINOA (*Chenopodium quinoa*; also called Inca wheat)—farmed on the slopes of the Andes Mountains and, more recently, on the flat plains of Saskatchewan, quinoa is not a grain but the seed of an herb plant in the Amaranth family. The seeds are one of the most nutritious crops available, being richer in protein than cereal grains and naturally gluten free. Quinoa is being pioneered in Saskatchewan, and its future as a cash crop is looking good.

QUINCE PRESERVES—in ancient Greece, quinces were called "apples of Cydonia" and were kept preserved in honey, a preparation that in later years would be called honey apple or *marmelada* by the Portuguese. The words passed into English during the 18th century when the British discovered that cooked quinces combined with sugar and vinegar produced a jell that they called "quidony" or "marmalade," and it was the precursor to all manner of jams, preserves and conserves.

R

RABBIT—during Canada's formative years, rabbit—of which there are several species across the country—was a constant presence on the tables of settlers. When fathers taught sons how to handle firearms, hunt and skin their quarry, it was always rabbit. Rabbit is good eats and is one of the healthiest meats on the planet. It is lower in cholesterol than either chicken or turkey and contains fewer calories than chicken. However good it may be, most Canadians have never eaten rabbit, and that is a national shame, seeing how it was once a foundation food. Rabbit is sold either as fryers or roasters, the former being less than 12 weeks old, the latter over 8 months old. Fryers are pink and tender and may be cooked like chicken, while roasters are usually not roasted but stewed or braised.

Rabbit Meat

- Canadians consume around 5 grams of rabbit meat per person annually; in France that figure is 5 kilograms.

RABBIT FRICASSÉE—fried rabbit in sauce, supper for almost any backwoods traveller at any time.

RECIPE

Rabbit Fricassée

Cut a wild or domestic rabbit into 6 pieces, dredge with flour and fry. Add milk or cream, cover and cook until tender. Remove the rabbit pieces and make gravy by adding flour to the pan.

RABBIT PIE—an every-other-night supper for early pioneer families and still a wonderful treat for modern-day culinary adventurers.

RECIPE

Rabbit Pie

Simmer a cut-up rabbit in water until tender; debone meat, season and lay aside. Fry 1 chopped onion in 3 Tbsp butter and mix in flour to make a roux. Add rabbit meat to sauce and pour into a buttered baking dish. Cover with pastry and bake until pastry is golden.

RABBIT STEW. See *bouillotte de lièvre*.

RACTOPAMINE—a drug added to cattle and swine feed to promote lean muscle tissue. Produced by Elanco Animal Health, a division of Eli Lilly and Company, the drug is banned in many countries because of the chemical's residue in meats causing an increase in human systolic blood pressure, along with various nerve discorders. That it works to inflate the profits of conglomerate agriculture means it can still be found in Canadian and U.S. pork, beef, chicken, turkey and farmed fish products.

RADICCHIO. See chicory.

RADISH (*Raphanus sativus*)—a quick-maturing root vegetable belonging to the massive Cabbage family and a favourite of Canadian home gardeners

market will have radishes in many colours, shapes, sizes and even nationalities, including the French breakfast radish, the Chinese or Japanese Daikon radish and the Sicily radish.

RAFFALD, ELIZABETH (1733–1781)—author of *The Experienced English Housekeeper* published in 1769, with an additional six editions published during her lifetime. Considered the finest cookbook published during the 18th century, the book was a must-read for housewives who were going to be immigrating to Canada.

RAGGED ROBINS—a favourite pioneer cookie made whenever dried or fresh coconut became available.

RAGOÛT DE BOULETTES—a meatball stew of Acadian origin that travelled to Louisiana and returned in a variety of forms: spicy or mild, pork, beef or both and sometimes with crayfish. *See also* crayfish boulettes.

because it can be intercropped with other vegetables and successively planted, enabling an almost constant supply through the growing season. The most familiar radish in Canada is the roundish, red-coloured radish, but a farmers'

CANADA'S FAVOURITE RADISH VARIETIES

- Cherry Belle—early, round and crunchy.

- Early Scarlet—early and round with a crisp, white flesh.

- French Breakfast—elongated with a white tip; one of the best snacking radishes.

- Long Scarlet—elongated with crisp, white flesh.

- White Hailstone—round and white with a mild taste.

RECIPE

Meatball Stew

Spread ¾ cup flour on a cookie sheet and bake in a 425°F oven until golden brown, about 10–15 minutes, stirring often to prevent burning. Next, cook 1 large minced onion in 2 Tbsp butter until translucent and transfer to a large bowl. Stir in 1 tsp each of ground cinnamon, cloves and nutmeg. Place 2 lbs ground pork into bowl along with 2 Tbsp dried parsley, 1 egg and ½ cup breadcrumbs, and mix well. Form 1-inch meatballs and roll them in the roasted flour, reserving the unused flour. Pour 6 cups chicken stock into cooking pot and bring to a boil over medium heat. Drop in meatballs along with a bay leaf and stir to keep meatballs from sticking to the bottom. Reduce boil to a simmer and cook meatballs for 20 minutes. Add 4 peeled and cubed potatoes and cook until tender, about 20 minutes. Remove meatballs and potatoes into a bowl. Remove bay leaf and discard. Mix the remaining roasted flour with ¼ cup cold water and gradually whisk into the simmering broth pot. Bring this gravy to a boil and keep stirring until thick. Return meatballs and potatoes to the gravy and serve the stew piping hot.

RAGOÛT DE BOULETTES ET PATTES DE COCHON (also called meatball and pigs feet stew)—a favourite of habitants and made with beef meatballs, pig trotters and onions, with or without vegetables.

RAILROAD CAKE—a jelly roll cake, but much lighter and named after the vehicle that brought the lightness of baking powder to farm communities—the railway.

RECIPE

Railroad Cake

Mix 1 cup each of sugar and milk, 2 cups flour, 3 beaten egg yolks, 2 tsp baking soda and 1 tsp butter. Fold in 3 whipped egg whites, pour batter into 2 shallow pans and bake immediately. While still warm, spread on jam or jelly and roll up cakes. Let cool and sprinkle with powdered sugar. Makes 2 cakes.

Railway Restaurants

• During the very early days of train travel, passengers were required to wait out the locomotive's frequent stops for fuel and water. These "whistle stops" would often feature a lunch counter offering sandwiches and quick meals not only to passengers but also to locals, and in many small western towns and villages they became the first restaurants.

RAINBOW TROUT (*Oncorhynchus mykiss*; also called steelhead)—adaptable to both fresh and salt water, this fish is a sportsman's dream and is so amenable to aquaculture that it's available at fish and supermarkets around the globe. Firm white flesh makes this fish easy to prepare in any manner, but a quick fry in butter tastes best.

RAINCOAST CRISP CRACKERS—small batch, all-natural ingredient crackers baked by Lesley Stowe Fine Foods in Vancouver, BC. They come in five scrumptious varieties, each one a taste sensation.

RAISIN PIE—an iconic pioneer dessert pie made by the Hudson's Bay Company, which insisted their outposts be stocked with various delights to reward voyageurs after a gruelling paddle.

Raisin pie sweetened with real sugar in a real butter crust, along with a free bottle of rum, was every voyageur's nightly dream that came true when he reached his destination.

RAISIN SAUCE—until World War I set in motion the gradual abandonment of all foods Canadian, this sauce was the nation's favourite for drizzling over a Sunday dinner ham.

Raisins

• Raisins had been hugely popular in Europe since the time of the Romans, and in the late 17th and early 18th centuries, the dried grapes became an intrinsic commodity of the triangular trade between the Caribbean, New England / Newfoundland and Africa. It was a foul business that enabled the slave trade, but it gave Canadian settlers ready access to Caribbean citrus, coconut, spices, raisins and other exotic foods that came along as deck cargo on the trading ships.

RECIPE

Raisin Sauce

Mix 2 Tbsp ham drippings with 2 Tbsp flour and ½ tsp dry mustard in a pot, and slowly add 1 cup apple cider. Bring to a boil then reduce heat, add ½ cup seedless raisins and simmer 10 minutes before serving.

RAMP, RAMPION. *See* wild leek.

RAPESEED (*Brassica napus*)—a leafy green member of the Cabbage family and popular as a salad green in both Britain and Canada. Because its seed oil is rich in erucic acid, the seeds were originally pressed for machine oil. Hybridizing by Canadian agro-scientists during the 20th century succeeded in removing the bitter erucic acid and created a sensational new salad and cooking oil called canola oil. *See also* canola oil.

RAPESEED OIL. *See* canola oil. *See also* cold-pressed canola oil.

RAPPIE PIE (also called *pâté à la rapure*)—an Acadian boiled chicken and potato pie much favoured by both New France settlers and modern Québécois housewives. In the early days, this dish required a long cooking time because the chicken was usually an old hen that had stopped laying eggs.

RECIPE

Rappie Pie

Dry several boiled and sliced potatoes in a cloth and place in a pot with chicken stock; simmer for 10 minutes. Spread a layer of potatoes into a well-greased bake tin, add a layer of boneless chicken and another of potatoes. Top with a mixture of minced onions, chopped salt pork or bacon, then season and bake for ½ hour at 350°F, or until the top is crispy brown.

RASPBERRY (*Rubus idaeus*)—a relative of the common blackberry and member of the Rose family. Raspberries, like blackberries, are not single fruits, but many drupelets gathered in clusters. When picked, raspberries leave their cores and are hollow, while blackberries come off whole. Raspberries are commercially cultivated across southern areas of Canada and are one of the most popular berries for eating fresh or in all manner of baked goods, jams and wines.

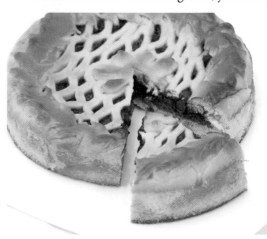

RASPBERRY VINEGAR—raspberry vinegar was a much-loved condiment in both Britain and Canada in the 19th century and was most often used to flavour Yorkshire puddings. Fill up a bottle with fresh raspberries (or any fresh berries), cover with a good wine vinegar, then leave it in the refrigerator for at least a month. When the time is up you will no longer need to refrigerate it. Leave the berries in the bottle and strain out whatever amount is required, as needed.

RAW MILK—a terrible name for nature's most perfect food and one promoted by dairy conglomerates because it provides moral licence to process milk into more profitable constituents. A better name is "unprocessed milk." *See also* milk.

RED RIVER CEREAL—a breakfast porridge mix of cracked wheat, rye and flax, and a favourite of western Canadians since its 1924 introduction to the city of Winnipeg. Now manufactured by Robin Hood Multifoods—a Canadian spoke in the Smuckers food empire—the cereal is still a good-for-you start for any day and is available across the country.

RED ROCK CRAB. *See* crab.

RED SALMON. *See* sockeye salmon.

REDFISH (*Sebastes* spp.)—three commercially fished species of a small Atlantic cousin of the Pacific redfish that are factory processed at sea into small fillets that are occasionally passed off as yellow perch, resulting in a creative marketing name change to "ocean perch." *See also* counterfeit fish.

REINDEER. *See* caribou.

RENNET—a digestive substance that contains rennin, an enzyme necessary for the digestion of milk in mammals through a curdling action that separates digestible solids from liquid: the curd and whey. Rennet is often used in the production of cheese, and for centuries, the most common source of rennet was the fourth stomach of unweaned calves. The stomachs were salted and dried and cut into thin strips for cheese making. Nowadays, the rennet is a liquid extract or powder and is more likely of vegetable origin.

RÉVEILLON—a French Canadian Christmas or New Year's party that features lots of family, food and fun. *Réveillons* are also celebrated in New Orleans, which still has a strong French population. The word *réveil* means "waking" and *réveillons* typically feature late nights and long dinners with extravagant foods such as lobster, escargot, foie gras and tortière. Not for the diet conscious as the food is nonstop and heavy on the calories, but who cares when you're having fun.

RHUBARB (*Rheum rhabarbarum*; also called pie plant)—a large-leafed, herbaceous perennial that arrived in Europe from China by way of the Silk Road and in North America via settlers, where it was so common an ingredient in pie that it was called "pie plant." Rhubarb is a vegetable, but Canadians like to think of it as a fruit for not only pies but also cakes, cobblers and sauces.

RHUBARB PIE—an easy-to-make dessert pie favoured by early settlers because the rhubarb plant grew fast and required little maintenance. Rhubarb crossed the country with early settlers and was always in the ground and growing before the roof went onto cabins.

RECIPE

Rhubarb Meringue Pie

In a pot, melt 1 Tbsp butter, add 1 cup sugar and 2 cups diced rhubarb and cook over medium heat until rhubarb is slightly soft and sugar is melted. Add 2 slightly beaten egg yolks and another ¼ cup sugar mixed with 1 Tbsp flour and cook until rhubarb mixture is almost a jelly. Pour into prebaked pie shell, top with meringue and brown in 300°F oven for about 15 minutes.

RHUBARB SAUCE—a simple pioneer dessert that is delicious when poured over ice cream but is also scrumptious by itself or when topped with a huge dollop of whipped cream.

RECIPE

Rhubarb Sauce

Cook 4 cups diced rhubarb in ¼ cup water with ½ cup sugar and lemon zest until rhubarb is tender, about 10 minutes. Serve as is or run through a food processor until smooth.

RICE PUDDING—a 17th-century English dessert that was originally baked in a sausage casing but that was naturalized to the Canadian food experience by the substitution of butter for traditional bone marrow, the addition of raisins or dried currants and the use of a pastry crust. This pudding, or pie, was a favourite with pioneers who often substituted wild rice for hard-to-come-by imported rice.

RECIPE

Crustless Rice Pudding

Mix together ½ cup long grain white rice, ½ cup sugar, 1 can evaporated milk (diluted with water to 4 cups), 1 cup raisins, 1 tsp vanilla and ¼ tsp salt and pour into a well-greased 9 x 13 baking dish. Sprinkle top with cinnamon and bake at 325°F for 1½ hours.

A B C D E F G H I J K L M N O P Q **R** S T U V W X Y Z

RITZ MOCK APPLE PIE—Nabisco printed this recipe on their Ritz cracker box until the 1970s, the original having been borrowed by Nabisco from a previous hard-times era when the dish was called "California pioneer apple pie," back in 1852. In that original recipe, the pseudo-apples in the filling were soda crackers.

RECIPE

Ritz Mock Apple Pie

Put 2 cups water, 2 cups sugar and 2 tsp cream of tartar in a saucepan and bring to a boil. Reduce heat, simmer 15 minutes, add 2 Tbsp lemon juice and the grated rind of 1 lemon and allow to cool. In a pastry-lined 9-inch pie tin, place 36 broken-up Ritz crackers, pour in sauce, dot with 2 Tbsp butter or margarine and sprinkle with ½ tsp cinnamon. Cover with pastry, slit for steam and bake in 425°F oven for 30–35 minutes or until top is golden brown. Serve warm.

ROAST BEEF, OLD ENGLISH-STYLE—scrape the mould from a haunch of well-aged beef and slather it with oil and whatever spices or herbs are on hand. Mount haunch on rotisserie and swing over a built-up fire. Alternatively, the meat can be placed into a community bread oven in the morning for pick up before supper. Community bread ovens were common in Europe, but only in England were they reserved on Sundays for the cooking of roasts, from whence comes the Sunday dinner roast, a tradition continued in English Canada. Community bake ovens were hot, with temperatures kept at 450–500°F for quick baking. Roasts were pulled out periodically and their pans drained of fat to keep from igniting. "Waste not, want not," and what to do with all the drained fat was solved by the invention of the Yorkshire pudding. No rising needed, just make a batter, pour into blazing hot Scotch pie moulds or iron pudding pans—with some melted fat in the bottom—and watch the magic. *See also* Yorkshire pudding with wild rice.

ROAST MOOSE—moose tenderloin is the prime cut and should be hung for a minimum of two weeks, then spit-roasted over coals or a gas barbecue or oven roasted. Moose are usually

butchered in the same manner as beef, with hunters receiving neatly wrapped and labelled packages. But moose meat is leaner than beef, and cooking methods and times vary according to the animal's age and method of slaughter.

ROAST PARTRIDGE—during Canada's formative years, all small game birds—grouse, quail, snipe, ptarmigan—common to Canada's northern areas were considered partridges and were a major food source for northern First Nations and residents of northern areas. Although there are native partridge species here, the most common in Canada, both wild and farm raised, is the non-native grey or Hungarian partridge (*Perdix perdix*), a member of the Pheasant family and native to Britain, not Hungary. The young birds were larded with bacon and then roasted in their own juices, one per diner.

ROAST VENISON—a saddle, or haunch, is best for roasting, cut from an animal that has been hung for a minimum of two weeks.

RECIPE

Roast Venison

Remove the bone and prepare a marinade of 1 sliced onion, 1 minced garlic clove, 1 bay leaf, 1 crushed clove and 4 juniper berries in a bottle of dry red wine or hard cider. Place meat in bowl and marinate overnight. When ready to roast, preheat oven to 450°F, tie meat into a compact shape and lard haunch with strips of bacon. Roast for 20 minutes and then reduce oven temperature to 325°F and cook for 15–20 minutes per pound.

DEER

Deer were everywhere during Canada's early settlement years, and to bag the evening meal, a farmer merely had to house the dogs for the night and step from the doorway in the early morning. Not much has changed—Canadian farmers with small apple orchards can still step out the back door and bag a deer because the delightfully agile creatures are unable to resist apple trees. They come in spring to nibble on bark and tender shoots and reappear in autumn to munch on succulent fruit. Nowadays, special fencing prevents deer from decimating large orchards, but in earlier times, only man's best friend enabled the evolution of the legendary Canadian apple pie.

ROAST WILD DUCK—around a quarter of a million wild ducks are harvested annually in Canada, and roasting is the preferred method of preparation.

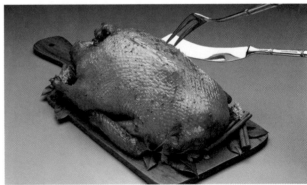

RECIPE

Roast Duck

Clean and stuff the birds with your favourite bread stuffing and pop them into a 400°F oven until they brown, then reduce heat to 250°F and bake for 2–2½ hours, until tender. To make gravy, deglaze the pan with water or wine, thicken with flour and season with salt and pepper.

ROAST WILD GOOSE—oiled, seasoned and roasted as for a regular recipe, Canada geese (*Branta canadensis*) harvested from the wild are a mighty tasty treat, especially larded over with strips of bacon. In the early days, Canada geese suffered the fate of bison and were nearly hunted to extinction but, thanks to conservation efforts, have made a spectacular comeback. Snow geese (*Chen caerulescens*) are a species hunted in the Far North and some east coast areas, while in the old days several species of swans were pioneer fare.

ROASTED PIG TAILS—a specialty of Waterloo County, Ontario. Real tails from real pigs are very yummy, but be careful with your teeth because they can break easily while munching on a tough pig tail.

ROASTED ROUNDER—an immature codfish roasted whole; a Newfoundland favourite dinner fish.

ROBIN HOOD FLOUR—a favourite of Canadian bakers since 1909, when Minneapolis grain miller F.A. Bean refurbished an old mill in Moose Jaw, Saskatchewan, and began producing quality wheat flour with the familiar red and green Robin Hood logo. *See also* Five Roses flour.

ROCK GUTS. *See* famine foods.

ROCK SAMPHIRE (*Crithmum maritimum*)—an edible plant found along coastal areas of Europe and North America and a favourite vegetable of coastal First Nations. Adopted by early settlers and still popular, the plant has a pleasant, hot and spicy taste that is perfect for green salads or pickling.

ROCK TRIPE (*Umbilicaria vellea*; also called *tripe de roche*)—rock lichen gathered by voyageurs to bolster pemmican stew. It isn't very tasty, but it was always underfoot and ready for picking. *See also* famine foods.

ROCKY MADSEN'S FISH CRISP GOURMET FISH SEASONING—available in three flavours: Honey Dijon, White Wine and Herbs, and Maple Smoke, with this last one doubling as a meat seasoning. It has become every Canadian fishing guide's favourite breading, and though hard to find on store shelves, it is easily ordered online.

ROE—the eggs or spawn contained within the ovaries of female fish, some of which are much

in demand, such as sturgeon roe (true caviar), and some less so, such as salmon, whitefish and turbot roe. *See also* caviar.

ROGERS SUGAR—the brand name used by the BC Sugar Refining Co. Ltd. since its establishment in 1891 in Vancouver by a young man from New Orleans named Benjamin Tingley Rogers. Today, the company is called Rogers Sugar Inc. and sells all manner of sugar products in western Canada under the Rogers brand, with its eastern subsidiary plants selling under the Lantic brand. *See also* sugar.

ROLLER MILLING—a method for milling grain perfected in Switzerland in 1834 and quickly adopted worldwide. The objections to this milling process concern the heat generated by the high-speed rollers, which is said to have a deleterious effect on the grain enzymes.

ROMAN CAULIFLOWER. *See* romanesco.

ROMANESCO (*Brassica oleracea*; also called Roman cauliflower)—a broccoli/cauliflower variant native to northern Italy and noted for its bizarre and bewitching shape. People who

like cauliflower and broccoli will love this vegetable. Even kids who hate broccoli and cauliflower take to the nutty sweetness of this variant, so look for it at your local farmers' market.

ROMBAUER, IRMA (1877–1962)—author of the all-time favourite North American cookbook *The Joy of Cooking*. Published at her own expense in 1931 and not in commercial publication until 1936, Irma's book had to wait until after World War II to be recognized for its brilliance. While no accurate sales figures are available, it is estimated that *The Joy of Cooking* has sold almost 11 million hardcover editions and that many or more in softcover.

ROOT BEER—a variation on spruce beer with sugar, spices, herbs and vanilla replacing the pungent spruce tips. Canadian settlers were drinking various root beers long before Pennsylvania pharmacist and vanilla broker Charles E. Hires decided to add a little vanilla, sarsaparilla, ginger and sassafras. He patented his recipe and made millions, much of that lucre coming from Canada as his original bottled extract became a huge hit with Maritimers. *See also* spruce beer.

ROSE HIP JELLY—a pioneer settler's favourite right across the country. Every autumn, when money was scarce and cupboards bare, the children of prairie farmers would scour the countryside for wild rose bushes and, with nimble fingers, harvest pails of rose hips. Rose hips are easily gathered, and the jelly is a preferred glaze for venison.

WILD ROSE HIPS

The wild rose bush (*Rosa* spp.) was ubiquitous in Canada, and First Nations used the hips—the fruit of the rose bush—to make tea, probably suspecting the hips provided a health benefit (they're loaded with vitamin C). Rose hips should be picked after a touch of frost has turned them a reddish colour, when they look like cherry-sized apples, an attribute they come by honestly as the two are related. Tart and tangy, rose hips are nicely tamed by sugar and are best used for jelly making because the straining process rids the mixture of a million seeds.

ROSE WATER—perfumed water prepared by steeping or distilling rose petals and used as a cooking ingredient, room freshener and cosmetic. Roses grow everywhere in Canada, and while distilling the essence from the fragrant flower sounds daunting and beyond the capabilities of both early settlers and contemporary citizens, it is a rather simple undertaking. Use it in recipes that call for rose water, or use to make cold cream. Pioneer women heated beechnut oil with beeswax and, while stirring constantly, dribbled in as much rose water as the emulsion could hold.

RECIPE

Rose Water

Place an inverted bowl at the bottom of a large stockpot and surround it with rose petals. Place another bowl right side up on top of the inverted bowl and fill pot (not bowl) with water to cover petals. Place lid on stockpot upside down (concave top is best), pile chipped or cubed ice on the inverted lid and begin the cooking process. Steam containing aromatic rose essence will condense on the stockpot lid and drip down into the catch bowl. This process will yield around 2 cups of rose water that should be bottled and capped to prevent evaporation.

ROUGHAGE—a word used to describe the indigestible carbohydrate material in food, such as bran. Roughage absorbs and holds water while passing through the human gut and acts as a laxative. Fibre is any indigestible material in food other than carbohydrates.

ROWANBERRY (also called dog berry, pig berry)—fruit of the mountain ash tree (*Sorbus americana*), also called rowan tree, used by pioneer settlers and modern-day foragers to make a tasty jelly that is great with meats, especially game meats. And yes, the mountain ash is that tree you probably have in your front yard, the one with the red berries that marks the coming of autumn like a signpost. Go pick them, but make sure it's after a frost so they're soft and ripe or the jelly will be bitter.

RUBBABOO—a trapper's stew or porridge made from a few handfuls of Indian meal and any-thing on hand: pemmican, a bit of last week's venison or whatever could be picked up along the trail. The name is derived from "burgoo," a British navy slang word for oatmeal gruel served up on 18th-century ships.

RUBY RED GRAPEFRUIT—during the 1930s, seeking to popularize a radiation-mutated grapefruit called Ruby Red, Florida citrus

RECIPE

Rowanberry Jelly

You'll need 2 lbs ripe berries picked either after a frost or left 24 hours in the freezer to tame the bit-terness factor. After the freezer, put the berries in a pot with some water, bring to a boil and then sim-mer until they are soft and mushy. Allow to cool a bit, then strain through muslin or a jelly bag and measure the collected juice. For every pint of col-lected juice add 1 lb sugar and heat slowly till melted, then up the heat to a boil and test for jell by placing a spoonful onto a saucer. When ready, pour into jars and refrigerate. Note: Fresh-picked rowan-berries require bletting before being turned into jam or jelly. See bletting.

KING WILLIAM'S LIQUID DIET

Obesity is a main impetus for the sudden popularity of certain foods and the exclusion of others in the national feedbag, the latter giving new meaning to the term "diet," cutting out certain foods to achieve weight loss. One of the most famous, and probably the first, dieter was the English king William the Conqueror, who, after attaining a weight that prevented him from riding horses, announced that he would abstain from all solid foods and go on a liquid diet of brandy and red wine. It worked, much to the disappointment of his food purveyors, because most of William's wealthier subjects who could actually afford to purchase fat-contributing foods had followed his lead into corpulence and simply continued emulating their boss. William's liquid diet financially devastated the local farmers, but England's surgeons were elated as profits from patching up drunken riders who toppled from their mounts went through the roof. That, as you may know, was the ultimate fate King William, who fell off his horse onto his head and died along with his liquid diet.

William's liquid diet was reintroduced in 1941 sans alcohol by Stanley Burroughs as the Master Cleansing Diet, or Lemonade Diet, a hugely successful weight-loss endeavour that lingered through the eons to become a favourite of modern-day celebrities wanting to shed pounds quickly. In 1964, San Francisco social gadabout Robert Cameron put the booze back into the liquid diet and, calling it the Drinking Man's Diet, made a fortune for both himself and North American livestock ranchers. In that same city but about 50 years earlier, art dealer Horace Fletcher advocated a diet wherein corpulent participants chewed their food 32 times (once for each tooth) and then spit it out. The spitting-out was short-lived, but the mastication part attracted hundreds of thousands of adherents and is still practised today.

growers promoted a variation of William the Conqueror's liquid diet, calling it the Grapefruit Diet. It was hugely successful and garnered hundreds of thousands of adherents, skewing Canadian milk and apple production for decades and putting grapefruit onto the shelves of every food store in both the U.S. and Canada. *See also* fad diets.

RUCKLE BEANS—similar to lima beans, and though they are not native to BC's Salt Spring Island, it is the only place on the planet that they are grown commercially. Brought to Salt Spring Island by Ontario farmer Henry Ruckle in 1872 , the beans have been part of the Ruckle family for over a century. What happened to the beans' Ontario progenitors is a mystery—not a trace survives. Their demise in Ontario could have had something to do with their tendency to turn into soup if over-boiled, but the folks on Salt Spring Island prefer them baked, so the Ruckle bean's survival is pretty much guaranteed. *See also* beans.

RUFFED GROUSE. *See* grouse.

RUM—the distilled fermentation of boiled sugar or molasses. Along with fish, furs and timber, rum was part of the economic engine that drove our nation to Confederation. During the 18th and 19th centuries, every British sailor and soldier got a pint of rum a day, fishermen got double or triple that, and every man, woman or child with a penny could buy a pint. Rum paid for our fish that fed slaves in the Caribbean, and rum bought the slaves to cut more Caribbean cane to make more rum to buy more cod.

Around and around it went, making the trading company owners filthy rich. It was a nasty business, but it led us to where we are today.

RUM BALLS—originally a sailor's dessert made by soaking hardtack in rum, molasses or maple syrup, today they still include the rum, but graham crumbs and cocoa replace the hardtack.

RUM IN WORLD WAR I

During World War I, the transportation of fresh food to the frontlines was often sub-orned by ammunition, but space was always found for thousands of gallon jars of 86-proof Jamaican rum. Canadians know about naval rum rations, but very few know that the practice was also extended to the army in World War I, especially to frontline troops, who often received double and triple rations. Although the labels claimed that Jamaica was the source, it was actually a product of Canadian distilleries and made from sugar beets supplied by large contract farms. Drinking rum made the mud and stench tolerable, the dismal food palatable and the onset of trench foot endurable. It also made going "over the top" into enemy machine-gun fire less of a lunatic proposition. Rum was liquid courage.

RUM SHRUB—in the 17th, 18th and 19th centuries, rum was usually poorly distilled and vile tasting. With some added sugar and citrus juice, the worst-tasting rum could be made into a palatable cocktail called "shrub," the father of all cocktails and probably so-called because of the many imbibers who woke up under some shrubbery. *See also* shrub.

RUTABAGA (*Brassica napus*; also called Swedish turnip)—rutabagas are a natural cross of turnip and cabbage with perhaps a touch of wild mustard thrown in for good measure. The Laurentian rutabaga is a 1920s variety and is as good as it gets.

RYE BREAD—made with rye grain (*Secale cereale*), rye bread is high in fibre and is denser and darker than wheat bread. *See also* bread.

RYE WHISKY—in our nation's formative years, most whisky was distilled from either 100 percent

or a good portion of fermented rye grain, hence the name rye whisky. Then along came cheaper grains, like corn and wheat, and rye slipped to a small percentage. However, for the aficionado of real Canadian whisky, Alberta Springs whisky made in Calgary, Alberta, is still in the straight rye whisky business. Try their reserve whisky and be ready for a lip-smacking experience.

Whisky

- By 1840, well over 200 whisky distillers operated in Canada, most producing a product distilled from rye grain mash. Most of those distillers started out as millers, grinding grain into flour, and the traditional payment was 10 percent of the grain: the grain tithe. Over time, as farmers increased yields of grain, the tithe began to pile up and became a problem for millers. Their inspired solution was to turn it into whisky.

- During Prohibition, Canada stopped short of banning the production and export of whisky. Cuba and Mexico were ostensibly the main destinations for Canadian whisky, but few ships ever got farther than the U.S., and because Prohibition was unpopular legislation, U.S. law enforcement generally turned a blind eye. Canadian distillers worked 24/7 to meet U.S. demand; grain farmers and boat builders prospered; and fishermen on both

coasts and the Great Lakes made fortunes transporting fish of a different colour. Distillers even packed bottles in burlap bags to make drops and pickups at sea easier.

- In Canada, unlike the U.S. or Britain where whisky is spelled with an "e"—as in Scotch whiskey or Bourbon whiskey—our word is spelled with no "e": whisky.

S

S&H GREEN STAMPS—from the early 1920s to the early 1960s, the Canadian housewife collected canned foods as a hedge against difficult times, a hard-to-break habit and probably the impetus for the national "better days" phenomenon using S&H Green Stamps. The stamps were a supermarket promotional tool—like today's loyalty point programs—designed to help housewives transition from pantries and corner stores to supermarket shopping any day of the week. It worked: housewives could still collect goods, albeit stockpiled in stamp form, and the supermarkets even provided a booklet to house their collection—a virtual pantry if you will.

SABLEFISH (*Anoplopoma fimbria*; also called black cod, butterfish)—a northern Pacific fish that is unique in that it is caught mostly by trapping in a manner similar to crab fishing. Sablefish have a high oil content and are excellent for grilling, roasting or pan searing. The majority of the catch is processed at sea, so the fish is seldom available on the fresh market.

SAGAMITÉ—a First Nations corn soup made not from kernels or cobs but from ground corn flour and animal fat. It was widely adopted by pioneer settlers.

SALAD BURNET (*Sanguisorba minor*)—a perennial member of the Rose family with leaves that taste like cucumber. Foraged by First Nations and cultivated by settlers, this herb has again become popular with chefs. It is used in a variety of ways, but mostly for salad greens.

SALALBERRY (*Gaultheria shallon*)—the salal shrub is an evergreen member of the Wintergreen family, and the berries were a important food source for coastal First Nations. Salalberries were gathered and dried in blocks for winter food, with a portion pounded into a tart, wintergreen-flavoured jam to cut the grease of roasted game. Salalberries look and taste a bit like blueberries and are so rich in pectin that they turn to jam when macerated, and no additional pectin is required to make jelly. Salal shrubs grow everywhere along the Pacific coast and can be identified by their dark green, waxy leaves.

SALMON—the common name for species of the Salmonidae family of fish, including Atlantic salmon (*Salmo salar*) and the Pacific salmons (*Oncorhynchus* spp.), as well as trout, char, grayling and whitefish. Salmon is an important historical and modern-day food and income source for many Canadians. Canadians love salmon; annually, we broil, poach, chowder, bake and grill around 6.5 kg per person, not including all those millions of cans. There's nothing wrong with the cans, given that most contain wild fish chock-full of the long-chained fatty acid known as omega-3, a healthy chemical compound found in oily fish and some plants. Wild salmon is an excellent source of omega-3 fatty acids, but because salmon is such tasty fare and easily obtainable, health benefits are

Salmon

- Wild salmon consume krill or shellfish whose diet consists of algae or plankton that contains carotenoids (the yellow, orange, and red pigments found in many plants), giving their flesh a natural pink or reddish colour. Farm-raised salmon, however, are fed a plant- or wild fish–based diet and therefore have little natural colour and no marketability, so artificial dyes are added to their food.

- It takes almost 4 kilograms of wild-caught food fish to produce 1 kilogram of farmed salmon.

- Ninety-nine percent of Atlantic salmon for retail sale are farmed, while only 20 percent of Pacific salmon are the product of aquaculture; most canned salmon is from the wild.

- Salmon are vulnerable to a parasitic nematode called *Anisakis*. If ingested from raw salmon by humans, it causes a debilitating gastrointestinal disease called anisakiasis—it is best not to consume raw salmon.

- Over the centuries, fishing has passed from a dangerous occupation to a dangerous

preoccupation of profiteering food conglomerates, and consumers of both the wild-caught and farmed varieties must employ due diligence in regard to source and origin of their fish, especially now that genetically engineered salmon are poised to enter the marketplace. Scientists have cut into the DNA of Atlantic salmon and inserted material from the faster-growing Chinook species, along with genetic material from an even faster growing eel-like fish, the ocean pout. The food conglomerates are going into the monster fish business, and because no farmed fish labelling laws exist in Canada, consumers are at their mercy and possibly in harm's way.

hardly our main reason for consuming it. Salmon are anadromous species, meaning they spend their lives in both fresh and salt water and are constant movers that need large fat reserves, a fortuitous situation for consumers because as everyone knows, the flavour is in the fat.

TIPS FOR COOKING SALMON

- When cooking fresh or thawed salmon, allow 4 minutes on high heat, 450°F, for each ½ inch of thickness, adding 5 minutes to cooking time if the fish is foil wrapped.

- Baking is best done using oiled foil. Brush fish with butter or oil, season with salt and pepper, wrap in foil and place on a baking sheet.

- Barbecuing salmon is easier when using a well-oiled barbecue basket to facilitate turning and basting. Fish are high-protein foods and need constant basting to keep from drying out. If not using a basket, remember to oil both the fish and the grill to prevent the dreaded stickage.

- Pan-frying any fish is as easy as dropping fillets or steaks into bubbling butter or oil, turning once and cooking until the fish turns opaque and flakes easily with a fork. Alternatively, fillets can be dredged in flour, egg, bread or cracker crumbs, along with whatever else seems apropos, such as herbs, Parmesan cheese or a squeeze of lemon.

- Steaming salmon has become popular: place fish in a steamer, cover with a tight lid and cook over boiling water for 8–10 minutes or until fish flakes with a fork.

- Poaching is easy: place fish in a pan of cold water or broth, bring to a simmer and cook until fish flakes with a fork.

- Because of their high fat content, salmon are good candidates for the freezer and will keep two months in a refrigerator freezer if double wrapped in freezer paper and foil. For longer periods, up to five months, a deep freezer is required.

RECIPE

Cedar Plank Salmon

Soak untreated cedar plank in water for at least 2 hours before using. Prepare your salmon fillets: remove any bones, wash in cold water, pat dry and season with salt and pepper, then coat generously with a half-and-half paste of Dijon mustard and brown sugar. Set the barbecue to medium-high and place the plank onto the grill, then close the lid. When the first whiff of smoke is detected from the barbecue, flip the plank over and place the fillets onto it, skin-side down. Close the lid and cook for 20–30 minutes. To make absolutely sure the fish is cooked, use a meat thermometer—the internal temperature should read 135°F.

SALMON JERKY—traditionally made by deep slicing salmon fillets, curing with maple or camas sugar and smoking over an alderwood fire for days. Nowadays, fillets are skinned, sliced and cured with brown sugar, smoked for a day, thin sliced and smoked again. It's still a tasty product, but not as good as the old days.

SALMON BURGERS—a salmon patty popularized by upscale BC restaurants and TV chefs. It is not a fish cake, as the salmon burger patty is constructed differently.

SALMON LOAF—popular during wartime and economic depression—not to mention with moms in a dither—the salmon loaf has endeared itself to generations of Canadians. Originally made with fresh fish and confined to coastal area kitchens, the loaf spread across the country when cheap canned salmon flooded the market toward the end of the 19th century.

RECIPE

Salmon Loaf

Combine 1 can drained salmon, 1 cup breadcrumbs, ¾ cup milk, 1 egg slightly beaten, ¼ cup minced onion and 2 Tbsp melted butter. Season with salt and pepper, fluff with a fork, transfer to a bread tin, pat into a loaf shape and bake at 350°F for 45 minutes.

SALMON PATTIES—canned salmon combined with egg, breadcrumbs, minced onion and seasonings. Patty cake, patty cake, roll them in flour, refrigerate for an hour and fry.

SALMON PIE—shepherd's pie using salmon, and sometimes covered with pastry. Popular in the days when salmon was plentiful, very popular during war and hard times when canned salmon was used, and still popular today because it's so easy and tasty.

RECIPE

Salmon Burgers

Place 1–1½ lbs half-frozen salmon fillets in a food processor and pulse to a mince. Transfer to a bowl and combine with 1 egg, ½ cup cornmeal, ¼ cup canola oil, 1 Tbsp sour cream, 2 tsp fresh dill and 1 tsp sea salt. Form patties, fry gently until brown, and serve on a soft roll.

A B C D E F G H I J K L M N O P Q R **S** T U V W X Y Z

Canned Salmon in BC

- BC's salmon industry began in 1824 when the Hudson's Bay Company (HBC) post at Langley began purchasing salmon from native peoples and salt curing it in barrels. By 1834, the HBC was packing and shipping 3000 to 4000 barrels annually.

- In 1870, Alexander Loggie, who had learned the canning process in his native New Brunswick, convinced a few other men to join him in a canning venture. Canned salmon took off like a rocket, and in less than a decade, three

BC canneries were packing and shipping 100,000 cases per year. By the early 1900s, dozens of canneries were established and packing almost 2 million cases per year.

SALMONBERRY JAM—an easy-to-make jam from the drupes, or berries, of the salmonberry bush (*Rubus spectabilis*), a member of the mighty Rose family. Salmonberries look like and have a taste similar to their raspberry relatives and can be foraged all over the Pacific Northwest. When foraging salmonberries, keep in mind that the yellowish berries are sweetest.

SALSIFY (*Tragopogon porrifolius*; also called oyster plant)—a root vegetable popular with Canadians until the root cellar was made redundant by the introduction of refrigeration. Brought along with other root vegetables in the early 18th century, salsify took to Canadian gardens like a native plant, surpassing its European parentage in both size and taste. Also called oyster plant because the taste is best described as a cross between oysters and asparagus, salsify has become a naturalized Canadian vegetable. Salsify roots resemble parsnips or carrots, and its grass-like leaves make good salad greens when cut and allowed to grow back as tender shoots. Salsify has lately become a favourite with some chefs and is once again being cultivated, albeit in small quantities.

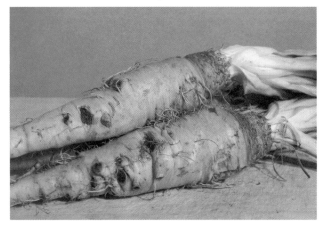

SALT BEEF (also called salt horse)—2-kg cuts of beef pickled in brine and packed into barrels. *See also* corned beef.

SALT COD—a codfish cleaned, split, rubbed with salt, washed and dried in the sunshine until dehydrated. The process was perfected by 16th-century Basque fishermen plying the coastal waters of Newfoundland. Before that, the most common method of preserving fish was to gut and air dry them, producing a hard, shrivelled product called stockfish. With the discovery of large European salt deposits in the early 17th century, the preserving process changed: gut, cover with salt for several weeks, rinse in seawater and dry on rocky beaches or raised racks called "flakes." This method produced a more easily reconstituted product familiar to most Canadians, the ubiquitous salt fish, the main ingredient in such dishes as bacalao, fish cakes and kedgeree. During the 18th century, the pickling process used to produce salt pork and beef was employed in the processing of fish; gutted, salted fish were simply packed into a barrel between layers of salt, pressed down with a screw press and topped off with saltwater.

RECIPE

Salt Cod Fish Cakes

Soak 2–3 lbs dried salt cod fillets at least 12 hours, changing the water several times. Boil 1 lb potatoes until soft and cook 1 small diced onion and 1 diced celery stalk in butter until soft. Boil salt cod 5 minutes, let cool and flake into pieces. Mash potatoes, onion, celery and fish together and mix in ¼ cup mayonnaise, 1 Tbsp Dijon mustard, ½ tsp Worcestershire sauce, ½ Tbsp finely chopped fresh dill, ½ Tbsp finely chopped fresh parsley, and salt and pepper to taste. Form into cakes and sear in a non-stick pan in a dash of canola oil.

A
B
C
D
E
F
G
H
I
J
K
L
M
N
O
P
Q
R
S
T
U
V
W
X
Y
Z

COD NATION

Canada is a nation founded on fish: after John Cabot's 1497 sojourn to the New World, one of his companions, the English merchant John Day, wrote to a friend that cod were so plentiful they could be taken from the sea in baskets weighted with stones. Dried codfish—more commonly called stockfish—was a staple food of 15th-century Europe, a king maker, as rulers of nations unable to feed their subjects were soon replaced by someone better at the job. Navies existed to protect a country's rights to productive fishing waters, and the most bounteous for the British lay off the southern coast of Iceland, an area also claimed by Norway, Sweden and the Netherlands. Naval engagements over fishing rights were common in that area, as was the seizure of entire fishing fleets. Fishing in those early days was a dangerous business: North Sea weather, hostile navies and wayward schools of cod were good reasons to seek out virgin fishing grounds, so both France and Britain sent their fleets westward to the New World. It was still dangerous but far more lucrative—Grand Banks cod could weigh 90 kilograms each, and filling a ship took only a few weeks.

The problem was that pickling the catch onboard and drying fish at home, as the Spanish and Portuguese did, was not an attractive option for the English, and for that reason, catching fish switched from the Grand Banks to offshore and processing became a land-based endeavour. Ships ballasted with salt left Britain in early spring and returned in late fall, their holds stuffed with dried and salted stockfish. Cheap salt cod flooded into English and French markets, and those markets soon ran short of people wanting to buy it. The British and French, poor or rich, did not particularly care for salt fish; the common people had their herring, and the landed gentry had aquaculture that gave them fresh trout or carp.

With local demand sated, 16th- and early 17th-century English ships loaded with salt cod went looking for new markets and found Africa. Ships of that era had rounded bottoms and required ballast to counteract the force of wind on sails, and cargo served that function. A ship without ballast stayed in port waiting for a new cargo. Salt cod vessels from the New World were soon sailing directly to African ports and returning to England with cargo as diverse as cocoa, ivory, dried fruits and lumber.

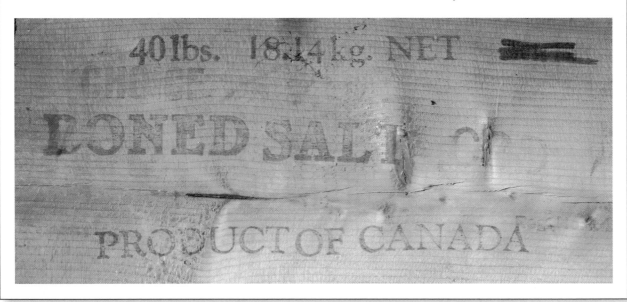

Salt Cod

- Before the Basque perfection of salting, codfish were simply air-dried, making the flesh difficult to keep and unappetizing. The salt, brought as ship ballast, enabled a longer shelf life and made for an extremely palatable product.

- The process of salting began with the unloading of codfish at the stage (the cleaning dock). On the stage, the fish were gutted, headed, split, washed and taken to the salting compound, where they were left to cure for a number of weeks. Cured, the fish were washed free of salt and taken to raised drying platforms called flakes. Drying, or making, fish was back-breaking work, as every storm required that the fish be gathered and redistributed after the weather cleared. At season's end, the salt cod was packed aboard a ship and sent to salt fish buyers in Europe in exchange for goods, a trust-in-God endeavour called "the voyage" because the ships would often run into foul weather and sink or be taken by pirates.

SALT COD CASSEROLE—an east coast favourite then and now, the dish is a simple preparation of cooked rice with an overlay of flaked salt cod, topped with a mix of chopped onions, green peppers and tomatoes, followed by another layer of rice, a drenching with white sauce and a half-hour bake in a moderate-temperature oven.

SALT HERRING. *See* Digby chicken.

SALT HORSE. *See* salt beef.

SALT PORK (also called white bacon)—brine-cured slabs of either streaky or pure fat unsmoked bacon cut into 2-kg pieces and packed into barrels.

RECIPE

Salt Pork and Cabbage

Place 2 lbs salt pork, 2 sliced onions, 2 minced garlic cloves, 1 tsp salt, ½ tsp savory, ¼ tsp pepper and 8 cups cold water into large pot, bring to a boil, then simmer until pork is tender, about 2 hours. Add 6 peeled and diced potatoes and 1 quartered medium cabbage during last half-hour of cooking and serve on a platter with cabbage surrounded by potatoes and topped with sliced pork.

SALT RISING BREAD—a complictaed no-yeast bread leavening method used by early pioneer settlers in which the salt kills off any yeasts, thereby allowing the bacterium *Clostridium perfringens* to raise the bread. *See also* bread.

RECIPE

Salt Rising Bread

Mix 1 cup each of cornmeal and water, pour into 2 cups boiling water, stir constantly for 5 minutes and remove from heat. Add 4 cups fresh milk still warm from the cow and 1 Tbsp each of sugar and salt. Let cool, stir in enough flour to make a batter and keep in a warm place for 4 hours. Add 2 cups buttermilk, 1 tsp baking soda and enough flour to make a soft dough. Mould onto a greased pan, let rise for 1 hour and bake.

SALT SPRING ISLAND CHEESES—sheep, goat and cows' milk cheeses made by artisan cheese makers using some of the finest milk on the planet. The Salt Spring Island Cheese Company makes delectable goat and sheep's milk cheeses, while the people at Moonstruck Organic Cheese Inc. produce a variety of marvellous cheeses with milk from their all-Jersey herd.

SALT SPRING ISLAND LAMB—the world's finest lamb. Salty air, lush forage and a temperate

Salt Spring Island

- Salt Spring Island is the largest and most populated of the Southern Gulf Islands and is located between Vancouver Island and the mainland in the Strait of Georgia.

Lamb

- Sheep destined for the dinner plate are graded according to age: baby lamb is 6–8 weeks old, spring lamb is 3–5 months, lamb is 5–12 months and yearling lamb is 1–2 years, while mutton is anything over 2 years.

climate all contribute to produce a succulent, flavourful meat that is beyond compare.

SALTED CAPLIN. *See* capelin.

SALTPETER—potassium nitrate, a crystalline salt used to make gunpowder, fertilizer and medicine, and for the preservation of various meats and sausages. *See also* nitrates and nitrites.

SAMPHIRE GREENS. *See* goose tongue.

SAND BAKED BEANS—dried beans or peas are soaked in water to soften, then are seasoned, sweetened and placed into a sealed bean pot and buried under a pile of superheated campfire rocks to cook.

SARDINE. *See* Atlantic herring. *See also* Pacific herring.

SASKATOON BERRIES

Saskatoons were dietary lifesavers for early voyageurs and trappers. The berry was a main constituent of pemmican, that easily carried and nutritious pounded meat ration produced by First Nations. Prairie settlers also relied on the berries, and for many of them, saskatoons were the only fresh fruit available. Gathered in large quantities, the berries were prepared using a method perfected by First Nations: clean the berries, boil them down to a sludge, pour into bread tins and dry in the sunshine like bricks. Berry bricks featured large in Prairie cuisine; chips from the berry bricks flavoured stews, coated roasted game and made wonderful dessert creations.

Nowadays, the berries are both foraged from the wild and cultivated. They are gaining popularity for their antioxidant, cancer-preventing qualities. Looks like a blueberry, tastes like a blueberry, but it is actually a super fruit in its own right because the saskatoon berry is packed full of nutritional qualities not found in blueberries.

SASKATOON BERRY (*Amelanchier alnifolia*; also called serviceberry)—the shrub is a member of the Rose family growing profusely from western Ontario to BC. Similar in colour and shape to blueberries, the purple-coloured saskatoon berries have a unique taste. They are easily gathered and made into marvellous jams, jellies, pies and puddings.

Saskatoon Origins

- The Saskatchewan city of Saskatoon derives its name from the saskatoon berry.

- The word "saskatoon" is the anglicized Cree word for the berry, *mis-sask-quah-too-mina*.

Saskatoon Berry Pie

Mix 1 cup sugar, ¼ cup cornstarch, ¼ tsp salt and juice of half a lemon in a bowl, then add 4 cups berries, stirring gently. Cover pie plate with bottom pastry and spoon in the berry mixture. Dot with butter and sprinkle with sherry if you like. Cover with top pastry, slit for steam and bake in preheated 400°F oven for 15 minutes. Reduce temperature to 350°F and bake 45 minutes more, until the crust is golden brown. Note: crust may be brushed with cream and sprinkled with sugar, egg washed or left plain.

SASKATOON BERRY PIE—the iconic berry pie of Canada's Prairie provinces and often combined with rhubarb to make another favourite, saskatoon rhubarb pie.

SAUSAGE—thanks to a few centuries worth of immigration from all corners of the globe, Canada has become a multicultural celebration of all things culinary—and nothing is as iconic to a culture as its sausages. Haggis, bangers, kielbasa, bratwurst, andouille, chorizo, salami and hundreds more are all as easily identified with their country of origin as their flags. Farmers' markets usually have old-school sausages, especially if there is an Amish or Mennonite presence. One of their specialties is the all-Canadian summer sausage.

SCALLOPS—of the 350 or so species of scallops, only four are of interest to Canadians: the Atlantic deep sea scallop (*Placopecten magellanicus*) and the Atlantic bay scallop (*Argopecten irradians*) on the east coast, and the pink scallop (*Chlamys rubida*) and the spiny scallop (*C. hastata*) on the west coast. The east coast species are easy to tell apart; the deep sea scallop, unlike its shallow water cousin, has no, or barely noticeable, radiating ribs on the shell. The Digby, Nova Scotia, inshore scallop fishing fleet is the largest in the world and supplies both fresh and frozen scallops, as well as roe, to a global market, whereas the offshore fishery concentrates mainly on shipboard flash-freezing. The small west coast scallops are fished from BC's Georgia and Johnstone straits by divers and boats towing small non-destructive bottom trawler nets called butterflies. Flash frozen, these tasty appetizer-sized scallops are catching on with chefs and are occasionally found in out-of-province fish markets. Fresh or frozen, scallops are delicious and easy to prepare.

TIPS ON BUYING AND CLEANING SCALLOPS

- When purchasing fresh scallops, it is a good idea to smell them. Fresh scallops should smell like the seaside—any sharp odour or a slight iodine smell indicates the bivalves have seen better days. If absolutely no odour is detected, chances are the scallops have been treated with sodium tripolyphosphate, a chemical that increases shelf life by enabling the scallops to hold water.

- Do not soak scallops in water like clams—they will suck it up like a sponge. To clean off dirt and sand, give them a quick rinse in cold water and dry quickly but thoroughly with paper towel.

RECIPE

Seared Scallops

Before cooking them, dry scallops with paper towel to keep the meat from splitting. Preheat an iron frypan, add a healthy dollop of canola oil and place your scallops. You may have heard that once placed in the pan scallops should not be moved until ready to flip, but that is hooey. Move them constantly until caramelized (about 2 minutes), then flip them over and repeat the process. When brown on both sides, remove scallops, dab onto a paper towel to remove excess oil and serve with a side of fiddleheads and pasta.

SCOFF. *See* Jiggs dinner.

SCONE—originally a quick-bake Scottish flat cake made with either barley, oats, wheat flour or a combination and served with plenty of butter. As the cake's popularity moved south into England, the preparation method changed from batter-drop griddle cake to oven-baked, white flour raised cake, and scones began appearing at afternoon tea alongside bowls of double cream and jam. Making the leap to Canada, it was back to griddle cooking but with the inclusion of local berries such as blueberries and cranberries. Nowadays, scones are still

A B C D E F G H I J K L M N O P Q R **S** T U V W X Y Z

A
B
C
D
E
F
G
H
I
J
K
L
M
N
O
P
Q
R
S
T
U
V
W
X
Y
Z

popular in the Maritimes but have been mostly been forgotten about in other provinces.

SCOTCH PANCAKES—back when a wood stove ruled the kitchen and the eldest family members still spoke with a brogue, this tea and breakfast cake was served along with fresh-churned butter and a jar of jelly or maple syrup. Mixed up in a jiffy with flour, sugar, a couple of eggs, a pinch of salt and enough milk to make a batter, they were better than bannock and the start of Canada's addiction to doughnuts.

SCOTCH PIE—originally, pie dough was a simple concoction of rough-milled rye flour, salt and water made several inches thick to withstand high baking temperatures. Called "coffins," the crusts

were containers meant to be reused or crushed up and added to stew as a thickener. By using soft wheat flour and adding lard and hot water to their pie dough, later Scottish immigrant bakers were able to mould edible dough into good-to-the-last-bite portable feasts. They especially excelled at meat pies, for, along with their locally raised mutton, all manner of wild game was available for pie making. For a nation on the move, the Scotch meat pie became a blessing because it stayed edible as long as coffin pies and required no utensils for consumption. *See also* coffin pastry.

RECIPE

Hot Water Pie Dough

Sift 4 cups flour and a pinch of salt into a warm bowl, make a well in the centre and slowly add ¾ cup lard melted in 1 cup hot water. Mix together, then roll out dough, cut into circles and form pie shells around the bottoms of ovenproof jars, reserving some dough for pie lids. Bake cases in 275°F oven. When cool, remove jars and fill pastry cases with chopped or ground meat (lobster, eel, oyster, salt cod), gravy and a pinch of nutmeg and cover tops with dough circles. Pinch closed, glaze pastry with milk and bake pies for another 40 minutes.

SCREECH—a rum once distilled in Newfoundland from the dregs that accumulated at the bottom of molasses barrels. Screech is still popular in Newfoundland, but it is now made and bottled in the Caribbean and distributed by the brand owner, the Newfoundland Liquor Commission.

SCRUNCHIONS, SCRUNCHIES—cubed salt pork or fatback bacon fried crispy and used as topping for brewis and dozens of other east coast specialty foods. Salt pork fried without cubing is called "vang."

SEA ASPARAGUS (*Salicornia virginica*; also called glasswort)—a marine plant harvested annually along the BC coast and Vancouver Island.

Sea asparagus resembles regular asparagus but has the salty, fresh taste of the sea that goes well with fish. Sea asparagus is shipped out frozen and is available online from several BC packers. *See also* goose tongue.

SEA BUCKTHORN (*Hippophae rhamnoides*)—the next "super berry" that is going to help Canadians survive the unrestrained use of pesticides by conglomerate farms, golf courses and municipalities. Growing full tilt in China and Russia, the bush with the orange berries that taste like passionfruit is already being planted in Saskatchewan and Ontario, and its fresh, health-preserving juice should be on the market in a few years.

A
B
C
D
E
F
G
H
I
J
K
L
M
N
O
P
Q
R
S
T
U
V
W
X
Y
Z

SEA CUCUMBER—around 30 sea cucumber species crawl about the ocean floor from Alaska to Mexico, but only one, the giant red, or California sea cucumber (*Parastichopus californicus*), is of interest to the BC commercial fishery and the Chinese merchant traders who buy almost the entire catch for its supposed aphrodisiac qualities.

SEA PARSLEY (*Palmaria palmata*; also called Nova Scotia sea parsley)—a natural mutation of dulse discovered by National Research Council of Canada scientists in 1978 and licenced to a Nova Scotia company, Ocean Produce International (OPI), for production by aquaculture. A uniquely Canadian product because it exists only in OPI's aquaculture tanks, sea parsley's burgundy-coloured florets run a gamut of tastes from celery to bacon to mussels to smoked oysters. It is available fresh, sun-dried or oven-toasted.

SEA PIE. See *cipaille*.

SEA SALT—all salt deposits are the remains of ancient oceans and differ from ordinary table salt in their lack of processing, which enables a composition of mostly sodium chloride with

traces of magnesium chloride, magnesium sulphate, potassium bromide and sodium bromide among other trace chemicals.

SEA URCHIN—there are red sea urchins (*Strongylocentrotus franciscanus*) and green sea urchins (*S. droebachiensis*). Green sea urchins are found on both coasts, mostly off of BC and New Brunswick, whereas the red urchin is only in the Pacific. Both red and green species are harvested inshore by divers and offshore by

trawlers, with 90 percent of the prepared catch being exported to Japan and the remainder going to Canadian sushi restaurants.

SEA URCHIN ROE (also called umi)—roe from green sea urchins is consumed from the spiny bottom dwellers using a spoon, cooked by upscale chefs or made into sushi, which is called umi.

HOW TO EAT SEA URCHIN ROE

It is like brain surgery: remove the top with a special tool or scissors, tip out the liquid and consume the five rose-coloured roe sacs (also called tongues) with a spoon. Mmmm, tastes like a hot afternoon at the fish market, though you can also try it marinated.

RECIPE

Sea Urchin Marinade

Mince half an onion, and in a small bowl mix onion, 2 Tbsp olive oil and 1 Tbsp each of dry sherry, lemon juice and chopped cilantro; then pop in your urchin tongues. Marinate no more than 30 minutes (the acidity of the lemon juice "cooks" the seafood). Serve on toasted French bread slathered with olive oil.

SEAFOOD CHOWDER—the Mi'kmaq plied the earliest French explorers with chowder while trying to part them from their iron, cloth and rope. If those explorers were around today, they would instantly recognize our chowders because the basic recipe has changed very little. The Mi'kmaq used seal oil for butter, wild leeks for onions, boiled hickory nuts for potatoes and wild mustard for spice, while the seafood would have been lobster, cod, haddock, oysters and clams. However, there would have been no cream in it, which nowadays is called Manhattan-style chowder.

SEAL FLIPPER PIE—despite the name, this east coast favourite contains not a shred of seal flipper. The word "flipper," in fact, refers to

A
B
C
D
E
F
G
H
I
J
K
L
M
N
O
P
Q
R
S
T
U
V
W
X
Y
Z

the front shoulder meat of seals, corresponding to a shoulder of lamb or pork. In Newfoundland, the actual flippers are called paws, with the fronts called "fippers" and the rear "daddles."

RECIPE

Seal Flipper Pie

Soak flipper meat in cold water and baking soda for an hour or so to dissipate any fishy taste, then remove the fat, cube the meat, dredge it in flour and brown it in a hot pan with onions and bacon. Cover the pan and bake for 2–3 hours. When done, top pie with pastry and bake for another 20 minutes to brown the crust.

SEAL FLIPPERS

Seal flippers are an early spring tradition in Newfoundland that residents are more than happy to keep secret. If the rest of Canada knew what tasty treats this tradition yielded up, the path to the Rock would be deep and wide. April is when the sealing boats return to port, and residents must be quick to the docks because seal flippers sell out quickly. Properly prepared, seal flipper is fork tender and one of the tastiest meats on the planet.

SEAWEED SALAD—a popular BC salad made with sliced tomatoes, cucumber and greens harvested from the ocean. Among the favourite seaweed greens are winged kelp, feather boa, nori, rockweed, sea cabbage, sea lettuce and rainbow seaweed. Sun dried, these seaweed varieties are available across Canada in specialty food stores or online.

SERVICEBERRY. *See* saskatoon berry.

SHAD (*Alosa sapidissima*; also called American shad)—the largest member of the Herring family, averaging about 2 kg, and a historically important east coast source of food and revenue. Shad are anadromous, meaning they live in the sea and spawn in fresh water, and for shad that is usually rivers in early spring, a few weeks after the alewife run. During the 1800s, up to 50 million tonnes of shad were caught annually and consumed fresh, pickled or smoked. Nowadays, with numbers drastically reduced by overfishing and habitat destruction, only small commercial fisheries still exist, with fish caught mainly for roe. In our Maritime provinces, the appearance of shad roe in fish markets is an anticipated culinary event and a sure sign that spring has arrived. Introduced to Pacific waters in 1871, shad have become established from Alaska to California but are not sought by commercial fishermen there.

SHARK FIN SOUP—the insatiable Chinese demand for shark fins to make soup is supplied in part by the Canadian Atlantic long-line fisheries targeting a shark species called porbeagle (*Lamna nasus*). The flesh is sold to European markets and the fins to the Chinese. About half the porbeagles caught on long-line hooks are by-catch, with the fins saved and the meat cut up for baiting hooks.

SHEDIAC LOBSTER FESTIVAL—a five-day extravaganza of all things lobster occurring every July in the town of Shediac, New Brunswick. Check online for exact dates.

SHEE FISH. *See* inconnu.

SHEEP SORREL (*Rumex acetosella*)—brought and planted by early pioneer settlers, sheep sorrel has a delightful lemony flavour and is used to make marvellous soups, salads, jams and pies. Not happy to remain in gardens, the plant escaped into the wild and became an invasive weed. Sheep sorrel is a small commercial crop in Canada, but it is widely foraged and can usually be found at farmers' markets.

SHEEPBERRY. *See* nannyberry.

SHELLFISH POISONING—there are four recognized syndromes of shellfish poisoning.

- Amnesic poisoning—the ingestion of a marine toxin called domoic acid causes short term and permanent memory loss and sometimes death.

- Diarrhetic poisoning—the consumption of toxic molluscs causes all the normal symptoms of food poisoning and then some, but is never fatal.

- Neurotoxic poisoning—the consumption of toxic molluscs may cause vomiting and slurred speech but no fatalities.

- Paralytic poisoning—the toxin accumulated by filter-feeding molluscs causes the standard symptoms associated with food poisoning and may progress to paralysis and death.

SHEPHERD'S PIE. *See* cottage pie. See also *pâté chinois*.

SHIP'S BISCUITS—what the British navy called hard-baked or hardtack biscuits, for which they operated their own bakeries. Both English and French merchant ships and fishing boats relied on commercial bakeries for hardtack supplies, with the French calling their biscuits *pain bateau*, and both also relied on the one-pot stew called lobscouse to soften the biscuits for consumption.

SHIPWRECK CASSEROLE—a layered, one-dish casserole with east coast roots, but popular across Canada.

A
B
C
D
E
F
G
H
I
J
K
L
M
N
O
P
Q
R
S
T
U
V
W
X
Y
Z

RECIPE

Shipwreck Casserole

Mix 1 can tomato soup with 1 can corn and pour half over a layer of potatoes, onions and rice. Layer with peas, ground beef or sausage and add remaining corn and soup mix. Bake at 350°F for 1½ hours, top with cheese and bacon, and brown for 15 minutes.

SHIRRIFF GOOD MORNING MARMALADE— a uniquely Canadian breakfast delight from one of the best family-run food businesses in Canada. Now owned by the U.S. food conglomerate Smuckers, the Shirriff label is still being pasted onto the marmalade with that unique flavour Canadians love, which is a rare occurrence in the grab-bag world of buying and selling Canada's heritage-brand foods.

SHISHAMO. See capelin.

SHORE LUNCH—shore lunches all have one common denominator: the freshest fish, filleted, breaded and finished in a waiting frypan in minutes. Many species of game fish are rife

for the fishing guide's pan depending on the anglers' catch, but for my money, walleye and trout are the best-tasting fish around. Where shore lunches differ is in the choice of breading and frying oils. Traditionally a guide's wife would make up the breading in a paper bag ready for shaking fillets, but most modern guides rely on a prepared mix and shake it in a plastic bag. As for the frying oil, modern guides will probably use canola, with some traditionalists adding a slice of fatback pork. In the old days, back before the 1970s, when butter was available in cans, butter was the frying medium of choice. The shore lunch is a taste sensation, as simple as fried fish and potatoes along with beans or corn from a heated can, and while it might sound mundane, it is a sensory revelation.

SHORE LUNCHES ACROSS CANADA

New Brunswick's Miramichi River is the Holy Grail for fly fishermen seeking the mighty Atlantic salmon. They are on the river in the early hours and are constantly working their rods, which makes for a hungry group of anglers. As the lunch hour approaches, they find it increasingly difficult to concentrate. On shore, their guide is concocting culinary magic: the obligatory fried potatoes are almost done, and the guide is busily slicing one of the group's catch into grilling steaks. With a flourish, he deftly places the salmon steaks onto a hot grill suspended over the open fire and alerts the group. "Fish on" has a different meaning on the Miramichi, and as the group reaches the campfire, that "fish on" is already cooked, ready to melt into mouths that, between bites, can only mutter, "Mmmm, good."

In La Belle Province, fishing lodges abound and their guides conjure up such memorable shore lunches that they make regulars out of occasional clients. Trout, splake, salmo and walleye are the favourites, but the guides are capable of turning any fish into a gastronomic

delight that may even include a blue cheese sauce. It may sound a bit strange, but then you probably have not tried Ermite, an extraordinary blue cheese produced in Québec by Benedictine monks.

Moving westward into Ontario, you will find that the Thousand Island fishing guides eschew butter for rendered slabs of fatback pork, whereas in the Prairie provinces, guides will fry potatoes in fatback while another cast-iron frypan is hot and bubbling with a half-inch of butter or canola oil, just waiting for the fish. In both cases, the walleye fillets have been bag-breaded in cornmeal, flour and pancake mix along with a touch of salt and cayenne pepper. In a matter of four to five minutes, those who have never partaken of a fishing guide's shore lunch will be feasting on what they will long remember as their best fish dinner ever.

In British Columbia, the shore lunch may undergo a change from grill or frypan to a cedar plank, with the fish of choice being salmon. The fish is split down the middle, carefully eviscerated, then nailed onto a cedar plank and placed upright next to the hot coals of a wood fire until it is cooked to perfection. If the weather is slightly inclement, which happens occasionally in BC, those lucky anglers awaiting the main course may be treated to salmon chowder. Once tried, never forgotten—subsequent salmon dinners and chowders will always be compared to that glorious taste of fish fresh from the sea.

A
B
C
D
E
F
G
H
I
J
K
L
M
N
O
P
Q
R
S
T
U
V
W
X
Y
Z

RECIPE

Salmon Chowder Shore Lunch

Usually prepared in advance and heated on site. Heat ¼ cup unsalted butter in stockpot, add 1 cup diced onion, 1 cup diced carrot, 1¼ cups diced celery, 1 Tbsp finely chopped fresh thyme and 1 bay leaf, then cook until onions are soft. Add 1 Tbsp apple cider vinegar and, while stirring, add 8 Tbsp flour, one at a time, and cook until thickened. Add 3 medium red potatoes, cut into 1-inch pieces, 6 cups whole milk and ¾ cup fish stock, bring to a simmer and cook until potatoes are fork tender. Remove from heat and let cool.

On site, set soup to heat and add 1 can whole kernel corn and 1 Tbsp finely chopped fresh parsley. Fry up 1 lb salmon fillets, skinned and cut into 1-inch cubes, and add to the chowder. Season with salt and pepper and serve piping hot with a dab of butter and crackers.

SHORT TIME PIE—even short of time, cooks can still be heroes with this famous short time pie crust, filled with vanilla ice cream and topped with sliced fruit.

RECIPE

Short Time Pie Crust

Place 1 cup prepared biscuit mix into a 9-inch pie plate along with ¼ cup butter and 3 Tbsp boiling water. Mix it up with a fork until dough ball forms, and press it into shape. Bake crust at 350°F for 10 minutes until golden.

SHRIMP (*Pandalus* spp.)—our main commercially caught shrimp is *P. borealis*, or pink shrimp. They are smaller than tropical varieties but have sweeter

RECIPE

Shrimp with Brown Butter and Pine Nuts

In a heavy skillet, heat 4 Tbsp butter until it browns, then add ⅓ cup pine nuts and stir until they also turn brown. Add 1½ lbs medium shrimp, peeled and deveined, and cook for 7 minutes or until tails curl. Sprinkle with 1 Tbsp lemon juice and serve with a side of miner's lettuce.

CANADA'S FAVOURITE SHRIMP SPECIES

- Coonstripe shrimp (*P. danae*; also called dock shrimp)—available in live tanks, great for barbecue or sushi.

- Humpback shrimp (*P. hypsinotus*; also called king shrimp)—available in live tanks, it is the best-tasting shrimp.

- Pink shrimp (*P. borealis*; also called northern shrimp, northern prawn)—usually peeled, cooked and frozen at sea, best for salads.

- Smooth pink shrimp (*P. jordani*)—usually peeled, cooked and frozen at sea, best for salads.

- Spot shrimp (*P. platyceros*; also called spot prawn)—main catch, frozen or fresh from May to mid-August.

TIPS ON BUYING SHRIMP

- Unless close to the source, most shrimp/prawns on display in fish market counters have been previously frozen in large, icy blocks. Thawed, they should be free of smells and black spots and firm to the touch; they should be consumed within 48 hours. It is better to ask your fishmonger if you can buy them still frozen.

- When buying frozen shrimp/prawns in bags, buy them with shells intact to preserve flavour and texture. If buying peeled, avoid those that are frosty with white spots, because that indicates thawing and refreezing.

A
B
C
D
E
F
G
H
I
J
K
L
M
N
O
P
Q
R

S

T
U
V
W
X
Y
Z

meat and are great for salads, cocktails and as an accompaniment for fish dishes. All Canadian shrimp are harvested from the wild, so a "Product of Canada" designation means the frozen shrimp you purchase were not raised in a ditch. Pink shrimp are caught in both Atlantic and Pacific oceans, but the main harvest is concentrated in the Atlantic.

SHRUB—a sugar-sweetened brandy, wine and spice punch of English origin, but naturalized through the substitution of backyard whisky or rum, applejack and maple sugar. The father of all cocktails, shrub was probably called so because, after a few too many, that is where imbibers would wake up: under a shrub. A favourite of pioneer men, barrels of shrub were stored away in barns and root cellars, providing settlers a welcome respite from hard times…hic!

SILKY SWALLOW WORT. *See* milkweed.

SILVER SALMON. *See* coho salmon.

SINGING HINNIES—a once-popular Nova Scotia pancake that combines flour, butter, currants, lard and sour cream into a stiff dough that is cut into rounds and fried. The frying cakes sizzle or "sing" as they cook, and "hinny" is slang for what goes onto the singers: honey.

SINGLE MALT WHISKY—a Scottish-style Highland whisky distilled on Cape Breton by

Glenora Distillery, the only distillery operation of its kind in North America.

SISCOWET—a rotund, very oily variety of lake trout (*Salvelinus namaycush*) caught only in the deepest sections of Lake Superior and smoked like herring.

SLOE—the unpalatable drupes or berries of the common blackthorn tree (*Prunus spinosa*) that were, and still are, used to flavour legal and illegal spirits, gin being the most common.

SLOW FOOD CANADA—just one of over 130 national organizations called Conviva that are dedicated to defending food and agriculture biodiversity. Slow Food stresses the need for taste education to combat the insanity of fast foods and helps in promoting the Canadian food experience, protecting local cuisines and safeguarding heritage and heirloom foods. With around 100,000 members worldwide, the movement has been successfully spreading the word

that the world's food supply is in trouble through awareness campaigns, tastings and dinners at the local level and large international events. Two great initiatives sponsored by the Slow Food Movement are the Ark of Taste, a catalogue of all manner of the best-tasting foods that are in danger of being eliminated by conglomerate agriculture, and the Presidia Project, an initiative to aid growers and artisan producers of those endangered food products.

SLUMGULLION—an east coast fishermen's stew made from fish scraps, usually cod.

SMALLAGE. *See* Indian celery.

SMELT—the smelts are a small, iridescent family (Osmeridae) of fish closely related to salmon that reproduce in prodigious numbers in both salt and fresh water.

SMOKED FOODS—wood smoke contains tarry chemicals that both contribute to taste and kill bacteria, enabling the preservation of meats and fish for long periods, a matter of some importance before the invention of refrigeration. Hanging meat and fish over an open fire fed logs of green wood was the original method and is called hot smoking, while the other more common method employs a chamber to concentrate smoke and is called cold smoking. The practice of smoking foods as a method of

preservation existed for a thousand years before anyone thought of using salt, with fish being the food item most smoked by ancient civilizations, especially oily fish such as herring. The Scottish and Irish cooked foods in peat burning fireplaces that were also good for smoking haddock and salmon, an amateur talent they brought along to Canada as immigrants. With the invention of refrigeration and speedier transport during the 19th century, smoking foods changed from a preservation method to one of taste, with lighter smoke and exotic woods being the order of the day.

Smoked Fish

- Just about any fish hauled from our oceans, lakes and rivers can be smoked hot or cold, brined or sugared.

- One of the biggest and best commercial fish smokers is a company named Grizzly in Saint-Augustin, near Québec City. Grizzly smokes wild and farmed salmon, halibut and trout by the cold-smoke method and has recently added a hot-smoke facility to process other fish, including sturgeon. Grizzly smoked fish is available at supermarkets and specialty food shops nationwide.

A
B
C
D
E
F
G
H
I
J
K
L
M
N
O
P
Q
R
S
T
U
V
W
X
Y
Z

SMOKED PORK JOWLS. See *oreilles de crisse.*

S'MORES—a campfire treat of roasted marsh-mallow and melted chocolate sandwiched between two graham crackers. While Americans like to think of this creation as theirs, anyone who has attended a Canadian summer camp knows the true origin of the gooey delight.

SNIPE IN SAUCE—a meal prepared by our pioneer settler ancestors with any of several small wading bird species known as snipes.

RECIPE

Snipe in Sauce

Melt ½ lb butter in a deep frying pan, then add 6 cleaned snipe, breasts down. Add 1 Tbsp each of chopped wild leeks (ramp) and dried apples. Cover and roast for 10–15 minutes, remove birds, deglaze pan with apple cider and use for a sauce.

SNIPE PIE—any crusted pie using small birds as the main ingredient. During our formative years, hunters firing gravel shot considered any flock of small birds fair game. Shore birds, migratory birds, blackbirds, songbirds—it mattered little. When stripped of feathers, they all looked and tasted pretty much the same.

SNOW APPLE (also called Fameuse apple)—a 17th-century French cultivar brought to Canada by early settlers, the snow is one of the few apple varieties that reproduce true from seed. Snows were widely grown in the Maritimes and Québec and are much appreciated for their sweet, crisp, snow-white flesh that makes for excellent snacking, cooking and cider. Forced into the background by the standardization of varieties by agricultural conglomerates as well as the tree's vulnerability to insect predation, the snow apple was relegated to being a heritage tree. Today, however, its fruit is being rediscovered at farmers' markets across the country as concerned artisanal growers strive to reintroduce this favourite eating apple.

SNOW PUDDING—from the earliest times, Canada has been an exporter of isinglass, a gelatin-like substance originally precipitated from the bladders of sturgeon or cod fished from the St. Lawrence River. Snow pudding was a favourite dessert of the Maritime provinces and made use of a plentiful supply of Caribbean citrus, sugar and local eggs. *See also* isinglass.

RECIPE

Snow Pudding

Dissolve 2 Tbsp isinglass or powdered gelatin in ¼ cup ice water. Add 1 cup boiling water, 1 cup sugar and ¼ cup cup lemon juice and stir. Beat 3 egg whites until stiff, then fold into gelatin mixture. Pour into wet cups and refrigerate. Make a crème anglaise by heating the 3 egg yolks with 1 cup milk, ¼ cup sugar and 1 tsp vanilla, and pour over the puddings when set.

SNOW TAFFY. See maple taffy.

SNOWBALLS—a product of the English candy maker Lee's, the Lee's Snowball has been a favourite Maritime sweet for generations; however, if Maritimers cannot get a Lee's fix, they will make their own snowballs.

> ### RECIPE
>
> #### *Snowballs*
>
> *Boil 3 cups sugar, ¾ cup butter and 1¼ cups milk to a temperature of 230°F. In a bowl, combine 3 cups rolled oats, 1 cup unsweetened coconut and ¾ cup cocoa powder, and mix well with liquid. Cool and form into balls, roll in additional coconut and chill.*

SNOWBERRY. *See* capillaire.

SOAPBERRY. *See* buffaloberry.

SOCKEYE SALMON (*Oncorhynchus nerka*; also called red salmon)—another competitor for best-tasting salmon, this species is the most sought after by commercial fisheries. Sockeye range along the entire west coast but are caught mainly in northern areas and rivers, where they spend three or four years before venturing out to sea. Sockeyes can reach a weight of 25 kg, live for about five years and feed mostly on zooplankton and krill, which accounts for their red-coloured flesh. Firm texture, a marvellous taste and flesh that is relatively free of toxins are attributes that make this species so much in demand by consumers and restaurant chefs. The fish is available fresh from June to the end of

August, but because more than half the catch not destined for the canneries is frozen, fillets and steaks are available year-round and, if not too long in the freezer, make for tasty fare, especially barbecued. Kokanee salmon—a small, 1–2-kg landlocked variety of sockeye found in some BC lakes—is an epicure's delight when pan-fried and is a not-to-be-missed gastronomic event if the opportunity ever arises. *See also* Pacific salmon, salmon.

SOLERA 2000—a fantastic artisanal balsamic vinegar crafted by Alois Thurn at his Okanagan Vinegar Brewery in Summerland, BC. Thurn crafts many other artisanal fruit vinegars and condiments, all of which must be purchased locally because he is too busy growing and crafting to run an online shop.

SOLOMON GUNDY—pirate food, originally called "salmagundi" and brought to the east coast by those brigands of the high seas, the Caribbean buccaneers. The dish became known as Solomon gundy in the Newfoundland dialect and was changed from a catch-all cold stew into a herring pickle.

RECIPE

Solomon Gundy

Clean 6 herring, cut into 1-inch pieces and soak in water 24 hours. Squeeze water from herring and place into a Mason jar with sliced onion in alternating layers. In a saucepan, heat 2 cups vinegar. Add ½ cup sugar and 2 Tbsp pickling spice. Let vinegar mixture cool, pour over fish and onions then seal and store jars in a cool spot. Best served with sour cream and extra fresh onions.

SOOKE HARBOUR HOUSE—hard to beat since 1979, when Vancouver Island innkeepers Sinclair and Frederique Philip decided their new restaurant would prepare and serve only local and Canadian meats, fish and produce. If one is ever shipwrecked, one can only hope to be washed up on the shore at Sooke Harbour House to be revived by a ration of maple-roasted salmon.

SOOPOLALLIE. *See* **buffaloberry**.

SORTILÈGE—a Canadian whisky and maple syrup liqueur popular with chefs and mixologists, blended in Québec.

SOUP 'N' SANDWICH—a hard, twice-baked bread called hardtack and pea, bean or portable soup (dehydrated soup stock) along with navy beans, salt pork and molasses were the sustaining foods on long sea voyages from the 16th to 18th centuries. It was a rudimentary soup 'n' sandwich or pork 'n' beans meal three times a day, with a little extra on Sundays—but only in fair weather. Ship captains were so leery of onboard fires that galley kitchens were locked up at the first sign of foul weather, and not even water was allowed to be boiled for tea. Atlantic storms could last days or even weeks, with crew and passengers making do with cold water, hardtack and cold salt pork while the quartermaster patrolled for illicit tea boilers. Steam power made fires less of a hazard, as there was less need for flammable canvas sails and ropes, allowing kitchens to remain open during stormy weather. Democracy reigned, with everyone able to claim a bit of railing to retch up whatever soup 'n' sandwich fare the ship's galley produced.

SOURDOUGH BISCUITS—bread rolls risen with an adapted yeast starter, a combination of wild and domestic yeasts. Made with flour, water and yeast, the starter has a sour milk smell, hence the name. Sourdough is a word synonymous with old-time, northern miners and pioneer settlers who used the starter. During the late 1960s, sourdough starter was rediscovered by adventurous bakers and has become immensely popular nationwide.

SHIPS' FARE THROUGH THE YEARS

Until the 19th century, passengers who thought ahead and purchased meat pies and a few bottles of rum or brandy before boarding the ship fared relatively well, especially the unmarried male passengers, and of those there were many: military officers headed for their postings, younger sons of merchants or noble families, Hudson's Bay Company employees and agents in the salt fish and timber trade. So many in fact, that as passenger service to Canada increased, a room was set aside for the single man's answer to riding out a storm—getting drunk. During a stormy passage, immigrant families huddled and prayed, while the single men caroused, sang and hung over the sides retching like dogs. It wasn't pleasant, especially if the captain and crew were also singing and hanging over the sides of what were commonly called "coffin ships" (as opposed to the safer, cleaner and therefore more expensive "good ships").

In 1838, a British concern, the Great Western Railway Company, launched the *Great Western*, a magnificent wooden-hulled steamer that provided patrons with reliable sailing dates and plenty of amenities for those who could afford upper-deck travel. In 1841, a Canadian named Samuel Cunard launched four steam-powered, wooden-hulled ships that provided some passenger amenities, such as dependable departure and arrival times and an onboard cow for fresh milk. However, Cunard was more interested in safety and the speedy delivery of the royal mail than with passenger comfort, and transatlantic travel remained a nightmarish soup 'n' sandwich experience until 1871, the year Britain's White Star Line launched the *Oceanic*, a sizeable iron-hulled vessel with a dining salon that spanned the entire width of the ship.

From then on, democracy was dead on transatlantic voyages. Only wealthy passengers who had purchased upper-deck cabins could dine in style and retch up overcooked roast beef from top decks. Those of lesser means made do with soup 'n' sandwich meals in the lower decks, and over the years, those decks got very low indeed. Third-class or "steerage" passengers were the meat and potatoes of the passenger liner business, but upper decks provided the promotional glamour those companies needed to attract well-heeled passengers, for which the company provided every amenity imaginable: electric lighting, ensuite baths, overstuffed Victorian furniture and, from the ship's kitchen, overcooked roasts, soggy vegetables and trifle.

A
B
C
D
E
F
G
H
I
J
K
L
M
N
O
P
Q
R

S

T
U
V
W
X
Y
Z

RECIPE

Sourdough Starter

Boil 2 large peeled potatoes until they fall apart. Place potatoes into a nonmetallic bowl and mash while slowly adding 2 cups water. Beat mixture while adding in 1⅔ cups unbleached flour, 3 Tbsp salt and ½ tsp active dry yeast. Set aside 24 hours for starter to acquire its characteristic sour taste. To keep starter alive, feed every other day with ¼ cup water and ½ cup flour.

SOUSED MACKEREL—an east coast pickled fish favourite, wherein mackerel fillets are cooked by boiling in vinegar, water and pickling spice, and served cooled on ice or at room temperature.

SOY MILK—prepared by grinding, soaking, boiling and filtering soybeans into a milky coloured product that bears a resemblance to dairy milk only in its protein content and is sold flavoured to cover an objectionable odour and taste.

Fortified Soy Beverage

Organic

Very high in calcium

Good source of protein

Low in fat

Gluten free

946 mL

SOYBEAN (*Glycine max*)—roasted as a snack food, ground into flour for bread-making or made into tofu, soybeans have made inroads into the Canadian food experience in part through the efforts of the Harrow Research Centre in Harrow, Ontario. Harrow has been very successful in producing in-demand soybean varieties. Veggie burgers and other food products made from soy are available at supermarkets everywhere.

SOYBEAN OIL. *See* vegetable oil.

SPICE CAKE—a molasses spice cake popular with Maritimers. Salt cod traded for West Indies molasses, ginger and spices provided early access to ingredients that became pervasive in east coast cuisine.

SPICY CHICKEN—not a Chinese dish but one made popular by ingredients easily obtained in Canada owing to the busy Caribbean trade, those being ginger, sugar and lemon, made into a basting sauce with plenty of butter.

SPINACH (*Spinacia oleracea*)—an edible plant in the Amaranth family that, according to urban myth, became a nutritional superstar owing to German scientist Emil von Wolff's misplacement of a decimal point in his 1870 measurement of the iron content of spinach leaves. With Popeye's help, spinach exploded in popularity. Today, Canadians include it in their gardens because it is nutritious, versatile and easy to grow.

CANADA'S FAVOURITE SPINACH VARIETIES

- Bloomsdale—a savoy-type spinach introduced to Canada from the U.S. mid-19th century.

- Bloomsdale Longstanding—a hybridized improvement introduced in the early 1920s.

- Merlo Nero—a heavier-leaved, savoy type that is good for cooking.

- Monstrueux De Viroflay—a smooth-leaved variety, its immature leaves are best for salads.

SPLIT PEA—a dried green or yellow pea mechanically split by a roller for quick cooking, often for soup. *See also* pea.

SPORK—short for spiced pork, a processed ham in a can that carried the logo "the meat with many uses." Spork was an opportunistic wartime product of the Burns Meat Packing Company that emulated U.S. meat packer Hormel's canned Spam (short for spiced ham). During World War II, Spam served the military and sustained Britain, fed kids at summer camp (along with Burns Chuckwagon Stew) and was a mother's favourite standby when time was short, soon becoming a hard-times food product duplicated by meat packers across Canada, the most ubiquitous being Spork. A similar product of Canada Packers called Klik is alive and well and sharing shelf space with the long-lived Spam.

SPLAKE—a hybrid fish; a cross between lake trout (*Salvelinus namaycush*) and brook trout (*S. fontinalis*) first developed in western Canada around 1946, but a breeding program was not earnestly undertaken until the late 1950s, when the federal Department of Lands and Forests began to rehabilitate the collapsed lake trout fishery in the Great Lakes. A wonderful game fish, the splake is also one of the best-tasting fish around and is much used by restaurant chefs.

SPOT PRAWN. *See* prawns.

SPOTTY DOG—a fruit-and-suet pudding and an east coast take on the English favourite, spotted dick. Maritimers usually add local berries to replace the chopped dates and figs called for in the traditional spotted dick recipe.

SPRAT. *See* Atlantic herring.

SPRING HERRING. *See* alewife.

SPRING SALMON. *See* Chinook salmon.

SPRUCE (*Picea* spp.)—large, coniferous evergreens whose needles were much used by First Nations and early settlers. Common native species include white spruce (*P. glauca*) and black spruce (*P. mariana*).

SPRUCE BEER—an alcoholic adaptation of a piney decoction brewed by First Nations before the arrival of Europeans. Introduced to Jacques Cartier during his second voyage to New France by members of the Iroquois nation, the non-alcoholic version of the brew cured Cartier's men of the dreaded scurvy. From that date on, spruce beer became a medicinal tonic for voyageurs, fur trappers and settlers, who quickly found that fermentation made the brew slightly more palatable.

RECIPE

Spruce Beer

Pound tender shoots of the black spruce tree to a resinous essence until you have 8 oz. Take 4 oz hops and boil for 30 minutes in 1 gallon water. Strain and add 16 gallons warm water, 2 gallons molasses and the spruce essence dissolved in 1 quart water. Pour into a clean cask, shake well, add ½ pint cider dregs and let stand for 1 week. When drawn off, add 1 Tbsp molasses per bottle.

SPRUCE GROUSE. *See* grouse.

SPRUCE GUM—the favourite chewing gum of First Nations and quickly adopted by pioneer settlers. Spruce resin is gathered, aged three to four days and popped into the mouth for a good chew. The Cree people not only chewed the gum, but also used it to extract sharp, pointed wild rice kernels from their eyes during the rice harvest. In Newfoundland, spruce resin gum collected for chewing is called "frankum."

SPRUCE TEA—a tea made by infusing the tender tips of white spruce, black spruce, hemlock or cedar in hot water.

Tree of Life

- A native cedar (*Thuja occidentalis*) credited with saving Jacques Cartier and crew from a grisly death by scurvy during their 1535 exploration of the St. Lawrence River is named for that occasion and called Arbor Vitae—now arborvitae—the tree of life.

SPRUCE TIP SALT—adds great flavour to salmon dishes; simply combine 4 Tbsp kosher salt with 4 Tbsp spruce tips and grind in a food processor.

SQUASH (*Cucurbita* spp.)—native to South America, the squash plant migrated north as a constituent of the "three sisters"—corn, beans and squash—the traditional planting combination of First Nations cultivators. Beans supply

nutrients to the squash and corn, which provides a growing support for the beans, and big-leaved squash plants shade tender corn shoots and conserve water. When the Europeans arrived in North America, they found many varieties of squash readily available, including pumpkin, butternut squash and acorn squash. Boiled, mashed squash beside a haunch of venison would have graced many a pioneer table.

RECIPE

Acorn Squash with Maple Butter

Slice each of 2 small acorn squash into 4 wedges, scoop out seeds and strings and arrange skin side down in a baking dish. Top each wedge with a dab of butter and a drizzle of maple syrup, cover with aluminum foil and bake in a 375°F oven for 30 minutes. Remove foil, bake a further 30 minutes and season with salt and pepper.

A B C D E F G H I J K L M N O P Q R **S** T U V W X Y Z

SQUASH CASSEROLE—a First Nations dish adapted to the tastes of early settlers by the addition of applesauce, egg, butter and seasoning to cooked and puréed squash.

SQUASH PIE. *See* pumpkin pie.

SQUASHBERRY. *See* partridgeberry.

SQUASHBERRY PUDDING (also called partridgeberry pudding)—a Newfoundland cake dessert usually topped with a rum and butter sauce. The cake recipe travelled west with early settlers and was adapted to include whatever fresh berries were handy, such as saskatoons, blueberries, raspberries, etc.

SQUASHBERRY WINE (also called partridgeberry wine, squatum)—a Newfoundland alcoholic beverage made from partridgeberries, a close relative of the cranberry. Newfoundlanders called them squashberries because they needed a good squashing to promote fermentation and to make the wine commonly called squatum.

SQUATUM. *See* squashberry wine.

SQUID—eight-armed cephalopods, of which there are around 300 species all closely related to molluscs. Squid are not long-lived, but their primary interest is reproduction, and for that reason they are one of the most sustainable fisheries with over 2 million tonnes of various species landed annually. As food, squid is usually marketed as calamari.

CANADA'S FAVOURITE SQUID SPECIES

Atlantic:

• Long-finned squid (*Loligo pealiei*)—a North Atlantic inshore fishery from Newfoundland south almost to Venezuela, with the catch processed by factory ships and quick frozen.

• Short-finned squid (*Illex illecebrosus*)—an Atlantic fishery, with the catch processed by factory ships and quick frozen.

Pacific:

• Humboldt squid (*Dosidicus gigas*; also called jumbo squid)—the largest species, which can weigh 40–45 kilograms.

• Neon flying squid (*Ommastrephes bartrami*)—the predominant offshore catch.

• Opal squid (*Loligo opalescens*; also called market squid)—the predominant inshore catch.

RECIPE

Deep-fried Calamari

Clean 3½ lbs squid and cut squid sacs into rings and tentacles lengthways if large. In a bowl, whisk together ½ cup sour cream and ½ cup whole milk, and add the squid. Pour 7 cups canola oil into a heavy saucepan (to a depth of 3–4 inches) and heat to 375°F. In a large bowl, sift together 2 cups flour, 2 tsp salt and 1 tsp cayenne pepper. Lift a small handful of squid from the milk mixture, shake off excess liquid and toss in flour mixture. Shake off excess flour, carefully add squid to hot oil and fry until golden. Repeat in small batches as the oil returns to 375°F, drain on paper towel and sprinkle with salt. Serve immediately with lemon wedges and tartar sauce.

grocery wholesaler Kelly, Douglas Co. Ltd. In 1976, Loblaw's sold Nabob Foods to Swiss chocolate company Jacobs Suchard, who five years later sold the brand to Canada Packers, who in turn sold it to CPC International (Hellmann's mayo, Karo syrup, Bosco, etc.), who made both Skippy and Squirrel peanut butter in Montréal in a plant owned by Best Foods, a subsidiary company of Canada Starch. In 2000, Unilever bought Best Foods and decided to dump Canada's Squirrel peanut butter in favour of the Americanized Skippy. People who buy Skippy are reminded of better days when they open jars of it and find the old Squirrel peanut butter squirrel on the freshness seal. *See also* peanut butter.

ST. ALBERT CHEESE—a dairymen's cheese cooperative in St. Albert, Ontario, producing outstanding Cheddar cheese since 1894. St. Albert cheese is a consistent prize-winner at both the British Empire Cheese Competition and the Royal Agricultural Winter Fair. The product is available at many Ontario and Québec retail locations and online.

ST. CATHERINE'S TAFFY—a pulled taffy candy traditionally made by Québec children to celebrate Saint Catherine's Day on November 25 each year.

ST. JACOBS FARMERS' MARKET. *See* Waterloo's farmers' markets.

SQUIRREL PEANUT BUTTER—it was Canada's favourite peanut butter, the one with the peanut on top and originally made in Vancouver by the Canada Nut Company. The brand became a nationwide favourite when it was marketed through Nabob Foods by Loblaw's-owned

ST. LAWRENCE MARKET—a year-round commercial bazaar market in Toronto that features a real Saturday farmers' market in a separate building across the street. The city has dozens of seasonal markets, with lists available online. *See also* market squares.

STARFLOWER. *See* borage.

STEAK AND KIDNEY PIE—as popular in Canada as in Britain, where it became the national dish during the 19th century and the darling of pub owners and goers. Historically, beef, ox, lamb or pig kidneys were used, but modern-day pub goers can expect to find only beef kidneys in their pies.

STEELHEAD. *See* rainbow trout.

STELLA'S CAFÉ AND BAKERY—half a dozen locations in a dozen years of business is what you get when you have talented bakers blending imagination with the finest ingredients. Stella's is a Winnipeg jewel that hopefully can stay out of the clutches of a conglomerate. Try the blue cheese and walnut sourdough bread.

STENCHEL (also called switchel)—a cheap Maritime drink made to quench the thirst of farm labourers. It is a mixture of molasses, vinegar and ginger stirred into cold water.

ST-HUBERT CHICKEN—a Québec restaurant chain serving rotisserie chicken along with the best gravy on the planet. In Québec, St-Hubert is comfort food *par excellence*, and the company, Rôtisseries St-Hubert, is in the top 10 of *Commerce Magazine*'s most admired Québec companies.

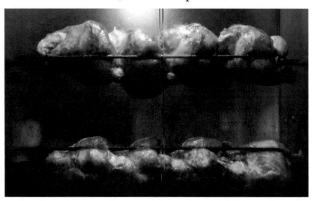

STOCKFISH—the historical name given to various fish that are air and sun dried on wooden racks or flakes, without salt, until they are stiff as boards, the most common being cod and haddock. Stockfish was a major trading commodity before distance to the New World fishing grounds and catch volumes required a change to the speedier salt drying method of preserving fish. Gone but not forgotten, air-dried stockfish are still produced in Norway and Iceland for customers in parts of Italy and Africa. *See also* salt cod.

STONE MILLED SPECIALTY GRAINS LTD—farm fresh and no gluten is what you get from this family-run company based in Manitoba that specializes in stone milling seeds of buckwheat, wild rice, pulses and corn.

STOVIES—a Scottish one-pot dish made Canadian by the use of wild game, especially bison.

RECIPE

Stovies

Melt 2 Tbsp fat drippings in a large cooking pot and soften 2 sliced onions. Add ½ lb cubed bison meat, season, layer on 2 lbs sliced potatoes, and pour on 12 oz stock. Bake for 1 hour, or until liquid is absorbed and potatoes are brown.

STRAWBERRY (*Fragaria* spp.)—wild or cultivated, strawberries are some of the tastiest and most popular fruits for eating fresh or in jams and pies, ice cream and milkshakes. Today's common garden strawberries are various hybrids of the European *F. vesca*, the North American *F. virginiana* and the South American *F. chiloensis*.

STRAWBERRY JAM—Canada's favourite breakfast jam since 1534, when Jacques Cartier found strawberries of excellent size and taste growing everywhere in New France.

STUBBY ORANGE—a famous fresh-squeezed orange juice and dairy cream soft drink manufactured during the 1930s by the Brown Brothers of Kingston, Ontario. The drink bottle was stubby and bore a cute cartoon character called Stubby on the label. The brand was successful and resulted in an entire Stubby line of soft drinks, with the grape Stubby being most famous. Today the Brown Brothers business survives as Brown's Fine Food Services, a cafeteria design and service company employing nearly 800 people.

STUFFED MEATLOAF—a Depression days or ration-extending meal popular right across the country. It's simple to make: line the bottom and sides of a bread tin with ground meat prepared as for meatloaf, stuff the middle with bread dressing and bake.

STURGEON (*Acipenser* spp.)—sturgeon were once so plentiful they were thought trash fish and used as field fertilizer, but now that we know better it may be too late because their numbers are shrinking drastically. Canada is home to five species: white (*A. transmontanus*) and green (*A. medirostris*) sturgeon in Pacific rivers and coastal waters, lake sturgeon (*A. fulvescens*) in the central provinces and Great Lakes, and shortnose (*A. brevirostrum*) and Atlantic (*A. oxyrinchus*) sturgeon in eastern rivers and coastal waters. In 1897, a white sturgeon weighing 1387 lbs (629 kg) was caught in the Fraser

River at New Westminster, BC. The largest Atlantic specimen on record weighed in at 353 lbs (160 kg).

STURGEON À LA SAINTE-MENEHOULD—a wine-poached sturgeon fillet served in a Sainte-Menehould sauce, a creamy concoction named for the patron saint of the French town where the sauce originated. During the 17th and early 18th centuries, sturgeon from the St. Lawrence River near Québec City were cleaned, salted and packed into barrels and used as a primary winter food item. The fish also yielded caviar, a much-appreciated luxury during the hard early days.

SUCCOTASH—an original First Nations dish of cooked beans and corn, but adapted to European settlers' tastes by the addition of butter, seasoning, a scrape or two of nutmeg and a bit of salt pork. Many variations exist, with many types of beans used and with tomatoes sometimes added.

SUCKLING PIG—the baby pig or piglet one finds at backyard barbecues. A suckling pig has not been weaned from its mother's milk.

SUCRE À LA CRÈME—a traditional Québécois cream fudge.

SUET SOUP—a basic vegetable soup with a good chunk of beef suet fried up with onions in lieu of stock.

SUGAR—carbohydrates whose molecules consist of carbon, hydrogen and oxygen in many forms and variations, the simplest of which are monosaccharides (single sugars), with dextrose, commonly called glucose, being most fundamental. In the human body, the digestive process reduces all carbohydrates to dextrose, which then goes straight into the blood stream. Fructose, sometimes called laevulose or fruit sugar, is another monosaccharide, as is galactose, one of the milk sugars. Ordinary white sugar, called sucrose, is a disaccharide (two-sugar molecule) made up of one dextrose and one fructose. Most refined (white) sugar is derived from either sugar cane, beets or corn. The intermediate products of cane refining are crude muscovado and Demerara sugars, with end products for both of those being molasses of different grades: light, medium and blackstrap. Various shades of brown sugar are produced along the refining path to white, each with a slightly different flavour. However, marketed golden or brown sugar is usually just refined white sugar with molasses added back for colour.

Sugar

- In Asia, sugar is often derived from refined palm tree sap that produces a hard brown sugar called jaggery, or simply palm sugar.

- After refining, some sugar is further processed into powder and mixed with a little starch for dryness: icing sugar.

- During Canada's formative years, the sugar arriving at our ports was part and parcel of the rum trade and so poorly refined that barrels would be quarter-full of molasses, which Newfoundlanders found useful for distilling a particularly potent rum called screech.

- Nowadays, corn is the source of most sugar used in food processing. Refining the starch of corn produces syrup that is high in fructose; further refining produces dextrose, a sugar with only half the sweetness of sucrose but with an ability to provide more bulk to food formulations.

SUGAR PIE. *See* maple syrup pie.

SUMAC TEA (also called fragrant sumac tea)—an excellent tea made by soaking the ripe, red fruit of the sumac tree (*Rhus aromatica*) in hot, not boiling, water for 15 minutes and then reheating the infusion. Surprisingly refreshing, it is very tasty and needs no sweetening. It's also delicious served cold as a summer beverage, with a taste reminiscent of lemonade.

SUMMER PUDDING—this pudding requires a small pudding or jelly mould and a variety of summer berries with good colour and flavour: raspberries, red or black currants, blackberries, mulberries, strawberries, etc.

RECIPE

Summer Pudding

Bring 2 Tbsp water and ⅔ cup sugar to a quick boil in a medium saucepan. Reduce heat, add 1 lb fresh summer berries and stew over gentle heat until soft but still retaining shape. Line pudding mould with thin-sliced white bread, making sure there are no gaps, then spoon in stewed berries and cover with more bread slices. Cover pudding with a saucer—the saucer should rest on the actual pudding, not the bowl—and weight it down with something. Refrigerate overnight. Before serving, turn the pudding out onto a serving plate and prepare whipped cream for topping.

SUMMER SAUSAGE—it is made everywhere and from various meats but is mostly a mix of seasoned beef and pork with a touch of sugar and pickling salt. The absolute finest summer sausage is produced by the Mennonite farmers of the Kitchener–Waterloo area of Ontario. Sausage meat is packed into "socks" weighing about 2.25 kg each, hung up to ferment and dry and then smoked to a dense and meaty goodness. *See also* sausage.

SUNCHOKE. *See* Jerusalem artichoke.

SUNFLOWER (*Helianthus annuus*)—native to North American prairie lands and cultivated by First Nations, the plant is the only oilseed plant native to Canada's prairies and is cultivated today for use as an oilseed, confection and birdseed. Sunflower seeds are rich in vitamins, while the oil is low in cholesterol and is recommended as a cooking and salad oil for healthy hearts. The sunflower seed business in Canada is booming; seeds are grown for both oil pressing and the confectionary trade. Oilseeds are small and black and specially hybridized for their oil content, while confectionary seeds are much larger and are usually white striped. There is another category of seeds that is also booming—birdseed—and demand is increasing every year.

SUNFLOWER SOUP—a First Nations sunflower seed and game meat soup widely adopted by settlers and later Europeanized by adding onions and replacing the game with chicken.

SUNNY BOY CEREAL—a breakfast fixture on Alberta tables since the 1920s. The Schroeder Milling Company, which also produces a line of quality bread, manufactures it from organic grains and also sells pancake mixes under the same label.

SUNROOT. *See* Jerusalem artichoke.

SUN-RYPE PRODUCTS LTD—an all-Canadian fruit juice mini-conglomerate based in BC's Okanagan Valley and operated by folks who really care about their customers. They produce the best apple juice and sauce anywhere, and why it's not available nationwide is a mystery.

SUPERMARKETS—after World War II, as personalized service at small corner food stores began to give way to larger, self-help food stores that would eventually be called "supermarkets," the Saturday morning farmers' markets became an almost forgotten affair. Instead of opening a stall on market day, local produce farmers packed up their wagons and travelled door-to-door just like the milkman. This practice survived in small towns and some cities through the 1950s and early 1960s, until a trip to the supermarket made door-to-door delivery of any foods seem antiquated. The boom times were underway in Canada in the 1960s; super-convenient supermarkets were being constructed everywhere. Hard times were a thing of the past and the pantry room could now be used for other purposes, such as a place to keep the new freezer, and who needed a whole side of beef when there were Swanson TV dinners? Supermarkets quickly became the go-to place for Canadian families to stock up on food and, unfortunately for them and the nation's farmers, those supermarkets also became the domain of business people only interested in profits and the globalization of trade to increase those profits. Keeping the labels and dumping local food processors and canneries for cheaper, imported food items helped turn the great Canadian food experience into a cuisine of weenie zaps, butter tarts and Nanaimo bars. *See also* Canadian canners, home freezers, market squares.

LOCAL AGRICULTURE AND BOOM TIMES

They're out there, dedicated, working part-time jobs and engaging in almost daily battles with banks, conglomerate food processors, GMO seed companies, property developers and ill-conceived government agricultural policies. They are Canada's small vegetable and fruit farmers, livestock and game ranchers, dairymen and poultry farmers, and we need them as we need air to breathe. Their average age is around 60, and their kids are educated and endowed with enough common sense not to follow in dad's footsteps, as the average Canadian farmer nets a miserable annual income.

In 1931, over 728,000 Canadian farms provided local populations with a cornucopia of fresh produce, meats and dairy products. Today, that number has shrunk to around 200,000, with most being monoculture industrial operations partnered with a processing conglomerate in a vertically integrated supply system. The processing conglomerates tell their partner farmers what and how much to grow or raise, what pesticides and fertilizers to use, when to ship and how much they're going to pay.

What happened to the smaller farmers? It was a combination of things, beginning with World War I and the subsequent Great Depression, when almost half the population was unemployed and people with little money for wholesome foods ate from cans. The Depression came with several years of drought, followed by World War II and more hard times. Then an entrepreneurial genius named Willard Garfield Weston looked at the U.S. sunshine states, with their expansive agricultural land, cheap labour and cheap gasoline. Pieced together by W.G. Weston, those factors translated into an opportunity called supermarkets. The food stores were already in place, a chain of 150 built by Theodore Pringle Loblaw, but they were small and sold only local seasonal produce, meats and a small selection of canned goods. Under Weston's control, Loblaw's food markets grew in size and number, drawing on an endless parade of produce-laden trucks from California and Florida. Cheap produce even in winter was the last straw for Canadian produce farmers, and most sold out to Big Food and moved into towns and cities. Over the years, little by little, Canada became more and more dependent on imported produce.

The 1960s were boom times: jobs were plentiful, there was a new car in every garage and Canadian families had a new bonding icon—the television. Television became the housewife's manual, with its commercials pointing the way to better, more modern ways of living. Magazines of the time also featured advertisements designed to get Canadians on the road to modernism. These full-page colour ads featured vivid displays of kitchen appliances and vehicles, especially home freezers and station wagons, the former being filled to the brim by a pretty housewife and the latter being emptied of supermarket grocery bags by an even prettier housewife.

SUPPLY MANAGEMENT—a closed-gate system of agriculture production wherein the original participants set the production figure and everyone coming after must pay for the privilege of producing a portion of the original production figure or quota. In Canada, cow's milk, chicken eggs, chickens and turkeys are produced by the supply management system, with each one having a governing board and enforcement division empowered to raid farms and levy fines.

SUPPORNE—a thick porridge made from Indian meal, with a look and taste similar to oatmeal porridge. For pioneer families, supporne was breakfast and was prepared every morning without fail. All you do is sprinkle Indian meal on salted boiling water and stir for 20 minutes. Supporne is a real rib-sticker when eaten with milk and sugar, honey or maple syrup.

SUSHI-GATE—the name given to the aftermath of a 2008 DNA study by two New York City high school students that found 25 percent of fish sold in local sushi shops and seafood markets was mislabelled. A more comprehensive study by the University of Guelph's Institute for Biodiversity found the fraudulent practice of mislabelling fish is a nationwide problem in both the U.S. and Canada, with around one-third of fish species mislabelled. *See also* counterfeit fish.

SWANS DOWN CAKE FLOUR—a favourite soft wheat cake flour of Canadian bakers since 1885, and now manufactured by Dover Mills of Cambridge, Ontario.

SWEDISH TURNIP. *See* rutabaga.

SWEET CREAM BUTTER—a type of butter used to craft some baked goods and different from normal butter in that it hasn't been ripened with a bacteria culture. Sweet cream butter may be salted or unsalted and is rather bland when compared to normal or cultured butter.

SWEET MARIE CANDY BAR—a fudge and peanut chocolate bar introduced by the Willard's Chocolate Company in 1931. Bought out by the George Weston Company in 1954, Willard's Sweet Marie bar is today manufactured by Cadbury, a division of Kraft Foods.

SWEET POTATO CASSEROLE—a variation of pumpkin pudding and a Thanksgiving dessert of both pioneer and modern-day families. Boiled and mashed sweet potatoes are mixed with butter, eggs, cream and maple syrup, molasses or brown sugar, topped with a mixture of nuts, coconut and maple syrup, molasses or brown sugar, and baked.

SWEET SORGHUM (*Sorghum bicolor*)—sorghum is one of the world's great food grains and is used for bread flour, animal fodder, sugar syrup and biomass for ethanol production. The bicolor variety is of interest to Canadian farmers now that it has been hybridized to grow in cooler climates.

SWEET VIBURNUM. *See* nannyberry.

SWEETBREADS—a butcher's word for the thymus gland and pancreas of young calves, lambs or pigs. Sweetbreads require immediate cooking after slaughter to prevent the meat from deteriorating. Blanching is recommended, with a plunge into cold water after 5–10 minutes of boiling. Then they can be stewed or sliced into cutlets, breaded and fried in butter.

SWITCHEL. *See* stenchel.

SWORDFISH (*Xiphias gladius*)—they are large billfish with a streamlined body that helps propel them through the water at high speeds when chasing prey. Swordfish are migratory and spend summers in Nova Scotia's warm Gulf Stream waters, where their annual presence supports a harpoon fishery with a long history. Swordfish are caught individually on the surface by a harpoon launched by hand from a chase boat. They are also caught in great numbers by commercial long liners, but Maritimers care little for fish long dead on a hook and insist their swordfish steaks come from harpooned fish, as they have for centuries. The next time you want swordfish for the barbecue, ask your fishmonger if his steaks are harpooned or caught by long line. If the latter, tell him to smarten up and get the good stuff.

COOKING SWORDFISH

Before World War II, swordfish was not popular with Canadians, most of whom did not know how to cook it. The common method was to fry it well and then a bit more in case of worms—that's right, worms—and though processors tried to nab them all, a few invariably snuck by to shock consumers. Nowadays fish processors know better than to let worms sneak by, and consumers have all kinds of information available on how to cook it: sear in a heavy fry pan and roast in the oven under a ton of butter until medium rare. It is still advisable to check not only swordfish but also all other species of large fish for marine worms, especially fish that migrate.

SXUSEM. *See* Indian ice cream.

T

TABAC DES BOIS (also called powdered mushrooms)—a Québec specialty, this mushroom powder can be wild or cultivated and is a favourite of restaurant chefs.

TABLES CHAMPÊTRES ET RELAIS DU TERROIR—two programs run by the *Association de l'agrotourisme et du tourisme gourmand* in Québec that promote country-style dining (*tables champêtres*) and buying from local farm shops (*relais du terroir*). Visitors can phone and reserve a home-cooked farmhouse meal at over 30 participating farms, and they can check out around 150 restaurants and farm shops scattered throughout the province that feature local and artisan foods on their menus and shelves.

TALL GRASS PRAIRIE BREAD COMPANY—Winnipeg's best bakery and quite possibly the finest bakery anywhere. Not that I haven't written those words about other exceptional Canadian bakeries, but they are constantly picked up by some multinational conglomerate and forced into mediocrity. As of 2013, Tall Grass is still independent and using the finest locally sourced ingredients to produce healthy bread products at their two Winnipeg locations. Be sure to try their cinnamon buns—they are simply scrumptious.

TANCOOK ISLAND SAUERKRAUT—cabbages love sea air, and those grown by German immigrant farmers on Nova Scotia's Tancook Island

get plenty of that salty air. When turned into sauerkraut, that cabbage exhibits amazing flavour. Unfortunately, or perhaps fortuitously because Nova Scotia is such a nice place to visit, you will have to go there to sample the amazing 'kraut.

TARTE AU SUCRE. See maple syrup pie.

TASTE OF NOVA SCOTIA—a successful initiative by Nova Scotia's food producers and restaurants to help foster awareness of locally produced food products at stores and farmers' markets.

TEABERRY. *See* wintergreen.

TEMPEH—a vegetable cheese similar to tofu but made by fermenting cooked soybeans in a mould. Less processed than tofu, tempeh is a brownish colour with a firm, chewy texture and a slightly sweet, made-in-Canada earthy flavour. *See also* soybean, tofu.

TERROIR—a French wine term meaning how a vineyard's immediate environment affects the flavour and aroma of wines produced from grapes of that vineyard. Over the years, the meaning has expanded to include all forms of agriculture and artisanal food production.

THE CANADIAN HOME COOK BOOK—compiled in 1888 by the ladies of Toronto and other major cities of Canada to raise money for Toronto's Sick Children's Hospital, it became Canada's best-selling cookbook of the 19th century. There have been many reprints, including one as recent as 2002.

THORNAPPLE. *See* hawberry.

THORNLOE CHEESE—a northern Ontario cheese maker specializing in traditional and speciality cheeses and a consistent winner at the Royal Agricultural Winter Fair. Their Cheddars are superlative, their blue cheeses addictive, and their Temiskaming St. George-style cheese is to dream of Portugal. Thornloe cheeses are available at some Ontario and Québec retail outlets and online. Look for their goat's milk blue cheese; it is a taste sensation.

THOUSAND ISLAND DRESSING—a salad dressing mix of mayonnaise, ketchup, Tabasco sauce and chopped pickle invented in the Thousand Islands area of Ontario and New York State.

Thousand Island Dressing

- Rumour has it that around 1900 when May Irwin, a New York stage actress, was visiting New York hotel owner George Boldt's fantastic mansion on Heart Island, his "one in a thousand islands," she received the recipe from Sophia LaLonde, the wife of her fishing guide. Sophia, who got the recipe from her Québécois mother, gave the recipe to Irwin, who gave it to Boldt, who then gave it to the head chef of his Waldorf Astoria Hotel, who graced it upon an appreciative public.

THREE SISTERS SOUP—a First Nations soup that uses the "three sisters" planting of corn, beans and squash.

> ## RECIPE
>
> ### Three Sisters Soup (Modern Version)
>
> *Cook ½ cup chopped onions and 1 tsp minced garlic in 3 Tbsp olive oil. Add 1 can each (with liquid) of corn, kidney beans and squash (or pumpkin), and water for desired consistency. Heat, season and serve with a dusting of pepper.*

THRILLS CHEWING GUM—a Canadian original, with a distinct rose water flavouring that most people equate to soap. A long time product of the London, Ontario, based O-Pee-Chee Company, the gum is now manufactured in Spain and distributed in Canada by Concord Confections based in Concord, Ontario.

TIFFIN—a synonym for lunch that evolved from the English word "tiffing," meaning to eat outside of mealtime hours. During the British occupation of India that began in 1750, the very English custom of a main meal at noon and light supper in the evening was reversed because of heat. The noon meal was called "tiffin" by polite society and "lunch" by the common soldier, a word derived from the Spanish *lonja*, meaning a thick slice of meat. Both words were used in Canada, with lunch eventually dominating.

TILAPIA—the common name for many species of cichlids, of which a few have become universal ditch fishes favoured by the global aquaculture industry for disease resistance and speedy growth. Tilapia are low in mercury because their diet is plant based, but that advantage to consumers is offset by their high levels of omega-6 fatty acids.

TIM HORTONS—Canada's favourite purveyor of doughnut holes and coffee—or, as we like to call them, Timbits and double-doubles. *See also* Maidstone Bakeries.

TIMPSULA. See *pomme-de-prairie*.

TIN COW—a term used by many western Canadians to describe canned evaporated milk. *See also* Carnation evaporated milk.

TOAST WATER—a medicinal concoction that gained popularity during the 18th century and hung around well into the 20th century as a way to supply nutrition to the sick and elderly. Pour boiling water over a few pieces of dry toast, allow to cool, filter and flavour with whatever is handy—a little fruit jam or jelly would do fine.

TOFU—a kind of vegetable cheese made by curdling soybean milk with a coagulant and separating the curds from the soy whey, producing a white, jelly-like substance with no flavour or discernable odour. Tofu is manufactured in nearly all Canadian cities and is available in four varieties: silken, used for creamy dishes; soft, used for soups; firm, used for stir-fry; and extra firm, also used for stir-fry. *See also* soybean, tempeh.

TOMATO (*Lycopersicon lycopersicum*)—the round, usually red fruit from a member of the Nightshade family, which includes peppers, potatoes, eggplants and the always mysterious mandrake, for which the tomato received an unwarranted

CANADA'S FAVOURITE TOMATO VARIETIES

- Amy's Sugar Gem—the best-tasting cherry tomato.
- Giant Green—a green tomato with fantastic flavour.
- Marianna's Peace—has large fruits prone to splitting but very tasty.
- Paul Robeson—a Russian heirloom that is so dark it is almost black.

- Pineapple—red and yellow streaks with a hint of pineapple flavour.
- Pink Brandywine—one of the best-tasting tomatoes ever.
- Prudan's Purple—a purple tomato with great taste.
- Red Currant tomatoes—they look more like a currant than a tomato, hence the name, and although small in size they pack a huge tomato flavour.

GREENHOUSE TOMATOES

Canadians have become so disenchanted with imported tomatoes that, according to polls, around 50 percent of consumers do without until local crops are harvested. Sensing opportunity, many Canadian growers turned to cultivating under glass, and today Canada is a world leader in greenhouse cultivation, with over a million square metres producing not only tomatoes but also peppers and cucumbers. Canadian greenhouse tomatoes, unlike imported, picked-green Californian or Mexican varieties, are allowed to ripen on the vines, producing a more expensive but nutrient-rich tomato with superior taste and texture.

However, even greenhouse produce pales when compared to the taste and texture of a naturally ripened, fresh-picked garden tomato, with the best of that lot being the heirlooms,

such as Brandywine or Marianna's Peace, both consistently judged the world's best-tasting tomatoes. These and other heirloom tomatoes are one-bite life changers that will have consumers searching farmers' markets for all manner of produce with long-forgotten flavours.

reputation as a food with aphrodisiac properties and the name "love apple." Introduced to Canada at the beginning of the 19th century, the tomato was slow to catch on until it was found superior to mushrooms and fermented fish in a condiment called ketchup.

RECIPE

Tomato Soup Spice Cake

Mix 2 cups flour, 1⅓ cups sugar, 4 tsp baking powder, 1 tsp baking soda, 1½ tsp allspice, 1 tsp cinnamon and ½ tsp ground cloves in a bowl. Add 1 can condensed tomato soup and ½ cup shortening and beat while scraping the sides of the bowl. Add 2 eggs and ¼ cup water. Beat until well mixed and pour into 2 greased and floured 9-inch cake pans and bake in a 350°F oven for 30–35 minutes.

TOMATO JAM. *See* Toronto marmalade.

TOMMY COD (*Microgadus tomcod*; also called winter cod)—a type of small cod found in North American coastal waters from Newfoundland to Virginia, with the greatest concentrations occurring in the Gulf of St. Lawrence and the St. Lawrence River. The fish is a favourite of Québec ice fishermen, who construct small villages on the frozen surface of various St. Lawrence feeder rivers.

TOPINAMBOUR. *See* Jerusalem artichoke.

TOPINAMBOUR BEIGNETS. *See* Jerusalem artichoke fritters.

TORONTO MARMALADE (also called tomato jam, Toronto jam)—a homemade condiment of boiled grated tomatoes, lemons and sugar. Popular during both World Wars because of the scarcity of tree fruits, this culinary endeavour produced an acceptable jam substitute.

TORONTO PIE—a hot-milk sponge cake, split in half and filled with strawberry or raspberry jam, that was popular in Toronto during the latter half of the 19th century.

RECIPE

Toronto Pie

Heat ½ cup milk until bubbles appear around the edges, then add 2 Tbsp butter. In a bowl, mix 1 cup flour, 1¼ tsp baking powder and ¼ tsp salt. In a separate bowl, beat 2 eggs, then add ⅔ cup sugar and ¼ tsp vanilla. Fold in dry ingredients, then stir in hot milk mixture. Pour batter into a 9-inch cake pan and bake at 350°F for 30–35 minutes. Let cool, turn out of pan, split cake into 2 layers and sandwich together with jam.

TOURTIÈRE—an iconic French Canadian pork pie with as many variations as there are towns in La Belle Province. One of the best—a layered meat and potatoes rib sticker—evolved in the

Saguenay–Lac-Saint-Jean region. While tourtière does have many variations, it is usually a combination of ground or cubed pork or beef, onions, salt, pepper and spices enclosed within a flaky crust. You can find many tourtière recipes online, and almost all are superior to the frozen tourtière sold in supermarkets.

Tourtière

- Tourtière likely arrived in the Lac-St-Jean area as a variation of sea pie, a layered meat and pastry provision for officers of English sailing ships that became entrenched in Atlantic coastal cuisine and was—and is still—called *cipaille*.

- *Tourte* is the French word for pigeon, once a main ingredient in tourtière. It is also the name of the pottery vessel used to bake the original pie *avec tourtes*.

TOUTON—a Newfoundland treat of fried yeast-risen bread dough served hot and drenched with molasses or maple syrup.

TRADITION STE-JULIE CREAM FUDGE—the best fudge in the world and a true Canadian success story that began in 1979, when Francine Nantel sold her first batch from her husband's convenience store. Francine's fudge had a "wow" factor, and the public was soon clamouring for so much more that the couple opened a small plant in Sainte-Julie, Québec. Over the years, the plant grew larger and the fudge flavours more numerous, but the Nantel family still holds to old-fashioned values and has preserved the "wow."

TRANS FATS—according to Statistics Canada, over 25 percent of Canadians between the ages of 31 and 50—the majority of our workforce—get over 35 percent of their daily calories from fat. That percentage far surpasses the threshold beyond which health risks increase, a fact reflected in the spiralling costs of healthcare. Trans fats in hydrogenated oils are the big killers, with a study by the British Medical Association determining that a daily diet of more than 5 g of trans fats provides populations with a 23 percent rise in the chance of heart disease. Fast-food consumers will find trans fats in all their orders, while consumers of factory foods—frozen fries, canned soups, pork and beans, crackers, cookies, frozen dinners, baked goods, etc.—will also find trans fats a pervasive ingredient that conglomerate food companies try to disguise with words

TASTE DEMENTIA

As Russell Baker, a columnist for *The New York Times*, put it, "The French fried potato has become an inescapable horror in almost every public eating place in the country. 'French fries' say the menus, but they are not French fries any longer. They are a furry-textured substance with the taste of plastic wood."

In a blindfolded taste test between natural and factory-processed foods, children will almost always pick the latter as their preferred choice. The modern child has been taste conditioned by non-nutritive breakfast cereals, dead milk, sugar and lard peanut butter, canned peas, frozen pizza and processed cheese. Most kids have no idea as to the tastes of real foods and are unable to define what is real and what is artificially flavoured, even when not blindfolded. One of the great icons of taste dementia is fruit-flavoured candy; most has a distinct artificial flavour that in no way resembles real fruit, with cherry, orange and grape being prominent. Modern-day conglomerate food processors employ an arsenal of concocted flavours, aromas and texture-providing chemicals designed to fool the senses of consumers.

such as "partially hydrogenated" or "fractionalized" oils. But a rose is a rose by any other name, so do your heart a favour and read food labels carefully, keeping in mind that ingredients are listed in descending order by weight.

TRAPPIST CHEESE—the name usually given to cheeses made by Trappist monks. The original was Port-Salut cheese from the Trappist abbey of Notre Dame du Port du Salut in Brittany, France. Oka, now owned by the mega co-op Agropur, was a Trappist cheese, and though still fabulous it has been supplanted by an even better Port-Salut–style, raw-milk cheese made by Trappist monks near Brandon, Manitoba, and called, quite simply, Trappist cheese.

TRASH FISH—a term used by commercial fishermen to describe any fish species lacking value. Today's long line fishery accounts for a huge number of trash fish such as porpoises, whales and sharks, which are differentiated from by-catch as they are tossed back dead or alive. Trawling vessels that scoop up entire schools of fish in their nets are now actively seeking trash fish for the aquaculture industry and experts fear repercussions as more valued fish are being deprived of food. *See also* by-catch fish.

TRIPE DE ROCHE. See famine foods. *See also* rock tripe.

TRITICALE—a Canadian Department of Agriculture crossbreed of wheat (Triti*cum*) and rye (*Se*cale), having the flavour of both. Produced by famed Scottish botanist Alexander Stephen Wilson during the late 19th century, triticale was perfected by the Swedish botanist Arne Muntzing during the 1930s and made commercially feasible by University of Manitoba plant breeders Leonard Sebeski and Burton Jenkins in the 1960s. Developed for Third World countries with marginal agricultural land, the new grain has undergone further advances. It is showing great promise as a feedstock for animals, as biofuel, as a new source of protein for humans in the form of nutritious breakfast flakes and is now

being cultivated on about a quarter-million acres of Canadian prairie land.

TROUT IN CORN HUSKS—a simple First Nations method of cooking trout adopted by settlers in what is now Ontario. After larding and seasoning the fish, wrap it in corn husks and tie the bundle at both ends; cover with campfire coals and cook for 15 minutes. *See also* corn husk cooking.

TUNA—Canada's west coast fishing fleet goes after the albacore tuna (*Thunnus alalunga*) mostly for canning and sushi purposes, while our east coast fleet pursues the legendary bluefin tuna (*T. thynnus*) to supply the Japanese fresh-frozen sashimi market. Bluefin numbers are alarmingly low, and Canadian licences issued to fishermen

for bluefin tuna are confined to one fish per day to be caught by rod and reel only. How many are caught by long line fishermen as by-catch is anyone's guess, but it must be plenty. Albacore tuna is the most prized Pacific tuna, with about 250 ships of various size taking part in a rod and reel catch conducted inshore and offshore. Offshore catch boats are usually accompanied by factory boats to clean and flash freeze the catch for the Japanese market.

TURBOT (*Psetta maxima*; also called Greenland halibut)—while not a commercially attractive species when cod was plentiful, the turbot became the fish to catch in the 1990s, precipitating a 1995 clash between Spain and Canada over a small section of the Grand Banks fishing grounds that lay outside of Canada's 200-mile (322-km) exclusive economic zone that almost led to a naval confrontation. A bottom-dwelling flatfish, the turbot has an extensive range and can weigh up to 25 kg. It has become increasingly important to east coast fishermen and the territory of Nunavut, and it is so in demand by Asian and European cooks that extensive aquaculture of turbot occurs on those continents and in South America. Wild-caught turbot can be either European halibut, Greenland halibut, Pacific halibut or Canadian halibut, all names adopted to avoid quota confusion.

TURKEY (*Meleagris* spp.)—almost all turkeys consumed in Canada are of one breed, the over-hybridized Broad-breasted White, a bird made so top heavy and short of leg that it can no longer reproduce naturally and must be artificially inseminated. The ancestor of all modern turkey breeds is the wild turkey indigenous to North America (*M. gallopavo*), with the genetic rungs of the ladder to the almost tasteless Broad-breasted White composed of some remarkable heritage breeds. Heritage breeds are intelligent, able to fly, survive on pasture and reproduce naturally, all qualities that make them the gourmet's choice for roasting, no matter that dark pinfeathers leave unattractive pigment marks on the carcasses.

CANADA'S FAVOURITE HERITAGE TURKEYS

- Bourbon Red—an excellent meat bird with lots of tasty dark meat.

- Broad-breasted Bronze—the last rung of the heritage ladder, it can still reproduce.

- Norfolk Black—a size improvement on the Spanish Black and just as tasty.

- Norfolk Bronze—a great meat bird that is making a comeback.

- Ridley Bronze—our own breed and one of the tastiest, but slow growing.

- Spanish Black—one of the tastiest meat birds on the planet.

- Standard Bronze—big and stately looking, the iconic bird of the 19th century.

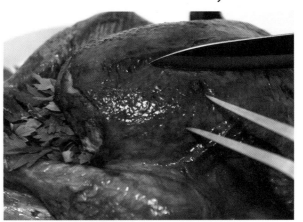

TURKEY *AU VIN*—a one-pot turkey masterpiece that in Canada's formative years would have featured wild turkey as the star attraction. Combined with onions, celery, carrots, mushrooms and a couple of cups of good red wine, this dish will tantalize diners even with a small commercial bird in the pot.

TURNIP (*Brassica rapa*)—an edible root vegetable suitable for culture in temperate climates. Brought to Canada by European settlers as both food and animal fodder, it has lost ground to the potato as a food crop but has always been a staple. Turnip greens are also edible; some varieties are grown specifically for their greens.

TURNIP CASSEROLE—ubiquitous in pioneer cuisine and easy to make. While not indigenous

to Canada, turnips carried west by settlers were soon a prominent menu item. By the latter part of the 19th century, turnips had become a staple on Canadian dinner tables.

RECIPE

Turnip Casserole

Boil and mash 2 turnips. Add 2 eggs, 1 cup applesauce, 6 Tbsp butter, 2 Tbsp brown sugar, 1½ tsp salt and ¼ tsp pepper, and top with butter-sautéed breadcrumbs. Bake at 350°F for 30 minutes, or until top is brown and crispy.

TURTLE SOUP—prepared from the meat of the common snapping turtle (*Chelydra serpentina*), the soup was so popular that Campbell's was canning it during the 1920s. Then the Great Depression made its preparation too problematic and costly, and it mostly disappeared from commercial offerings and restaurant menus. Nowadays, the snapping turtle is a species of concern, and though it can still be taken for private soup pots, no commercial hunting is permitted anywhere in Canada.

TYEE SALMON. *See* Chinook salmon.

U

UDDER GUY'S ICE CREAM—a Vancouver Island ice cream delight made from the finest ingredients by Judy Piggot, the hardest-working gal to ever buck the dairy conglomerates.

UMI. *See* sea urchin roe.

UPSIDE DOWN CAKE—a popular then and now cake where the bottom becomes the top after

baking and usually features an attractive pattern consisting of fruit and berries, which in modern times is often candied cherries and/or pineapple.

UPTOWN FARMERS' MARKET. *See* Waterloo's farmers' markets.

V

VAN DYK'S WILD BLUEBERRY JUICE—Canada Grade A Nova Scotia wild blueberries are gently pressed, flash pasteurized and bottled in 500 mL tamperproof glass bottles by the Van Dyk family of Caledonia, Nova Scotia. High in phytochemicals, especially anthocyanin, wild blueberries have powerful antioxidant and anti-inflammatory properties that protect against diseases such as cancer, heart disease, diabetes and Alzheimer's.

Nutraceuticals

- Canada is a major producer of several functional food crops—such as flaxseed, borage, evening primrose, hempseed and blueberries—that are processed into nutraceuticals to benefit the health of consumers.

VANILLAN—the largest flavour component of natural vanilla beans synthesized from wood pulp and used to make artificial vanilla extract and as a flavouring agent in foods and beverages.

VEAL—the tender meat of male dairy calves. To give milk, dairy cows must calve, and half of newborn calves are males and superfluous to the industry because insemination of milk cows is accomplished by artificial means. Young female calves,

or heifers, are generally kept as replacements for aging cows, while the unlucky male bull calves are sold off to veal producers.

VEAL PATTY-CAKES—finely chop some leftover veal, add to it some heavy cream and a beaten egg to moisten, sprinkle on a bit of salt, pepper, marjoram and mace and make patty-cakes to fry in butter.

VEGETABLE GUMS—used in almost all processed foods to stabilize, emulsify, thicken, jell and suspend solid particles and are derived from various natural sources. A few examples are agar, carrageenan, guar gum, gum Arabic and tragacanth.

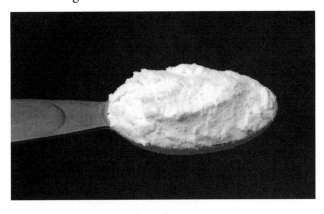

VEGETABLE OIL—any oil derived from plants, including canola oil, sunflower oil and soybean oil, all of which are produced in Canada.

SOYBEAN OIL VS. TROPICAL OIL

During the 1970s, in response to mounting scientific evidence that soybean and other vegetable oils lowered immunity and contributed to cancer, soybean producers decided to shift the spotlight onto their chief competitors: the tropical oil producers. The beaners spent millions to convince the buying public that saturated fatty palm and coconut oil caused high cholesterol levels in blood, leading to heart disease. They did a first-rate job. High cholesterol is certainly a risk factor in heart disease, but it is not a cause; however, to this day, because of that hugely successful misinformation campaign, most people still believe saturated fat causes heart disease. Soybean producers were so successful that hydrogenated soybean oil found its way into 40 percent of food products containing oils, causing myriad health problems for consumers and setting off a Canadian oilseed agricultural revolution that eventually claimed almost a quarter of the nation's arable land for the growing of soybeans and canola.

tenderloin while the haunch is the upper back leg or ham. The loin rack is best when roasted, while the tenderloin is best when cut into medallions and grilled. All other cuts of venison are best as stewing meat. To avoid culinary confusion, meat from any species of the Cervidae family is called venison. Meat from moose, elk, deer and caribou is all venison and cooked to the same rules.

VENISON—the prime cuts of venison are the loin, also called the saddle, and the haunch, the former being a two-part affair of rack and

RECIPE

Venison Liver Paté

Grind or finely chop ¾ lb salt pork (or lean pork) and 1½ lbs venison liver together. Place meat into mixing bowl and add 2 cloves crushed garlic, 2 Tbsp brandy, ½ tsp salt, ¼ tsp pepper and a pinch each of dried rosemary and nutmeg. Cut some pork fat into thin strips and line paté moulds or bread pan, then press in meat mixture. Place moulds or bread pan into a shallow roasting pan and pour 1 inch of boiling water into roasting pan. Cook in a 325°F oven until mixture sets in centre, 3–4 hours. Cool thoroughly before removing from moulds or pan and place on ice or refrigerate.

VENISON LOIN WITH WINE SAUCE—the best cut of venison marinated, roasted and served in a wine sauce in the manner of the earliest French dinner club, the Order of Good Cheer.

RECURSE

Venison Loin with Wine Sauce

Mix up a marinade of olive oil, sliced carrots, celery, onions, garlic, thyme and bay leaves. Marinate loin in the refrigerator for 24 hours. Sprinkle with salt and pepper, and sear on all sides. Roast in a pre-heated 425°F oven for 7–10 minutes, then reduce oven to 300°F and cook for another 10 minutes per pound; it should be medium rare. Slice against the grain and serve with wine sauce.

To make sauce, boil 3 cups beef stock until reduced by half and set aside. Cook ¼ cup minced shallots, 1 minced garlic clove and 1 thyme sprig until soft. Add 2 large, coarsely chopped tomatoes and cook for 5 minutes. Add 1 cup red wine, ¼ cup port wine and 3 Tbsp sherry wine vinegar, and boil until reduced by half. Add reserved stock and 2 Tbsp red currant jelly and simmer for 1 hour, skimming when necessary.

RECIPE

Venison Pot Roast

Rub a haunch of venison with vinegar, red pepper and salt, and lard with strips of salt pork (or bacon) rolled in seasoned bread crumbs. Prepare a marinade of red currant jelly, ½ cup dry red wine and 1 tsp each of juniper berries, thyme, peppercorns, garlic, salt and molasses (or brown sugar). Allow venison to marinate overnight. Brown haunch on all sides in a Dutch oven, pour on marinade, cover and roast at 350°F for 12 minutes per pound. Remove lid for the last 15 minutes.

VENISON POT ROAST—served with potatoes or any other root vegetables, pot roast is a classic Sunday night pioneer dinner that is as delicious today as it was in earlier times.

VERJUS—a kind of vinegar made from the juice of acidic unripe grapes or from crabapple juice. Common in France where verjus, sometimes spelled "verjuice," is squeezed from culled grapes, it is slowly becoming available in Canada at farmers' markets but requires some searching. Verjus makes a great salad dressing; it pairs with oil like a dream and supplies the acid without the punch of vinegar.

VIA RAIL. *See* Canadian National Railway.

VICTOR ET BERTHOLD CHEESE—a semi-soft, award-winning raw Ayrshire cow's milk cheese made at the Fromagerie du Champ à la Meule, in Notre-Dame-de-Lourdes, Québec.

VICTORY GARDENS—during the two World Wars, backyard gardens accounted for over 30 percent of the fresh produce consumed

A B C D E F G H I J K L M N O P Q R S T U **V** W X Y Z

A
B
C
D
E
F
G
H
I
J
K
L
M
N
O
P
Q
R
S
T
U
V
W
X
Y
Z

POST-WAR HOARDERS

Old habits die hard, and as World War I and the Great Depression changed Canada's rural topography from small family farms to large industrial farms, displaced rural populations moved into towns and cities and brought along their self-sustaining rural mentality of root cellars, icehouses and backyard vegetable gardens as nutritional insurance against hard times and starvation. The hoarding of canned goods and growing of vegetables became a national obsession.

By 1939, when Canada entered World War II, almost every urban household had a victory garden along with a closet, back room or cellar set aside for storing canned goods. Canada's wartime ration board frowned upon

the hoarding of canned foods, and while many warning pamphlets were distributed, it was never—unlike exceeding meat, sugar and gasoline quotas—an unlawful practice. To counter the emptying of shelves by hoarders, storekeepers imposed their own ration system, usually two cans per customer. Telephones were still a rare commodity, and if a household had one, it was probably a party line, a shared affair that allowed housewives to plot, plan and beat storekeepers at their ration game by making daily rounds to different shops.

by Canadians and helped win those wars. It was Canadians doing their bit to help both the war effort and local communities by reducing the pressure on the public food supply. It was also a way to supplement meals while dealing with wartime rations, especially of canned goods.

VIN DE MIEL. See hydromel.

VINARTERTA—a traditional Icelandic torte cake of thin, cookie-like layers separated by a prune-based filling. It is usually made at Christmas, but it can be found every August at the annual Icelandic Festival at Gimli, Manitoba.

New Iceland

- In 1875, anxious to attract settlers to Manitoba, the Canadian government gave a good chunk of the western shore of Lake Winnipeg to a group of Icelandic immigrants. For the next 22 years, the area was called New Iceland and was closed to all but Icelandic peoples and governed by Icelandic laws.

- Today it's called Gimli, and every August they celebrate all things Icelandic with lots of fried fish, Viking hoopla and feting of Icelandic dignitaries.

VINEGAR PIE—a prairie adaptation of lemon pie, made before the railway brought in fresh lemons. Prepared as regular lemon pie, but with lemon essence and vinegar to raise acidity and tartness.

VINTNERS QUALITY ALLIANCE (VQA)—a designation created in 1988 to regulate the wines of Ontario and expanded in 1990 to regulate those produced in BC. VQA designations require that if a wine has the grape variety listed on the label, it must contain a minimum of 85 percent of that variety. If a designated growing area is listed, 95 percent of the fruit must come from that area. If the vineyard is named, 100 percent of contents must originate from that vineyard.

VIRGINIA HAM—a term for what many Canadians called dry-cured country hams back in the day. The term references the famous peanut-fed hogs raised around the town of Smithfield, Virginia, that provided hams of exceptional quality.

VOYAGEUR STEW—originally a game stew with salt bacon, pemmican, wild rice and dried peas, the recipe now includes beef broth, various vegetables and herbs.

A
B
C
D
E
F
G
H
I
J
K
L
M
N
O
P
Q
R
S
T
U
V
W
X
Y
Z

W

WACKY CAKE (also called blue Monday cake, crazy cake, lazy cake)—a mix-in-the-pan chocolate cake popular during the 1950s and promoted by cooking maven Kate Aitken as the first cake young girls should learn how to bake.

WAFFLES—Canadians have carried on a long-time love affair with waffles. In the early days, stovetops were the cooking vehicle and Indian corn batter was poured into an iron mould constructed by a local blacksmith. Nowadays, batter can be any grain and waffles are cooked in electric waffle makers, but the maple syrup topping has stayed the same, and that is really what a waffle is all about.

WALLEYE (*Sander vitreus*; also called doré, pickerel)—an important food source for First Nations and familiar to early pioneer settlers

because the fish also ranges in lakes and rivers in Europe. Walleye abound in the Great Lakes, and in northern waters, they are the dominant species. Walleye flesh is white and flaky and is considered by many people to be the world's tastiest freshwater fish. They are caught commercially in many areas of Canada. Walleye are also an important game fish and account for millions in tourist revenues, especially to Saskatchewan, where the species is the provincial fish.

BLUE PICKEREL

In years past, a variety of walleye nicknamed blue pickerel found in the Great Lakes watershed was so popular that it was totally fished out by the late 1950s. During that time, my father had a standing order with the Erie Beach Hotel in Port Dover for blue pickerel. Whenever commercial fishermen caught one in their nets, the Erie Beach would call my dad, and he would drop everything and race the seven miles to Port Dover to feast on the rarity. His last rush to the blue occurred in spring 1958, after which the Erie Beach never called again.

WALLEYE IN BEER BATTER—a favourite shore lunch recipe of fishermen. Wherever there are fishermen, there is bound to be beer. *See also* shore lunch.

RECIPE

Walleye in Beer Batter

Beat 3 eggs until frothy, then add ½ can beer and 1 tsp salt. In another bowl, combine 1 cup each of cornmeal and flour with 1 tsp salt. Dip skinless walleye fillets into liquid batter, roll in dry mix and fry in butter until golden and the fish flakes with a fork.

WALNUT MAYONNAISE—in Canada's formative years, cooks would prepare a homemade mayonnaise by whisking together walnut oil and egg

yolks, but nowadays using a prepared mayo is the way to go. Walnut mayonnaise is easy to make and very tasty.

RECIPE

Walnut Mayonnaise

Mix 1 cup prepared mayonnaise, ½ cup sour cream, ½ cup very finely chopped walnuts and a spoonful each of chopped green onions and parsley.

WALNUT OIL—drizzled on salads and ice cream, fresh-pressed walnut oil is sensational and was once an easily obtained favourite of Canadian cooks until men felled all the walnut trees (*Juglans* spp.) to make furniture. Today, most walnut oil is of European origin and very expensive. Tiny amounts of locally pressed oil do make an occasional appearance at Canadian farmers' markets; the walnut oil found at farmers' markets will probably be from fast-growing Persian walnut trees and not the native black walnut (*J. nigra*) or butternut (*J. cinerea*), but no matter: if the former is found, buy some, and if it's the latter, buy lots.

WAPATO (*Sagittaria latifolia*; also called broadleaf arrowhead)—the plant has tuberous roots similar to the potato and was a much-used source of food for both west coast First Nations and early BC settlers. Wapato tubers can be

boiled, but roasting is preferred because it removes bitterness and makes them taste remarkably like potatoes. West-coasters should watch for them at farmers' markets and try them as a side for barbecued meats or salmon.

WAPITI. *See* elk.

WAR CAKE (also called Depression cake)—a recipe first popular in World War I when some baking ingredients were missing from store shelves. War cake bakers used flour, corn syrup, water, salt, cloves and nutmeg to produce a heavy, fruitcake-type dessert with good keeping qualities.

WAR RATIONS—Canadian soldiers fared well during the first two years of World War II, with each one receiving a daily ration of 1 lb of fresh or frozen meat, 4 oz of bacon, 2 cans of salmon, 1 can of pork and beans, 1 can of fruit and a bar of chocolate, as well as sugar, pickles, jams and loaves of bread produced at frontline bakeries. But when Germany blockaded Britain with U-boats and action at the front stalemated, artillery became the mouths that needed feeding. The flood of not-bad rations was quickly reduced to a trickle, and troops had to rely on so-called iron rations instituted in World War I. *See also* iron rations.

WATER AVENS. *See* Indian chocolate.

WATER OATS. *See* wild rice.

WATERCRESS (*Nasturtium officinale*)—an edible perennial and close relative of mustard, from whence comes the pungency of watercress. It was introduced to Canada by the earliest settlers, who considered the plant both a salad ingredient and a medicine for various ailments.

WATERCRESS SOUP—a fresh-tasting cress and potato soup favoured by pioneer settlers and modern-day upscale chefs.

RECIPE

Watercress Soup

Cook 2 chopped onions in 2 Tbsp butter. Add 2 bunches watercress and 2 peeled and diced potatoes and cook, stirring, for 5 minutes. Add 2 cups chicken broth and lower heat. Simmer for 15 minutes. Run mixture through a sieve, food mill or blender, return to pot and add 2 cups milk, and salt and pepper to taste. Serve hot with a dab of butter.

WATERLOO'S FARMERS' MARKETS—empty the trunk before you head off to the Uptown Market and the St. Jacobs farmers' markets in Waterloo because this is where the Mennonites come to show the world what hard work and manure can do on a farm. Across the street from one another and run by the same people, these markets sell more fleas than food, but the seasonal produce is first rate. *See also* market squares.

WEESUKAPUKA. *See* Labrador tea.

WELLESLEY APPLE BUTTER & CHEESE FESTIVAL—it's always on the last Saturday in September, and it's such a celebration of all things country that even city folk get caught up in a whirlwind of activities. There's a little something for everyone at this festival to honour the town's major industries: the J.M. Schneider Cheese Factory and A.W. Jantzi & Sons, packers of Wellesley Brand apple products. Come early for the pancake breakfast and hit the farmers' market at the arena to stock up on all foods Mennonite.

WESTERN SANDWICH—a waste-not, want-not sandwich invention of early prairie settlers. In the heat of summer and without refrigeration, fresh eggs spoiled quickly. To avoid having to discard them, pioneer cooks disguised the off-flavour by mixing them with onions, salt pork, peppers, etc.

WESTON'S HOME-MADE BREAD—from tiny acorns come great oaks, and in 1884 when George Weston began operating his own bakery, his brand name was Real Home-Made. In 1897, he opened Weston's Model Bakery after the installation of modern bakery equipment and within a few years the whole of southern Ontario was able to purchase Real Home-Made bread in standard sized loaves.

WHEAT (*Triticum* spp.)—wheat is available in many strains: hard or soft, red or white, winter or spring. The most common in Canada is Hard Red Spring wheat, with the province of Saskatchewan being its primary source. Most wheat is ground into flour.

A B C D E F G H I J K L M N O P Q R S T U V **W** X Y Z

A
B
C
D
E
F
G
H
I
J
K
L
M
N
O
P
Q
R
S
T
U
V
W
X
Y
Z

CANADA'S FAVOURITE WHEAT VARIETIES

- Durum—a hard wheat used to make semolina, which is used to make pasta.

- Hard Red Spring—produces high-gluten flour good for bread baking.

- Hard Red Winter—a high-protein strain, also good for bread and to increase the protein content of soft wheat pastry flours.

- Hard White—a medium-protein wheat used for baking bread and brewing beer.

- Soft White—a low-protein wheat used for pastry flour.

- Soft Red Winter—a low-protein strain used to bake cakes, muffins and pie pastry.

HISTORY OF WHEAT IN CANADA

Canada's contribution to a better staff of life is so immeasurably steeped in misery and sacrifice that it warrants a worldwide day of remembrance for its pioneers. Wheat arrived on the Canadian prairies in 1812. It was a native English variety brought by the original Scottish settlers to the Selkirk colony at the junction of the Red and Assiniboine rivers. They planted winter and spring wheat, and both crops failed. They planted again the next year, and again, the crops failed—but the fertile land yielded up a good supply of potatoes and turnips.

Undaunted by the two previous failures, the settlers hove to their ploughs and set wheat seed once again, but in spring 1815, they were attacked by Métis rebels and were driven off their land. Rescued by a relief column sent by Lord Selkirk, the settlers returned to find their wheat growing well enough to give them a harvest. The next year, in spring 1816, the Métis attacked again, causing heavy damage. In fall 1817, with the wheat standing tall in the fields, a hurricane struck and levelled everything.

In spring 1818, something completely unexpected descended on the fields like a black cloud—grasshoppers, so many they consumed the prairie like fire. The farmers were done; the grasshoppers had left them with very little seed for next year's planting, and they moved off their land to hunt buffalo. The next spring, they returned to plant what little seed they had, only to have the grasshoppers return.

In 1820, with no seed, the settlement sent men to the U.S. to purchase bushels of seed to be barged up the Red River in time for a late spring planting. That fall, the grasshoppers returned—only for a short time, but the crop had been late into the ground and the yield was only enough for next year's seed; the men went back to hunting buffalo. It went like that for another two decades. Even when the weather held, diseases such as rust and smut destroyed crops.

In 1842, a miracle occurred—not on the prairies but in the tiny settlement of Otonabee, near Peterborough, Canada West (Ontario). The Otonabee farmer's name was David Fife, and the miracle was a packet of Ukrainian wheat called Halychanka scooped from a ship in Glasgow harbour by a friend and sent to David in spring 1842. Not sure if the variety was winter or spring, he popped some seeds into the ground, only to find it was winter wheat and it failed to ripen. Undaunted, he planted the remainder in fall only to have all but three ears of grain eaten by his cow when it came up the next spring. Come spring 1844, he remembered the three saved ears and planted them in a small experimental plot. Those seeds grew well, but most succumbed to the ever-present rust disease before harvest.

Saving the seeds that survived rust, David Fife popped them into the ground and the next fall was rewarded with his miracle: the wheat stalks in his plot grew faster, taller and stronger than any of his normal Siberian wheat variety and showed no signs of rust or smut. He immediately planted his entire crop, and the next fall saw a bumper crop with enough seed to share his good fortune with neighbours, who called their bumper crops of rust-free wheat "Red Fife" after the grain's red colour and the miracle worker from Otonabee.

WHEAT BERRIES—kernels of wheat straight from the farmer's field. Before being added to salads or various other culinary preparations, wheat berries are first softened by long boiling (1½ hours), then cooled and seasoned. If not eaten right away, they can be frozen for later use.

WHEAT BREAD—any bread made from any variety of the hybridized seeds of the wheat plant. Wheat (and wheat bread) has as much

history in Canada as its people: both arrived around the same time. The first wheat seeds went into the ground at Port Royal, Nova Scotia, in spring 1606, and the first loaves of Canadian wheat bread were baked that fall. Since then, both our people and those seeds have evolved, the former into a great nation and the latter into the best bread-making wheat on the planet. *See also* bread.

WHEY—milk is composed of liquids and solids, and when the two are separated (curdled) for cheese making, the watery part is called the whey and the solid parts are called curd. Along with cheese, Canada's conglomerate dairies produce about 1.5 billion kg of whey, of which about half is powdered, 10 percent is fed to pigs and the remainder is either dumped into sewers or sprayed onto fields. Dairy conglomerates are making fortunes from Canada's antiquated supply system and should be required by law not to waste this product, even if the financial returns are slim.

WHISKY. *See* applejack, cherry whisky, rye whisky, single malt whisky, Yukon Jack whisky.

WHITE BACON. *See* salt pork.

WHITE HATTER STEW—a baked, pastry-topped beef stew and the official grub of the Calgary Stampede. One-pot meals were a mainstay of chuckwagon cooks, and that tradition continues at the Stampede. White hatter stew is usually served up in individually baked containers to the sea of white-cowboy-hatted visitors.

WHITE WALNUT. *See* butternut.

WHITE WHEAT—a type of wheat lacking genes for colouring bran, which is normally a reddish colour. Canadian farmers grow two types of white wheat: Canadian Prairie Spring White, for use in the flatbread market; and Canadian Western Hard White, for making noodles and leavened breads. Canadian conglomerate bakers are marketing whole-wheat bread made with white wheat, and though it looks like baker's fog white bread, it is 100 percent whole wheat with colourless bran. *See also* wheat.

WHITEFISH (*Coregonus clupeaformis*)—the predominant catch of Canadian lake fisheries is whitefish. The province of Manitoba supplies roughly half the Canadian commercial catch, and most of it is exported to the U.S. for processing into gefilte fish. What remains in Canada can be found gutted and whole in the freezer sections of most supermarkets. Whitefish is inexpensive and makes a delectable change from marine species. One of the best and easiest methods for cooking whitefish is breading with cornmeal and frying, but grilled, baked or fried, it matters not—this popular freshwater delight is sure to please.

WHOOPIE PIE—a traditional Mennonite iced cookie still available at farmers' markets where Mennonites sell their farm and kitchen products.

WHORE'S EGGS. *See* cosy eggs.

WILD ASPARAGUS. *See* milkweed.

WILD BERRY JUMBLE PIE—a pie made with any combination of: bakeapples, blackberries, blueberries, buffaloberries, cranberries, red and black currants, dewberries, elderberries, gooseberries, huckleberries, jostaberries, lingonberries, mooseberries, mossberries, nagoonberries, nannyberries, partridgeberries, raspberries, salalberries, salmonberries, saskatoons, strawberries, squashberries and teaberries. And there are dozens more, along with many suitable only as famine food. When berries are picked as found, several kinds will go into the pail, and who wants to sort berries? Just pour them into the pie crust in one delicious jumble, and an epicurean masterpiece will emerge from the oven. It's not strictly Canadian—jumble pie has been around for ages—but the berries are distinctly Canadian and provide us rightful claim to this luscious wild berry pie.

Wild Berries

- Wild berries added zest to pemmican and provided early settlers a welcome addition to corn mush and rabbit stew. Dried berries made a passable substitute for raisins in dessert recipes, while fresh berries made marvellous jams and jellies with or without added sweeteners.

- Wild berry bushes also provided Canadian settlers with a virtual pharmacy for common ailments; their bark, berries and leaves contain all manner of medicinal properties. Highbush cranberry tea cured swollen glands and dampened the effects of mumps. A wine fermented from sweet, ripe hawberries could be cheerfully imbibed to cure pains, ague and bladder problems. Pin cherries cured scurvy and the common cold. Chokecherries cured diarrhea, while a decoction of black cherry root would prevent diarrhea. The roots of blueberry plants infused in water produced a palatable tea that reputedly cured both cholera and hiccups. And lowbush cranberries cured dysentery, a common ailment among early settlers.

- Settlers near Ontario's Lake Erie region had a special treat in the bayberry, or wax myrtle. Its wax-covered berries not only cured scrofula but, when mixed with beeswax, also produced scented candles, a fortuitous discovery for occupants of tiny cabins, even in modern times.

- Most of Canada's wild and cultivated berries are related members of the Rose family, while the cranberry, huckleberry and blueberry are members of the Heath family.

WILD BOAR (*Sus scrofa*)—most Canadians think of wild boar as being an Italian specialty foraged from the hillsides of Umbria and Tuscany, but they are not paying attention to the offerings of local game ranchers, many of whom are raising boar for butchering. Canadians who would rather hunt their own are invited to do so at various game ranches located in almost every province. Hunters wishing a more natural hunt only have to head for the prairies, where feral pigs have become a real problem that farmers would love to have solved.

WILD CELERY. *See* Indian celery.

WILD CITRON. *See* mayapple.

WILD COTTON. *See* milkweed.

WILD GARLIC. *See* Canada onion.

WILD GAME—during Canada's formative years, putting dinner on the table meant a short trek out the door with a musket. The forest was

a good provider then, as it is today, and although today's trek to get to the forest can be much longer, for many Canadians it still puts a staggering variety of meat and fowl on the table: rabbit, deer, moose, caribou, elk, bear, goose, turkey, duck, grouse and partridge, all from populations kept sustainable through constant monitoring by provincial and federal game management authorities. Once the backbone of Canadian cuisine, game meats have slipped off the culinary map into almost total obscurity, with most Canadians having never sampled anything wilder than a domestic rabbit. Because the selling of most wild game is prohibited in Canada, the only way to taste wild game meat is either to go hunting or through a gift from hunters. Modern-day hunters and hunting regulations advocate that game has a sporting chance; that's good, but the downside is that targeted animals are seldom killed instantly, which means their meat is often full of stress hormones that impart an off or gamey flavour to the meat. Hunting game with bow and arrow has become increasingly popular, and friends and families of bow hunters will probably already know the gamey taste. The alternative is farm-raised game meats, which are widely available for purchase. That undesirable gamey flavour is not present in the meat of ranched or farmed animals because slaughtering is done in a humane and stress-free manner. To those many diners who have never sampled the historical cornerstone of Canadian cuisine, here is a taste revelation just waiting for you: farm-raised game meats and birds are melt-in-the-mouth yummy.

A B C D E F G H I J K L M N O P Q R S T U V **W** X Y Z

THE CERVID TRADE

New Zealand cervid (deer) ranchers have been extraordinarily successful, exporting over $300 million annually in prepared meat and byproducts, such as antlers. These antlers are much in demand in Asia, especially South Korea, where they are processed into pharmaceutical products. They're considered a sustainable product because every year without fail, farmed male deer and elk grow new antlers that can be painlessly removed by ranchers. Equally high was the Asian demand for the roasts and chops of said cervids.

Sensing opportunity, hundreds of Alberta and Saskatchewan ranchers entered the cervid farming business. It thrived, making more money for ranchers than beef, and was on its way to emulating New Zealand's success when a nightmare illness called Chronic Wasting Disease (CWD) made an appearance in 1996 in a herd of Saskatchewan farm-raised elk. CWD is related to Mad Cow Disease, and although there is no scientific evidence that these diseases can be transmitted to humans, the fear generated by Mad Cow Disease resulted in Korea and other Asian countries closing their borders to all North American beef products in 2005. Because the importation of cervid products was also blocked, Canadian cervid ranchers were caught with all their eggs in one basket, crashing the entire industry.

Down but not out, deer ranchers have reformed and are targeting home markets with meats that have tested free of CWD. In addition, provincial governments have made CWD testing sites available for hunters and recommend that all animals be tested before consumption.

Unethical Huntsmen

- A few decades ago, deer hunters would put out blocks of salt and construct hiding places called blinds well in advance of open season. When that date rolled around, they were able to shoot deer from a blind while the animal was happily licking up salt and oblivious to danger. Although today this practice is considered cruel and unethical—and rightly so—these dinners no doubt tasted superb.

- Moose were even easier to target because savvy hunters only had to await the first snowfall and the road salting trucks. The salt was irresistible to moose, and hunters could drive around and pick out their contented prey.

WILD GINGER (*Asarum canadense*; also called Canada snakeroot, Indian ginger)—from its root, a flavouring agent can be extracted that has a remarkable ginger flavour. Employed by First Nations and early settlers as a cookery seasoning and wine/beer additive, peeled wild ginger root was an important trade item for many years.

WILD GINGER ALERT

Wild ginger root was recently found to contain aristolochic acid, a known carcinogen, and efforts have been made by government agencies to deter foraging of this once-popular seasoning.

WILD JALAP. *See* mayapple.

WILD LEEK (*Allium tricoccum*; also called ramp, rampion)—a member of the Onion family and much used by First Nations and settlers to flavour

game and stews. Although identical in flavour, wild leeks growing in western Canada sport narrow leaves, while the eastern variant has broader leaves.

Wild Leek

- Not just a good substitute for garlic, the wild leek is also purported to provide almost mystical health benefits: it lowers blood sugar, corrects hypertension, speeds healing of wounds and cures both freckles and the common cold.

WILD LICORICE. *See* licorice root.

WILD MUSTARD. *See* charlock.

WILD RAISIN. *See* nannyberry.

WILD RICE (*Zizania* spp.; also called Canada rice, Indian rice, water oats)—while not true rice, wild rice is a close relative. Globally, four species exist:

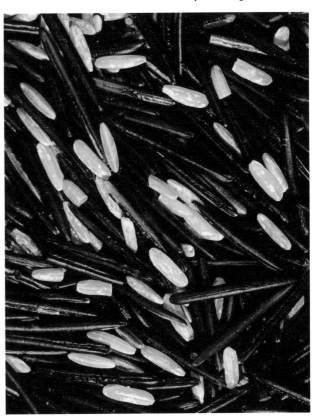

wild rice (*Z. aquatica*), northern wild rice (*Z. palustris*), Texas wild rice (*Z. texana*) and an Asian species, Manchurian wild rice (*Z. latifolia*). Never of any commercial or dietary importance, Texas wild rice has all but disappeared. The Manchurian species, though at one time a staple food for the Chinese, became less so with the advent of easier-to-grow rice species, and it too has all but disappeared. Not so with the wild and northern species—both were mainstay foods of First Nations and Canadian and American settlers, and they have continued to grow in popularity, with the northern species being the most commonly harvested. In Canada, both Saskatchewan and Manitoba provide discriminating consumers and chefs worldwide with natural wild rice that is both tasty and nutritious. Wild rice is high in protein, low in fat, a good source of potassium and the vitamins riboflavin, thiamin and niacin, and makes a wonderful side for any main dish, especially wild duck.

Wild Rice

- Ricers have generational claim to productive areas and, while not necessary in modern times, ricer families used to bind rice stalks into bundles as a way of marking territory. Each family used a unique form of binding, such as different strips of bark or ways of tying the bundles.

- Ricing is not without its hazards; the grains are sharp enough to pierce skin, and some grains harbour rice worms that can inflict nasty bites. Needless to say, ricers go well protected even in sweltering heat. In Manitoba and Saskatchewan, First Nations are the major harvesters, and their ricing garb has remained relatively unchanged for the better part of 200 years: lots of protective clothing and plenty of spruce gum to remove barbs from the eyes.

HARVESTING AND PROCESSING WILD RICE

The ricing, or harvesting, of wild rice is a technique perfected by First Nations and is called "knocking." Old-style knocking entails driving a flat-bottomed canoe into a stand of wild rice, bending the stalks over the craft with one long stick and knocking that stick with another called the knocker. Done properly, rice grains fall off the stalks and into the bottom of the canoe in neat piles. Done improperly, the stalks may break, negating a second or third ricing. Nowadays, most ricers use flat-bottomed airboats with a mechanized knocker and collecting tray, but the need for proper technique remains unchanged: a ricer must knock with the boat at the proper speed or risk damaging the plants. Wild rice is a self-seeding annual plant, and knockers must take care to allow some grains to remain as seed for their next season's crop.

Once harvested, rice grains must be dried to prevent mildew. Before the arrival of the Europeans, drying was accomplished by layering the grains on a large platform over several small fires. With the Europeans came large iron pots that enabled the "parching," or slow roasting, of rice grains, the process still in use today. Slow roasting drives out moisture, destroys the germ—thus preventing germination—and hardens off the kernel.

The hull loosens and falls away during "hulling," a process that used to involve tedious hours of treading on rice grains until they became separated from their hulls but is now accomplished by machines at local buying depots or tribal mills, cooperative facilities set up to process wild rice. "Winnowing," or cleaning, the grains of chaff is also done by a depot or mill machine, but in the old days, it usually involved throwing the grains into the air, allowing the wind to remove chaff and other bits of undesirable matter.

In times past, wild rice grains were then packed into animal skin sacks or birch bark containers and buried in the ground below the frost line so they would keep for long periods. Nowadays, grains processed by depot machines come in paper sacks or boxes not designed to protect them for long periods, but that is never a problem because naturally harvested wild rice is much in demand.

RECIPE

Wild Rice and Forest Mushroom Pilaf

Soak and rinse 1 cup wild rice in three changes of hot tap water to remove starch. In a saucepan, cook 1 lb fresh forest mushrooms and 1 small leek in 1 Tbsp butter until soft and beginning to brown, about 7–8 minutes. Add rice, ¼ cup chopped parsley and enough water to cover by 1 inch. Bring to a boil, reduce heat to low, cover and simmer until rice is tender, about 45 minutes. Drain water and season, then fluff with a fork and serve immediately.

WILD ROSE SYRUP—a sweet, flavourful syrup made by steeping the petals of the wild roses (*Rosa* spp.) that are common across the country.

RECIPE

Wild Rose Syrup

Gather and wash 4 cups of rose petals. In a heavy-bottomed saucepan combine petals, 2 cups distilled water, 2 cups sugar and the juice of 1 lemon, and cook at just below a simmer for 1 hour. Strain the petals from the liquid and bring to a boil until thickened.

RECIPE

Wine Jelly

Soften 2 envelopes of powdered gelatin in ½ cup cold water for 5 minutes, then add it to 1 cup boiling water along with ⅔ cup sugar, ¼ cup each of orange and lemon juice, and 2 cups good red wine. Add a pinch of salt and stir until blended. Pour into jelly jars, or into a jelly mould for a decorative touch, and refrigerate.

WILD SPINACH. *See* lamb's quarters.

WILD TURNIP. See *pomme-de-prairie.*

WILLY KRAUCH SMOKED FISH—salmon, mackerel and eel, and according to Craig Claiborne, late food writer of the *New York Times*, nobody smokes them better than Willy Krauch does. Willy passed away a few years ago, but his three kids are still keeping Tangier, Nova Scotia, the subject of food columnists around the globe.

WINDSOR BEAN. *See* horse bean.

WINE JELLY—with Ontario and BC overflowing with wines, it might be a good idea to dust off this old recipe. Although it originally called for Gamay grape wine, almost any red will do nicely.

WINEGARDEN ESTATE WINERY & DISTILLERY—located in the rich farmland of New Brunswick near Baie Verte and operated by Roswitha Rosswog, Canada's only female distiller. The estate store features over 70 varieties of grape and fruit wines, eau-de-vie, brandies, liqueurs and bitters, all crafted from fresh New Brunswick produce.

WINNIPEG GOLDEYE (*Hiodon alosoides*)— a small, freshwater fish with a deep body and large, yellow eyes. Endemic to rivers and lakes from Ontario to BC, goldeyes are caught commercially in Manitoba and Saskatchewan and processed in Winnipeg. There, gutted fish are brined, dyed an orange colour, smoked over oak fires, boxed and shipped worldwide.

WINNIPEG GOLDEYE AND CRAB CAKES— an Alberta discovery that raises crab cakes to a culinary level that surpasses the American effort by miles—sorry, by kilometres.

> ### RECIPE
>
> #### Winnipeg Goldeye and Crab Cakes
>
> *Cook 1 diced onion, 1 diced bell pepper and 1 diced stalk of celery in butter until soft. Add 2 tsp chopped fresh tarragon, zest of 1 lemon and 1 tsp Worcestershire sauce, and set aside to cool. In a large bowl, mix 1 lb each of cleaned crab meat and Winnipeg goldeye with the onion mixture, 2 eggs, 2 tsp Dijon mustard, 3 cups breadcrumbs (or enough to hold mixture together), and salt and pepper to taste. Form into cakes. Place seasoned flour on one plate and seasoned breadcrumbs on another plate. Make an egg wash in a shallow bowl. Dredge crab cakes in seasoned flour, then dip into egg wash, then roll in seasoned breadcrumbs. Pan fry in butter until golden brown, then transfer to a 375°F oven and bake for 8–10 minutes or until done.*

WINTER COD. *See* tommy cod.

WINTERGREEN (*Gaultheria procumbens*; also called boxberry, checkerberry, partridgeberry, teaberry)—a low-growing, cross-Canada evergreen groundcover with bright red berries that persist well into winter and provide pickers with a waxy, sweet chew. During the late-19th and early-20th centuries, both the leaves and the berries were commercially foraged to make flavouring for jelly, candy, toothpaste and gum.

Wintergreen flavouring is still popular, but it is now made artificially.

WINTERGREEN CANDY—a Turkish delight–style candy perfected by herbalist and 1960s TV personality Euell Gibbons.

WINTERGREEN TEA—a hot water decoction of the fermented leaves of the wintergreen plant, and a much-used settlers' tonic for whatever ailed them.

WINTERGREEN WINE—a favourite of pioneer women for the way it livened up functions such as quilting and canning bees, and old-time herbalists recommended wintergreen wine be given to invalids as a pick-me-up.

WISHAKAPUKA. *See* Labrador tea.

WOLFFISH. *See* Atlantic wolffish.

Wintergreen Relief

- Got a toothache? A wintergreen leaf placed on the affected tooth will alleviate the pain like magic.

- The essential oil in wintergreen, oil of wintergreen, is 99 percent methyl salicylate, which is in the same chemical family as aspirin.

- Wintergreen also supposedly increases blood circulation to the gums, an attribute that probably gave rise to the toothpaste flavouring.

XYZ

XIPHIAS GLADIUS—the scientific name for swordfish, and our excuse for an entry under X. *See also* swordfish.

YELLOW PERCH. *See* perch.

YORKSHIRE HOG—so favoured and hybridized by Canadian hog producers, it has become known as the Canadian Yorkshire. The pig is a quick grower and produces high quality, lean meat.

YORKSHIRE PUDDING. *See* roast beef, Old English-style.

YORKSHIRE PUDDING WITH WILD RICE—east met west in a Canada West settler's kitchen, and the dish remained a favourite until hearth cooking was replaced by kitchen stoves and meat juices no longer dripped off roasts but pooled in pots. To make this dish, simply include precooked wild rice in any standard Yorkshire pudding recipe, pour into pudding pans or a casserole dish and bake until tall, brown and scrumptious looking.

RECIPE

Yorkshire Pudding

Make while the roast beef is resting. Mix 1 cup flour and ½ tsp salt in a large bowl. Whisk 2 eggs and 1 cup whole milk in a small bowl. Pour wet ingredients into dry ingredients, stirring until just mixed; do not overmix. Heat pudding pan until hot, pour in ¼-inch of melted fat (or butter), then fill half full with batter. Bake at 450°F for 20 minutes, then reduce oven temperature to 350°F and bake a further 20 minutes until golden brown. Serve immediately with slices of roast beef and gravy.

A
B
C
D
E
F
G
H
I
J
K
L
M
N
O
P
Q
R
S
T
U
V
W

RECIPE

Yukon Gold Fries

Cut 6 large Yukon Gold potatoes into strips and place into a plastic bag with 3–4 Tbsp olive oil (maybe some onion and garlic too) and shake. Lay strips on a well-greased baking sheet, season and bake at 375°F for 15 minutes, then flip and bake another 15 minutes, or until crisp. Sprinkle on some coarse sea salt and serve hot.

YUKON GOLD POTATO—a Canadian original developed by botanist Gary Johnston at the University of Guelph during the early 1960s and now grown worldwide. *See also* potato.

YUKON GOLD POTATO FRENCH FRIES—in the hierarchy of diabolical "wish we hadn't thought of that" modern-day inventions, frozen French fries are right up there with gas-powered leaf blowers, sliced bread and escalators—shameful inventions that are really icons of laziness. Frozen French fries are a waste of money because a better product can be made at home simply by cutting up a potato.

YUKON JACK WHISKY—named after celebrated Yukon pioneer Captain Jack McQuesten, this 100 proof, honey-based whisky liqueur is the celebrated "puts hair on your chest" drink of Canada's Far North.

ZUCCHINI—a variety of summer squash developed in Italy from North American origins. Now grown in gardens across Canada for its edible flowers and fruit, it is best picked small before it has a chance to grow out of control and you end up abandoning it on neighbours' doorsteps in the middle of the night. *See also* squash.

X
Y
Z

SOURCES

Barss, Beulah M. *The Pioneer Cook*. Calgary: 1931; Calgary: Detselig Enterprises Ltd., 1980.

Barrenechea, Teresa. *The Basque Table*. Boston: Harvard Common Press, 1998.

Berton, Pierre and Janet. *Canadian Food Guide*. Toronto: McClelland and Stewart, 1966.

Breckenridge, Muriel. *The Old Ontario Cook Book*. Toronto: McGraw-Hill Ryerson Limited, 1976.

Casselman, Bill. *Canadian Food Words*. Toronto: McArthur & Company, 1998.

Casselman, Bill. *Canadian Words and Sayings*. Toronto: McArthur & Company, 2006.

Davidson, Alan. *The Oxford Companion to Food*. London: Oxford University Press, 1999.

Duncan, Dorothy. *Canadians at Table*. Toronto: Dundurn Press, 2006.

Ellis, Eleanor A. *Northern Cookbook*. Edmonton: Hurtig Publishers, 1967.

Erichsen-Brown, Charlotte. *Medicinal and Other Uses of North American Plants*. New York: Dover Publications, 1979.

Ferguson, Carol and Margaret Fraser. *A Century of Canadian Home Cooking*. Toronto: Prentice Hall Canada Inc., 1992.

Freedman, Paul. *Food*. Berkeley: University of California Press, 2007.

Fritsch, Klaus with Mary Goodbody. *Morton's Steak Bible*. New York: Clarkson Potter, 2006.

Hirigoyen, Gerald. *The Basque Kitchen*. New York: HarperCollins, 1999.

Jordan, Peter and Steven Wheeler. *The Ultimate Mushroom Book*. London: Anness Publishing Ltd., 1998.

Kurlansky, Mark. *Cod*. Toronto: Alfred A. Knopf, 1997.

Lafrance, Marc and Yvon Desloges. *A Taste of History*. Montréal: Les Éditions de la Chenelière and Canadian Park Services, 1989.

Laura Secord Candy Shops. *Laura Secord Canadian Cook Book*. Toronto: McClelland and Stewart, 1984.

Murray, Rose. *A Taste of Canada*. Vancouver: Whitecap Books, 2008.

Nearing, Helen and Scott. *The Maple Sugar Book*. New York: Schoken Books, 1950.

Ogle, Jennifer. *Canadian Cookbook*. Edmonton: Lone Pine Publishing, 2006.

Pringle, Laurence. *Wild Foods*. New York: Four Winds Press, 1978.

Purity Flour Canadian Cook Book. Toronto: Coles Publishing Company Limited, 1975.

Robin Hood Multi Foods. *Robin Hood Cook Book*. Vancouver: Whitecap Books, 2003.

Rolland, Jacques L. *The Cook's Essential Kitchen Dictionary*. Toronto: Robert Rose Inc., 2004.

Staebler, Edna. *Food That Really Schmecks*. Toronto: The Ryerson Press, 1968.

Stewart, Anita. *Our Mothers' Kitchen*. Toronto: Random House, 1991.

Stewart, Anita. *The Flavours of Canada*. Vancouver: Raincoast Books, 2000.

Traill, Catharine Parr. *The Backwoods of Canada*. London, England: Charles Knight, 1836; Toronto: Penguin Canada, 2006.

Traill, Catharine Parr. *The Canadian Settlers Guide*. Toronto: Toronto Times, 1857; Toronto: McClelland and Stewart, 1996.

The Cook Not Mad. Kingston: James Macfarlane, 1831; Toronto: The Cherry Tree Press, 1973.

Upton, L.F.S. *Micmacs and Colonists*. Vancouver: University of BC Press, 1979.

PHOTO CREDITS

All photos are sourced from Photos.com, with the exception of the following: Laura Peters 375a; Nanette Samol 106b, 247a; Volker Bodegom 43a, 195, 205, 232, 236c, 249b, 258a, 264a, 282b, 291a, 318b, 322c, 326c, 327a, 328a&b, 334b, 340c, 341a, 346, 348a&b, 354a, 368a, 376b, 380a&b, 382a, 384b&c, 388a&b, 389c, 390b, 395a&c, 396b, 399a&b, 406b, 407b,c&d, 408a&b, 409a&b, 410, 413, 414a, 415a.

© Photos.com: Ablestock.com 8b, 62b, 156b; Achim Prill 362c; Acnakelsy 82b, 404b; adam muir 295b; aida ricciardiello caballero 332c; akit 134; Aksakalko 307b; al62 375b; Alain KRAFFT 162b; Alain Turgeon 202a; Alasdair Thomson 84b; alberto gagna 116b; Aleksandr Volkov 353; Aleksey Malakhov 327b; Alena Dvorakova 152; Alexander Blinow 173b, 260a, 312a; Alexander Raths 102, 139, 180b; Alexey Fedorov 260b; alexnika 268b; alfio scisetti 270b; Alice Day 311b; Alicja Bochenek 106a; Alistair Williamson 282a; Amy Randall 266a; Andre Nantel 359a; Andrea Skjold 54a, 138, 390a; Andrew Klafter 125a; AndrewFurlongPhotography 117b; Andrey Popov 36b; Andrey Spiridonov 391a; Andrey89 161b; Andrii Gorulko 208b; Andrii Lychak 386b; Andris Tkacenko 24b, 153b, 318c; Andy Raatz 398c; andyKRAKOVSKI 131b, 365a; Anna Idestam-Almquist 112b; Anna_Kurz 394c; ANNA-PONCHINA 67c; AnsonLu 294b; antikainen 275b; Anton Ignatenco 292b, 401; Antonio Gravante 322b; Antonio Muñoz palomares 238b; Antonio Scarpi 326a; Arkady Chubykin 249c; Arseniaya Pavlova 135a; aspenrock 121; audaxl 26a; Александр Перепелица 411a; Bambi Golombisky 61; Barbro Bergfeldt 120a; Baris Arslan 297a; Bernd Jürgens 111b; beti gorse 73b, 223a, 224, 244, 384a; bill martin 101; Birgit Brandlhuber 59b; bluerabbit 184a; Bob Ingelhart 14b, 127a, 308b; Bochkarev Photography 276a; Boris Kaulin 119b; Boris Ryzhkov 331a, 397a; Brandon Blinkenberg 79b; Branislav Senic 406a; Brent Shetler 369c; Brian Brown 304a; Brien Chartier 19a; Bronwyn8 132c; Brooke Fuller 30b; Buzz Productions 92; Can Balcioglu 242b; Carlos Rodriguez 142a; Carol Heesen 93a; Cathy Yeulet 140, 402b; Celso Pupo Rodrigues 363a; Cezar Serbanescu 111a; CGissemann 114b; Chad Zuber 141a; charlenger 269b; Charles Brutlag 117a, 308c, 330a; chengyu zheng 38a; Cheryl A. Meyer 153a; Chicetin 176a; Chorboon Chiranuparp 377a; Chris Elwell 46b, 82d; Chris Evans 67b; Chris Fertnig 39a; Chris Poletti 164; Christian Musat 171; Christina Hallock 200b; Christina Powell 122b; Christopher Russell 74a; Ciaran Griffin 394a; Claude Dagenais 382c; Claudio Baldini 227a; clemarca 197; coffeechcolate 280b; Comstock Images 66b, 77a, 169, 259a, 262a, 358c 417b; cynoclub 300a; D. Robert Park 126b; Dan Moore 91b; DanBachKristensen 50a; Daniel Alvarez 397b; Danilin Vasily 379b; Danny Hooks 119c; Darren Platts 217b; darren wise 147, 400b; Darryl Brooks 113b; Dave White 305c; David Chin 266b; david franklin 202b; David Smith 113a; David Stephen Morgan 211a; David Stuckey 319b; Davidenko Andrey 174a; Debbie Woods 160a; Deborah Reny 35; Dennis Donohue 319a; Derek Holzapfel 355a; Diane Labombarbe 22b; Diego Mejia 20c; Digital Paws Inc. 83b; Dimitar Marinov 240a; Dimitry Romanchuck 146a; Dirk Ott 223b; Dmitriy Kalinin 351; Dmitriy Yakovlev 112a; Dmitry Knorre 229b; Dmitry Vinogradov 237b; Dominic Sender 43c; dornes 178a; Doug Edgar 13; Douglas Freer 330b; Dusan Kostić 104a; Dusan Zidar 317b; EbertStudios 230a; Eduardo Leite 362a; Ekaterina Fribus 110b; Elena Elisseeva 85d, 86a, 144b, 178b, 264b, 267b, 321b, 403; Elena Korostelev 187a, 328c; Elena Schweitzer 93b, 132b, 236b, 301; emiu 143b; Eric Isselée 80a; Erin Wilkins 259b; Ernst Fretz 193b, 349; etiennevoss 25, 128b, 287a; EuToch 299a; Evgeniy Lankin 65c; Evgeny Kozhevnikov 354b; Ewa Brozek 132a; Ewa Walicka 231a; eyal fischer 400a; eyewave 249a; Falk Kienas 59a; fedir sabov 313; Fedor Kondratenko 302b; Fekete Tibor 404a; feng qi 36a; Feng Yu 53b; fotolinchen 216; francesco turci 294a; FRANCO DI MEO 179a; Frank Cutrara 296b; Frans Rombout 88a, 90a, 228a, 233, 324c, 340b; FrantiA!ek Czanner 75b; fred goldstein 379a; Freddy Eliasson 291b; Gene Lee 320a; George Burba 412; George Doyle 119a; Georgios Kollidas 11c; gerenme 155b, 281a, 314c; gonul kocak 374a; Gordon Heeley 75a; Gßbor Kardos 53a; Hans-Joachim Schneider 57a; Hedwig Schipperheijn 196; Heike Rau 185a; HelleM 51b; Hemera Technologies 5a&b, 10b, 12a&b, 16b, 21a, 23c, 26b, 28a, 31a, 94a, 100a, 219, 300b, 307a, 308a, 325, 338b, 347, 398b, 411b; hexvivo 378c; Iakov Filimonov 302c; Igor Dutina 368b; Igor Tarasyuk 211b; Ihor Hromyk 41a; Ildiko Papp 319c; Ilie Victor Oancea 369a; Ina Peters 291c, 387a; inerika 253; Ints Tomsons 73a; Ivan Kmit 212a; Ivan Mateev 237c; Ivaylo Ivanov 314b; Jacek Chabraszewski 175, 341b; Jack Cobben 116a; Jack Puccio 137, 226, 371c; JackJelly 220; Jacqueline Kemp 48a; Jaime Pharr 192a; James Davis 358a; james steidl 289b, 318d; Jamie Hide 27; Jan Kaliciak 414b; Jan Tyler 329a; JANE MCILROY 6a; Jane White 332b; Jason Rothe 317c; Jean-Pierre Vaillancourt 201a; Jeffrey Banke 71a, 339b; Jeffrey Hahn 163; jeka1984 191a; Jill Battaglia 204b, 278b; Jill Chen 315b; Jiri Bursik 64b; Joanna Glab 62a; Joe Belanger 34b, 373c; Joe Biafore 51a; Joe Gough 293b, 310, 416; Joel Johndro 123a; John Anderson 364a; John Bloor 225a; John Cave 245a; John Foxx 47, 89c, 151a, 378a; John Gollop 143a; john shepherd 15b; John Young 85c; Jolanta Dabrowska 336a; joloei 386a; Jonathan Daniels 189a; Jörg Beuge 278c; Jose Miguel Barcelo 373a; Josef Hanus 199; Jowita Stachowiak 366; Joy Prescott 295a, 344b; jreika 350b, 372b; Ju-Lee 32b, 228b, 316a; Juan Carlos de la Calle Velez 333b; Juanmonino 262b, 267a; Juliane Jacobs 334a; Julie de Leseleuc 415b; Jultod 343b;

Jupiterimages 7a, 8a, 11a, 12c, 20a, 23a, 24a, 26c, 39c, 40b, 42, 43b, 44b, 45, 58b, 68b, 69, 70b, 71b, 80c, 81, 85a, 99b, 105, 114c, 136, 154, 162a, 165c, 179b, 180a, 186, 198, 209, 247c, 252, 254, 283b, 289a, 306b, 309a, 312b, 318a&e, 326b, 331b, 344a, 360, 372a, 395b, 402a, 405; kabVisio 323; Karen Gentry 273a; Karen Sarraga 125b; Karl Nilsen 146b; Kathy Reesey 371b; katkov 107; keattikorn 283a; Ken Marsh 330c; Ken Pilon 18; Kenn Stilger 141b; Kim Hammar 7b; Kim Lawler 365b; Klaus Larsen 286b; Kristen Pierson 240b; krodere 392b; Krzysztof Slusarczyk 188; L. Lynnette Peizer 389b; laperla_foto 235a; Laura Clay-Ballard 31b; Lauri Patterson 258b; Lcc54613 79a; Le Do 324b; Leandro Hernandez 382c; LeeAnn Townsend 124; LeeAnnWhite 298b; leekris 96; lena5 387b; Leonid Nyshko 67a, 170a, 187c; Levent Konuk 56b, 176b; Lijuan Guo 76b; Lilyana Vynogradova 335a, 376a; lionel Boivineau 286a; lisa combs 373b; Lisa F. Young 314a; Liubomir Turcanu 212b; lsantilli 217a; Lubos Chlubny 155a; Luca Francesco Giovanni Bertolli 239c; LUNAMARINA 78b; Lux_D 52; Lydia Goolia 84c; Lyudmila Suvorova 204a; Maksym Kravtsov 287b&c; Malgorzata Slusarczyk 55b; Mara Radeva 352c; Marc Lautenbacher 172; marco palazzi 165a; Marek Kosmal 63b; Marek Uliasz 86b; MarenWischnewski 378b; Maria Jeffs 103; marilyn barbone 273b; Maris Zemgalietis 50b; Mariya Volik 292a; Mark Fairey 250b; Mark Halbe 98; Mark Hatfield 127b; Mark Hayes 265b; Martin Turzak 317d; martine oger 158; marucyan 82a; mathieu boivin 320b; Matjaz Kopricvc 120c; matka_Wariatka 185b; Matt Gibson 396a; Matthew Bechelli 128a; Matthias Happach 191b; Mauro Rodrigues 129; Mayya Morenko 15a; Media Bank 56a; Meliha Gojak 239b; Melinda Fawver 73c; Melissa Fiene 64a; Michael Gray 289c, 298a, 394b; Michael Olson 263; Michael Zurawski 317a; Michael_at_isp 192b; mikafotostok 236a; Mikkel Svensson 256a; minadezhda 279b; Mona Makela 148b, 358a; morningarage 78a; msheldrake 46a; Mykola Velychko 60b; Mypurgatoryyears 65b; NA 20b, 23b, 248a, 305a; Naomi Bassitt 122a, 221; Natalia Artamonova 370; Natalia Bratslavsky 17a, 108; Nathan Allred 239a; Natikka 275a; Neil Kendall 97a; Nicolas McComber 157; Nicole Tebo 320c; Nikolay Suslov 227b; nyul 229a; ODrachenko 24d; Oleg Fedorkin 371a; Oleg Kruglov 104b; Olga Aleksandrovna Lisitskaya 309b; Olga Danylenko 299b; Olga Nayashkova 115; Olga Popova 68a; OlgaMiltsova 72b, 377b; olvas 276b; onepony 19b, 44a, 126a, 242a, 321a; oran tantapakul 95; Paul Abbitt 256b; Paul Binet 90b, 316b; Paul Brighton 6b, 290a; Paul Cowan 238c, 352b, 393a; Paul Laliberte 359b; Paul Lennon 391b; Paulina Lenting-Smulders 274; pavelr28 32c; PeJo29 50c; Petar Zigich 63a; Peter Elvidge 261; Peter Kim 126c; Peter Spiro 11b; Peter Zijlstra 149, 237a, 322a, 339a, 393b; Phil Augustavo 284; Phil Dickson 279a; Phil Reid 85b; Philip Stridh 39b; photolog 285; PhotoObjects.net 182; Photos.com 9b, 14a, 16a, 17b&c, 22a, 23d, 24c, 29a&b, 65a, 97b, 100b, 173a, 207, 210, 214, 243, 265a, 367, 389a; Pierre Cardon 272a; PinkBadger 336b; Piter1977 324a; pkkokkz 269a; Polka Dot Images 36a, 55a, 235b, 404c; Preto_perola 87b; Pumba1 135b; R Sean Galloway 194; Rafael Laguillo 131a; Rainer Junker 241a; Ralf Cornesse 38b; rattanapat 49a; raul taborda 329b; Raywoo 49b; Rebble 246; Richard Gunion 156a, 356; Richard Sidey 271; Rikke Breiting 167a; Rob Bouwman 91a; Robert Crum 304b; Robert Marrott 174b; Robert Redelowski 417a; Robert Sarno 225b; Robyn Mackenzie 54c, 165b, 311a, 392a; Rolf Aasa 54b; Romain Baghi 364b; romrodinka 234a; Ron Jupiterimages 118b; ronpaulk 333c; Ruslan Olinchuk 361; RusN 40a; Ruzanna Arutyunyan 187b; Ryan Rodrick Beiler 166; sakakawea7 87a; Sally Scott 89b, 190; samuel areny 333a; Samuel Perry 10a; Sarah Marchant 144a; sasel77 332a; Scott Jantzen 338a; Sema Ozenir 336c; seraficus 181; Serhiy Zavalnyuk 80b; Shannon Lane 114a; Silvio Verrecchia 350a; Simone van den Berg 88a; SMarina 281b; SonbeamCLOSED 278a; spetnitskaya nadya 238a; spflaum1 136; Sreedhar Yedlapati 60a; stanislaff 37, 148a; Stefan Stendahl 288; stephane duchateau 344c; Stephanie Frey 77b; Stephen Pothier 230b; Steve Bower 268a; Steve Lovegrove 275c; Steve Ross 248b; steven mayatt 383; Steven Miller 302d; Stock_Creative 33b; Stockbyte 41b, 94b, 123b, 168, 245b, 335b, 337, 352a; Stuart Brown 203a; sumnersgraphicsinc 381; sutsaiy 99a; Svetlana Feofanova 241b; svetlana foote 74b, 277a; SVETLANA KOLPAKOVA 150a; Svetlana Kuznetsova 88b; Sylvain LapensAe-Ricard 255; Szabolcs Szekeres 213; Tatiana Belova 145; Tatiana Emshanova 305b; Tatyana Nikitina 58a; The_Pixel 30a; thierry vialard 398a; Thinkstock Images 34a, 66a, 70a; Thomas Peter 215; Thomas Steinke 142b; thumb 4; tibu 363b; Timothy Epp 208a; Tom Brakefield 355b, 400c; Tom Tietz 78c, 130; Tomo Jesenicnik 150b, 290b; Torsten Wittmann 28b; trabachar 167b; TT 72a, 161a, 345, 374b; tuja66 362b; Ty Smith 57b; unknown 189b; Uros Petrovic 118a; Vadim Balantsev 120b; Valentyn Volkov 32a, 203b, 218, 222, 250a, 280a, 303, 342, 357; Valeriy Evlakhov 30c; Valeriy Kirsanov 183; Vassiliy Vassilenko 48b; Vebjørn Karlsen 201b; videophoto 281c; vikif 315a, 407a; Viktar Malyshchyts 297b; Viktor Petoe 110a; Viktor Pravdica 33a; Viktorija Kuprijanova 277b; VikZa 82c; Vitali Dyatchenko 21b, 170b; Vitalii Netiaga 343a; vkph 160b, 369b; Vladone 385; VMarin 53c; voltan1 109; wawritto 83a; Weerapat Wattanapichayakul 84a; Wieslaw Zieba 292c; William Berry 76a, 89a, 302a; Worapat Maitriwong 340a; xie2001 270a; Yaiza Fernandez Garcia 247b; yamanstock 293a; Yan Gluzberg 184b; Yasonya 234b, 324d; Yoko Bates 193a; Yuriy Chaban 9a; YuriyS 151b; Yury Minaev 200a; zack schnepf 57c; Zedcor Wholly Owned 36c, 272b; Zeljko Radojko 133, 177; zhekos 296a; zkruger 231b.

ABOUT THE AUTHORS

A.H. Jackson

Alan Jackson has searched remote jungles for new orchid species, raised bananas in Ecuador, pioneered vanilla beans in New Guinea and introduced Canadians to the tropical delights of passion fruit, guava and cherimoya. Born into a family of food processors, he experienced the food business from harvest to table and witnessed the events that transformed Canadian agriculture from free market enterprise to conglomerate ownership. Weather and gardens are intrinsic to food production and Alan writes on those subjects, drawing on his experiences as a commercial pilot and owner-operator of a large greenhouse/garden centre. Alan attended the University of Guelph, Leicester College and Clark University, and resides in Toronto with his wife, M.

James Darcy

James Darcy is a dedicated food folklorist who has a lifetime of international food and travel experience to draw upon in contributing to this book.